THE
ESSENTIALS
OF ENGLISH

A WRITER'S HANDBOOK

Ann Hogue

LONGMAN ON THE WEB

Longman.com offers online resources for teachers and students. Access our Companion Websites, our online catalog, and our local offices around the world.

Longman English Success offers online courses to give learners flexible study options. Courses cover General English, Business English, and Exam Prep

Visit us at **longman.com** and

LCCC LIBRAF
DISCARD

Longman

The Essentials of English: A Writer's Handbook

Copyright © 2003 by Pearson Education, Inc.
All rights reserved.
No part of this publication may be reproduced,
stored in a retrieval system, or transmitted in any
form or by any means, electronic, mechanical,
photocopying, recording, or otherwise, without
the prior permission of the publisher.

Pearson Education
10 Bank Street
White Plains, NY 10606

Vice president, instructional design: Allen Ascher
Senior acquisitions editor: Laura Le Dréan
Director of development: Penny Laporte
Senior development editor: Françoise Leffler
Vice president, director of design and
    production: Rhea Banker
Executive managing editor: Linda Moser
Production manager: Ray Keating
Production coordinator: Melissa Leyva
Production editor: Lynn Contrucci
Director of manufacturing: Patrice Fraccio
Senior manufacturing buyer: Dave Dickey
Cover design: Elizabeth Carlson
Cover photo: Don Bonsey/Getty Images
Text design: Ann France
Text composition: TSI Graphics
Text font: 11/12 Minion
Text credit: Pages 309–310: *Designer Babies*
    from "Gender Vendors" by psychologist Joshua
    Coleman, PhD, *San Francisco Chronicle*,
    Oct. 1, 2000.

Library of Congress Cataloging-in-Publication Data
Hogue, Ann.
    The essentials of English : a writer's handbook
    / Ann Hogue.
        p. cm.
    ISBN 0-13-030973-7
    1. English language—Rhetoric—Handbooks,
    manuals, etc. 2. English language—Grammar—
    Handbooks, manuals, etc. 3. English language—
    Textbooks for foreign speakers. 4. Report
    writing—Handbooks, manuals, etc. I. Title.

PE1408.H664 2002
808'.042—dc21

                                        2002069478

Printed in the United States of America
2 3 4 5 6 7 8 9 10—RRD—07 06 05 04 03

Reviewers

Isabella Anikst, American Language Center—UCLA
Extension; Amy Bach, University of Wisconsin; Victoria
Badalamenti, LaGuardia Community College; Dorrie Brass,
UMBC, English Language Center; Lauren Brombert,
DePaul University; Mimi Bunker, DePaul University;
Valerie Chamberlain, University of Wisconsin; Jennie
Chang, Orange Coast College; Barry Coppock, DeVry
University; Mary-Erin Crook, Pasadena City College;
Elizabeth Cummings, University of Houston; Anna
Degrezia; Raul Delabra; Douglas Evans, Rio Hondo
College; David Fein, UCSD English Language Program;
Barbara Freedman, Lakeview Learning Center; Andrew
Freund, American Language Center—UCLA Extension;
Sally Gearhart, Santa Rosa Junior College; Sarah Golden,
UCSD English Language Program; Patricia Goldstein,
University of Wisconsin; Amy Grisk, University of
Wisconsin; Sheri Hai, Rio Hondo College; Jami Hanreddy,
University of Wisconsin; Lisa Heyer, SFSU; Rosemary
Hiruma, California State University—Long Beach,
American Language Institute; Robert Holcomb, Rio Hondo
College; Stephanie Howard, American Language Center—
UCLA Extension; Taiki Imoto, Orange Coast College;
Glenna Jennings, UCSD English Language Program; Gye
Hyon Jo, DePaul University; Cathy Johnson, Pasadena City
College; Kathy Reyen Judd, Truman College; Linda
Farhood-Karasavva, Lecturer—Queens College, Hunter
College, and New School University; Elke Katsuren, LACC;
Cathy Kaye, University of Wisconsin; Liz Kelley, UCSD
English Language Program; Joo-Young Kim; Daryl Kinney,
LACC; Brock Klein, Pasadena City College; Claudia Kupiec,
DePaul University; John Lanier, Lakeview Learning Center;
Kathy Larson, DePaul University; Kim Lawgali, UCSD
English Language Program; Judy Lejeck, DeVry University;
María Lerma, Orange Coast College; Lena Lor, Orange
Coast College; Komi Magloe, Pasadena City College;
Jennifer Eick-Magan, DePaul University; Elizabeth Ballon
Mariscal, UCSD English Language Program; Dana
Marterella, LACC; Michael Martin, American Language
Center—UCLA Extension; Claudia McCarthy, DeVry
University; Brian McDonald, UCSD English Language
Program; Alice McGrath, Lakeview Learning Center;
Michele McMenamin, Rutgers University, PALS; Alan
Meyers, Truman College; Alfredo Miranda, Orange Coast
College; Daniel Mulalic, Orange Coast College; Kenneth
Ng, Orange Coast College; Katelyne Nguyen, Orange Coast
College; Carla Nyssen, California State University—Long
Beach, American Language Institute; Rodolfo Pacheco,
Orange Coast College; Kevin Paris, Brookhaven College;
Sally Patterson, LACC; Stuart Phillips, University of
Massachusetts; Renée Pinchero, DePaul University; Megan
Riordan, DePaul University; Esther Robbins, Prince
Georges Community College; Mark Roberge, SFSU; Alison
Robertson, Rio Hondo College; Dzidra Rodins, DePaul
University; Michael Rose, UCSD English Language
Program; Shelagh Rose, Pasadena City College; Nuha Salibi,
Orange Coast College; Peg Sarosy, SFSU; Rod Sciborski, Rio
Hondo College; Betti Sheldrick, DePaul University; Kathy
Sherak, SFSU; Mark Sondrol, University of Wisconsin;
Patricia Sotelo, Orange Coast College; Marlene Sprigle,
UCSD English Language Program; Donna Steiner, DeVry
University; Jody Stern, UCSD English Language Program;
Sara Storm, Orange Coast College; Bogumila Szalas,
Lakeview Learning Center; Paul Thomas, DePaul
University; Ethel Tiersky, Truman College; Grace
Tomlinson, LACC; Deborah van Dommelen, SFSU; JoDee
Walters, San Diego State University, American Language
Institute, English for Academic Purposes; Alia Yunis,
American Language Center—UCLA Extension; Pat
Zebrowski, Rutgers University, PALS

CONTENTS

PREFACE

To the student

A handbook, like a dictionary, is a reference book. Specifically, a handbook is a reference book for writers because it contains all, or almost all, of the information that writers need to produce a correct and polished piece of writing. The piece of writing might be a single paragraph, an essay, a business letter, or a research paper. Independent writers as well as high school and college students will find *The Essentials of English* a useful addition to their bookshelves.

If you aren't sure where to put quotation marks, or which words to capitalize, or whether to write *one hundred* or *100*, this handbook will tell you. If you aren't sure how to begin an essay or a business letter, you can find suggestions here. It will also show you the correct formats for both. A handbook is also a concise grammar book, useful for looking up everything from verb forms to article use.

While appropriate for native and nonnative speakers alike, *The Essentials of English* was written with the needs of ESL students especially in mind. For this reason, it differs from other handbooks in several ways:

- Items that are potentially troublesome to nonnative speakers (articles, phrasal verbs, subordinate clauses, and so on) are given a lot of space, while items that rarely trouble new learners (dangling participles and nonstandard verb forms, for example) are given minimal space—or none at all.
- Vocabulary is controlled; common, everyday language is used in both explanations and examples.
- Explanations are short and use everyday vocabulary and simplified sentence structures.
- Examples are chosen from current topics of multicultural interest.
- Passive voice is avoided in explanatory material.
- Several reference lists especially helpful to nonnative speakers (phrasal verbs, adjective + preposition combinations, and transition signals, for example) appear at the back of the book.

Contents

The Essentials of English has eight main parts.

> **PART 1: The Basics** defines and gives examples of grammar terms that all students of English need to know. If you aren't sure what noun clauses or gerund phrases are, read about them here.
>
> **PART 2: Clear Sentences** teaches you how to write well-formed sentences that communicate your meaning clearly.

PART 3: Grammar is a concise grammar book. You will find most grammar rules here.

PART 4: Punctuation explains the different punctuation marks used in English. If you aren't sure when to use a semicolon, look the rules up here.

PART 5: Mechanics explains the rules for using capital letters, hyphens, underlining or italics, and spelling. It also tells you when to use abbreviations and whether to write numbers as numerals or words.

PART 6: Writing and Revising is a concise writing book. It reviews the techniques and forms for writing expository paragraphs and essays in English.

PART 7: Formats shows the correct formats for both academic and business writing. The section on research papers explains the basic procedures and form of a research or term paper.

PART 8: Reference Lists has lists of useful information for your quick reference: irregular verbs, adjective + preposition combinations, phrasal verbs, commonly confused words, and so on.

How to use this handbook

To find answers to specific questions, you can take the following routes.

- Scan the table of contents in the front of the book to find the general area of your question—grammar, punctuation, format, and so on. Then turn to the appropriate part or section. OR
- Scan the table of contents at the beginning of each main part to find the specific topic of your question—verb tenses, article use, word order, introductory paragraphs, business letters, and so on. Then turn to the appropriate section. OR
- Check the alphabetical Index at the back of the book to find the exact topic of your question—present perfect tense, *the*, transition signals with time order, business letter greetings, and so on. Then turn to the appropriate page(s). OR
- In the Editing Symbols section on pages 410–413, look for references to specific sections for help in correcting errors and making revisions marked or suggested by your instructor.

"Special Tips" boxes warn you to be especially careful. They appear after items where students sometimes make errors, such as using a simple present tense verb in a sentence containing *since*. Other Special Tips explain confusing points, such as the differences among *too, very,* and *enough.* Still others give useful hints. *Never put an adverb between a verb and its object* is an example of a Special Tips hint.

Mini-practices follow many sections, giving you the opportunity to test your understanding of the rule or rules just explained. Check your answers in the Answer Key at the back of the book.

Acknowledgments

This handbook is the result of the combined efforts of a multitude of people—students, teachers, and editors. I am very grateful to all of them sharing for their knowledge with me.

During the planning stages, numerous students and teachers met in focus groups around the country to critique the first draft of the manuscript, and their sound advice caused me to make extensive revisions. Also, many specific suggestions from individual reviewers were incorporated into the final copy. My sincere thanks to each of them. (*See list of reviewers on page ii.*)

I am also grateful to colleagues Caroline Gibbs, Mary Fitzpatrick, and Sara Oser for their insightful comments on early drafts. I owe special thanks to my friend and Northwestern University graduate Patrick MacLeamy for the term paper model, to students Jacob Bien and Erin Pallas of the Branson School in Ross, California, for their chemistry lab report, and to psychologist Josh Coleman for allowing the adaptation of his article on gender selection.

Most importantly, my editors at Longman have been extraordinary in their dedication to this project over the past three years. Laura Le Dréan has put in countless hours, traveling around the country to gather vital feedback, providing not just good information, but wise judgment and (occasionally sorely needed) encouragement. To her I owe very, very special thanks. Special thanks are also due to Françoise Leffler for her expert knowledge and critical eye. Her editing skills added immeasurably to the book's content and form. Finally, thank you, Lynn Contrucci, for your hours of hard work in actually getting the work of the rest of us onto the page. I truly appreciate your expert management of the many steps in the production process.

Last of all, thank you, Andrew, for continuing to be my wisest counselor and constant friend.

Ann Hogue

PART 1　The Basics

1   Words

English has several kinds of words, which are called the "parts of speech": nouns, pronouns, verbs, adverbs, adjectives, articles, prepositions, conjunctions, and interjections.

Individual words can become different parts of speech depending on their function in a sentence. For example, the word *question* can be either a noun or a verb.

noun
▶ The **question** was easy.

verb
▶ The police **questioned** several people.

1a   Nouns

A noun names a person, place, thing, or idea. Examples of nouns are *teacher, school, book, color, life,* and *truth.*

Common nouns and proper nouns

A noun that names a *particular* person, place, or thing is a proper noun. Proper nouns begin with capital letters. All other nouns are common nouns.

Common nouns	Proper nouns
man	Michael Jordan
country	Indonesia
statue	Statue of Liberty

Count nouns and noncount nouns

A common noun can be count or noncount. Count nouns name people, places, and things that you can count (*one book, two books*). Count nouns can be singular or plural, and you can use an indefinite article (*a, an*) with them.

Noncount nouns name things that you cannot count. For example, you cannot count *sunshine* or *oxygen.* Noncount nouns are never plural, and you cannot use *a* or *an* with them.

Count nouns	Noncount nouns
book	sunshine
person	oxygen
idea	information

Gerunds

Words that end in *-ing* can be nouns. These nouns are called gerunds.

▶ **Swimming** is good exercise.

▶ I enjoy **cooking.**

Reference: Learn more about nouns in the following sections: Count and noncount nouns, *Section 14*; Gerunds, *Section 12a*; Proper nouns, *Section 33c*; Plural nouns, *Section 38c*; Possessive nouns, *Section 28a.*

PRACTICE—Section 1a

Find and underline the nouns in the following sentences. There are seven common nouns and two proper nouns.

EXAMPLE

<u>Teaching</u> is a <u>profession</u> that brings great <u>satisfaction</u>.

1. Quebec is a province in eastern Canada.
2. I usually get my best ideas in my dreams.
3. Experience is the best teacher.
4. Exercising immediately after eating is unwise.

1b Pronouns

A pronoun replaces a noun or noun phrase. The replaced noun is called the antecedent.

▸ **John** lost **my bag** when **he** took **it.**

In this sentence, *he* replaces *John,* and *it* replaces *my bag.*

Some pronouns can be adjectives when they modify nouns.

▸ Where's **my book?**
▸ I didn't enjoy **that movie.**

There are eight kinds of pronouns.

PRONOUNS	
Personal pronouns	I, me, you, he, him, she, her, it, we, us, they, them ▸ **She** gave **it** to **them. They** got **it** from **her.**
Possessive pronouns	my, mine, your, yours, her, hers, his, its, our, ours, their, theirs ▸ Let's study at **your** house. **Mine** is too noisy.
Demonstrative pronouns	this, that, these, those ▸ I love **this** picture, but I don't like **those.**
Interrogative pronouns	who, whom, whose, which, what ▸ **Who** went to the movies with you? **Which** movie did you see?
Relative pronouns	who, whom, whose, which, that ▸ George, **who** is my best friend, is a dog.

(continued)

(*continued*)

PRONOUNS	
Indefinite pronouns	all, another, any, anyone, anybody, anything, both, each, either, everybody, everyone, everything, few, many, neither, nobody, none, no one, nothing, one, several, some, somebody, someone, something ▶ **Everyone** here speaks **several** languages.
Reflexive pronouns	myself, yourself, himself, herself, itself, ourselves, yourselves, themselves ▶ He hurt **himself.** They painted the house **themselves.**
Reciprocal pronouns	each other, one another ▶ They promised to take care of **each other.**

Reference: Learn more about pronouns in the following sections: Pronouns, *Section 16*; Pronoun agreement, *Section 17*; Pronouns: Unclear reference, *Section 18*.

PRACTICE—Section 1b

Find and underline eleven pronouns in the following sentences.

EXAMPLE

Has <u>anyone</u> seen <u>my</u> sunglasses? <u>I've</u> lost <u>them</u>.

1. Whose car can I borrow? You can borrow mine.
2. Is that your final answer?
3. She taught herself to play the piano.
4. All of his former girlfriends came uninvited to his wedding.

1c Verbs

A verb expresses an action or names a state of existence.

Action	State of existence
jump	be
laugh	seem
love	appear

Verbs are the most changeable words in English. We change their form to express meanings such as these:

- Is the time of the action the past, the present, or the future?
- Does the action happen every day? Is it happening right now?
- Did it happen just one time or several times?
- Did one person or more than one person perform the action?
- Does the verb express an action performed by the subject (*John hit the ball*) or received by the subject (*The ball was hit*)?

Main verbs and helping verbs

Main verbs

A sentence always has at least one main verb (MV). Main verbs carry the basic meaning, and their form can change.

▶ I **am** cold.
▶ He **is** cold.
▶ They **were** cold.

▶ I **work.**
▶ He **works.**
▶ They **worked.**

Helping verbs

With main verbs, we often use one or more helping verbs (HV) to make the different tenses, to make questions, and to express meanings such as possibility, advisability, permission, and requirement.

   HV   MV
▶ I **was** working.

   HV   MV
▶ **Do** they work?

        HV   HV   HV   MV
▶ They **should have been** working.

        HV   MV
▶ We **must** work.

The helping verbs are (1) the forms of *be, have,* and *do* and (2) the modals.

FORMS OF *BE, HAVE,* AND DO	MODALS
be, am, is, are, was, were, been, being **have, has, had** **do, does, did**	can, could will, would shall, should may, might must, ought to had better
Be, have, and *do* can change their form. I **am** working. He **is** working. They **were** working.	Modals never change their form. I **must** work. He **must** have worked. They **must** be working.

NOTE: Helping verbs are also called auxiliary verbs.

Regular and irregular verbs

Verbs have five basic forms: the base form, the *-s* form, the past tense form, the past participle, and the present participle. These forms are called the "principal parts" of verbs. The principal parts of verbs are either regular or irregular.

	BASE FORM	-S FORM	PAST TENSE	PAST PARTICIPLE	PRESENT PARTICIPLE
Regular verbs	love walk	loves walks	loved walked	loved walked	loving walking
Irregular verbs	eat go	eats goes	ate went	eaten gone	eating going

- The base form is the form that you find in a dictionary.
- The *-s* form is the base form + *-s* or *-es*.
- The present participle is the base form + *-ing*.
- The other two forms can be regular or irregular. Regular verbs add *-d* or *-ed* to make the past tense and past participle. Irregular verbs make these forms in many different ways, so you have to memorize them. There is a list of irregular verbs in *Section 46* at the back of the book.

Transitive and intransitive verbs

Transitive verbs

Verbs are either transitive or intransitive. Transitive verbs have a direct object. A direct object (DO) is a noun or pronoun that receives the action of the verb. For example, the verbs *love* and *buy* are transitive because you love someone and you buy something.

    S   V   DO   S   V   ⌐— DO —⌐
▶ I **love** you.   ▶ They **bought** a new car.

Intransitive verbs

Intransitive verbs do not have a direct object. You cannot put a noun or pronoun directly after them. For example, the verbs *go* and *die* are intransitive because you cannot go something or die something.

    S   V   S   V
▶ He **went** home before he **died**.

Some verbs can be either transitive or intransitive depending on their use in a particular sentence.

    S   V   DO   S   V
▶ She **studied** art.   ▶ She **studied** in Italy.

Linking verbs

A linking verb is a verb that links the subject to a subject complement. A subject complement is either a noun that renames the subject or an adjective that describes the subject.

SUBJECT	LINKING VERB	SUBJECT COMPLEMENT
Dogs	**are**	social animals. (*noun*)
Your dog	**looks**	lonely. (*adjective*)

The most common linking verb is *be*. Other linking verbs include the verbs of the senses—*feel, look, smell, sound,* and *taste*—and the verbs *become, remain,* and *seem*.

Special Tip

Some languages allow you to omit a linking verb when the meaning is clear without it, but English requires a verb in every sentence.

  am
▶ I hungry.
  ^

  looks
▶ The baby sleepy.
         ^

 Contractions

Sometimes a verb hides in a contraction.

I'm	=	I am	**I'd**	=	I had OR I would
he's	=	he is OR he has	**she'd**	=	she had OR she would
they're	=	they are	**they'd**	=	they had OR they would
I've	=	I have	**I'll**	=	I will
you've	=	you have	**you'll**	=	you will
there's	=	there is OR there has	**who's**	=	who is OR who has

Reference: Learn more about verbs in the following sections: Verb forms and tenses, *Section 11*; Special situations with verbs, *Section 12*; Subject-verb agreement, *Section 13*; Verbs with direct and indirect objects, *Section 9c*; List of irregular verbs, *Section 46*; List of verb + preposition combinations, *Section 47*; List of phrasal verbs, *Section 48*.

PRACTICE—Section 1c

Find and underline all the verbs in the following sentences. Mark the main verbs *MV* and the helping verbs *HV*. Look for verbs in contractions, and mark the verb part of the contraction. There are twenty-one main verbs and eighteen helping verbs.

EXAMPLE

 HV   *MV*   *HV* *MV*   *HV* *MV*
I <u>don</u>'t <u>know</u> if I <u>can</u> <u>come</u> to your party. I'<u>ll</u> <u>ask</u> my parents.

1. Pardon me. Your dog is eating my shoe.
2. Oh! I'm sorry! I'll stop him.
3. He must be very hungry. Didn't you feed him this morning?
4. Yes, I did, but he hasn't been eating much lately. I don't think he likes dog food.
5. Well, he certainly likes my shoe. Maybe you should try a different brand of dog food.
6. Tom and I are having a potluck barbecue next weekend.
7. That's great! Who's coming? Am I invited?
8. Didn't you get our invitation? You should have received it long ago.
9. Well, it hasn't come yet.
10. That's too bad. I hope you can still come.

1d Adjectives

Adjective + noun

Adjectives modify (give more information about) nouns and pronouns. They answer the questions *Which one? How many? What kind?*

▶ They live in the **yellow** house. (*Which house?*)

▶ There are **twelve** eggs in a dozen. (*How many eggs?*)

▶ He drives a **racing** car. (*What kind of car?*)

Nouns and pronouns can be adjectives.

▶ a **shoe** store   ▶ **math** teachers

▶ **my** book   ▶ **some** money

Words ending in *-ing* and *-ed* can be adjectives. These adjectives are called participles or participial adjectives.

▶ a **frightening** experience   ▶ a **sleeping** baby

▶ a **used** car   ▶ a **broken** heart

Proper adjectives are usually capitalized.

▶ a **Shakespearean** play   ▶ my **Spanish** class

Compound adjectives are adjectives made from two or more words connected by a hyphen that function together as one word.

▶ a **two-word** verb   ▶ a **part-time** job

▶ a **well-known** actor   ▶ a **three-story** building

Linking verb + adjective

Adjectives can follow linking verbs (*be, look, seem, appear, taste, smell, sound, feel,* and so on).

▶ The flowers **are** *beautiful.*

▶ The soup **tastes** *salty.*

Adjective + preposition

There are many idiomatic adjective + preposition combinations.

　　good at   *happy* about   *tired of*   *married* to

▶ He's very **good at** math.

Reference: Learn more about adjectives in the following sections: List of adjective + preposition combinations, *Section 49*; Agreement of adjectives, *Section 20a*; Comparisons, *Section 21*; Compound adjectives, *Section 34a*; Order of adjectives, *Section 20b*; Participles: *boring* or *bored?*, *Section 20c*; Position of adjectives, *Section 19a*; Proper adjectives, *Section 33c*.

PRACTICE—Section 1d

Find and underline the adjectives (including nouns and pronouns used as adjectives) in the following sentences and draw an arrow to the word each one modifies. There are nine adjectives.

EXAMPLE

An important event in the life of an average American boy is the day he gets his first car.

1. My car isn't new or beautiful, but I love it anyway.
2. Its body is in terrible condition.
3. The back bumper is rusty, and the front window is cracked.

1e Articles

An article is a special kind of adjective. There are two kinds of articles: definite and indefinite. The only definite article is *the*. The two indefinite articles are *a* and *an*.

▸ I received **a** check in **the** mail yesterday, but I don't know what **the** check is for.

Reference: Learn more about articles in *Section 15*.

PRACTICE—Section 1e

Find and underline all the articles in the following sentences. There are three indefinite and seven definite articles.

EXAMPLE

A police officer rang our doorbell in the middle of the night.

1. He said a neighbor's pet had escaped, and he was searching the neighborhood for it.
2. He showed us a picture of the escaped pet.
3. It was an enormous snake!
4. We closed the front door, turned on every light in the house, and sat with our feet in the air for the rest of the night.

1f Adverbs

Adverbs modify (give more information about) verbs, adjectives, and other adverbs. They answer the questions *How? When? Where? How often?*

	Question	Answer
▸ Children learn new languages **easily**.	How do children learn?	*easily*
▸ He speaks English **very well**.	How does he speak?	*well*
	How well?	*very*

(continued)

	Question	Answer
▶ They saw the **recently** discovered comet.	When was the comet discovered?	*recently*
▶ They went **upstairs.**	Where did they go?	*upstairs*
▶ She is **always** late.	How often is she late?	*always*

Adverbs in *-ly*

Add *-ly* to adjectives to form many adverbs. Notice that *y* changes to *i*.

> quick—**quick*ly***
> careful—**careful*ly***
> nice—**nice*ly***
> easy—**eas*ily***

Other adverbs

Many adverbs do not end in *-ly*.

almost	**inside**	**now**	**too**
always	**late**	**outside**	**twice**
downstairs	**near**	**sometimes**	**upstairs**
far	**never**	**then**	**very**
fast	**often**	**there**	**well**
here	**once**	**today**	**yesterday**

Conjunctive adverbs

There is a special group of adverbs called conjunctive adverbs, which are words like *however, therefore, consequently,* and *furthermore.* Conjunctive adverbs are like conjunctions because they show logical relationships between clauses.

Reference: Learn more about adverbs in the following sections: Position of adverbs, *Section 19b*; Comparisons, *Section 21*; Conjunctions, *Section 1h*.

PRACTICE—Section 1f

Find and underline 10 adverbs in the following sentences. Draw an arrow to the word each adverb modifies.

> **EXAMPLE**
>
> The new student talks <u>very softly</u>.

1. I love the smell of freshly baked bread.
2. It never rains in July.
3. I can swim fast, but I can't swim very far.
4. The children went outside to play.
5. She almost always gets up too late to eat breakfast.

1g Prepositions

Prepositions show relationships such as direction, time, location, or ownership.

Most prepositions are one word (*of, from, in, on*), but some prepositions are two words (*next to, because of, according to*) or even three words (*in front of, in addition to*). Here is a list of common prepositions.

about	beneath	in front of	past
above	beside	inside	since
according to	between	in spite of	through
across	beyond	instead of	throughout
after	by	into	till
against	despite	like	to
along	down	near	toward
along with	due to	next to	under
among	during	of	underneath
around	except	off	unlike
as well as	except for	on	until
at	for	onto	up
because of	from	out	upon
before	in	out of	with
behind	in addition to	outside	within
below	in back of	over	without

Preposition + noun

A preposition is usually combined with a noun or noun phrase to make a prepositional phrase.

▶ The library is *on* **this floor.**

▶ It is unusual to see a person *with* **green eyes.**

Verb + preposition

Prepositions also occur in combination with verbs. Some of these combinations have idiomatic meanings and follow special rules; they are called phrasal verbs.

   look up   look up to   look down on   look forward to   look after

Adjective + preposition

There are many idiomatic adjective + preposition combinations.

   good at   happy about   tired of   interested in   married to

Reference: Learn more about prepositions in the following sections: Prepositional phrases, *Section 2d*; List of adjective + preposition combinations, *Section 49*; List of verb + preposition combinations, *Section 47*; List of phrasal verbs, *Section 48*.

> **!** **Special Tips**
>
> **1.** *To* can be a preposition or part of an infinitive.
>
> ▶ We went **to** the supermarket **to** buy some fruit.
>
>   The first *to* is a preposition. It is followed by a noun phrase (*the supermarket*). The second *to* is part of the infinitive *to buy*.
>
> **2.** Some prepositions are also subordinating conjunctions.
>
>   A subordinating conjunction is followed by a subject and a verb, and a preposition is followed by a noun or noun phrase. There is no verb after a preposition.
>
>   subordinating
conjunction   S   V
>
> ▶ We went shopping **after** we ate lunch.
>
>   preposition   noun
>
> ▶ We went shopping **after** lunch.

PRACTICE—Section 1g

Find and underline twelve prepositions in the following sentences.

EXAMPLE

Finding a parking place <u>on</u> campus <u>after</u> 9:00 a.m. is a daily challenge <u>for</u> students who drive <u>to</u> school.

1. I usually buy a parking permit for my car before the first day of school.
2. Unfortunately, I was so busy that I forgot to buy one at the beginning of the semester.
3. On the first day of school, I walked out of the building after class and saw a police officer standing next to my car.
4. She was putting a ticket on the glass under the windshield wipers.

1h Conjunctions

Conjunctions connect words and word groups and show the relationship between the connected elements. There are four kinds of conjunctions:

1. Coordinating conjunctions: **and, but, so, or,** etc.

2. Correlative conjunctions: **not only . . . but also,** etc.

3. Subordinating conjunctions: **because, when, if,** etc.

4. Conjunctive adverbs: **however, therefore,** etc.

Coordinating conjunctions

There are seven coordinating conjunctions. They are sometimes called the "fan boys" because their first letters spell the words "fan boys."

<u>f</u>or	<u>a</u>nd	<u>n</u>or	<u>b</u>ut	<u>o</u>r	<u>y</u>et	<u>s</u>o

Coordinating conjunctions connect two or more grammatically equal words and word groups. That is, they connect nouns with nouns, verbs with verbs, prepositional phrases with prepositional phrases, independent clauses with independent clauses, and so on.

▶ **Chicken, rice, tomatoes, *and* onions** are the main ingredients in this recipe.
▶ I enjoy swimming **in the ocean *but* not in a pool.**
▶ Our coach always says, "It doesn't matter if you **win *or* lose.** Just do your best."
▶ **I finally passed the TOEFL, *so* next semester I can start college.**
▶ She was **tired, *yet* happy.**
▶ **We got wet, *for* we hadn't brought our raincoats.**
▶ **Marie didn't come to work yesterday, *nor* did she call.**

Reference: Learn more about coordinating conjunctions in the following sections: Compound sentences, *Section 6a*; Connecting words with coordinating conjunctions, *Section 6b*; Parallel forms, *Section 6d*; List of connecting words, *Section 52*.

Correlative conjunctions

Correlative conjunctions always connect in pairs. For this reason, they are sometimes called "paired conjunctions."

both . . . and	either . . . or	whether . . . or
not only . . . but also	neither . . . nor	

Like the "fan boys," correlative conjunctions connect grammatically equal words and word groups. Correlative conjunctions can connect only two items; "fan boys" can connect more than two.

▶ My mother can speak ***both* French *and* Vietnamese.**
▶ She has lived ***not only* in Vietnam *but also* in France.**
▶ It's always ***either* too hot *or* too cold** in our classroom.
▶ This sofa is ***neither* comfortable *nor* beautiful,** so let's get rid of it.
▶ She couldn't decide ***whether* to buy a car *or* to take a vacation.**

Reference: Learn more about correlative conjunctions in the following sections: Connecting words with correlative conjunctions, *Section 6c*; Parallel forms, *Section 6d*; List of connecting words, *Section 52*.

Subordinating conjunctions

A subordinating conjunction is the first word in a dependent clause and shows the relationship of the clause to the rest of the sentence. For instance, the subordinating conjunction *because* tells you that the following words will give a reason, and the subordinating conjunction *when* shows a time relationship.

Time	Reason	Partial contrast	Manner
after	as	although	as, just as
as, just as	because	even though	as if
as soon as	since	though	as though
before			
since	**Condition**	**Direct opposition**	**Distance, frequency**
until	if	while	as + adverb + as
when	unless	whereas	
whenever			**Purpose**
while	**Result**		so that
	so + adjective + **that**		in order that
Place	so + adverb + **that**		
where	such a(n) + noun + **that**		
wherever	so much/many/little/few + noun + **that**		
anywhere			
everywhere			

▶ **Whenever** I travel, I don't like to carry a lot of cash.
▶ I use my ATM card to get money **because** ATMs are everywhere.
▶ I can get money **even though** the banks are closed.
▶ **If** you travel a lot, you should get an ATM card from your bank.

Reference: Learn more about subordinating conjunctions in the following sections: Complex sentences, *Section 7a*; List of connecting words, *Section 52*.

! *Special Tips*

1. Some subordinating conjunctions signal more than one relationship. For example, *as* can express time, manner, or reason.

   ▶ The room grew quiet **as** the teacher passed out the tests. (*time*)
   ▶ We wrote our names and today's date **as** the teacher instructed us to. (*manner*)
   ▶ **As** we hadn't studied, we didn't do well on the test. (*reason*)

2. Some prepositions are also subordinating conjunctions. See Special Tip 2 on page 12.

Conjunctive adverbs

Conjunctive adverbs are special adverbs that act like conjunctions. They show the relationship between independent clauses.

also	however	meanwhile	otherwise
besides	indeed	moreover	similarly
consequently	instead	nevertheless	therefore
furthermore	likewise	nonetheless	thus

▸ We were enjoying the sunset at the beach. **Meanwhile,** a thief was breaking into our car. (*1*)

▸ The thief stole our clothes. He **also** stole our money and our travelers' checks. (*2*)

▸ We reported the theft to the police. We probably won't get our things back, **however.** (*3*)

▸ We can't identify the thief; **besides,** our vacation ends and we have to fly home tomorrow. (*1*)

Note the different positions of the conjunctive adverb in the second clause: (*1*) at the beginning, (*2*) after the subject, (*3*) at the end.

Reference: Learn more about conjunctive adverbs in the following sections: Compound sentences, *Section 6a*; Compound sentences with semicolons, *Sections 26a and 26b*; List of connecting words, *Section 52*.

PRACTICE—Section 1h

Find and underline eight conjunctions in the following sentences.

EXAMPLE

My best friend didn't go to college; <u>instead</u>, he started his own business.

1. He opened his first store when he was still in high school, and now he owns three stores.
2. He both sells and rents computer hardware, but he doesn't sell software.
3. He is successful because he is honest and because he works hard.
4. Last year he made a lot of money; as a result, he was able to buy his parents a house.

1i Interjections

An interjection is a word or phrase that expresses surprise or emotion. Interjections can be strong or weak. Put an exclamation point after a strong interjection and a comma after a weak one.

▸ **Ouch!** That hurts!   ▸ **Gosh,** I'm sorry.

Interjections are seldom used in formal academic and business writing.

2   Phrases

A phrase is a group of words that belong together by meaning and does not contain a subject + verb combination.

▶ **in the morning**
▶ **a new idea**
▶ **to meet you**

> ## ! *Special Tip*
>
> Note the different meanings of *phrase, clause,* and *sentence.*
>
> - A **phrase** is a group of words that doesn't have a subject-verb combination. A phrase is part of a sentence, and a sentence usually has many phrases.
>
>   ▶ **before breakfast**
>
>   There is no subject-verb combination.
>
>   ▶ I take a walk **before breakfast.**
>
>   The phrase is part of a sentence.
>
> - A **clause** has a subject and a verb. A clause can be a sentence by itself when its meaning is complete.
>
>   ▶ **I eat breakfast.**
>
>   The meaning is complete, so this clause is also a sentence.
>
>   ▶ **before I eat breakfast**
>
>   There is a subject and a verb, but the meaning is not complete. This clause is not a sentence.
>
> - A **sentence** has at least one clause and can have several clauses.
>
>   ▶ **Before I eat breakfast, I take a shower.**
>
>   This sentence has two clauses.

2a   Noun phrases

A noun phrase is a noun + its modifiers. It can be a subject (S), a subject complement (SC), or an object (O).

```
        ┌─────── S ───────┐         ┌──────────── O ────────────┐
```
▶ My oldest daughter teaches a high school physics class.
```
        ┌─────── S ───────┐   ┌─ SC ─┐
```
▶ My youngest son is a dancer.

2b Infinitive phrases

An infinitive phrase is an infinitive + its objects and modifiers. Infinitive phrases can have many different functions in a sentence.

Subject	▶ **To learn a language well** requires years of study and practice.
Direct object	▶ I expected **to get an A in Professor Lee's class.**
Subject complement after *it*	▶ It is necessary **to pay your tuition before Friday.**
After certain adjectives	▶ I'm happy **to meet you.**
To express a purpose	▶ He went to the store **to buy some milk.**

Reference: Learn more about infinitives and infinitive phrases in *Section 12b.*

2c Gerund phrases

A gerund phrase is a gerund + its objects and modifiers. A gerund phrase acts like a noun; that is, it can be a subject, a subject complement, or an object.

┌─────────── S ───────────┐
▶ **Playing tennis with my boyfriend** is my favorite weekend activity.

┌─────────── O ───────────┐
▶ I especially enjoy **playing doubles with him.**

Reference: Learn more about gerunds and gerund phrases in *Section 12a.*

2d Prepositional phrases

A prepositional phrase is a preposition + a noun or noun phrase. Prepositional phrases have many purposes. They can tell a place or a time, give a description, or show possession.

Place	▶ Yesterday there was an accident **in front of my house.**
Time	▶ It happened late **at night.**
Description	▶ A car **with no headlights** hit someone.
Possession	▶ I don't know the name **of the victim.**

Prepositional phrases that give more information about a noun follow the noun, as in the last two examples above. Prepositional phrases that tell a place or a time usually appear near the end of a sentence. However, you can sometimes move place and time phrases to the front.

Reference: Learn more about moving prepositional phrases in *Sections 9a and 9c.*

2e   *-ing* and *-ed* phrases

An *-ing* or *-ed* phrase is a shortened adjective or adverb clause. It consists of a present or past participle + objects and modifiers. Sometimes it begins with a subordinating conjunction.

Some *-ing* and *-ed* phrases act like adjectives; that is, they give more information about a noun or pronoun.

-ing phrase   ▶ The student **sitting next to the window** is asleep.

This phrase gives more information about the noun *student.*

-ed phrase   ▶ **Very embarrassed,** he apologized to the teacher.

This phrase gives more information about the pronoun *he.*

Other *-ing* and *-ed* phrases tell a time or a reason. They may or may not begin with a subordinating conjunction.

-ing time phrase   ▶ **Before leaving,** the student apologized to the teacher again.

This phrase tells *when* something happened. It gives a time.

-ed reason phrase   ▶ **Worried about his grade,** the student apologized a third time the next day.

This phrase tells *why* something happened. It gives a reason.

Reference: Learn more about *-ing* and *-ed* phrases in *Sections 7c* and *7d.*

2f   Appositive phrases

An appositive phrase is a noun phrase that renames another noun.

▶ My mother loved to watch the television show **Who Wants to Be a Millionaire.**

This phrase renames *television show.*

▶ Fugu, **one of the most expensive fish dishes in Japan,** is also one of the most deadly.

This phrase renames *fugu.*

Reference: Learn more about appositives and appositive phrases in *Section 7b.*

3   Clauses

A clause is a group of words that contains a subject and a verb.

    S V   S   V
▶ **she left**   ▶ **because she was tired**

EXCEPTION: In commands, the subject is not expressed. We understand that the subject is *you*.

        S   V
▶ (You) **Be careful.**

There are two kinds of clauses: independent and dependent. A sentence must have at least one independent clause, and it can have one, two, three, or even more clauses.

3a   Independent clauses

An independent clause contains a subject and a verb and can be a sentence by itself. Independent clauses are sometimes called main clauses.

    S V   S V
▶ **She left.**   ▶ **It was late.**

3b   Dependent clauses

A dependent clause contains a subject and a verb, but it cannot be a sentence by itself because the meaning is not complete. There are three kinds of dependent clauses: adverb, adjective, and noun clauses. They begin with a subordinating word (SW) such as *because* or *that* or a relative pronoun (RP) such as *whom*. Dependent clauses are sometimes called subordinate clauses.

	SW S V
Adverb clause	. . . **because she was tired** . . .
	RP S V
Adjective clause	. . . **whom we saw in the library** . . .
	SW S V
Noun clause	. . . **that it was late** . . .

A dependent clause must be connected to an independent clause to make a complete sentence.

▶ Jane went home early **because she was tired.**

▶ Professor Jones, **whom we saw in the library,** is my chemistry teacher.

▶ We didn't realize **that it was late.**

Dependent adverb clauses

Adverb clauses always begin with a subordinating conjunction such as *after, although, as, because, everywhere, if, so that,* or *when.* Like single adverbs, adverb clauses answer the questions *When? Where? Why? How?* They can also express a condition, contrast, purpose, or result.

When ▶ You can read a magazine *while* **you are waiting.**

Where ▶ My dog follows me *wherever* **I go.**

Why ▶ *Because* **it rained,** we didn't go to the beach.

Condition ▶ Study hard *if* **you want to get an A.**

Contrast ▶ *Although* **Anna studied hard,** she didn't get an A.

Reference: Learn more about adverb clauses in the following sections: Complex sentences, *Section 7a*; Time clauses, *Section 11c*; Conditional sentences, *Section 11c*.

Dependent adjective clauses

Dependent adjective clauses are also called relative clauses. They begin with a relative pronoun (*who, whom, whose, which, that*) or relative adverb (*when, where*).

Like single adjectives, adjective clauses modify (give more information about) nouns and pronouns. The modified noun or pronoun is called the antecedent.

▶ Anyone *who* **wants to go on the class trip** should sign up by Friday.

▶ A lot of people use America Online, *which* **is an Internet service provider.**

▶ The man *whom* **you met at my birthday party** is my best friend's fiancé.

▶ I get depressed in the winter, *when* **it rains every day.**

Reference: Learn more about adjective clauses in *Section 23*.

Dependent noun clauses

A noun clause is a dependent clause that acts like a noun. That is, it can be a subject, subject complement, direct object, or object of a preposition. Noun clauses begin with one of these subordinating words: *that, if, whether, who, whom, whose, which, what, where, when, why, how, how much, how many, how far, how long, how often, how soon,* and so on.

┌────── subject ──────┐
▶ *Whether* **they will win** is still uncertain.

┌── subject complement ──┐
▶ The result was exactly *what* **we had expected.**

▶ I don't know *when* they will arrive.
┌──────── direct object ────────┐

┌──────────── object of preposition ────────────┐
▶ They disagreed about *how much* money they should save each month.

Reference: Learn more about noun clauses in the following sections: Complex sentences, *Section 7a*; Clauses of importance, *Section 11c*; Reported speech, *Section 11c*.

PRACTICE—Section 3b

Underline the dependent clauses in the following sentences. One sentence has no dependent clauses.

EXAMPLE

It's easier to understand a country's culture <u>when you know its history.</u>

1. American schoolchildren have a long summer vacation because many families lived on farms at the beginning of the nation's history.
2. The children worked on the farms during the busy summer growing season.
3. Even though there are few farming families in the United States today, schools still close for three months during the summer.
4. In modern times, some people think that children don't need such a long summer vacation.

4   Sentences

A sentence is a group of words that has a subject and a verb and expresses a complete thought. These are sentences:

▶ **They arrived.**
▶ **It's easy.**
▶ **Stop!**

These are NOT sentences:

✗ **Is easy to meet people.**

There is no subject.

✗ **I nervous when talking in front of people.**

There is no verb.

✗ **When they arrived after a long flight from Hong Kong.**

What happened when they arrived? This is not a complete thought.

4a Sentence parts

A sentence has two main parts: a subject and a predicate. The subject is the noun or pronoun that names who or what the sentence is about. The predicate is the verb and its objects, complements, and modifiers.

Subjects

Unlike other languages, every sentence in English must have a subject. The only exception is a sentence that expresses a command: **Stop!** In this kind of sentence, we understand that the subject is "you."

A **simple subject** (SS) is a single noun or pronoun.

⌐ SS ¬
▶ The little **dog** in the house next door barks all day long.

⌐ SS ¬
▶ The longest **book** that I have ever read is *War and Peace.*

A **complete subject** is the simple subject + its modifiers.

⌐———————— complete subject ————————¬
▶ **The little dog in the house next door** barks all day long.

⌐———————— complete subject ————————¬
▶ **The longest book that I have ever read** is *War and Peace.*

To find the complete subject of a sentence, first find the verb. Then ask a question with *Who?* or *What?* using the verb and the words after the verb. The answer is the complete subject.

Question	Answer
▶ Who barks all day long?	The little dog in the house next door (*complete subject*)
▶ What is *War and Peace?*	The longest book that I have ever read (*complete subject*)

To find the simple subject, remove all modifying words, phrases, and clauses from the complete subject. Modifiers include articles (*a, an, the*), adjectives (*little, longest*), prepositional phrases (*in the house, next door*), and dependent clauses (*that I have ever read*). The remaining noun or pronoun is the simple subject.

▶ ~~The little~~ dog ~~in the house next door~~ (*simple subject:* dog)
▶ ~~The longest~~ book ~~that I have ever read~~ (*simple subject:* book)

Using this technique to find the simple subject is especially helpful when the complete subject is very long.

SS
▶ ~~The~~ true reason ~~that I don't want to go out with your cousin Jack next Friday night even though he is a very nice person~~ is that I'm busy that evening.

Recognizing the simple subject will help you avoid several kinds of mistakes such as subject-verb agreement errors.

SS   V
▶ **Both** of my sisters **are** married.

The simple subject is *both,* not *sisters,* and requires the plural verb *are.*

SS   V
▶ **Neither** of my brothers **is** married.

The simple subject is *neither,* not *brothers,* and requires the singular verb *is.*

Reference: Learn more about subjects in the following sections: Inverted (verb-subject) word order, *Section 9b*; Subject-verb agreement, *Section 13.*

PRACTICE—Section 4a

Underline the complete subject and write SS above the simple subject of each sentence.

EXAMPLE

SS
One of the newest winter sports is snowboarding.

1. Snowboarding, which is especially popular among young people, requires good balance.
2. Special areas to be used exclusively for snowboarding are now available in most ski resorts.
3. A good skier is not automatically a good snowboarder.
4. The techniques of snowboarding are different from the techniques of skiing.
5. Most of the people in the world eat rice as their staple food.
6. Methods of cooking rice differ from culture to culture.
7. Also, different cultures are accustomed to eating different types of rice.
8. Asian people, who use chopsticks to eat, prefer sticky rice.
9. Therefore, short-grain and medium-grain rice, which sticks together better than long-grain rice, us used in most Asian cuisines.

Predicates

A predicate consists of at least a verb.

▶ My pet goldfish **died.**

In addition to a verb, a predicate may also include a direct object, indirect object, subject complement, or object complement. A predicate may also include other modifiers such as expressions of time and place.

▶ The name of the noisy dog that lives next door **is Fifi.**

▶ Fifi **barks and runs back and forth in her yard all day long, from six o'clock in the morning until six o'clock in the evening.**

4b Sentence patterns

Various kinds of predicates create different sentence patterns. There are six basic sentence patterns in English.

Pattern I

	SUBJECT	PREDICATE
Pattern I	Subject	Intransitive verb
	Dogs The baby	bark. is sleeping.

In the simplest pattern, there is only a subject and an intransitive verb. An intransitive verb is a verb that cannot have a direct object. Examples of intransitive verbs are *go, arrive, sleep, fall,* and *die.*

Pattern 2

	SUBJECT	PREDICATE	
Pattern 2	Subject	Linking verb	Subject complement
	Our neighbor's dog Dogs	looks are	lonely. (*adjective*) social animals. (*noun*)

In this pattern, the verb is a linking verb (*be, become, appear, seem, look, feel, taste,* and *smell*). Linking verbs are followed by subject complements. Subject complements complete the meaning of the subject by either describing it (when they are adjectives) or renaming it (when they are nouns).

Pattern 3

	SUBJECT	PREDICATE	
Pattern 3	Subject	Transitive verb	Direct object
	Dogs We	need visited	attention. our aunt.

In this pattern, the verb is transitive. Transitive verbs are followed by direct objects. A direct object names the receiver of the verb's action. To find the direct object, make a question using *Whom?* or *What?* and the verb and subject.

Question	Answer
▶ What do dogs need?	attention (*direct object*)
▶ Whom did we visit?	our aunt (*direct object*)

Pattern 4

	SUBJECT		PREDICATE	
Pattern 4	**Subject**	**Transitive verb**	**Direct object**	**Object complement**
	Our neighbors Our neighbors	leave named	their dog their dog	alone. (*adjective*) Fifi. (*noun*)

In this pattern, there is an object complement, which can be an adjective or a noun. Object complements complete the meaning of the direct object by either describing it (when they are adjectives) or renaming it (when they are nouns).

Pattern 5

	SUBJECT	PREDICATE		
Pattern 5	**Subject**	**Transitive verb**	**Indirect object**	**Direct object**
	They They	should give bought	Fifi her	more attention. a new leash.

In this pattern, there is a transitive verb, an indirect object, and a direct object. An indirect object names *to whom* or *for whom* the action was done. To find the direct object, ask a question using *Who?* or *What?* and the verb and subject. To find the indirect object, ask a question using *To whom?* or *For whom?*

Question	Answer
▶ What should they give?	more attention (*direct object*)
▶ To whom should they give more attention?	Fifi (*indirect object*)
▶ What did they buy?	a new leash (*direct object*)
▶ For whom did they buy it?	her (*indirect object*)

Reference: Learn more about the word order of direct and indirect objects in *Section 9c.*

Pattern 6

	SUBJECT	PREDICATE	
Pattern 6	***There* or *It***	**Verb (usually *be*)**	**Subject**
	There It	isn't is	any hot water. (nice) to meet you.

In this pattern, the subject comes after the verb. The words *there* or *it* are not the subjects; they are "empty" words that fill the position where you usually find the subject. In the first example, the real subject is *any hot water.* In the second example, the real subject is *to meet you* (*To meet you is nice*).

Reference: Learn more about sentences beginning with *There* and *It* in *Section 9b.*

4c   Question patterns

There are three kinds of questions in English: *yes/no* questions, information questions, and tag questions.

Yes/no questions

Yes/no questions are questions that can be answered *yes* or *no*. They begin with a verb.

▶ **Is** she your sister?
▶ **Are** you coming?
▶ **Were** they at home?
▶ **Does** he know the answer?
▶ **Have** you finished your homework?
▶ **Can** your children swim?

Information questions

Information questions ask for information and begin with a question word such as *who, what, where, when,* and *how.* Information questions are sometimes called *wh-* questions.

▶ **Who** is she?
▶ **When** are you coming?
▶ **Where** were they?
▶ **Which** movie did they see?
▶ **How long** have they been gone?
▶ **How well** can your children swim?

Tag questions

A tag question is a statement with a "tag" added at the end. We use "tag" questions in informal conversation. When we ask a tag question, we expect the other person to agree with us. We almost never use tag questions in formal writing.

Positive statement	+	Negative "tag"	Negative statement	+	Positive "tag"
▶ It's a nice day,		isn't it?	▶ It isn't too windy,		is it?
▶ You work downtown,		don't you?	▶ He doesn't like his job,		does he?
▶ We finished the lesson,		didn't we?	▶ We didn't miss anything,		did we?
▶ Your children can swim,		can't they?	▶ Your children can't swim,		can they?
▶ She has met his parents,		hasn't she?	▶ They haven't met before,		have they?
▶ You are going to work,		aren't you?	▶ You aren't going to quit,		are you?
▶ He will graduate soon,		won't he?	▶ He won't go to law school,		will he?

4d Kinds of sentences

In addition to the six patterns of a simple sentence, there are four kinds of sentences in English. We form the different kinds by combining dependent and independent clauses in different patterns.

Simple sentences

A simple sentence is one independent clause.

├─────────────── independent clause ───────────────┤
▶ A sports teacher invented the game of basketball about 100 years ago.

Compound sentences

A compound sentence is two independent clauses connected in one of three ways.

├─────────── independent clause ───────────┤
▶ The game of basketball was invented in the United States, **but**

├────── independent clause ──────┤
it is now popular all over the world.

├─────────── independent clause ───────────┤
▶ Basketball was invented in the United States; **however,**

├────── independent clause ──────┤
it is now popular all over the world.

├──────── independent clause ────────┤ ├──────── independent clause ────────┤
▶ Basketball was invented in the United States; it is now popular all over the world.

Complex sentences

A complex sentence is one independent clause and at least one dependent clause.

├───── independent clause ─────┤ ├──────── dependent clause ────────┤
▶ A sports teacher invented the game because he wanted his students to have a sport

├──────────── dependent clause ────────────┤
that they could play indoors during the cold months of winter.

├───── independent clause ─────┤ ├──────── dependent clause ────────
▶ The first baskets were peach baskets, which were attached to the walls of the

├───────────┤
school gymnasium.

Compound-complex sentences

A compound-complex sentence has at least two independent clauses and at least one dependent clause.

├───── independent clause ─────┤ ├──────── dependent clause ────────┤
▶ The first baskets were peach baskets, which were attached to the walls of the

├──────────┤ ├────── independent clause ──────┤
school gymnasium, and the first basketballs were soccer balls.

Reference: Learn more about sentences in *Sections 5–10.*

PART 2 — Clear Sentences

5   Connecting Ideas

A sentence can express one idea—*I like coffee*—two ideas—*I like coffee, but I don't drink it at night*—or several ideas—*I like coffee, but I don't drink it at night because it keeps me awake.* The way you connect ideas is important because good connections make the relationships among ideas clear.

Sometimes, writers want to show that ideas in a sentence are equally important. At other times, they want to show that one idea is more important than another idea. In English, when we want to show that ideas are equally important, we use coordination. When we want to make one idea more important than another, we use subordination.

5a   Coordination

In coordination, we use the same kind of word, phrase, or clause to express ideas of equal content or importance. These three ideas are equal in content:

(a) We play baseball in the spring and summer.

(b) We play football in the fall.

(c) We play basketball in the winter.

When we combine these three ideas into one sentence, we write them as matching word groups connected by commas and *and* to show that they are all equal.

▶ We play baseball in the spring and summer, football in the fall, **and** basketball in the winter.

5b   Subordination

In subordination, we show that ideas are not equal by subordinating less important information. We put main ideas in independent clauses and supporting ideas in dependent clauses and phrases.

Deciding which ideas are main ideas usually depends on your topic or point. Here are two ideas:

(a) Basketball is a winter sport.

(b) Basketball was invented one hundred years ago.

If your topic is "the seasons when different sports are played," the main idea is sentence (a). The information in sentence (b) is secondary information. When you combine the ideas, you write the main idea (a) as an independent clause and the supporting information (b) as a dependent (subordinate) clause.

┌──── (a) ───┐ ┌──────────────── (b) ─────────────────┐ ┌──── (a) ────┐
▶ Basketball, which was invented one hundred years ago, is a winter sport.

If your topic is "the history of basketball," the main idea is sentence (b), so you make (b) the main clause and (a) the dependent clause.

┌── (b) ──┐ ┌────── (a) ──────┐ ┌──────── (b) ────────┐
▶ Basketball, which is a winter sport, was invented one hundred years ago.

5c Coordination or subordination?

The following charts show the main ways to coordinate and subordinate ideas in English. To study each way in detail, go to the section referred to in parentheses.

COORDINATION

Use coordination to connect ideas of equal importance. There are three ways to do this.

1. Make a compound sentence: Connect two independent clauses with a coordinating conjunction, a conjunctive adverb, or a semicolon (*Section 6a*).

   ▶ Green tea is popular in Asia, **but** black tea is more common in North America.
   ▶ Green tea is popular in Asia; **however,** black tea is more common in North America.
   ▶ Green tea is popular in Asia; black tea is more common in North America.

2. Connect words or word groups with a coordinating conjunction (*Section 6b*).

   ▶ Green tea **and** black tea come from the same plant **but** are processed differently.

3. Connect words or word groups with a correlative ("paired") conjunction (*Section 6c*).

   ▶ **Both** green tea **and** black tea contain chemicals that are good for you.

SUBORDINATION

Use subordination to connect ideas of unequal importance. There are four ways to do this.

1. Make a complex sentence: Write less important information as a dependent clause and connect it to an independent clause (*Section 7a*).

   ▶ **Because green tea is healthy,** it is becoming popular outside Asia.
   ▶ Green tea contains a lot of antioxidants, **which slow the aging process.**
   ▶ Some doctors believe **that green tea fights cancer.**

2. Write less important information as an appositive or appositive phrase and connect it to an independent clause (*Section 7b*).

   ▶ Green tea and black tea come from the same plant, ***Camellia sinensis.***

3. Write less important information as an *-ing* or *-ed* phrase and connect it to an independent clause (*Section 7c*).

   ▶ **Interested in knowing more about green tea,** doctors began studying its chemistry.

4. Write less important information as a shortened adverb clause and connect it to an independent clause (*Section 7d*).

   ▶ **After analyzing green tea's chemistry,** doctors recognized its health benefits.

Do not use coordination to connect ideas that are very different. The relationship between the ideas is not clear, so the reader cannot tell which idea is more important. Use subordination to connect dissimilar ideas.

Not clear ✗ I was born in Cuzco, **and** a big festival takes place there every June.

Clear ▶ I was born in Cuzco, **where** a big festival takes place every June.

Not clear ✗ Calama, Chile, used to be the driest place on earth, **and** it had had no rain at all for four hundred years.

Clear ▶ Calama, Chile, used to be the driest place on earth **because** it had had no rain at all for four hundred years.

6   Connecting Ideas by Coordination

Use any of the following ways to connect ideas when they are equal in content or when you want to give them equal importance.

6a Making compound sentences

A compound sentence is a sentence that has two independent clauses. The clauses can be connected in three different ways: with a coordinating conjunction, with a conjunctive adverb, or with a semicolon.

Compound sentences with a coordinating conjunction

The most common way to make a compound sentence is to connect two independent clauses with a coordinating conjunction: *and, but, so, or, yet, for,* or *nor.* There is usually a comma before the conjunction. You can omit the comma when the clauses are very short.

Each conjunction signals a different relationship between the two clauses.

RELATIONSHIP	COORDINATING CONJUNCTION
Addition	**and**
Contrast	**but**
Result	**so**
Choice	**or**
Surprise	**yet**
Reason	**for**
Addition of a negative	**nor**

Addition ▶ My father loves kitchen gadgets. ~~He~~ *, and he* buys a new one almost every week.

Contrast ▶ A few of the gadgets are useful. ~~Most~~ *, but most* of them just take up space.

Result ▶ We ran out of space for them in the kitchen. ~~He~~ *, so he* started to store them in the living room.

Choice ▶ My mother asked my father to please stop buying gadgets. ~~She~~ *, or she* would throw them out.

Surprise ▶ Of course, Dad came home the next week with three new ones *, yet* Mom wasn't upset.

Reason ▶ Maybe she realized that buying little gadgets is harmless. ~~None~~ *, for none* of them cost a lot of money.

Addition of a negative ▶ After all, he doesn't buy sports cars. ~~He doesn't~~ *, nor does he* bring home a new yacht every week.

! *Special Tips*

1. Avoid beginning sentences with *and, but,* or *so.*

Experienced writers sometimes begin sentences with *and, but,* or *so* for special emphasis. In formal academic and business writing, however, it is not a good idea to begin sentences with a coordinating conjunction. Connect the sentences instead.

▶ Every summer, we went to the beach./And sometimes we camped there all night. ***, and***

▶ When I was a child, I wanted to be a movie star./But when I grew up, my ideas changed. ***, but***

▶ I am the youngest daughter in my family./So, I didn't have many responsibilities as a child. ***, so***

2. Don't put a comma between two verb phrases.

Before you add a comma, make sure that the second verb has a subject; in other words, make sure that the second part is an independent clause.

▶ Tom has applied to veterinary school,/and hopes to be accepted next year.

A comma is incorrect in this sentence because there aren't two independent clauses. There is only one subject (*Tom*) for two verbs (*has applied* and *hopes*).

3. Punctuate *for* and *because* differently.

The conjunction *for* means *because,* but *for* is not used very often to express this meaning. Make sure that you put a comma in front of *for* but not in front of *because.*

▶ My apartment is cold**, for** the heater is broken.
▶ My apartment is cold **because** the heater is broken.

4. Follow special rules for *nor.*

When you combine two negative sentences with *nor,* use inverted word order after *nor* (put the verb in front of the subject) and omit the second *not.*

▶ My parents didn't teach me how to swim,/I didn't learn at school. ***, nor did I***

You can omit repeated words if they are not needed for meaning.

▶ As a result, I can't swim, nor my brothers and sisters can't swim.

You can omit the repeated word *swim* because it is not necessary for meaning.

▶ I haven't visited my parents for two years, nor they haven't visited me.

You cannot omit *visited me* because it is not identical to *visited my parents.*

Compound sentences with a conjunctive adverb

In this kind of compound sentence, you connect two independent clauses with a conjunctive adverb such as *however, therefore,* and *for example.* There is a semicolon before the conjunctive adverb and a comma after it.

Each conjunctive adverb signals a different relationship between the two clauses.

RELATIONSHIP	CONJUNCTIVE ADVERBS
Addition	**also, besides, furthermore, in addition, moreover**
Contrast (complete)	**however, in contrast, on the other hand**
Contrast (partial)	**however, nevertheless, nonetheless, still**
Result	**as a result, consequently, therefore, thus**
Sequence	**afterward, meanwhile, then, subsequently**
Comparison	**likewise, similarly**
Example	**for example, for instance**

Addition
▶ Community colleges offer preparation for many jobs; **moreover,** they prepare students to transfer to four-year colleges or universities.

Contrast (complete)
▶ Most community colleges do not have dormitories; **in contrast,** most four-year colleges do.

Contrast (partial)
▶ Colleges try to find housing for all students; **nevertheless,** students sometimes have to find a place to live on their own.

Result
▶ Native and nonnative English speakers have different needs; **therefore,** most schools provide separate classes for each group.

Sequence
▶ The workers put five victims into an ambulance; **afterward,** they found another victim alongside the road.

Comparison
▶ Hawaii has a lot of sunshine and very friendly people; **similarly,** Mexico's weather is very sunny and its people are quite hospitable.

Example
▶ Colors can have different meanings; **for example,** white is the color of weddings in some cultures and of funerals in others.

Reference: For a complete list of conjunctive adverbs and examples of sentences using them, see *Section 52.*

Compound sentences with a semicolon alone

A third way to make a compound sentence is to connect the clauses with a semicolon alone.

▶ My family's favorite dinner is anything homemade; my favorite dinner is anything from a takeout place.

However, using a semicolon alone is possible only when the relationship between the two clauses is clear without a connecting word. When the relationship isn't clear, you must use a connecting word.

Not clear ✗ My mother had a full-time job; she cooked dinner every night for our family.

Clear ▶ My mother had a full-time job; **nevertheless,** she cooked dinner every night for our family.

There is little difference in meaning in the three ways of making a compound sentence, but there is a difference of style. Beginning writers use coordinating conjunctions to connect clauses; more experienced writers also use the other two ways.

Reference: Learn more about compound sentences in the following sections: Commas in compound sentences, *Section 25a*; Semicolons in compound sentences, *Sections 26a and 26b*; Overuse of *and, but,* and *so, Section 8d*.

PRACTICE—Section 6a

Practice writing compound sentences. Combine each pair of sentences into one sentence. Use any of the three ways, but use each way at least once.

EXAMPLE
My family loves to eat. I hate to cook.

My family loves to eat, but I hate to cook. OR

My family loves to eat; however, I hate to cook.

1. Pit bulls, which are fighting dogs, can be very aggressive. They are not good pets for families with children.
2. Pit bulls must always be on a leash. They are very unpredictable.
3. Never trust pit bulls. They can attack without cause.
4. Pit bulls are known to be dangerous. Rottweilers and giant schnauzers can also be problem dogs.
5. My little Chihuahua is small. He thinks he is a pit bull.
6. He runs around and growls ferociously. Most people just laugh at him.
7. Actually, Chihuahuas can be dangerous at times. They are not very tolerant of children.

6b Connecting words with coordinating conjunctions

Connect equal words or word groups with coordinating conjunctions such as *and, or, but,* and *yet.*

Each coordinating conjunction signals a different relationship between the words or word groups.

RELATIONSHIP	COORDINATING CONJUNCTION
Addition (positive)	**and**
Addition (negative)	**or**
Choice	**or**
Contrast	**but**
Surprise	**yet**

Addition (positive) ▶ I like cold milk **and** hot coffee.

Addition (negative) ▶ I ***don't*** like hot milk **or** cold coffee.

Choice ▶ We can stop to rest, continue hiking for another half an hour, **or** go home.

Contrast ▶ I enjoy swimming in the ocean **but** not in a pool.

Surprise ▶ It's sunny **yet** cool today.

 Special Tips

1. Punctuate with care.

When connecting words and word groups with these conjunctions, follow the comma rule for items in a series (*Section 25f*).

If you connect two items, use no comma.

▶ red and white

If you connect three items, you must use at least one comma. The second comma is optional.

▶ red, white(,) and blue

If you connect four or more items, the last comma is required.

▶ red, white, blue, and black

NOTE: In British English, you never use a comma before *and* when connecting items in a series.

(continued)

(*continued*)

2. Use parallel form.

Be sure the connected words or word groups have parallel form (*Section 6d*).

Not parallel ✗ Do you prefer **living alone** *or* **a roommate?**

Parallel ▶ Do you prefer **living alone** *or* **having a roommate?**

PRACTICE—Section 6b

Fill in each blank with a coordinating conjunction that fits the context. There is more than one possible answer for item 4.

EXAMPLE

The foolish boys didn't take a map, a flashlight, __or__ a cell phone on their hike.

Suzanne _____ Anna are roommates at an English language school. Suzanne,
      1.
who was born in Switzerland, speaks German _____ French. Anna, who is from
                      2.
Thailand, doesn't speak German _____ French. They share a small dormitory room
                      3.
_____ can't even say "Good morning" to each other. They had better find someone
4.
to translate for them _____ learn English fast! [*These are choices.*]
            5.
On the first morning, the two girls dressed quickly _____ went to the dining
                                6.
room for breakfast. They could choose a continental-style breakfast with juice,
toast, _____ coffee _____ tea _____ an American-style breakfast with juice, toast,
    7.   8.   9.
eggs, potatoes, _____ meat. Anna doesn't drink coffee _____ tea, so she asked for
          10.   11.
a glass of orange juice.

6c   Connecting words with correlative conjunctions

Connect equal words or word groups with correlative conjunctions: *both . . . and, not only . . . but also, either . . . or, neither . . . nor,* and *whether . . . or.*

Correlative conjunctions are sometimes called "paired conjunctions" because they always occur in pairs. Paired conjunctions give special emphasis to the words and word groups they connect. Compare these two sentences:

▶ Japanese food is delicious to eat **and** beautiful to look at.
▶ Japanese food is **not only** delicious to eat **but also** beautiful to look at.

In the second sentence, you pay more attention to the phrases *delicious to eat* and *beautiful to look at* than you do in the first sentence because they are joined by *not only . . . but also* instead of by just *and.*

Each correlative (paired) conjunction signals a different relationship between the words and word groups it connects.

RELATIONSHIP	CORRELATIVE CONJUNCTIONS
Addition	**both ... and, not only ... but also**
Positive choices	**either ... or**
Negative choices	**neither ... nor**
Which one of two choices	**whether ... or**

Addition
> ▶ The Italian film *Life is Beautiful* made me **both** laugh **and** cry. It contained **not only** comic **but also** tragic scenes.

Positive choices
> ▶ **Either** my father **or** my mother will meet me at the airport. (*One person will come to the airport.*)

Negative choices
> ▶ **Neither** my father **nor** my mother will meet me at the airport. (*No one will come to the airport.*)

Which one of two choices
> ▶ I can't decide **whether** to go to summer school **or** to get a summer job.

When you use paired conjunctions, make sure the connected words or word groups have parallel form (*Section 6d*).

PRACTICE—Section 6c

Fill in each blank with a paired conjunction that fits the context. Use each pair once.

EXAMPLE

To get to the city center from here, you can _either_ catch a streetcar at the corner _or_ walk two blocks to the subway station.

True vegetarians eat nothing from animals. In other words, they eat _____ meat _____ dairy products. _____ my cousin _____ his wife are vegetarians. They don't
    1.   2.
eat meat. My cousin's wife is not a true vegetarian, however, because she _____ eats fish _____ drinks milk.
    3.

Most restaurants in my city have two separate dining areas. Customers can sit _____ in the smoking area _____ in the nonsmoking area. My boyfriend smokes,
    4.
but I don't. We can never decide _____ to make me uncomfortable in the smoking area _____ to make him miserable in the nonsmoking area.
    5.

6d   Using parallel forms

When you connect ideas by coordination, you must use parallel, or matching, forms. This means that you must join nouns with nouns, verbs with verbs, prepositional phrases with prepositional phrases, and so on.

Not parallel ✗   Kayo is **beautiful, young, *and* a talented violinist**.
adjective   adjective   ⌐——noun phrase——⌐

Parallel   ▶   Kayo is **beautiful, young, *and* talented**.
adjective   adjective   adjective

Parallel   ▶   Kayo is **a beautiful young woman *and* a talented violinist**.
⌐——noun phrase——⌐   ⌐——noun phrase——⌐

Not parallel ✗   She has played with orchestras *both* **in Europe *and* Asia**.
prep. phrase   noun

Parallel   ▶   She has played with orchestras in *both* **Europe *and* Asia**.
noun   noun

Parallel   ▶   She has played with orchestras *both* **in Europe *and* in Asia**.
prep. phrase   prep. phrase

Parallel forms with *and, but, or,* and *yet*

When you connect ideas with *and, but, or,* and *yet,* write the connected ideas in parallel form.

▶   Newborn babies don't do much during their first few weeks; they only **eat,**
verb
sleep, wet, *and* cry.
verb   verb   verb

The following sentences show errors in parallel form and ways to fix them.

Noun phrases   ▶   The students like Ms. Gibbs's class because of her friendly
manner, ~~she explains clearly~~, and her funny jokes.
her clear explanations

Prepositional phrases   ▶   My grandfather earned his living by fishing and ~~he sold~~ little wooden birds that he carved.
by selling

Infinitives   ▶   The students like to listen and to speak but not ~~writing~~ in English.
to write

Gerunds   ▶   The students like listening and speaking but not ~~to write~~ in English.
writing

Verbs   ▶   Will you fly, travel by train, or ~~renting~~ a car?
rent

Adjectives   ▶   My great-grandfather was uneducated, yet ✗ wise ~~person~~.

Parallel forms with *not only . . . but also, either . . . or*

When you connect ideas with *both . . . and, not only . . . but also, either . . . or, neither . . . nor,* and *whether . . . or,* use parallel forms after both parts of the paired conjunction.

                           noun   noun

▶ My grandmother can speak *both* **French** *and* **Vietnamese** fluently.

The following sentences show errors in parallel form and ways to fix them.

Prepositional phrases ▶ College students use computers not only for schoolwork

                                 for games.

            but ~~they~~ also ~~play games on them.~~

                                        he missed too many labs

Adverb clauses ▶ He failed physics either because ~~of too many missed labs~~ or because he never opened the textbook.

Adverbs ▶ E-mail allows you to communicate both quickly and

                                economically.

            ~~without paying a lot of money.~~

Verbs ▶ When I first arrived at college, I was so homesick that I could neither sleep nor ~~I didn't want to~~ eat.

Infinitive phrase ▶ I couldn't decide whether to stay at school or

                        to

             ~~maybe I should~~ return home.

! *Special Tips*

1. Omit repeated words.

   You can omit repeated words that are not necessary for parallel structure.

   ▶ The students like Ms. Gibbs' class because of her friendly manner, ~~her~~ clear explanations, and ~~her~~ funny jokes.

   ▶ My grandfather earned his living by fishing and ~~by~~ selling little wooden birds that he carved.

2. Move one conjunction.

   Sometimes you only have to move one conjunction of the pair to make forms parallel.

   ▶ My professor advised me (either) to take chemistry or marine biology next semester.

   ▶ Living in a dormitory (not only) is cheaper but also less lonely for new students.

PRACTICE—Section 6d

A. Underline the parallel forms in the following paragraph.

EXAMPLE

Do dogs chase cats <u>because they are natural enemies</u> or <u>because it's fun</u>?

When deciding what kind of pet to get, most people consider only dogs, cats, and fish. Cats are soft, cute, and playful. Dogs are fun but can be destructive. They like to dig holes in the garden and chew holes in the furniture. Fish are excellent pets because they don't make much noise, they don't eat a lot, and they won't ruin your carpets.

B. Edit the sentences in this paragraph for mistakes in parallel form. Some sentences have no errors.

EXAMPLE   *eventual space needs.*

When choosing a pet, consider the pet's growth and ~~how much space it will eventually need~~.

If you prefer a more exotic pet, consider these choices. A giraffe is useful not only for reaching things from high shelves but also to see over the heads of people at a parade. A pet lion is a good choice if you live alone, for pet lions give their owners both companionship and home security. If you like water sports, cold weather, and having a companion who is always well dressed, a penguin is the pet for you. If you have a new baby in your household, consider either a goat or a kangaroo. A "nanny" goat can baby-sit, a milk producer, and you don't have to mow your grass. You can use a kangaroo's pouch either for carrying the baby or keeping the baby's bottle warm.

7 Connecting Ideas by Subordination

Use any of the following ways to connect ideas when you want to make one idea less important than other ideas.

7a Making complex sentences

Write less important information as a dependent clause and connect it to an independent clause to make a complex sentence. There are three kinds of dependent clauses: adverb, adjective, and noun.

We use each kind of clause to add a different kind of information.

- Adverb clauses add information about time, reason, manner, and so on.
- Adjective clauses add descriptive information about a noun or pronoun.
- Noun clauses report information such as what someone thinks or says, among other functions.

Complex sentences with adverb clauses

An adverb clause tells *when, where, why, how, how far, how often,* and so on. It always begins with a subordinating conjunction that expresses the relationship between the adverb clause and the independent clause. (See *Section 52* for a list of subordinating conjunctions and the relationships they express.)

Time	▶ *As soon as* **we sat down to eat dinner,** the telephone rang.
	▶ After driving over one hundred miles without finding a gas station, were almost home **when we ran out of gas.**
Place	▶ My dog follows me *wherever* **I go.**
Reason	▶ My girlfriend and I went to a disco *because* **she wanted to dance.**
Result	▶ The music was *so* **loud** *that* we couldn't talk.
Partial contrast	▶ *Although* **it was noisy and crowded,** we had a good time.
Direct opposition	▶ *Whereas* **my girlfriend is a good dancer,** I have two left feet.
Manner	▶ I followed the instructions exactly *as* **they were written.**
Distance	▶ We parked *as close* to the theater *as* **we could.**
Frequency	▶ He practices English *as often as* **he can.**
Purpose	▶ We went home early *so that* **we could get a good night's sleep.**
Condition	▶ *If* **it rains,** we won't go to the beach tomorrow.

The punctuation of a complex sentence with an adverb clause depends on the order of the clauses. When an adverb clause comes first, separate the clauses with a comma. When an independent clause comes first, don't separate the clauses with a comma.

▶ **Because Jill was studying for final exams,** she didn't answer her telephone all day.

▶ Jill didn't answer her telephone all day **because she was studying for final exams.**

EXCEPTION: Adverb clauses of direct opposition beginning with *while* or *whereas* are always separated with a comma, even when they follow an independent clause.

▶ One of my roommates studies day and night, *whereas* **the other two like to party.**

▶ My sister is an excellent cook, *while* **I can't even fry an egg.**

Reference: Learn more about adverb clauses in the following sections: Verb tenses in time clauses, *Section 11c*; Conditional sentences, *Section 11c*.

! Special Tips

1. Watch out for fragments (*Section 8a*).

Not correct ✗ Since Julia has been working out at the gym every day.

An adverb clause cannot be a sentence by itself.

To correct ▶ Since Julia has been working out at the gym every day/ *, she has lost weight.*

Connect the adverb clause to an independent clause.

2. Use the right conjunction.

Not correct ✗ Although the weather was beautiful, we asked the teacher to move class outside.

Although is the wrong conjunction. *The weather was beautiful* is a reason that we asked the teacher to move class outside. *Although* connects a contrast, not a reason. The sentence needs a conjunction that connects a reason, such as *because*. Compare:

┌──── reason ────┐ ┌──── result ────┐
Because I was tired, I went to bed early.

┌──── contrast ────┐
Although I was tired, I stayed up late to finish my homework.

To correct ▶ ~~Although~~ *Because* the weather was beautiful, we asked the teacher to move class outside.

Choose a conjunction that fits the context.

3. Put the conjunction in front of the right clause.

Not correct ✗ Because I took my umbrella to work, it looked like rain.

Because is in the wrong clause, the clause of result. *Because* is a conjunction that introduces a reason. Here it should be in front of *it looked like rain.*

┌──── reason ────┐ ┌──── result ────┐
It looked like rain. I took my umbrella to work.

To correct ▶ ~~Because~~ I took my umbrella to work/*because* it looked like rain. OR

▶ Because I took my umbrella to work/ *it looked like rain,* ~~it looked like rain~~ ⊙

Move the conjunction to the right clause. If you have trouble deciding which clause is a reason and which is a result, ask yourself: What happened first? This is the reason. Then ask: What happened last? This is the result.

4. Don't use too many conjunctions.

Not correct ✗ Although I have studied Spanish for six years, but I still don't speak it well.

Both clauses start with a conjunction (*although* and *but*). In English, we use only one conjunction to connect two clauses.

To correct ▶ Although I have studied Spanish for six years, b~~u~~t I still don't speak it well. OR

~~Although~~ I have studied Spanish for six years, but I still don't speak it well.

Delete one of the conjunctions.

PRACTICE—Section 7a (1)

A. Underline two adverb clauses in the following paragraph.

EXAMPLE

The passengers started applauding <u>as soon as the airplane landed</u>.

After the war in Vietnam ended, many Vietnamese came to the United States to live. Many of these newcomers wanted to settle where they could live near others from their homeland. As a result, large Vietnamese communities developed in the California cities of Los Angeles and San Jose.

B. Edit the sentences in the following paragraph for adverb clause errors. Every sentence has an error. The first mistake has been corrected as an example.

       C   *because*

~~Because~~ ¢onflicts often develop in immigrant families͵ old and new cultures are

different. For example, when young people want to choose their own careers and marriage partners. Although the children grow up learning the new culture, but their parents and grandparents hold on to the customs of their homeland.

C. Combine the sentences in each pair to make one complex sentence with an adverb clause. There is more than one way to combine each pair.

EXAMPLE

Young people are caught between two cultures. They sometimes suffer.

When young people are caught between two cultures, they sometimes suffer. OR

Young people sometimes suffer because they are caught between two cultures.

1. A friend of mine couldn't go to parties. Her parents didn't allow her to go out.
2. Her last class ended. She had to go directly home every day after school.
3. She had to help her mother. Her brothers played sports and visited friends after school.

Complex sentences with adjective clauses

Adjective clauses modify (give descriptive information about) a noun or pronoun. The modified noun or pronoun is called the antecedent. Adjective clauses should come immediately after their antecedents.

adjective clause   adjective clause

▶ Roberto, **who loves to surf**, lives in an apartment **that overlooks the Pacific Ocean.**

Who loves to surf modifies (gives descriptive information about) *Roberto*. *Roberto* is its antecedent. *That overlooks the Pacific Ocean* modifies (gives descriptive information about) *an apartment*. *An apartment* is its antecedent.

Adjective clauses are sometimes called relative clauses. They begin with a relative pronoun (*who, whom, whose, which, that*) or a relative adverb (*where, when*).

▶ Students *who* **have an A average** do not have to take the final exam.
▶ The salesperson *whom* **we spoke to** was very helpful.
▶ Do you know the name of the student *whose* **essay won a prize?**
▶ I am afraid to take advanced calculus, *which* **is required for my major.**
▶ Did you read the book *that* **the teacher recommended?**
▶ Jerusalem is a city *where* **three of the world's religions have holy sites**.
▶ July 4 is the day *when* **Americans celebrate their independence from Great Britain.**

Don't put commas around an adjective clause that is necessary to identify its antecedent.

▶ Students **who work more than twelve hours a week** should not take more than three classes.

We need the information *who work more than twelve hours a week* to identify which students should not take more than three classes. Therefore, do not use commas.

Put commas before and after an adjective clause that is not necessary to identify its antecedent but merely gives extra information about it.

▶ Michael, **who works twenty hours a week,** should not take more than three classes.

The name *Michael* identifies the person who should not take more than three classes. The fact that he works twenty hours a week is merely extra information about him. Therefore, use commas.

Reference: Learn more about adjective clauses in *Section 23.*

PRACTICE—Section 7a (2)

Underline the adjective clauses in the paragraphs and draw an arrow to the antecedent of each. Circle the relative pronoun or adverb. There are nine adjective clauses in the two paragraphs.

EXAMPLE

The Hawaiian Islands, (which) comprise 8 major and 124 minor islands, became the fiftieth state of the United States in 1959.

    The island that most tourists visit is Oahu, where the capital city of Honolulu is located. The largest island is Hawaii, which is also the name of the state. One of the most interesting islands is Niihau, which is called the "Forbidden Island" because no one is allowed to visit the island without special permission. Niihau is privately owned by one family, the Robinsons. The Robinsons want to help the native Hawaiian families who live on their island to preserve their culture by keeping outsiders away. Although everyone can speak English, Hawaiian is the everyday language of Niihau.

    Not many Americans know that Hawaii was once a monarchy. The most famous king of Hawaii was Kamehameha I, who united all the islands into one kingdom about 1800. The last queen, whose name was Liliuokalani, ruled until 1893, when she was overthrown by a group of businessmen with the help of the U.S. military. Today, there are many native Hawaiian groups that want to see the United States give Hawaiian land back to their people.

Complex sentences with noun clauses

A noun clause is a dependent clause that acts like a noun; that is, it can be a subject, an object, or an object of a preposition. Noun clauses are often used in academic and business writing to report information, ideas, and the words of others.

Noun clauses begin with one of these subordinating words: *that, whether, if* (informal), and question words such as *who, which, what, where, when, why, how, how much, how often, how soon,* and so on.

▶ Everyone knows *that* **global warming is a serious problem.**

▶ Recent measurements have shown *how much* **ice has melted in the Arctic.**

▶ World leaders have been meeting to discuss *what* **action governments should take.**

▶ Environmentalists wonder *whether* **we can reverse the damage or not.**

We often use noun clauses to report what someone says. This kind of noun clause is called "reported speech" or "indirect speech." There are special rules for verb tenses in reported speech.

▶ The *Journal of Environmental Science* reports *that* **the winter temperatures in the North Sea have risen 8.4 degrees in six years.**

We also use noun clauses after expressions such as *It is important . . . , It is urgent . . . , It is necessary . . .* In this kind of noun clause, called a "clause of importance," you must use the base (simple) form of the verb.

▶ It is necessary **that he *finish* all the antibiotic medicine.**   (NOT *finishes*)

▶ It is important **that we *be* ready to leave at six o'clock.**   (NOT *are*)

Never use a comma before a noun clause.

▶ I hope̸/**that I will get good grades this semester.**

The independent clause determines the end-of-sentence punctuation. If the independent clause is a statement, use a period. If the independent clause is a question, use a question mark.

▶ **I don't know** where she lives.

▶ **Do you know** where she lives?

Reference: Learn more about noun clauses in the following sections: Clauses of importance, *Section 11c*; Reported speech, *Section 11c*.

! *Special Tip*

Be aware of word order.

Always use statement word order (subject + verb), not question word order (verb + subject), in a noun clause even when a noun clause begins with a question word. Also, noun clauses don't need *do, does,* and *did* because they are not questions.

              it is.
▶ I don't know what time ~~is it.~~

           I can
▶ Could you please tell me where ~~can I~~ find an ATM machine?

            the students were
▶ The teacher didn't understand what ~~were the students~~ talking about.

          they said.
▶ Maybe she couldn't hear what ~~did they say.~~

              something costs.
▶ In some cultures, it is not polite to ask how much ~~does something cost.~~

PRACTICE—Section 7a (3)

A. Find and underline four noun clauses in the following paragraph.

EXAMPLE

Do you think <u>that parents should choose their children's future careers</u>?

> When I was young, I didn't know what I wanted to be. I wasn't sure whether I wanted to be a singer, an actor, or a musician. I just knew that I wanted to be famous. My parents, however, decided that I should study business.

B. Edit the noun clauses in the following paragraph for mistakes. There are three errors. The first mistake has been corrected as an example.

> My parents decided that I should become a businessman without asking me
>
>   *ed*
> what d̶i̶d̶ I want to do with my life. My parents don't know me very well. They
>   ^
> don't know who am I? They don't understand that I am an artist in my heart.
> I hope, that I will find a way to fulfill their wishes and my dreams.

7b   Using appositives

An appositive or appositive phrase is a noun or noun phrase that renames another noun or noun phrase. We use appositives to identify and to add more details about a noun.

                              appositive phrase
▶ The game of golf, **formerly an "old man's sport,"** is changing.

          appositive
▶ Golf star **Tiger Woods** has made the game popular among young people.

You can make an appositive by shortening an adjective clause. Just delete *who* or *which* and the verb *be*.

▶ Even young women are learning to play golf, ~~which was~~ **traditionally a man's sport.**

You can also make an appositive by combining sentences, writing the less important information as an appositive.

> Se Ri Pak is a rising star. + She is a young woman golfer from Korea. =
▶ Se Ri Pak, **a young woman golfer from Korea,** is a rising star.

Put commas before and after an appositive that is not necessary to identify the first noun but merely gives extra information about it.

▶ Mark McGwire and Sammy Sosa, **two power hitters,** changed the game of baseball forever.

Don't use commas with appositives that are necessary to identify the first noun.

▶ Power hitters **Mark McGwire and Sammy Sosa** changed the game of baseball forever.

Reference: Learn more about this comma rule in *Section 25c.*

PRACTICE—Section 7b

A. Circle the appositives and appositive phrases in the paragraph, and draw an arrow to the nouns or noun phrases they rename. One sentence has two appositives.

EXAMPLE

The Roxy, a new eight-screen movie theater, recently opened in the city center.

My teenage daughter saw the film *Titanic* twelve times. The film starred two of Hollywood's most popular young actors, Leonardo DiCaprio and Kate Winslet. The love story of the beautiful young heiress Rose and the handsome young artist Jack touched the hearts of young people everywhere. The film, one of Hollywood's biggest hits in years, received fourteen Oscar nominations.

B. Combine each pair of sentences into one sentence. Make the second sentence an appositive or appositive phrase and insert it into the first sentence. Add commas if the appositive is extra information.

EXAMPLE

Our family kitchen is always full of delicious smells. It is my favorite room in the house.

Our family kitchen, my favorite room in the house, is always full of delicious smells.

1. My mother loves to cook. My mother is a professional chef.
2. She makes the best lasagna. Her lasagna is a flavorful combination of ground beef, tomatoes, cheese, and pasta.
3. My father won't eat her lasagna. My father is a vegetarian.

7c   Using *-ing* and *-ed* phrases

Phrases containing *-ing* or *-ed* words are called participial phrases because the *-ing* or *-ed* words are the present and past participle verb forms. They act like adjectives; that is, they add descriptive information to a noun or pronoun.

present participial phrase
▶ The students, **thinking that class had ended,** packed up their books and left.

past participial
phrase
▶ Shakespeare's English was very different from the English **spoken today.**

You can make this kind of phrase by shortening certain adjective clauses.

1. Delete *who, which,* or *that.* (You can shorten adjective clauses only when a relative pronoun—*who, which,* or *that*—is the subject of its clause.)

2. Change the verbs as follows:

a. Change an active voice verb (simple present, simple past, or future tense) to an *-ing* word.

> *planning*
> ▶ Anyone w~~ho plans~~ **to travel in the tropics** should know about malaria.

> *leaving*
> ▶ The Smiths, w~~ho will leave~~ **next week for the Amazon,** got some malaria pills from their doctor.

> *believing*
> ▶ Mr. Smith, w~~ho believed~~ **malaria was a disease of the past,** didn't take the pills.

b. If the verb is in the present or past continuous tense, delete the helping verb *be* and leave the *-ing* word.

> ▶ The bus hit a pedestrian w~~ho was~~ **crossing the street.**

c. If the verb is in the passive voice (present or past tense), delete the helping verb *be* and leave the *-ed* word.

> ▶ A person w~~ho is~~ **bitten by a malaria-carrying mosquito** can get the disease.

> ▶ Mrs. Smith, w~~ho was~~ **worried about getting sick,** took malaria pills every day.

Put commas before and after *-ing* and *-ed* phrases that do not identify the noun or pronoun but merely give extra information about it. Extra information phrases can appear either before or after the noun they modify.

▶ George, **planning to graduate in June,** has already started looking for a job.

▶ **Planning to graduate in June,** George has already started looking for a job.

Don't use commas around a phrase that is necessary to identify its antecedent. Necessary phrases always follow the noun they describe.

▶ Students **planning to graduate in June** must make an appointment with the registrar.

Reference: Learn more about this comma rule in *Section 25c.*

7d Using shortened adverb clauses

Shortened adverb clauses tell *when* or *why*. They give a time or a reason.

Time ▶ **After leaving home,** I began to appreciate my family.

Reason ▶ **Being the oldest child in my family,** I often had to take care of my younger siblings.

You can shorten time clauses and reason clauses. Here's how to do so.

1. Delete the subject. (This is possible only when the subjects of both clauses are the same person or thing.)

2. Change the verbs as follows.

   a. Change an active voice verb (simple present, simple past, or future tense) to an *-ing* word.

   speaking
   ▶ When ~~I speak~~ on the telephone, I try to speak slowly and clearly.

   b. If the verb is in the present or past continuous tense, delete the helping verb *be* and leave the *-ing* word.

   ▶ Some students like to listen to music **while ~~they are~~ doing homework.**

   c. If the verb is in the passive voice (present or past tense), delete the helping verb *be* and leave the *-ed* word.

   ▶ **When ~~he was~~ questioned by the police,** the murderer confessed to his crime.

3. Delete reason words (*because, since,* and *as*) but keep time words (*before, after, while, when,* and *since*).

   Needing
   Reason ▶ ~~Because I needed~~ a quiet place to study, I often yelled at my noisy siblings.

   yelling
   Time ▶ After ~~I had yelled~~ at them, however, I always felt guilty.

! ***Special Tips***

1. Make sure the subjects of both clauses are the same person or thing before shortening an adverb clause.

   coming
   ▶ Before ~~I came~~ to the United States to study, I had never lived on my own.

   The subjects are the same person, so it is possible to shorten the adverb clause.

   ▶ Before **I** came to the United States, **my parents** gave me a lot of advice.

   The subjects are different people, so it is not possible to shorten the adverb clause.

2. The location and punctuation of shortened adverb clauses can vary. In most cases, you can put the phrase at the beginning of a sentence and put a comma after it.

PRACTICE—Section 7d

A. Find and underline four *-ing* or *-ed* phrases and shortened adverb clauses in the following paragraph.

EXAMPLE

<u>Hoping to graduate in three years</u>, Jack took extra classes every semester.

    Four-year-old Sarah loved to dress up in her mother's clothes and play "grown-up." One day, while wearing her mother's high-heeled shoes, Sarah fell down the stairs. Knocked unconscious, Sarah lay very still. Sarah's mother, believing that her daughter was dead, began to scream. Sarah woke up when her mother began screaming. Frightened by her mother's screaming, Sarah began screaming, too.

B. Shorten adjective and adverb clauses wherever possible in the following paragraph. There are five clauses that can be shortened.

EXAMPLE

      studying
After ~~he studied~~ night and day for two and a half years, Jack decided to quit shcool and travel.

    Because she finally realized that screaming was useless, Sarah's mother quieted down and called an ambulance. While she waited for the ambulance, she checked her daughter for injuries. Fortunately, she didn't find any. Just to be safe, however, the ambulance crew took Sarah to the hospital. Poor little Sarah, who was strapped to a gurney (a bed on wheels) and put into the ambulance, screamed all the way there. She stopped screaming only after her mother promised to bring her some ice cream. Because he was concerned about broken bones, the doctor ordered X rays. After she looked at the X rays, however, the doctor told Sarah's mother that nothing was broken and that she could take Sarah home.

---

8   Common Sentence Problems

In this section are examples of four common problems in sentence structure and style and the best ways to correct them.

 Computer Note

Grammar checkers are not very good at finding errors in sentence structure. They are able to recognize some fragments and some run-together sentences, but sometimes grammar checkers make mistakes, too! They occasionally mark sentences that are correct as "possible" fragments or "possible" run-together sentences.

8a   Fragments

A fragment is a group of words that looks like a sentence but is in fact only part of a sentence. There are several kinds of fragments.

Dependent clause by itself

Not correct ✗ Shopping for a new car online saves time. **Because you can compare models and prices from home.**

> The second "sentence" is in fact a dependent clause. A dependent clause cannot be a sentence by itself. It must be connected to an independent clause.

To correct ▶ Shopping for a new car online saves time,/**Because you can** *because* **compare models and prices from home.**

> Connect the dependent clause to the independent clause.

Missing subject *it*

Not correct ✗ More and more people are shopping online these days. **Is easy, fast, and economical.**

> The subject *it* is missing in the second "sentence." In some languages, you can omit a subject that is a pronoun. In English, you must always have a subject (except in commands).

To correct ▶ More and more people are shopping online these days. **Is easy, fast,** *It is* **and economical.**

> Add the missing subject *it*.

Missing subject *there*

Not correct ✗ Old, established companies like Sears and J. C. Penney have put their entire catalogs online. **Also on the Internet have many new companies that sell their products only on the Web.**

> There is no subject for the verb *have* in the second "sentence." The verb *have* is also the wrong verb. The verb should be a form of *be*.

To correct ▶ Old, established companies like Sears and J. C. Penney have put *there are* their entire catalogs online. **Also on the Internet have many new companies that sell their products only on the Web.**

> Change *have* to *there are*.

Missing verb

Not correct ✗ **It cheaper for companies to sell online because they don't have the high overhead of a retail store.**

There is no verb. In some languages, you can omit the verb *be*. In English, you must always include it.

To correct ▶ **It ˄*is* cheaper for companies to sell online because they don't have the high overhead of a retail store.**

Add a verb.

Missing subject and verb

Not correct ✗ You can buy almost anything online. **For example, food, automobiles, books, clothes, airline tickets, and even insurance.**

There is no subject or verb in the second "sentence."

To correct ▶ You can buy almost anything online. **For example, *you can buy* food, automobiles, books, clothes, airline tickets, and even insurance.**

Add a subject and a verb.

-ing phrases

Not correct ✗ It is possible that we will do most of our shopping online in the future. **Without having to travel to a store.**

There is no subject or verb in the second "sentence." An *-ing* word by itself is either a gerund or a participle—not a verb.

To correct ▶ It is possible that we will do most of our shopping online in the future,/ ~~Without~~ *without* having to travel to a store.

Connect the *-ing* phrase to a sentence.

OR

▶ It is possible that we will do most of our shopping online in the future. *We won't have to* ~~Without having to~~ travel to a store.

Rewrite the *-ing* phrase to make it a complete sentence with a subject and a verb.

! Special Tips

1. Look for danger words like *because, although, which, if,* and *when.*

Make sure that a sentence beginning with one of these words has at least one independent clause. If it doesn't, it is a fragment.

Fragment?	▸ My son is majoring in mechanical engineering. Because he is good at math and understands how machines work.
Danger word	*because*
Question	Is there an independent clause in the sentence containing the danger word?
Answer	No.
Conclusion	This is a fragment. It is not a complete sentence.

2. Try to turn a sentence into a *yes/no* question without adding any new words except *do, does,* or *did.*

If it is possible to make a *yes/no* question, it is a complete sentence. If it is not possible, it is a fragment.

Fragment?	▸ My daughter wants to study industrial design. If she gets accepted at a good college.
Yes/no question	Does my daughter want to study industrial design?
Conclusion	A *yes/no* question is possible. The sentence is complete. It is not a fragment.
Yes/no question	Does if she gets accepted . . . ?
Conclusion	A *yes/no* question is not possible. This is a fragment.

PRACTICE—Section 8a

There are six fragments in the following paragraphs. Find and correct them. There is more than one way to make the corrections. The first fragment has been corrected as an example.

Four hundred years ago, a game began when people started throwing a ball against a church wall to entertain themselves during religious festivals. This game became known as jai alai, which means "merry festival" in the Basque language.

It was

Jai alai is a ball game similar to handball and racquetball. ~~Was~~ invented by the Basque people, who live in the northern part of Spain. Although jai alai began in Europe. Is now popular in many Latin American countries. Especially in Mexico has many jai alai teams. Athletes who play jai alai must be very quick and have excellent eye-hand coordination. Because it is one of the fastest of all ball games. The ball, or pelota, has been clocked at over 180 miles per hour. Is the hardest ball used in any sport. Because the pelota is so hard, the walls of a jai alai court are made of granite. Just like the original church walls.

8b   Run-together sentences

A run-together sentence is a sentence error that happens when you connect two independent clauses incorrectly. Sometimes the two clauses have nothing between them. Sometimes there is a comma between them but no connecting word. The second type is sometimes called a comma splice.

There is more than one way to correct a run-together sentence.

If the ideas are equal, use one of the techniques of coordination. For example:

Not correct ✗ **Chen is an excellent student he is a star athlete.**

> There is nothing between the two independent clauses—no connecting word and no punctuation mark.

, and

To correct ▶ **Chen is an excellent student ʌ he is a star athlete.**

> Add a coordinating conjunction (and a comma if there isn't one).

; in addition

▶ **Chen is an excellent student ʌ he is a star athlete.**

> Add a semicolon, a conjunctive adverb, and a comma.

;

▶ **Chen is an excellent student ʌ he is a star athlete as well.**

> Add a semicolon.

If one idea gives secondary information, use a technique of subordination. For example:

Not correct ✗ **Chen gets straight A's, he studies all the time.**

> There is a comma but no connecting word.

because

To correct ▶ **Chen gets straight A's ʌ he studies all the time.**

> Make one idea an adverb clause.

OR

, who studies all the time,

▶ **Chen gets straight A's ʌ he studies all the time.**

> Make one idea an adjective clause.

! *Special Tip*

Make it a habit to check for run-together sentences in your own writing.

Look for words like *then, also,* and *therefore* in the middle of a sentence. These words frequently occur in run-together sentences. Ask yourself three questions: (1) Are there two clauses? (2) Are both clauses independent? (3) How are the clauses joined?

Run-together? ▶	We finished our homework, then we played video games for a while.	
Danger word	*then*	
Question 1	Are there two clauses?	**Answer** Yes.
Question 2	Are both clauses independent?	**Answer** Yes.
Question 3	How are the clauses joined?	**Answer** With a comma only.
Conclusion	This is a run-together sentence.	

and
To correct ▶ We finished our homework, then we played video games for a while.

Run-together? ▶	Our homework is to read Chapter 6, and there is also a test on Friday.	
Danger word	*also*	
Question 1	Are there two clauses?	**Answer** Yes.
Question 2	Are both clauses independent?	**Answer** Yes.
Question 3	How are the clauses joined?	**Answer** With a comma and a coordinating conjunction.
Conclusion	This is not a run-together sentence. The sentence is correct.	

PRACTICE—Section 8b

The following paragraph contains three run-together sentences. Find the errors and correct them, using any appropriate technique. There is more than one way to make corrections. The first error has been corrected for you as an example.

      Teaching children good behavior is one of the main jobs of parents; schools also share this responsibility. Every culture has its own methods of doing this. In some cultures, parents and teachers hit children who misbehave. In other cultures, parents don't hit their children, instead, they exclude them from the family group. In U.S. schools, teachers may not hit children physical punishment is against the law. They can make them do extra lessons or send them to the principal's office.

8c   Choppy writing

Choppy writing is writing in which there are a lot of short sentences. Short sentences are not errors, but writing too many of them together is not good style. Readers have to work harder to understand the relationship among the ideas because there are no connecting words to help them.

Problem paragraph

> George Washington and Abraham Lincoln were two famous U.S. presidents. Their lives were very different. Washington's parents were rich landowners. Lincoln's family was poor. Washington and Lincoln had similar ideas about slavery. Washington had owned slaves. He gave his slaves their freedom. Lincoln freed all slaves. He issued the Emancipation Proclamation on January 1, 1863. Washington was known for his honesty. Lincoln's nickname was "Honest Abe."

To correct   Combine sentences, coordinating equal ideas and subordinating secondary information.

The similarities and differences discussed in this paragraph are more or less equal in content. It is best to connect these ideas using coordinating words such as *however, but,* and *and.*

▶ They were famous presidents.   **however**   Their lives were different.

▶ Washington's parents were rich.   **but**   Lincoln's family was poor.

▶ Washington freed his own slaves.   **and**   Lincoln freed all slaves.

▶ Washington was honest.   **and**   Lincoln was honest.

Other sentences express secondary information. It is best to subordinate these ideas by writing dependent clauses beginning with *who* and *when.*

▶ Washington freed his slaves.   **who**   He had owned slaves.

▶ Lincoln freed all slaves.   **when**   He issued the Emancipation Proclamation.

Revised paragraph

> George Washington and Abraham Lincoln were two famous U.S.
> *; however, their*
> presidents/ ~~Their~~ lives were very different. Washington's
> *, but*
> parents were rich landowners/ Lincoln's family was poor.
> Washington and Lincoln had similar ideas about slavery.
> *, who*   *, and*
> Washington had owned slaves/ ~~He~~ gave his slaves their freedom/
>   *when he*
> Lincoln freed all slaves/ ~~He~~ issued the Emancipation
>   *, and*
> Proclamation on January 1, 1863/ Washington was known for his
> honesty. Lincoln's nickname was "Honest Abe."

PRACTICE—Section 8c

The following paragraphs contain choppy writing. Improve them by combining sentences. There is more than one way to make the revisions. One revision has been made as an example.

> Washington and Lincoln were leaders during times of crisis. Washington was
>   , *which*
> the top general of the army during the Revolutionary War./It̶ began in 1775.
>
> Lincoln was president during the U.S. Civil War. It began in 1861.
>   The young country was in danger of breaking apart after these two wars. It needed a strong leader to stay united. Washington was a strong president. Lincoln was a strong president. Both men believed in keeping the country together. Both men worked very hard to keep the country from splitting apart.
>   America finally won its independence from England. Washington helped write the U.S. Constitution. The Constitution made the federal government strong. The Civil War ended in 1865. Lincoln's strong leadership helped reunite the North and the South.

8d   Overuse of *and, but,* and *so*

Using too many *and*s, *but*s, and *so*s in a sentence, like choppy writing, is not an error, but it is not good style. The sentences are too long, and the relationship among the ideas is not clear because so many clauses are independent. It's hard to tell which are the main ideas and which are supporting information.

Problem paragraphs
> There are now over 31 million Spanish-speaking people living in the United States, and their number is rapidly increasing, and by the year 2050, they will be the largest minority group, and they will make up one-fourth of the nation's population.
>   A small town in Texas has many residents from Mexico, and they speak Spanish, so the town decided to make Spanish its official language, but the same thing will probably not happen in many other places in the United States.

To correct
Reduce the number of *and*s, *but*s, and *so*s. Divide long sentences into two or three shorter ones. Coordinate equal ideas and subordinate supporting information.

Revised paragraphs
> There are now over 31 million Spanish-speaking people living in the United States, and their number is rapidly
>   . *By*
> increasing/ a̶n̶d̶ b̶y̶ the year 2050, they will be the largest
>   *making*
> minority group, a̶n̶d̶ t̶h̶e̶y̶ w̶i̶l̶l̶ m̶a̶k̶e̶ up one-fourth of the nation's population.
>   *Since a*   *who*
> A small town in Texas has many residents from Mexico,/ a̶n̶d̶

~~they~~ speak Spanish, ~~so~~ the town decided to make Spanish its
                    . However,
official language/ ~~but~~ the same thing will probably not happen
in many other places in the United States.

PRACTICE—Section 8d

The following paragraph is an example of overuse of *and*, *but*, and *so*. Improve the paragraph using any appropriate technique. There is more than one way to make the revisions. The first revision has been made for you as an example.

. After

My family has always worked hard/ ~~and after~~ we came to the United States, we bought a small grocery store. My father worked in the store all day, and my mother worked there for a few hours in the afternoon, and she also took care of the house. There were five children in the family, and we all went to the store every day after school. My oldest brother enjoyed selling things, and I liked keeping the shelves neat, so we enjoyed our afternoons in the store, but our younger brothers and sisters hated being there because they wanted to be outside playing with their friends.

9 Word Order

 Computer Note

Grammar checkers cannot recognize mistakes in word order. A computer cannot know if the three words *he, is,* and *where* should have the word order of a question (*Where is he?*) or the word order of a noun clause (*where he is*).

Using the correct word order is important in English because word order can change meaning. Compare:

▶ **Sammy Sosa hit the baseball.** (*and he made a home run*)
▶ **The baseball hit Sammy Sosa.** (*and he went to the hospital*)

Reference: Learn about the word order of adjectives in *Sections 19a* and *20b* and about word order with adverbs in *Section 19b*.

9a Normal word order

Normal word order in an English sentence is as follows:

SUBJECT	VERB	OBJECT(S)/ COMPLEMENTS	PLACE EXPRESSION	TIME EXPRESSION
We	watched	a video	at home	last night.

This order is not very flexible. Only a few variations are possible (*Sections 9b and 9c*). Here are two rules that you *must* follow.

1. Never put anything between a verb and its objects.

┌─ V ─┐   ┌────── O ──────┐
▶ I **bought** yesterday **all my textbooks.**

2. Put place expressions before time expressions.

┌── time ──┐ ┌── place ──┐
▶ We went **after class to the bookstore.**

9b   Inverted (verb-subject) word order

Normal word order is subject-verb. In six situations, the word order is inverted (verb-subject).

Questions

In most questions, the subject follows the verb, and *do, does,* and *did* may be necessary (*Section 4c.*)

	VERB	**SUBJECT**	
	Are	**you**	hungry?
	Can	**I**	go to the movies with you?
Which car	**did**	**they**	buy?
How long	**has**	**Marta**	been sick?

EXCEPTIONS

1. Questions in which *who* or *what* is the subject use normal subject-verb word order.

┌S┐ ┌── V ──┐   ┌S┐ ┌── V ──┐
▶ **Who is knocking** at the door? **What happened** to you?

2. Tag questions use normal subject-verb word order in the main part of the question, but not in the tag part.

┌S┐ ┌── V ──┐
▶ **You are coming** to the party tonight, aren't you?

Sentences beginning with *There*

The subject follows the verb in sentences beginning with *There is, There are, There was, There will be,* and so on. We use this kind of sentence when we want to say that something exists. The word *there* is not the subject; it is an "empty" word that fills the position where you usually find the subject. The real subject follows the verb (*Section 4b, Pattern 6*).

	VERB	SUBJECT
There	are	seven continents.
There	is	a reason for everything.

We also use this kind of sentence with a place expression such as *in the plaza* and *in his eyes*.

⌐V¬ ⌐————— S —————⌐
▶ There **were hundreds of demonstrators** in the plaza.

⌐V¬⌐S¬
▶ There **was fear** in his eyes.

However, it is usually better to put the real subject first and replace *be* with an "action" verb such as *jammed* and *showed*.

▶ **Hundreds of demonstrators jammed** the plaza.

▶ **Fear showed** in his eyes.

Sentences beginning with *It*

The subject follows the verb in certain sentences beginning with *It* + linking verb.

	VERB		SUBJECT
It	wasn't	easy	to find a parking space.
It	is	important	that everyone arrive on time.
It	seems	wrong	to do it that way.

Reference: Learn more about these kinds of sentences in the following sections: Infinitives (as subject complements), *Section 12b*; Clauses of importance, *Section 11c*.

Sentences beginning with a place expression + an intransitive verb

The subject can follow the verb in sentences containing a place expression and an intransitive verb. Verbs in this pattern are usually ones such as *stand, sit, lie, appear, rise,* and *shine*. Putting a place expression at the beginning of a sentence gives it special emphasis.

PLACE EXPRESSION	VERB	SUBJECT
Next to the motorcycle	stood	a tall man in a leather jacket.
In the distance	rise	the snow-covered mountains.

You can also use normal word order in these sentences.

▶ **A tall man in a leather jacket stood** next to the motorcycle.

▶ **The snow-covered mountains rise** in the distance.

Sentences beginning with a negative word

We can begin a sentence with a negative word or phrase to emphasize it. Put the verb before the subject, and use *do, does,* and *did* if necessary. In the following sentences, notice how putting *never* first gives it special emphasis.

▶ She has *never* seemed so upset.

▶ *Never* has she seemed so upset.

Here are other examples:

NEGATIVE	VERB	SUBJECT	
At no time	were	the children	in danger.
Nowhere	could	we	find an empty seat.
Not only	did	he	win, but he also set a new world record.
No longer	do	we	have to listen to their complaints.
Rarely	does	it	rain in the desert.
Seldom	do	new parents	get eight hours of sleep.

Conditional sentences

In a conditional clause when the verb is *were, should,* or a past perfect tense (*had known, had written, had seen,* and so on), you can emphasize the hypothetical condition by omitting *if* and using inverted word order.

NORMAL PATTERN	INVERTED PATTERN
If **I were** rich, I would travel.	**Were I** rich, I would travel.
If **he should** call, tell him that I am not at home.	**Should he** call, tell him that I am not at home.
If **I had known** her name, I would have introduced you to her.	**Had I known** her name, I would have introduced you to her.

Reference: Learn more about conditional sentences in *Section 11c.*

PRACTICE—Section 9b

Edit the following paragraphs for errors in word order. There are six errors.

EXAMPLE

I miss very much (my family.)

    I received last week a letter from my best friend, who lives in Italy. He enclosed a funny photo of himself. The photo shows my friend holding both his arms out to one side with his hands pointing up. In the background is the famous Leaning Tower of Pisa. It looks as if he is keeping from falling over the tower.

I was happy to get his letter. Not often I hear from this friend—usually just once a year at Christmas. I am thinking about going next summer to Europe. If I go, I will certainly visit him. We haven't seen for almost ten years one another. We used to get together often, but since he moved to Italy, we have seen each other only once when he came home to attend his sister's wedding. Not only he moved to Italy, but he also got married. Now he is the father of two children and has no time to travel.

9c Word order of direct and indirect objects

Many verbs can have both a direct object and an indirect object.

- A direct object names the receiver of the verb's action.
- An indirect object tells *to whom* or *for whom* the action is done.

An indirect object (IO) comes in front of a direct object (DO).

$$\text{IO} \quad \text{DO}$$

▶ A used car dealer sold **me a car that doesn't run.**

If you replace the indirect object with a prepositional phrase (PP), put it after the direct object.

$$\text{DO} \quad \text{PP}$$

▶ My friend is going to fix **the car for me.**

Indirect objects with or without a preposition

With some verbs, you can write an indirect object with or without a preposition. Most verbs use the preposition *to;* a few verbs use the preposition *for.*

USE *TO* WITH THESE VERBS			USE *FOR* WITH THESE VERBS		
bring	pay	serve	build	draw	order
give	promise	show	buy	find	pour
guarantee	read	teach	cook	get	save
hand	refund	tell	do	make	type
lend	sell	throw			
offer	send	write			
owe					

▶ The soldiers *gave* **the children** some candy.
▶ The soldiers *gave* some candy **to the children.**

▶ Please *get* **me** a jacket. I'm cold.
▶ Please *get* a jacket **for me.** I'm cold.

Indirect objects that require a preposition

With other verbs, you *must* use a prepositional phrase with *to* or *for*.

USE *TO* WITH THESE VERBS			USE *FOR* WITH THESE VERBS		
admit	introduce	report	cash	fix	pronounce
announce	mention	say	change	keep	repeat
describe	prove	speak	close	open	sign
explain	recommend	suggest	correct	prepare	translate

to us
▶ The poet *explained* us the poem.
    ^

                                          to us
▶ She also *described* us the process of writing poetry.
                                       ^

                              for her
▶ The polite boy *opened* her the door.
                        ^

                                  for me
▶ Could you please *change* me this $20 bill?
                              ^

PRACTICE—Section 9c

Edit the following sentences for errors. Two sentences are correct.

EXAMPLE
My parents sent to me a leather jacket for my birthday.

1. I often give homeless people a dollar or two.
2. Could you please explain me the difference between "lend" and "borrow"?
3. The polite student opened for the teacher the door to the classroom.
4. The teacher said "Thank you" to him.
5. Every night, the mother reads to the children a story before they go to sleep.

9d   Varying sentence openings

Most sentences in English follow the same subject-verb-object/complement pattern. For variety, begin some sentences with a word or phrase that is not the subject. Don't overdo it, though! Don't begin every sentence with a different element.

Notice that when you move something to the front of a sentence, you usually add a comma after the word, phrase, or clause that you move. (Learn more about this comma rule in *Section 25b*.)

Time word or phrase

▶ We wrote a summary of the article first.
▶ **First,** we wrote a summary of the article.

▶ We wrote three questions about it later on.
▶ **Later on,** we wrote three questions about it.

Prepositional phrase of time or place

▶ I can see the ocean from my bedroom window.
▶ **From my bedroom window,** I can see the ocean.

▶ They waited for two days for news about their family.
▶ **For two days,** they waited for news about their family.

Transition expression

▶ We had to cancel our plans as a result.
▶ **As a result,** we had to cancel our plans.

Infinitive phrase

▶ A person must be able to accept differences in order to live in a new culture.
▶ **In order to live in a new culture,** a person must be able to accept differences.

▶ You have to work hard to get an A in Ms. Fitzpatrick's class.
▶ **To get an A in Ms. Fitzpatrick's class,** you have to work hard.

Adverb

▶ They waited anxiously for news about their family.
▶ **Anxiously,** they waited for news about their family.

▶ Start a sentence occasionally with an adverb.
▶ **Occasionally,** start a sentence with an adverb.

Adverb clause

▶ You will improve your writing style if you vary your sentence openings.
▶ **If you vary your sentence openings,** you will improve your writing style.

-ing/-ed phrase

▶ I went to bed after finishing my homework.
▶ **After finishing my homework,** I went to bed.

▶ Alexei, worried about his grade in lab class, went to see the instructor.
▶ **Worried about his grade in lab class,** Alexei went to see the instructor.

Notice how changing a few sentence openings improves this paragraph.

Original	A new Internet business is creating a furor in colleges and universities. Students no longer need to go to class at some universities. They can miss a class and still get a copy of the lecture notes free. Several new Internet companies recently started to publish lecture notes on the Internet. The companies pay a student who is enrolled in a class $300 a semester to take notes and post them on the companies' Web sites. Other students can download the notes free because the companies' costs are paid by advertising.
Revised	A new Internet business is creating a furor in colleges and universities. **At some universities,** students no longer need to go to class. They can miss a class and still get a copy of the lecture notes free. **Recently,** several new Internet companies started to publish lecture notes on the Internet. The companies pay a student who is enrolled in a class $300 a semester to take notes and post them on the companies' Web sites. **Because the companies' costs are paid by advertising,** other students can download the notes free.

PRACTICE—Section 9d

Improve this paragraph by beginning two or three sentences with an element other than the subject *I.*

I took the test for my first driver's license yesterday. I was so nervous during the driving test that I drove the wrong way on a one-way street. I made an illegal U-turn to correct my mistake. I ran over the curb when trying to parallel park. I also forgot to signal before turning into the parking lot at the end of the test. I failed to get my license even though I got 100% on the written test.

10   Word Choice

With over 600,000 words, English has one of the largest vocabularies of all the languages in the world. This fact makes choosing appropriate words a special challenge. The suggestions in this section may help you choose wisely.

10a Dictionaries and thesauruses

Dictionaries

A good dictionary is useful for a writer not only during the writing but also during the revising and editing processes. There is a tremendous amount of information in a dictionary. A dictionary can help you not only with word meanings and spelling but also with word forms. For example, if you need the noun form of the adjective *clear,* you can find it in a dictionary. A good dictionary can also help you choose appropriate words. It will tell you which words are informal, slang, and obsolete (no longer used in modern English).

Special dictionaries for students of English as a second language are available. These dictionaries give easy-to-understand definitions and a lot of example sentences. They also help with special problems, such as the difference between *say* and *tell.* Also, if you need to know whether to write *married to* or *married with* or *She recommended to go* or *She recommended going,* an ESL dictionary will tell you.

Thesauruses

A thesaurus is a book of synonyms. In some thesauruses, words are listed alphabetically. In other thesauruses, words are grouped by meaning; that is, words with similar meanings are listed near each other. Most computer word-processing programs contain a thesaurus, or you can purchase one on disk or CD-ROM.

However, thesauruses often simply show lists of synonyms and do not explain differences in meaning and usage, so there is a danger that you will use a word incorrectly. It is never a good idea to use a word from a thesaurus that is unfamiliar to you. Use a thesaurus only to remind yourself of words that you already know.

 ! *Special Tips*

1. Use an English–English dictionary while writing and revising.
   Don't depend on your bilingual dictionary to give you the best information.

2. Don't use big words that you find in a dictionary or thesaurus just because they seem impressive.
   Use only words that are familiar to you.

10b Informal language and slang

 Computer Note

Some computerized grammar checkers allow you to check your writing at different levels of formality (casual, formal, and technical, for example). However, even if you have set your computer to check for formal language, it does not always tell you when you have used an informal word like *guy* or *kid.*

Informal language is everyday spoken language and includes expressions such as *OK, kids, guys,* and *hang out.* Slang is language used by particular groups such as teenagers and surfers, and people outside the group don't always understand it.

Don't write the same way you speak. Don't use informal language in formal academic or business writing, and don't use slang.

Informal ▶ I had to baby-sit the younger ~~kids~~ *children* last weekend while my ~~mom~~ *mother* went shopping.

Slang ▶ We should ~~hit the books~~ *study*, or we will ~~bomb the final~~ *fail the final examination*.

10c Gender-sensitive (sexist) language

 Computer Note

Most grammar checkers are able to point out some, but not all, gender-sensitive words.

The movement for equality for women has made people more aware of gender-sensitive language, which is language that unnecessarily differentiates between women and men. For instance, many people feel that using words such as *waitress* suggests that women have a lower social position.

Try to use gender-neutral words, especially in the following situations.

Words with *-man* and *-ess*

Avoid using the word *man* and words containing *man* to refer to all human beings. Choose a gender-neutral word or expression instead. See the list.

▶ War is a tragedy for all ~~mankind~~ *humanity*.

GENDER-SENSITIVE	GENDER-NEUTRAL
businessman	**businessperson**
chairman	**chair, chairperson**
freshman	**first-year student**
mailman	**letter carrier**
mankind	**humankind, humanity, human beings, people**
manpower	**personnel, human resources**
policeman	**police officer**
salesman	**salesperson, sales associate, sales clerk**

Avoid words that end in *-ess*. Choose a gender-neutral word or expression instead. See the list.

    flight attendant

▶ The ~~stewardess~~ brought me an extra blanket.

GENDER-SENSITIVE	GENDER-NEUTRAL
actress	**actor**
hostess	**host**
stewardess	**flight attendant**
waitress	**waiter, server**
seamstress	**tailor**

NOTE: Female titles (*princess, duchess, countess*) and names of female animals (*lioness, tigress*) are acceptable.

Pronouns

As you know, pronouns agree in gender and number with their antecedents.

▶ **Mrs. Smith** is a lawyer. *She* works for a large law firm in the city.

▶ **Mr. Smith** is a teacher. *He* teaches math at a high school.

▶ **Mr. and Mrs. Smith** live in Los Angeles. *They* have lived there for ten years.

What if the antecedent is gender-neutral? What pronoun should you use with an antecedent such as *person, student, anyone,* or *everyone?*

▶ **A student** must take certain steps in order to graduate in June. First, *he? she?* must . . .

▶ **Everyone** who takes a sports class has *his? her?* own gym locker.

Here are some suggestions:

1. Make the sentence plural. This way is preferred.

    ▶ **Students** must take certain steps to graduate in June. First, *they* must . . .

    ▶ All **students** who take a sports class have *their* own gym locker.

2. Use both pronouns (*he or she, him or her, his or her*). Using both pronouns is awkward if they occur often in a paragraph, so most writers try to avoid it.

    ▶ **A student** must take certain steps in order to graduate in June. First, *he or she* must . . .

3. Rewrite the sentence.

    ▶ If *you* want to graduate in June, *you* must take certain steps. First, *you* must . . .

Occupations

Avoid stereotyping occupations as all-male or all-female. Use both pronouns or make the sentence plural.

> *he or she*
> ▶ A nurse today must operate complex medical equipment. For example, ~~she~~ must be able to program computers that dispense medications.

> *students do*   *they are*   *jobs*
> ▶ If ~~an~~ engineering ~~student does~~ well in school, ~~he is~~ guaranteed ~~a job~~ after graduating.

PRACTICE—Sections 10b–10c

Edit the following sentences for gender-sensitive language, informal language, and slang.

EXAMPLE

Employees   want their paychecks   their   accounts
~~Any employee~~ who ~~wants his paycheck~~ deposited directly into ~~his~~ bank ~~account~~ must fill out this form.

1. Every employee is responsible for cleaning his own uniforms.
2. Each department elects a new chairman every four years.
3. Yoshi hangs out with several other guys at the gym.
4. There are seven kids in my family.
5. What time are you gonna leave?

PART 3 Grammar

11   Verb Forms and Tenses

11a   Verb forms

 Computer Note

Grammar checkers recognize some, but not all, errors in verb forms. Grammar checkers may call form errors subject-verb agreement errors. For example, they may call *They living with her parents* a subject-verb agreement error.

Main verbs

Every sentence in English has at least one main verb. Main verbs in English have five forms.

	BASE FORM	-S FORM	PAST TENSE	PAST PARTICIPLE	PRESENT PARTICIPLE
Regular verbs	**work**	**works**	**worked**	**worked**	**working**
Irregular verbs	**go**	**goes**	**went**	**gone**	**going**

- We make the *-s* form of both regular and irregular verbs by adding *-s* or *-es*, and we make the present participle by adding *-ing*.
- We make the past tense and past participle forms of regular verbs by adding *-d* or *-ed*. Sometimes there are spelling changes when you add *-(e)s*, *-(e)d*, or *-ing*. (Learn about spelling changes in *Section 38b*.)
- Irregular verbs make the past tense and past participle forms in many different ways, so you must memorize them. (*Section 46* lists irregular verbs.)

Helping verbs

With main verbs, we use one or more "helping verbs" to make different tenses, to make questions, and to express meanings such as possibility, advisability, and necessity.

    HV   MV
▶ I *was* working.

    HV   MV
▶ *Do* they work?

    HV HV HV   MV
▶ They *should have been* working.

    HV   MV
▶ We *must* work.

The helping verbs are (1) the forms of *be, have,* and *do* and (2) the modals.

FORMS OF *BE, HAVE,* AND *DO*	MODALS	
be, am, is, are, was, were, been, being	**can, could**	**will, would**
have, has, had	**shall, should**	**may, might**
do, does, did	**must, ought to**	**had better**
Be, have, and *do* can change their form.	Modals never change their form.	
I **am** working	I **must** work	
he **is** working	he **must** have worked	
they **were** working	they **must** be working	

NOTE: Helping verbs are also called auxiliary verbs.

11b Verb tenses

 Computer Note

Grammar checkers do not recognize verb tense mistakes. You must check for these errors on your own.

The tense of a verb shows the time of an action or condition. Tense also gives information such as whether an action happened just once, happened repeatedly, has stopped happening, or is still happening. The following chart summarizes the twelve tenses in English.

Summary of tenses

SIMPLE TENSES		PERFECT TENSES	
Simple present	I work	**Present perfect**	I have worked
Simple past	I worked	**Past perfect**	I had worked
Simple future	I will work	**Future perfect**	I will have worked
PROGRESSIVE TENSES*		**PERFECT PROGRESSIVE TENSES**	
Present progressive	I am working	**Present perfect progressive**	I have been working
Past progressive	I was working	**Past perfect progressive**	I had been working
Future progressive	I will be working	**Future perfect progressive**	I will have been working

*Progressive tenses are also called continuous tenses.

Nonprogressive verbs

Certain verbs are generally not used in the progressive tenses. These verbs do not express actions. Instead, they express emotions, mental processes, the five senses, possession, and a few other nonaction meanings. These verbs are also called nonaction verbs or stative verbs.

EMOTIONS				
love like miss	hate dislike	fear envy	mind care	▶ I **love** you. (NOT I am loving you.) ▶ She **misses** her friends back home. (NOT She is missing her friends back home.)
MENTAL PROCESSES				
know think* understand	believe doubt	mean realize	remember forget	▶ I **don't understand.** ▶ Do you **remember** your first day at school?
THE SENSES				
feel* hear	see*	smell*	taste*	▶ I **hear** loud music from the party next door. ▶ Dinner **smells** delicious!
POSSESSION				
own	possess	have*	belong	▶ That car **belongs** to my friend. ▶ They **have** a nice house.
OTHERS				
be* exist consist of include	seem look* appear*	need prefer want	cost owe	▶ You **seem** sad today. ▶ My family **consists of** my mother, my father, and me. ▶ He **needs** a job.

You can use verbs with an asterisk (*) in the progressive tenses with a different meaning.

	Nonaction meaning	Action meaning
think	▶ I **think** he's handsome, don't you?	▶ I **am thinking** about my future.
feel	▶ I **feel** sick.	▶ She **is feeling** her baby's skin.
	▶ I **am feeling** sick. In informal speech, you can use *feel* in tenses with progressive nonaction meaning when talking about health.	
see	▶ **Do** you **see** any taxis?	▶ She **has been seeing** a psychiatrist.
smell	▶ The flowers **smell** good.	▶ She **was smelling** the flowers when a bee stung her.
taste	▶ This soup **tastes** terrible.	▶ The cook **is tasting** the soup.
have	▶ We **don't have** a telephone.	▶ I'm **having** a problem with my boyfriend.
	▶ They **have** two children.	▶ **Are** you **having** a good time?
be	▶ She **is** rude. She is a rude person. It's a permanent characteristic.	▶ She **is being** rude. Right now, she is acting rudely. It's a temporary behavior.
look	▶ The children **look** sleepy.	▶ The children **are looking** at a picture book.
appear	▶ The kitten **appears** to be hungry.	▶ A famous singer **is appearing** in tonight's opera.

The present tenses

In each of the four present tenses, the verb shows a different relationship to present time.

The simple present tense

	base form	-s form
Statements	I work.	He works.
Questions	Do you work?	Does he work?
Negatives	They don't work.	He doesn't work.

1. Use the simple present tense to describe actions or conditions that are usual, habitual, or permanent.

   ▶ He **works** late every night.

   ▶ She **has** green eyes.

   We often use adverbs of frequency such as *often, usually, always,* and *frequently* with the simple present tense.

   ▶ The teacher *usually* **wears** a suit to school.

   ▶ He *frequently* **arrives** early.

2. Use the simple present tense to state general truths. The time is unimportant.

   ▶ The sun **rises** in the east and **sets** in the west.

   ▶ Parents **love** their children.

3. We sometimes use the simple present tense for a future action, especially for events on a schedule or timetable.

   ▶ His plane **leaves** at 9:30 tonight.

   ▶ How many stops **does** his flight **make?**

4. We use the simple present tense for a future action in certain time clauses. (See page 94.)

   ▶ The party will begin *as soon as the guest of honor* **arrives.**

! Special Tips

1. Remember to use the *-s* form with *he, she,* and *it* in the simple present tense.

   ▶ My sister believe͜ that you can know your future. She visit͜ a fortune teller every week.
   (-s)   (-s)

2. For special rules for the location of adverbs of frequency in a sentence, see *Section 19b.*

The present progressive tense

am/is/are + present participle		
Statements	I am working.	He is working.
Questions	Are you working?	Is he working?
Negatives	They aren't working.	He isn't working.

1. Use the present progressive for an action that is happening at the moment of speaking. The action is temporary.

   ▶ The teacher **is wearing** blue jeans today.

   ▶ She **is looking** for her car keys.

2. Use the present progressive for an action that is happening during the present period of time but not necessarily at the exact moment of speaking. The action is temporary.

▶ Their son **is studying** in France this year.

▶ She **is looking** for a husband.

3. We sometimes use the present progressive for a future action. We usually add a time word to show future time, but sometimes future time is clear from the context.

▶ My in-laws **are coming** for dinner **tonight**.

▶ They**'re coming** at *seven o'clock*.

▶ They**'re bringing** a cake for dessert.

The simple present vs. the present progressive

Because we use it for habitual actions, the simple present implies that an activity is more or less permanent. Because we use it for actions that are happening now (but may not continue in the future), the present progressive implies that an action is temporary. Compare the following uses.

▶ She **lives** with her parents. This sentence implies that she lives with her parents permanently.

▶ She **is living** with her parents. This sentence implies that she is living with her parents temporarily—perhaps until she finishes school.

▶ She **works** in a bank. Banking is her profession.

▶ She **is working** in a bookstore. This is a temporary job—perhaps while she is going to school.

PRACTICE—Section 11b (1)

Complete each sentence with the correct form of the verbs in parentheses. Choose between the simple present and the present progressive. The subject is provided if necessary.

EXAMPLE

I always *listen to* (*listen to*) music when I *study* (*study*) at home. What song *are you listening to* (*you listen to*) right now?

1. Water _____ (*boil*) at 100° Celsius and 212° Fahrenheit.

2. The water _____ (*boil*). Let's make tea.

3. Sara usually _____ (*sit*) in the front row, but today she _____ (*sit*) in the back.

4. What _____ (*you think about*)? You _____ (*have*) such a dreamy expression.

5. School always _____ (*begin*) on the day after the Labor Day holiday.

The present perfect tense

have/has + past participle		
Statements	I have worked.	He has worked.
Questions	Have you worked?	Has he worked?
Negatives	They haven't worked.	He hasn't worked.

1. The present perfect links the past and the present. Use it for an action that started at some unspecified time in the past. The action or its effects carry over into the present. The action may or may not still be happening.

   ▶ Americans **have become** dependent on their cars. (*Their dependence affects many things in U.S. society today.*)

   ▶ She **has lost** a lot of weight. (*She looks thin now.*)

   ▶ **Have** you **seen** the movie that's playing at the Roxie? (*Would you like to see it with me tonight?*)

2. We often use the words *ever, never, already*, and *yet* with present perfect verbs.

   ▶ **Have** you *ever* **eaten** chocolate-covered ants?

   ▶ I **have** *never* **been** to China.

   ▶ We **have** *already* **done** this exercise.

   ▶ He **hasn't seen** his newborn son *yet*.

3. Use the present perfect for actions that started in the past and are still going on now. Use *for* and *since* to tell how long the action has been happening.

   Use *for* + an amount of time: *for twenty-four hours, for two days, for a week, for five years, for a while, for centuries.*

   Use *since* + a specific start time: *since Monday, since last year, since my birthday, since 12:30, since 2001.*

   Since can also introduce a clause: *since they got married, since he stopped eating.*

   ▶ I **have lived** in the same apartment *for two years*. (*I still live there.*)

   ▶ They **have been** married *since 1983*. (*They are still married.*)

   ▶ He **hasn't eaten** anything *for twenty-four hours*.

   ▶ He **hasn't eaten** anything *since six o'clock last night*.

   ▶ He **has lost** ten pounds *since he stopped eating*.

4. Use the present perfect for repeated actions and for actions that will probably happen again. We often add words or phrases (*five times, several*) or adverbs of frequency that imply repetition (*always, usually, sometimes*). We also use expressions like *so far*.

▶ I've **done** the same math problem *five times*.

▶ She's **taken** *several* art classes.

▶ I've *always* **tried** to do my best.

▶ We've **written** three essays *so far*.

5. We sometimes use the present perfect for actions that have happened very recently, especially when the action or its effects influence the present. We often add adverbs such as *just, recently,* and *lately*.

▶ I'm not hungry. I've *just* **finished** dinner.

▶ They **have** *recently* **bought** a new house.

▶ **Have** you **seen** any good movies *lately*?

 Special Tips

1. Don't use *since* with an amount of time. Use *for*.

>   *for*
▶ I have been here ~~since~~ three weeks.

2. Don't use the simple present in a sentence containing *since*. Use the present perfect.

> *have been*
▶ I ~~am~~ here since September 5.

The present perfect progressive tense

	have/has + *been* + present participle	
Statements	I have been working.	He has been working.
Questions	Have you been working?	Has he been working?
Negatives	They haven't been working.	He hasn't been working.

1. Use the present perfect progressive for an action that began in the past and is still happening now. In many cases, you can also use the present perfect.

▶ Mother and I **have been cooking** since early morning.

▶ I **have been thinking** a lot about my future.

▶ You **have been working** too hard.

▶ She **hasn't been sleeping** well lately.

2. Sometimes there is no difference in meaning between the present perfect and the present perfect progressive.

▶ My family **has lived** in Canada for six years.

▶ My family **has been living** in Canada for six years.

The present perfect vs. the present perfect progressive

Sometimes there is a difference in meaning between these two tenses.

Use the present perfect progressive to emphasize that the action is still going on. ▶ Mother and I **have been working** hard all day. (*We are still working.*)	Use the present perfect to emphasize that the action is complete. ▶ Mother and I **have worked** hard all day. (*Now we are resting.*)
Use the present perfect progressive to emphasize the action. ▶ She **has been writing** poetry for several years. ▶ "Someone **has been sitting** in my chair," said the mama bear.	Use the present perfect to emphasize the result. ▶ She **has written** several good poems. ▶ "Someone **has broken** my chair," said the baby bear.
Use the present perfect progressive to tell how long something has been happening. ▶ How long **have** you **been studying** English? ▶ I've **been studying** it for three years.	Use the present perfect to tell amounts (how much, how many, and how many times something has happened). ▶ How many computer classes **have** you **taken?** ▶ I've **taken** one.

PRACTICE—Section 11b (2)

Complete each sentence with either the present perfect or the present perfect progressive form of any verb that fits the content. The subject is provided if necessary. There is more than one correct answer for one sentence.

EXAMPLE

Why _haven't you called_ (*you*) me in the past few days?

1. Professor Hill _____ the same class for twenty years.

2. Professor Hill _____ several textbooks about his subject.

3. How many times _____ (*Eric and Johannes*) the TOEFL?

4. _____ (*you*) ever _____ a shark?

5. I'm sorry I'm late. How long _____ (*you*)?

The past tenses

In each of the four past tenses, the verb shows a different relationship to past time.

The simple past tense

	Regular verbs: base form + *-ed*	Irregular verbs: irregular form*
Statements	I worked. He worked.	I went. He went.
Questions	Did you work? Did he work?	Did you go? Did he go?
Negatives	They didn't work. He didn't work.	They didn't go. He didn't go.

*For a complete list of irregular verbs, see *Section 46*.

1. Use the simple past tense for actions that happened at a specific time in the past. The action started and ended in the past.

    ▶ She **went** to the dentist.
    ▶ When **did** they **get** married?

    We often use time expressions such as *six years ago, yesterday, last year, in 1999,* and *at midnight* with the simple past. The past time may also be clear from the context without a time expression.

    ▶ My family **moved** to Canada *six years ago*.
    ▶ She **arrived** unexpectedly *yesterday*.
    ▶ **Did** you **live** in a dormitory *last year*?
    ▶ They **got** married *in 1999*.

    The time can be a point in time (*at 6:12 a.m.*) or a period of time (*for several hours*). The important thing is that the action started and ended in the past.

    ▶ The sun **rose** this morning *at 6:12 a.m.*
    ▶ We **watched** TV *for several hours.*

2. Use the simple past tense for habitual past actions. You can also use *would* and *used to* for this meaning (*Section 11d*).

    ▶ I **watched** cartoons every morning when I was a child.
    ▶ I **would watch** them all morning long.
    ▶ Mother **used to turn off** the TV about noon.

The simple past vs. the present perfect

The simple past and the present perfect are used in different situations.

Use the simple past when the action happened at a specific time in the past. ▶ They **took** a vacation last year.	Use the present perfect when the action happened at an indefinite time in the past. ▶ They **have traveled** a lot.
Use the simple past to say that something started and finished in the past. This sentence means that they aren't married any longer: ▶ They **were married** for thirty years.	Use the present perfect tense to say that something started in the past and is still happening now. This sentence means that they are still married: ▶ They **have been married** for thirty years.
Use the simple past for repeated past actions that will probably not happen again. This sentence means that I will not rewrite my essay again: ▶ I **rewrote** my essay three times. (*I am finished revising it.*)	Use the present perfect for repeated past actions that may or will probably happen again. This sentence means that I might rewrite my essay again: ▶ I **have rewritten** my essay three times. (*I am still working on it.*)

The past progressive tense

was/were + present participle		
Statements	I was working.	He was working.
Questions	Were you working?	Was he working?
Negatives	They weren't working.	He wasn't working.

1. Use the past progressive tense for an action that was in progress at a specific time in the past.

   ▶ Carlos started his homework at 8:00. He stopped at 10:00. At 9:00, Carlos **was doing** homework.

   ▶ I **was living** in Toronto at this time last year.

2. We often use the past progressive and the simple past together when one past action interrupts another past action.

   ▶ The sun **was shining** when I *woke up* this morning.

   ▶ We **were watching** TV when a friend *called*.

Use the past progressive for the action that started first and the simple past for the interrupting action. You can write this kind of sentence in two ways.

- Use *when* to begin the clause with the simple past verb.
  ▶ I was living in San Francisco **when** a big earthquake **happened**.

- Use *while* to begin the clause with the past progressive verb.
  ▶ A big earthquake happened **while** I **was living** in San Francisco.

3. When two past actions are in progress at the same time, use the past progressive for both.
  ▶ I **was living** in San Francisco **while** my boyfriend **was living** in Seattle.

PRACTICE—Section 11b (3)

Complete each sentence with the correct form of the verbs in parentheses. Other words are provided if necessary. There is more than one correct answer for some sentences.

A. In the following sentences, choose between the simple past and the past progressive.

EXAMPLE

We _were walking_ (*walk*) across the street when a car _appeared_ (*appear*) out of nowhere and almost _ran into_ (*run into*) us.

1. We _____ (*shout*) at the driver, but she _____ (*not hear*) us.

2. She _____ (*talk*) on her cell phone while she _____ (*drive*).

3. She _____ (*not pay attention*) to us poor pedestrians.

4. While we _____ (*recover*) from that near-death experience, we _____ (*see*) another car speeding toward us, so we quickly _____ (*jump*) onto the sidewalk.

B. In the following conversation, choose among simple past, present perfect, and present perfect progressive.

MECHANIC: How long _____ (*you have*) problems with your car?
           1.

CUSTOMER: This is the first problem I _____ (*ever have*).
          2.

MECHANIC: How long _____ (*you own*) this car?
           3.

CUSTOMER: I _____ (*buy*) it two years ago.
          4.

MECHANIC: I see that your oil is low. How many times ———— (*you check*) the oil
                                                              5.
since you bought the car?

CUSTOMER: Well, I ———— (*check*) it once.
                      6.

MECHANIC: What? Only once in two years? No wonder your car ———— (*develop*)
                                                                    7.
a problem!

CUSTOMER: This is my first car, so I ———— (*not learn*) how to take care of it yet.
                                         8.

The past perfect tense

had + past participle		
Statements	I had worked.	He had worked.
Questions	Had you worked?	Had he worked?
Negatives	They hadn't worked.	He hadn't worked.

1. Use the past perfect tense when one action in the past happened before another action in the past. Put the earlier action in the past perfect and the later action in the simple past.

   ▸ We **had** just **finished** dinner when we *decided* to go to a movie.

   ▸ By the time we *arrived* at the theater, the movie **had** already **started**.

   The second action doesn't have to be in the same sentence. Sometimes it is clear from the context or from a time expression.

   ▸ We **hadn't seen** a good movie in several weeks.

   When you use *before* or *after*, you do not have to use the past perfect because the time relationship is clear. You can use the simple past tense instead.

   ▸ We **(had) called** the theater *before we left* home.

2. You can think of the past perfect as the past of the present perfect.

   ▸ I am proud of myself. I **haven't missed** a class all semester. (*present time*)

   ▸ I was proud of myself. I **hadn't missed** a class all semester until last Friday, when I had a car accident. (*past time*)

The past perfect progressive tense

had been + present participle		
Statements	I had been working.	He had been working.
Questions	Had you been working?	Had he been working?
Negatives	They hadn't been working.	He hadn't been working.

1. Use the past perfect progressive to emphasize the duration of an action that was in progress before another action or time in the past.

▸ The child's eyes **were** red because she **had been crying**.

▸ She and her brother **had been fighting** over a toy.

2. Use the past perfect progressive to tell how long a past action had been happening before another past action happened.

▸ When we finally **found** seats, the movie **had been playing** for about ten minutes.

3. You can think of the past perfect progressive as the past of the present perfect progressive.

▸ He is arriving tonight. He **has been visiting** his family in Bogotá. (*present time*)

▸ He arrived last night. He **had been visiting** his family in Bogotá. (*past time*)

PRACTICE—Section 11b (4)

Complete each sentence with the correct form of the verbs in parentheses. Other words are provided if necessary. There is more than one correct answer for some sentences.

In sentences 1–3, choose between the simple past and the past perfect.

EXAMPLE

She __drove__ (*drive*) her car to school because she __had missed__ (*miss*) the bus.

1. We _____ (*arrive*) at the airport too late to say goodbye; their plane _____ (*already take off*).

2. The foolish young couple _____ (*know*) each other only two weeks when they

_____ (*decide*) to get married.

3. Then, just two weeks after they _____ (*get*) married, they _____ (*want*) to get divorced.

In sentences 4–7, choose between the past progressive, the present perfect progressive, and the past perfect progressive.

    4. When my alarm clock rang this morning, I _____ (*sleep*) for twelve hours.

    5. When my alarm clock rang this morning, it _____ (*rain*). I could hear the raindrops on the roof.

    6. Wake up, Carlos! You _____ (*sleep*) since eight o'clock last night. It's time to get up.

    7. I_____ (*have*) the most wonderful dream when my alarm clock woke me up this morning.

The future tenses

There are four ways to express simple future actions.

1. Use *be going to* + base form.   ▶ I **am going to work** for my uncle.

2. Use the simple future tense.   ▶ I **will work** in his warehouse.

3. Use the present progressive tense.   ▶ I **am working** tonight.

4. Use the simple present tense.   ▶ My shift **starts** at midnight.

Be going to

	am/is/are + going to + **base form**	
Statements	I am going to work.	He is going to work.
Questions	Are you going to work?	Is he going to work?
Negatives	They aren't going to work.	He isn't going to work.

Be going to is the most common way to express future time. We use it especially in informal speech. *Be going to* shows an especially close connection of future plans with present time.

1. Use *be going to* to make predictions that are going to happen immediately.

  ▶ Hurry! We**'re going to miss** our plane!

  ▶ The bus is out of control. It**'s going to crash**.

2. We also use *be about to* + base form to emphasize that an action is going to happen very soon.

  ▶ Hurry! We**'re about to miss** our plane!

  ▶ The bus is out of control. It**'s about to crash**.

The simple future tense

will + base form		
Statements	I will work.	He will work.
Questions	Will you work?	Will he work?
Negatives	They won't work.	He won't work.

1. Use *will* for predictions that are certain because they are usual or normal.

   ▶ The cat **will come** home when he gets hungry.

   ▶ The teacher **will give** us a quiz on Friday. (*She always does.*)

2. Use *will* to make offers and promises.

   ▶ We**'ll help** you move into your new apartment.

   ▶ I**'ll write** you every day and **call** you every weekend.

Reference: Learn about other uses of *will* in *Section 11d*.

Present tenses with a future meaning

1. Use the simple present tense for events on a schedule or timetable, such as school classes, buses, trains, movies, and work shifts. You can also use *will*.

   ▶ Vacation **begins** on June 15.

   ▶ Their flight **leaves** at 6:30 a.m.

   ▶ How many stops **does** the bus **make**?

2. Use the simple present (or sometimes the present perfect) in a time clause to express a future action. Do not use *be going to* or *will* in a time clause. (See *Section 11c* for more information about time clauses.)

   ▶ We'll have a party *when your friends* **come** *to visit*.

   ▶ *After we* **finish** *our work*, we're going to go to a movie.

   ▶ *After we* **have finished** *our work*, we're going to go to a movie.

3. We often use the present progressive for a future action. We usually add a future time word or phrase, but sometimes future time is clear from the context.

   ▶ I **am working** late *tonight*.

   ▶ They **aren't getting** married *until June*.

   ▶ Where **are** we **meeting** for lunch?

Be going to vs. *will* vs. the present progressive

Sometimes we can use either *be going to* or *will* or the present progressive with no difference in meaning. Sometimes there is a difference.

1. Use *be going to* or *will* to make predictions.

   ▶ Do you think it's **going to rain** tonight?

   ▶ Do you think it'**ll rain** tonight?

   - If the event will happen immediately, you cannot use *will*.

   ▶ Watch out! That bus **is going to hit** us!

   ▶ It's starting to rain. We'**re going to get** wet.

   - If the event will not happen immediately, you can use either *be going to* or *will*.

   ▶ I'**m going to miss** you when you leave.

   ▶ I'**ll miss** you when you leave.

2. Use *be going to, will,* or the present progressive for future intentions.

   ▶ What **are** you **going to do** this summer?

   ▶ What **will** you **do** this summer?

   ▶ What **are** you **doing** this summer?

   - We prefer the present progressive or *be going to* when we have made a previous plan.

   ▶ I'**m meeting** with my adviser this afternoon. (*previous plan*)

   ▶ I'**m going to talk** about changing my major.

   - We prefer *will* when there is no particular plan or when we decide to do something spontaneously (at that moment).

   ▶ I'**ll see** you later. (*no particular plan*)

   ▶ We're going out for pizza. Does anyone want to come with us? I'**ll come!** (*spontaneous decision*)

The future progressive tense

	will be + present participle	*be going to* + *be* + present participle
Statements	I will be working. He will be working.	I am going to be working. He is going to be working.
Questions	Will you be working? Will he be working?	Are you going to be working? Is he going to be working?
Negatives	They won't be working. He won't be working.	They aren't going to be working. He isn't going to be working.

Use the future progressive to express an activity that will be in progress at a specific time in the future.

▶ Tomorrow morning at 10:00, we **will be sitting** in an airplane on our way to New York.

▶ By this time next year, I **am going to be living** in New York.

The future perfect tense

	will have + past participle	
Statements	I will have worked.	He will have worked.
Questions	Will you have worked?	Will he have worked?
Negatives	They won't have worked.	He won't have worked.

Use the future perfect to express an activity that will have happened before a specific time in the future.

▶ My parents **will have been** married for fifty years next June 30.

▶ By this time next year, I **will have finished** college and **gotten** my first job.

The future perfect progressive tense

	will have been + present participle	
Statements	I will have been working.	He will have been working.
Questions	Will you have been working?	Will he have been working?
Negatives	They won't have been working.	He won't have been working.

Use the future perfect progressive to emphasize how long an activity will have happened by a specific time in the future. There is sometimes no difference between the future perfect progressive and the future perfect.

▶ By midnight tonight, they **will have been working** on the same problem for more than forty-eight hours.

▶ By midnight tonight, they **will have worked** on the same problem for more than forty-eight hours.

Sometimes, there is a difference.

- When you want to emphasize *how long* something will have been happening, use the future perfect progressive.

▶ I **will have been living** in the United States for seven years by the time I graduate from college.

- When you want to tell *amounts* (how much, how many, how many times), use the future perfect.

▶ My parents **will have spent** more than $250,000 on my education.

PRACTICE—Section 11b (5)

Complete each sentence with correct forms of the verbs in parentheses. Other words are provided if necessary. Choose any appropriate way to show future time. There is more than one correct answer for some sentences.

EXAMPLE

What time _will the concert begin_ (*the concert begin*)?

1. Please hurry! By the time we _____ (*get*) there, the concert _____ (*already start*).

2. I forgot my teacher's name. I _____ (*remember*) it as soon as I _____ (*see*) his face.

3. I'm sure our daughter _____ (*call*) tonight because she always calls on Mother's Day.

4. _____ (*we have*) time to get a pizza before the show _____ (*start*)?

5. My son's class _____ (*go*) on a field trip to the zoo tomorrow.

6. The weather report says that it _____ (*rain*) tomorrow, so the school may cancel the trip.

7. My cousin _____ (*arrive*) today from Australia.

8. I _____ (*pick him up*) at the airport.

9. By the time his plane _____ (*land*), he _____ (*travel*) for thirty hours.

10. He _____ (*be*) tired.

! **Special Tip**

Don't shift back and forth between tenses unnecessarily.

Be consistent: If you begin a paragraph using past tenses, continue using past tenses throughout. If you begin a paragraph using present tenses, don't change to past tenses unless the meaning requires it.

▶ **We started our hike at 6:00 a.m. and hiked for an hour or so. Then Jeff, our**
        spotted   *signaled*
  leader, ~~spots~~ bear tracks and ~~signals~~ for us to stop.

PRACTICE—Section 11b (6)

Edit the following paragraphs for incorrect verb tenses and unnecessary shifts between present and past. The first mistake has been corrected for you as an example.

    We finished dinner, washed our dinner dishes, and stored our leftover food in bear-proof metal containers before crawling into our tents for the night. We were
                                     heard
almost asleep when suddenly, we ~~hear~~ the rattling of pots and pans just outside our tent. We looked out and see an enormous black bear pawing through our campsite kitchen. Of course, it is looking for food. We try to remember what to do: stay quiet, make noise, or run? No one could remember. Then I realize that I have put a candy bar in my shirt pocket during the afternoon and that I am still wearing the shirt with the candy in it. I close my eyes, say my prayers, and prepare to die.

Suddenly, I am hearing the roar of a car engine and the screech of tires. Two park rangers are jumping out of their truck and begin banging cooking pots together. They have heard that a bear is in the area, so they have been patrolling the campground all night. The noise scares the bear away.

After I am sure that the bear has left, I crawl out of my tent. I was so happy to see those two park rangers! I want to give them something to thank them for saving my life, but they are not very pleased when I take the candy bar out of my pocket and offer it to them.

11c Special tense combinations

Time clauses

A time clause is a dependent clause that begins with a time word (*when, after, as soon as,* and so on). The verb tense in a time clause may be different from what you expect.

Future time clauses

Use the simple present (or sometimes the present perfect) in a future time clause. The simple present is preferred.

▶ The test will begin **as soon as everyone *sits* down.** (*preferred*)

▶ The test will begin **as soon as everyone *has sat* down.**

Do not use *will* or *be going to* in a future time clause.

　　　　　　　　　　　　　　　　　　　　　　　　　is
▶ We will have a celebration when the test ~~will be~~ over.

　　　　　　　　　　　　　　find out
▶ I won't celebrate until I ~~will find out~~ if I passed.

　　　　　　　　　　　　　　　　　　　look at
▶ I am going to say a little prayer before I ~~am going to look at~~ my score.

Past time clauses with *before* or *after*

In sentences with a past perfect verb and a simple past verb, you can use the simple past tense for both verbs when *before* or *after* are the time words because the difference in times is clear.

▶ Our cat **ran** away *after* we **had scolded** him.

▶ Our cat **ran** away *after* we **scolded** him.

► He **had been** gone for three days *before* he **came back home**.

► He **was** gone for three days *before* he **came back home**.

Time clauses with *since*

In time clauses beginning with *since,* the verb can be in the present perfect (like the verb in the independent clause), or it can be in the simple past tense. It is in the simple past tense when the time clause action ended in the past.

► We haven't seen our cat *since* **he disappeared last Friday**.

It is in the present perfect tense when the action began in the past but continues into the present.

► I haven't slept *since* **he's been gone**.

PRACTICE—Section 11c (1)

Complete each sentence with the correct form of the verbs in parentheses.

1. We _____ (*not see*) Linda since she _____ (*start*) her new job.

2. My history paper was due today. After I _____ (*finish*) writing it last night, I _____ (*ask*) my roommate to check it.

3. My English paper is due tomorrow. After I _____ (*finish*) writing it tonight, I _____ (*ask*) my roommate to check it.

4. The young couple in the apartment next to mine had a baby last week. They

   _____ (*not sleep*) for more than two hours since the baby _____ (*come*) home from the hospital.

Conditional sentences

A conditional sentence is a sentence with an *if*-clause. An *if*-clause is a dependent clause that states a condition for a result to happen or not happen. In the sentence *If it rains tomorrow, we won't go to the beach,* the condition is the weather. The result is going or not going to the beach.

Basic patterns of conditional sentences

There are four basic patterns of conditional sentences. Each pattern has a different combination of verb forms depending on whether the time is present, future, or past and on whether the condition is true or not true.

	VERB FORM IN THE IF-CLAUSE	VERB FORM IN THE RESULT CLAUSE
I. Present time, true condition	*present* ▶ If (when) you **have** a college education,	*present* you **earn** more money.
2. Future time, true condition	*present* ▶ If you **get** at least 90% on the final exam,	*future* you **will get** an A in the class.
3. Present time, untrue condition	*simple past* ▶ If Paul **weren't** so lazy, (*Paul is lazy.*)	*would + base form* he **would get** better grades.
4. Past time, untrue condition	*past perfect* ▶ If the test **had been** easier, (*The test was hard.*)	*would have + past participle* I **would have gotten** a good grade.

I. Present time, true condition

Use this pattern to show that a condition is true. The meaning is "When this condition happens, the result is always the same." Notice that you can use any present tense in the *if*-clause.

CONDITION: present	RESULT: present
▶ If Paul **studies,**	he **gets** straight A's.
▶ If he **has studied,**	he **is** more relaxed during tests.
▶ If he **is studying,**	we **try** to be quiet.

You can use present-time modals (*can, may, must, should*) in the result clause.

▶ If Paul has to study, we **should** be quiet.

You can use the word *when* in place of *if* in this pattern. You cannot use *when* in the other three patterns.

▶ **If (When)** you take twelve or more units, you are a full-time student.

You can put either the *if*-clause or the result clause first.

▶ **If you have a student visa,** you can't work.
▶ You can't work **if you have a student visa.**

You can also make questions.

▶ **Where can you work** if you have a student visa?
▶ **Can you work** on campus if you have a student visa?

2. Future time, true condition

This pattern means "If this condition happens, then this result will probably happen." The result is not certain; it may or may not happen.

CONDITION: present	RESULT: future
▶ If Paul **studies**,	he **will graduate** in four years.
▶ If he **graduates** in four years,	his parents **are going to buy** him a new car.

We sometimes use this pattern to make promises, to make predictions, and to negotiate.

- ▶ If you **marry** me, I **will treat** you like a queen. (*promise*)
- ▶ If you **marry** Tom, you **will be** sorry. (*prediction*)
- ▶ If I **wash** the dishes, **will** you **clean up** the kitchen? (*negotiation*)

You can use the modals that express probability (*may, might*) in the result clause.

- ▶ If Paul gets a new car, he **might** sell his old one to me.
- ▶ If you watch the sky tonight, you **may** see a shooting star.

You can also use the modal *should* in the *if*-clause. Notice that you can omit *if*, but then you must move *should* in front of its subject.

- ▶ If **it should** rain, we won't go to the beach.
- ▶ **Should it** rain, we won't go to the beach.

You can reverse the order of the clauses, and you can make questions.

- ▶ Which math classes will you take **if you get a high score**?
- ▶ **If you get a low score**, are you going to take algebra?

3. Present time, untrue condition

This pattern tells the reader, "The condition is not true at the present time."

CONDITION: simple past	RESULT: *would* + base form
▶ If we **went** to Disneyworld, (*We aren't going to Disneyworld.*)	we **would visit** the Epcot Center.
▶ If I **were** the teacher, (*I am not the teacher.*)	I **would** never **give** homework.

We use this pattern to give advice and to express dreams.

- ▶ If I **were** you, I **would apologize** immediately. (*advice*)
- ▶ If I **had** a million dollars, I **would travel** around the world first class. (*dream*)

You can use the modals that express possibility (*could, might*) in the result clause.

▶ If we went to Disneyworld, we **could** also visit the Kennedy Space Center.
▶ If we visited the Space Center, we **might** see a shuttle launch.

You can also use *should* and *could* in the *if*-clause.

▶ If we **should** be lucky enough to see a launch, we would take lots of photos.
▶ If you **could** have three wishes come true, what would you wish for?

You can reverse the order of the clauses, and you can make questions.

▶ **If you suddenly became rich,** what would you do?
▶ What would you do **if you suddenly became rich**?

The verb *be* is irregular in this pattern. Use *were* (not *was*) for all persons, singular and plural.

▶ If **I** *were* the teacher, I wouldn't give homework or tests.
▶ If **he** *were* smart, he would take my advice.

Before *were,* you can omit *if,* but then you must move *were* in front of its subject.

▶ If **I** *were* smarter, I would be richer.
▶ *Were* I smarter, I would be richer.

4. Past time, untrue condition

This pattern tells the reader, "The condition was not true in the past."

CONDITION: past perfect	RESULT: *would have* + past participle
▶ If we **had had** the money, (*We didn't have the money.*)	we **would have taken** a nice vacation.
▶ If we **had taken** a vacation, (*We didn't take a vacation.*)	we **would have gone** to Paris.

We use this pattern to express past mistakes, to express past dreams, and to apologize.

▶ If I **had studied** harder, I **would have gotten** a better grade. (*past mistake*)
▶ If I **had been** able to choose my major, I **would have studied** biochemistry. (*past dream*)
▶ If we **had known** you needed help, we **would have come** immediately. (*apology*)

You can use *could have* and *might have* in the result clause.

▶ If we had studied harder, we **could have** passed the test.
▶ If we had studied harder, we **might have** passed the test.

You can also use *could have* in the *if*-clause.

▶ If we **could have** gone in June, Bill might have come with us.

You can reverse the order of the clauses, and you can make questions.

▶ I would have come to visit you **if I had had more time**.
▶ How much money could we have saved **if we had bought our computer at a discount store?**

You can omit *if* before any past perfect verb, but then you must move *had* in front of the subject.

▶ If **I had had** more time, I might have gotten a higher grade on the test.
▶ **Had I had** more time, I might have gotten a higher grade on the test.

5. Mixed time, untrue condition

You can mix past, present, and future times when the condition is untrue.

▶ If I **had studied** harder, I **wouldn't be** worried about my grades now.
▶ If I **were planning** to stay here one more year, I **wouldn't have sold** my car.
▶ We **could drive** to the mountains next weekend if I **hadn't sold** my car.

 Computer Note

Grammar checkers do not mark verb errors in conditional sentences. For example, they might miss an error such as this one: *We would have gone to the meeting if we would have known about it.*

PRACTICE—Section 11c (2)

Complete the conversation with the correct form of the verbs in parentheses. There is more than one correct answer for some of the items.

Andrew and Martha are driving to San Francisco on their vacation. They are having an argument.

ANDREW: We are lost, and it's your fault.

MARTHA: My fault? Why is it my fault?

ANDREW: Because you told me to turn right an hour ago. If you ___had told___ (*tell*) me

to turn left instead of right, we _____ (*not get*) lost. The problem is that you

<u>1.</u>

don't know how to read a map. If you _____ (*know*) how to read a map, we

<u>2.</u>

_____ (*be*) there by now.

<u>3.</u>

Ten minutes later.

MARTHA: If we _____ (*not be*) at the hotel by six, they _____ (*cancel*) our reservation.

<u>4.</u> <u>5.</u>

ANDREW: If they _____ (*cancel*) our reservation, we _____ (*can sleep*) in the car.

<u>6.</u> <u>7.</u>

MARTHA: Sleep in the car? Never! If you _____ (*remember*) to bring the cell phone,

<u>8.</u>

we _____ (*could call*) the hotel and _____ (*tell*) them to hold our room.

<u>9.</u> <u>10.</u>

Replacements for *if*

Unless

Unless means "if not."

▶ **Unless** you study, you won't pass the class. (*If you don't study, you won't pass the class.*)

▶ You can't get a refund **unless** you have a receipt. (*You can't get a refund if you don't have a receipt.*)

Provided (that)/as long as

Use *provided, provided that,* or *as long as* in place of *if* when the condition is very strict. *As long as* is more informal than *provided* and *provided that.*

▶ I will lend you my car **provided (that)** you bring it back by 4:00.

▶ I'll tell you a secret **as long as** you promise not to tell anyone else.

In case/in the event that

Use *in case* or *in the event that* to explain preparations for something that might happen in the future.

▶ We'll bring some snacks **in case** we get hungry.

▶ We should leave early **in the event that** there is a lot of traffic.

You can also use *in case* or *in the event that* to give a reason for past preparations.

▶ We brought some snacks **in case** we got hungry.

▶ They left an hour early **in the event that** there was a lot of traffic.

PRACTICE—Section 11c (3)

Complete the sentences with *unless, as long as, in case,* and *in the event that.* Use each expression once.

Some students are planning a surprise birthday party for a friend. The party will be next Sunday night.

1. What will we do _____ she's not at home on Sunday?

2. She always studies at home on Sunday _____ she has a date.

3. Someone will have to stay with her all afternoon _____ she decides to go to the library.

4. Good idea! She won't go out _____ she has a guest.

Wishes

A wish states the opposite of reality. Therefore, use the same verb forms after the verb *wish* as you use after clauses for unreal conditions.

	REAL SITUATION	WISH
Present time	*I am taking five classes.*	▶ I **wish** (that) I **weren't taking** so many classes.
	I can't concentrate.	▶ I **wish** (that) I **could concentrate.**
	I have to write a paper.	▶ I **wish** (that) I **didn't have to write** a paper.
Future time	*My boyfriend will not call tonight.*	▶ I **wish** (that) my boyfriend **would call** tonight.
Past time	*I ate too much.*	▶ I **wish** (that) I **hadn't eaten** too much.

We often use *I wish . . . would* and *I wish . . . wouldn't* to express a request or a complaint.

▶ I **wish** you **would call** more often. (*request*)
▶ I **wish** she **wouldn't drive** so fast. (*complaint*)

Wish vs. hope

Wish states a future situation that will probably not happen, so after *wish,* use *would* and *could. Hope* states a future situation that may happen, so after *hope,* use *will, can,* or the simple present tense.

WISH	HOPE
▶ I wish (that) my boyfriend **would call** tonight. (*He probably won't call.*)	▶ I hope (that) my boyfriend **will call** tonight. (*It is possible that he will call.*)
▶ I wish (that) you **could come** to my party. (*You probably can't come.*)	▶ I hope (that) you (**can**) **come** to my party. (*It is possible that you can come.*)

Reported speech

 Computer Note

Grammar checkers do not mark errors in reported speech. For example, they might miss the error in this sentence: *Tom said that he is going home.*

There are two ways you can report what another person has said or written: in direct quotation or in reported speech. In direct quotation, you repeat the person's exact words and enclose them in quotation marks.

▶ Tom said, **"I'm going home."**
▶ We replied, **"We're sorry you are leaving so early."**

In reported speech, you report what the person said or wrote without quotation marks. You usually have to change some of the words, especially pronouns and verbs. Reported speech is also called indirect speech.

▶ Tom said **(that) he was going home.**
▶ We replied **(that) we were sorry he was leaving so early.**

Reporting verbs

You can use any of the following verbs to introduce a direct quotation or reported speech.

STATEMENTS				QUESTIONS
acknowledge	claim	indicate	reply	ask
add	complain	maintain	report	inquire
admit	conclude	mean	say	question
announce	confess	note	state	want to know
answer	declare	observe	suggest	wonder
argue	deny	promise	tell	
assert	exclaim	remark	warn	
believe	explain	repeat	write	

Reference: For an explanation of when to use *say* and *tell,* see *Section 54.*

Direct quotations vs. reported speech

Besides the use of quotation marks, there are other differences between direct quotations and reported speech.

1. Pronouns and possessive words change to fit the meaning.

Direct quotations	Reported speech
▶ John said, "**I** will be five minutes late because **I** have to get **my** car."	▶ John said **he** would be five minutes late because **he** had to get **his** car.
▶ Mary and Alice said, "**We** don't want to be late to **our** class."	▶ Mary and Alice said that **they** didn't want to be late to **their** class.

EXCEPTION: When the speaker is reporting his or her own words, pronouns do not change.

▶ I told him, "**I** can't wait."	▶ I told him that **I** couldn't wait.
▶ **We** said, "**We** don't want to be late."	▶ **We** said that **we** didn't want to be late.

The word *this* changes to *that,* and *these* changes to *those.*

▶ She said, "**This** gift is for you."	▶ She said that **that** gift was for me.
▶ The students asked, "Are **these** the right books for English 1A?"	▶ The students asked if **those** were the right books for English 1A.

2. The word *here* changes to *there,* and time expressions change to fit the meaning.

Direct quotation	Reported speech
▶ He said, "I left my backpack **here**."	▶ He said that he had left his backpack **there**.
▶ The teacher said, "I'm too busy to help you **now**, but I will have some free time **tomorrow**."	▶ The teacher said that she was too busy to help us **then** but that she would have some free time **the next day**.
▶ She said, "I did it **yesterday**."	▶ She said that she had done it **the day before**.
▶ They said, "We returned it **a week ago**."	▶ They said that they had returned it **a week earlier**.

EXCEPTION: In informal spoken English, we sometimes do not make these changes. We say, *They said that they returned it a week ago.*

3. When the reporting verb (the verb that introduces the quotation or reported speech) is past tense, the verbs change.

DIRECT QUOTATION		REPORTED SPEECH	
He said,	"I **work** hard."	He said (that)	he **worked** hard.
	"I **am working** hard."		he **was working** hard.
	"I **have worked** hard."		he **had worked** hard.
	"I **have been working** hard."		he **had been working** hard.
	"I **worked** hard."		he **had worked** hard.
	"I **was working** hard."		he **had been working** hard.
	"I **will work** hard."		he **would work** hard.
	"I **am going to work** hard."		he **was going to work** hard.
	"I **can work** hard."		he **could work** hard.
	"I **may work** hard."		he **might work** hard.
	"I **must work** hard."		he **had to work** hard.
	"I **have to work** hard."		he **had to work** hard.
	"I **should work** hard."		he **should work** hard.
	"I **could work** hard."		he **could work** hard.
	"I **might work** hard."		he **might work** hard.
	"**Work** hard."	He told me	to **work** hard.
	"Please **work** hard."	He asked me	to **work** hard.
He asked,	"**Do** you **work** hard?"	He asked whether	I **worked** hard (or not).
	"When **do** you **work**?"	He asked me	when I **worked**.

4. Use the word *that* to connect reported speech to the introductory clause. You can omit *that* when the meaning is clear without it.

▶ She said **that** she was busy.

OR

▶ She said she was busy.

5. Verbs don't change in four situations:

a. When the reporting verb is in the present tense or the future tense, the verb in reported speech does not change.

▶ Roger: "I **can come** to the party."   ▶ Roger *says* that he **can come** to the party.

Direct quotation	Reported speech
▶ Spelling teacher: "The word 'Mississippi' **has** four *s*'s and two *p*'s."	▶ Our spelling teacher said (that) the word "Mississippi" **has** four *s*'s and two *p*'s.
▶ Science teacher: "Water **boils** at a higher temperature in the mountains."	▶ Our science teacher said (that) water **boils** at a higher temperature in the mountains.
▶ Math teacher: "I always **give** easy tests."	▶ Our math teacher said (that) she always **gives** easy tests.

b. When the reported information is a fact, a general truth, or a customary action, the verb in reported speech is often in the "timeless" simple present.

c. Verbs in dependent time clauses do not change. (However, notice that the verbs in the independent clauses *do* change.)

▶ John said, "I broke three glasses **while I *was washing* the dishes last night**."	▶ John said that he had broken three glasses **while he *was washing* the dishes the night before last**.
▶ He added, "I cut myself **when I *picked up* the broken glass**."	▶ He added that he had cut himself **when he *picked up* the broken glass**.

d. In informal spoken English, we don't always change simple past to past perfect, especially when the event happened very recently.

▶ She said, "I just **saw** Mary."	▶ She said that she **had** just **seen** Mary. (*formal*)
	▶ She said that she just **saw** Mary. (*informal*)

> **!** *Special Tip*

Don't mix direct quotation and indirect speech in the same sentence.

that time was up and that

▶ At exactly ten-thirty, the teacher said ~~time's up and~~ we should put down our pencils and close our test booklets.

OR

, "Time's up. Put down your pencils and close your test booklets."

▶ At exactly ten-thirty, the teacher said ~~time's up and we should put down our pencils and close our test booklets.~~

Reference: Learn more about direct quotations in the following sections: Using quotations in a research paper, *Section 45e*; Quotation marks, *Section 29a*.

PRACTICE—Section 11c (4)

Change the direct quotations in each sentence into reported speech.

The day before a big exam . . .

EXAMPLE

The teacher said, "The exam is at eight o'clock tomorrow morning."

The teacher said that the exam was at eight o'clock the next morning.

1. The students said, "We won't be awake then."
2. The teacher told the students, "You should eat breakfast before the test."
3. The students asked, "Can we bring coffee and bagels to the exam?"
4. The teacher replied, "No, you can't."

The day of the exam . . .

5. The students complained, "We didn't have time to eat breakfast."
6. The teacher said, "The exam has started."
7. She told them, "Please be quiet."
8. The students said, "We can't be quiet because our stomachs are growling."

The day after the exam . . .

9. The teacher said, "You did well on the exam."
10. Then she said, "I am going to give all of you A's."
11. The students replied, "We prefer A+'s."
12. The teacher smiled and said, "This is not possible."

Clauses of importance

 Computer Note

Grammar checkers cannot recognize when a subjunctive verb is needed, so they might mark *I suggested that he go* as a subject-verb agreement error and suggest changing it to *he goes. He go* is correct.

After certain introductory clause verbs and adjectives, the verb in the following dependent clause is in the subjunctive form. The subjunctive form of a verb is the same as the base form—*be, go, do,* and so on. These clauses are also called subjunctive clauses.

INTRODUCTORY CLAUSE	DEPENDENT CLAUSE OF IMPORTANCE
▶ Our teacher demanded	that we **be** quiet during the test.
▶ It is very important	that Joanna **see** her adviser as soon as possible.

The introductory clause verbs and adjectives that follow this pattern express the ideas of importance or advisability.

VERBS			ADJECTIVES	
advise	order	request	advisable	mandatory
ask	prefer	require	desirable	necessary
command	propose	suggest	essential	urgent
demand	recommend	urge	important	vital
insist				

> *lose*
▶ It is **essential** (that) my husband ~~loses~~ weight.

> *exercise*
▶ The doctor **has suggested** (that) he ~~exercises~~ more often.

> *go*
▶ She also **recommended** (that) he ~~goes~~ on a diet.

▶ Now my husband **insists** (that) we ~~will~~ change doctors.

Notice these points:

1. The introductory clause verb can be in any tense.

2. You can omit *that*.

3. Put *not* before a subjunctive verb to make it negative.

> ▶ She recommended that he *not* **smoke**.

4. In informal spoken English, we often use *should* + base form instead of the more formal subjunctive. Speakers of British English prefer *should*.

> ▶ She also recommended that he **should go** on a diet.

5. We often use an infinitive phrase instead of a clause. Learn more about infinitive phrases in *Section 12b*.

SENTENCES WITH A CLAUSE	SENTENCES WITH AN INFINITIVE PHRASE
▶ She asked **that we be quiet.**	▶ She asked **us to be quiet.**
▶ It is important **that a father spend time with his children.**	▶ It is important **for a father to spend time with his children.**

PRACTICE—Section 11c (5)

A. There is a water shortage in the city. Complete the sentences using these suggestions for conserving water. Use a subjunctive verb form in each sentence. Take special care with sentences that contain negatives.

conserve water   recycle water whenever possible
don't wash cars   don't water gardens

  1. The city water department ordered that homeowners _____.

  2. It also requested that no one _____.

  3. The mayor urged that each person _____.

  4. It is vital that we all _____.

B. Edit the following paragraph for errors in the subjunctive verb forms. There are four mistakes. The first one has been corrected as an example.

                       call

    It was important that John ~~called~~ home immediately because his wife was having a baby. When he called, his wife urged that he comes home right away. He drove eighty miles per hour until a police officer stopped him for speeding. After he explained his urgency, the police officer smiled, tore up the ticket, and advised that he doesn't drive quite so fast. "Your wife is probably feeling stressed," said the police officer, "so it is advisable that you are calm. Good luck!"

Let, help, make, have, and get

These five verbs have special patterns.

Let and help

After *let* and *help,* use the base form of a verb. After *help,* an infinitive is also possible.

▶ **Let** the soup **cook** slowly.

▶ Please **help** me **carry** these groceries. OR Please **help** me **to carry** these groceries.

Make, have, and get

Make, have, and *get* can have the meaning "cause someone to do something" or "cause something to be done." For this reason, they are called causative verbs.

When the meaning is "cause someone to do something," use the base form of a verb after *make* and *have,* and use an infinitive after *get.*

▶ I **made** my husband **cook** dinner last night.

  The verb *make* means that I forced my husband to cook. He had no choice.

▶ I **had** him **feed** the baby, too.

  With the verb *have,* there is no force. I asked my husband to take care of the baby, and he did it.

▶ By the time he **got** the baby **to stop** crying, it was after midnight.

The verb get means "persuade": He finally persuaded the baby to stop crying.

When the meaning is "cause something to be done," use a past participle after *have* and *get*. We use this verb combination to say that another person does something for us. We don't do it ourselves, and it is not important who does it for us. *Have* and *get* have the same meaning.

▶ Josh **will have** his car **repaired** tomorrow.

Someone else will repair Josh's car.

▶ I **get** my teeth **cleaned** every six months.

Someone cleans my teeth every six months.

PRACTICE—Section 11c (6)

Complete each sentence with the correct form of the verb in parentheses. Use the base form, infinitive, or past participle.

EXAMPLE

We always let the children <u>*plan*</u> (*plan*) our vacation every summer. There's always a lot to do.

1. Of course, we help them _____ (*choose*) a place we will all enjoy.

2. I make my husband _____ (*take care of*) the car.

3. He gets the car _____ (*wash*), the oil _____ (*change*), the tires _____ (*check*), and the engine _____ (*tune up*).

4. I have my oldest son, Jason, _____ (*cut*) the grass and _____ (*take*) the dog to the kennel.

5. Jason is a little lazy, so he gets his younger brother Christopher _____ (*do*) his work whenever he can.

6. We have our mail and newspaper deliveries _____ (*stop*).

7. We don't get our electricity _____ (*turn off*), however.

8. We all help _____ (*carry*) our bags to the car on the morning of our departure.

11d Modals

There are eleven modals: *can, could, will, would, shall, should, may, might, must, ought to,* and *had better.* English uses modals to show a speaker's attitude toward what he or she is saying. They show attitudes such as doubt (*That can't be true!*), necessity (*We must buy our tickets today*), and possibility (*He may be sick*).

Forms of the modals

Modals can occur in these tenses.

Simple modals show present or future time.	modal + base form ▶ We **can go** now. (*present*) ▶ We **should go** soon. (*future*)
Progressive modals express an activity in progress at the moment of speaking. They also show action that will be in progress at a specific time in the future.	modal + be + present participle ▶ He **must be sleeping**. (*present progressive*) ▶ We **should be going** soon. (*future progressive*)
Perfect modals express a past action.	modal + have + past participle ▶ They **must have worked** last night. (*present perfect*)
Perfect progressive modals express an activity that was in progress at a specific time in the past.	modal + have been + present participle ▶ They **might have been sleeping** when we called. (*present perfect progressive*)

Here are some important points to remember about the modals.

1. Always use the base form of a verb directly after a modal. This is true for all tenses.
   > *speak*
   ▶ He could ~~spoke~~ Spanish when he was a child.
   ▶ He might **be** working late.
   ▶ You may **have** caught a cold.
   ▶ He could **have** been trying to call us.

2. Never use -*s*, -*ed*, or -*ing* endings with modals.
   > *can*
   ▶ He ~~cans~~ speak English very well.

3. Never use *do, does,* or *did* with modals to make questions or negatives.
   To make a question, move the modal in front of the subject.
   To make a negative, add *not* after the modal. *Not* is sometimes abbreviated *n't: can't, shouldn't, couldn't.* An exception is *will* + *not* = *won't.*
   > *Can*
   ▶ ~~Does~~ he ~~can~~ speak French, too?
   > *can't*
   ▶ No, he ~~doesn't can~~ speak French.

4. Never use *to* after a modal (except in *ought to*).

   ▶ Can you please ~~to~~ tell me where I can find a taxi?

5. Never use two modals together.

   ▶ Jane might ~~will~~ help us look for an apartment tomorrow. OR

   ▶ Jane ~~might~~ will help us look for an apartment tomorrow.

PRACTICE—Section 11d (1)

Edit the following paragraph for errors in the form of the modals. There are seven mistakes. One sentence has two mistakes, and some sentences have none. The first mistake has been corrected for you as an example.

Because of the danger of international terrorism, passengers have to go through
can
several airport security checks before they ~~cans~~ board the plane. They must
arrived at the airport at least two or three hours early. It can takes a lot of time to
check in all the passengers, especially on an international flight. Passengers don't
must leave their luggage unattended because a terrorist might can put a bomb
inside. The ticket agent will ask three questions: Did you pack your luggage
yourself? Has your luggage been under your control since you packed it? Has any
person asked you to take anything on the airplane? Every passenger must to be
able to answer "no" to all three questions. Also, they must showing a picture ID.

Meanings of the modals

The following chart shows the different meanings of the modals.

CAN/CAN'T

a. Ability

<table>
<tr>
<td>Both can and be able to mean "ability." We use can more often, but we use be able to in two situations:</td>
<td>▶ Paula can understand Spanish, but she can't speak it.

▶ Paula is able to understand Spanish, but she isn't able to speak it.</td>
</tr>
<tr>
<td>• to express ability in the present perfect or the past perfect tense (because can has no past participle form)</td>
<td>haven't been able to
▶ We <s>haven't could</s> find a cheap apartment yet.</td>
</tr>
</table>

(*continued*)

(*continued*)

• to express ability and possibility together (because we cannot use two modals together)	*be able to* ▶ He might ~~can~~ come to the party.
b. Strong possibility	▶ It **can rain** every day during the rainy season.
c. Request (informal)	▶ **Can** I **borrow** your dictionary?
d. Permission (informal)	▶ You **can stay** out tonight until ten o'clock.
e. Suggestion	▶ You **can work** during the day and take classes at night.
f. Impossibility *Can't* expresses impossibility in the present.	▶ You **can't be** hungry. You just ate a huge dinner.

COULD / COULDN'T

a. Ability Use either *could* or *be able to* to say that someone had a general ability to do something in the past. Use only *be able to* to say that someone succeeded in doing a specific thing in the past. Do not use *could*. Both negative forms can be used in both situations.	▶ My brother **could** usually **beat** me at chess. ▶ My brother **was** usually **able to beat** me at chess. *was able to* ▶ One time I ~~could~~ beat him. ▶ I **couldn't / wasn't able to speak** English a year ago. ▶ I **couldn't / wasn't able to finish** the test on time.
b. Possibility *Could* expresses more doubt than *can*.	▶ It **could rain** tonight.

c. Polite request ▶ **Could** I **borrow** your dictionary?

Could is more polite
than *can*.

d. Polite suggestion ▶ We **could meet** in the coffee shop after class.

e. Impossibility ▶ You **couldn't be** hungry. You just ate a huge
dinner.
In addition to *can't,*
couldn't expresses
impossibility in the
present.

MAY / MAY NOT

a. Request (formal) ▶ **May** I **borrow** your dictionary?

May is a very formal ▶ **May** I **offer** you my congratulations?
way to make a request.

b. Permission (formal) ▶ You **may not leave** the house until you finish
your homework.

c. Possibility ▶ The teacher is absent today. He **may be** sick.

In addition to *can* and ▶ It **may rain** tonight.
could, we use *may* for
possibility in the present
or future.

MIGHT / MIGHT NOT

Possibility ▶ He **might have** the flu, or he **might** just **have**
a bad cold.
We also use *might* for
possibility in the present ▶ It **might rain** tonight.
or future. *Might* expresses
more doubt than *may*.

SHOULD / SHOULDN'T; OUGHT TO / OUGHT NOT TO

Should and *ought to* have the same meaning, but we use *should* more often. We don't
use *ought to* in questions or in negative sentences.

a. Advice/opinion ▶ You **should get** more sleep.

▶ You **ought to get** more sleep.

▶ How much homework **should** children **do**?

▶ Children **shouldn't eat** too much candy.

(continued)

(*continued*)

b. Duty/moral obligation	▶ Parents **should protect** their children.
	▶ Parents **ought to protect** their children.
c. Expectation	▶ Our guests **should arrive** at any minute.
	▶ Our guests **ought to arrive** at any minute.

HAD BETTER / HAD BETTER NOT

Strong advice *Had better* is stronger than either *should* or *ought to. Had better* gives this warning: "Serious consequences will follow if you don't take this advice." *Had* is often shortened to *'d*, especially in speaking.	▶ You are driving too fast; you **had better slow down**. ▶ We**'d better not be** late to class again.

MUST / MUST NOT; HAVE TO / DON'T HAVE TO; HAVE GOT TO

Have to and *have got to* are included here because they share the meaning "necessity" with the modal *must*. They are modal-like but are not true modals because they can change their form (*I have to, he has to, I have got to, he has got to,* and so on). Also, *have to* needs *do, does,* or *did* to make negatives and questions.

a. Necessity Both *must* and *have to* express necessity. *Must* and *have to* have almost the same meaning. *Must* is a little stronger and a little more formal. You can use both *must* and *have to* in questions. Use only *have to* for past time. (*Must* has no past form.)	▶ You **must be** sixteen years old to get a driver's license. ▶ You **have to be** sixteen years old to get a driver's license. ▶ Please, doctor. You **must come** immediately! ▶ You **must pay** us a visit us soon. ▶ **Must** you **be** so bossy? ▶ **Do** you **have to be** so bossy? ▶ My grandfather **had to walk** five miles to school every day. ▶ However, he **didn't have to do** five hours of homework every night.

Don't have to, didn't have to, and *haven't had to* mean "no necessity." The negative of *must* has two different meanings. See items b and c.	▶ Since my neighbor won the lottery, he **hasn't had to work**.
Have got to is another way to express necessity in present time. In American English, *have got to* is used mainly in informal speaking.	▶ I**'ve got to go** now.

b. Certainty

Must frequently means "it is 95% certain, it is almost sure that . . ."	▶ John gets a lot of traffic tickets. He **must be** a bad driver.
Must not means "it is 95% certain that X doesn't happen."	▶ John always gets F's. He **must not study** at all.

c. Prohibition

	▶ You **must not drive** without a license.
Must not can mean that something is prohibited, not allowed. You cannot use *don't have to* to mean prohibition.	*must not* ▶ You ~~don't have to~~ drive on the sidewalk.

WOULD / WOULDN'T; WOULD RATHER / WOULD RATHER NOT; USED TO / DIDN'T USE TO

Would rather/would rather not and *used to/didn't use to* are included here because they share some meanings with other modals.

a. Polite request

	▶ **Would** you **cook** dinner tonight?
Another way to make a polite request is *would (you) mind +* present participle. See also item e.	▶ **Would** you **mind cooking** dinner tonight?

b. Willingness to do something

	▶ I**'d do** anything for you.
Would is often shortened to *'d,* especially in conversation.	▶ **Would** you **rob** a bank for me? ▶ Well, no, I **wouldn't do** that.

(continued)

(*continued*)

c. Past habitual activity
Used to also expresses a past habitual activity. It has the same meaning as *would*.

► My brother and I **would play** hide-and-seek on warm summer evenings at my grandparents' house.

► We **used to play** other games, too.

We make the question and negative forms of *used to* like a regular past tense verb, with *did* or *didn't* + base form.

► What childhood games **did** you **use to play**?

► We **didn't use to play** many games.

d. Preference

► I'd **rather not go out** tonight.

Would rather expresses preference in the present and future.

► I'd **rather stay** at home.

e. Permission

► **Would you mind if** we **left** class early?

You can use the expression *Would you mind if* + a simple past verb to request permission to do something. You can also use *Do you mind if* + a simple present verb.

► **Do you mind if** we **leave** class early?

WILL / WON'T

The main use of *will* is to express future time (*Section 11b*). In addition, *will* expresses the following meanings. *Will* is often shortened to *'ll* and *will not* is often shortened to *won't*.

a. Request

► **Will** you **marry** me?

b. Offer

► We**'ll help** you move into your new apartment.

c. Refusal to do something

► My car **won't start** (*refuses to start*). I need a ride.

d. Promise

► I**'ll write** you every day, and I**'ll call** you every weekend.

SHALL

Speakers of British English use *shall* more often than Americans. Americans use *shall* only in very formal English—in legal documents, for instance, and in certain first-person questions.

Use *shall* in first-person questions asking "Do you want me/us to ... ?"

▶ **Shall** I **get** your coat? (*Do you want me to get your coat?*)

▶ What **shall** we **have** for dinner? (*What do you want us to eat for dinner?*)

PRACTICE—Section 11d (2)

Complete the conversations using the appropriate modals and the correct forms of the verbs in parentheses. There are several possible answers to some of the sentences.

A young couple is planning an automobile trip.

ROBERT: Where _should_ we _go_ (go) ? We _could spend_ (spend) a week touring the Southwest, or ...

SUSAN: That _____ (be) fun! We _____ (see) the Grand Canyon. Maybe we _____
              1.   2.   3.
(hike) down into the canyon!

ROBERT: We _____ (visit) our cousins in Phoenix. They have invited us several times,
          4.
and we have never been to see them.

SUSAN: _____ we _____ (visit) relatives on our vacation? I don't want to. I _____
               5.   6.
(see) the Grand Canyon.

ROBERT: We _____ (do) both. First, we _____ (visit) the Grand Canyon, and then
          7.   8.
we _____ (drive) to Phoenix and spend a few days with our cousins.
      9.

On the road to the Grand Canyon.

SUSAN: When _____ (get) there?
      10.

ROBERT: We _____ (be) there in a couple of hours.
      11.

SUSAN: _____ we _____ (stop) soon? I am hot, tired, and hungry.
             12.

ROBERT: We _____ (stop) in the next town. There _____ (be) an air-conditioned
          13.   14.
restaurant there.

Perfect modals

The perfect forms of modals express past time.

CAN'T HAVE / COULDN'T HAVE	
Impossibility in the past	▸ You **can't have finished** that book already. ▸ We **couldn't have succeeded** without your help.
COULD HAVE	
a. Possibility, ability, or opportunity for someone to do something (but did not do it) in the past	▸ Our team **could have won**, but we made a mistake in strategy. ▸ I **could have gone out** last night, but I was too tired.
b. Suggestion	▸ You **could have studied** harder and **gotten** a better grade.
MAY HAVE / MAY NOT HAVE	
Possibility that someone did or didn't do something in the past	▸ The teacher is absent today. He **may have gone** to a teacher's conference.
MIGHT HAVE / MIGHT NOT HAVE	
Possibility. *Might have* expresses more doubt than *may have*.	▸ He **might have gone** to a teacher's conference.
SHOULD HAVE / SHOULDN'T HAVE; OUGHT TO HAVE / OUGHT NOT TO HAVE	
a. Advice, opinion, or a good idea in the past that didn't happen	▸ I feel awful today. I **shouldn't have eaten** so much last night, and I **should have gone** home earlier. ▸ Yes, you **ought to have gotten** more sleep.
b. Duty/moral obligation in the past	▸ We **should have called** the police. ▸ We **ought to have called** the police.
c. Expectation of an event in the past. It is unknown and unimportant whether the event actually happened.	▸ Edgar has worked hard. He **should have gotten** a raise last month. ▸ Our guests **ought to have arrived** by now.

MUST HAVE / MUST NOT HAVE	
Certainty (95%)	▸ Tom got an A on the last test. He **must have** studied.
	▸ Ann got an F. She **must not have** studied.

WOULD HAVE / WOULDN'T HAVE; WOULD RATHER HAVE / WOULD RATHER NOT HAVE	
a. Willingness to do something in the past	▸ I **would have done** anything to make her happy.
b. Preference *Would rather have* expresses preference in the past.	▸ We **would rather have flown** first class, but we couldn't afford to.
	▸ We **would rather not have taken** such a late flight.

Progressive modals

Progressive modals express activities in progress.

1. Use a present progressive modal for an activity in progress at the moment of speaking or for one that might be in progress at a named time in the future.

   ▸ John doesn't answer his telephone. He **may be sleeping**.
   ▸ We **might be moving** soon.

   In some cases, the simple modal form is also possible.

   ▸ We **might move** soon.

2. Use a perfect progressive modal for an activity in progress when another action happened to interrupt it in the past.

   ▸ John didn't answer his telephone yesterday evening. He **may have been sleeping** when we called.
   ▸ He **couldn't have been sleeping** so early in the evening, but he **might have been watching** TV.

PRACTICE—Section 11d (3)

Complete the conversations using any appropriate modal and the correct form of the verbs in parentheses. There are several possible answers to some of the sentences.

After their visit to the Grand Canyon, Robert and Susan start toward Phoenix. While driving through the hot Arizona desert, they have this conversation.

SUSAN: I didn't know it _would be_ (be) so hot in Arizona in July.

ROBERT: I _____ (*fix*) the air conditioner before we started on the trip.
1.

Oh-oh. We _____ (*be*) lost. I _____ (*take*) the wrong road a few miles back.
2. 3.

SUSAN: You _____ (*check*) the map when we stopped for lunch.
4.

ROBERT: Well, you _____ (*look for*) road signs instead of always listening to the radio
5.
with your eyes closed.

A few minutes later

ROBERT: Oh-oh. We _____ (*have*) another little problem. We _____ (*run out*) of gas.
6. 7.

SUSAN: What? We _____ (*find*) a gas station fast, or we _____ (*spend*) the night in
8. 9.
the desert!

ROBERT: Our cousins _____ (*get*) worried. They _____ (*wonder*) where we are. We
10. 11.
_____ (*arrive*) in time for dinner, and it's almost midnight.
12.

SUSAN: We _____ (*call*) them before our cell phone went dead.
13.

11e Passive voice

🖥 Computer Note

Grammar checkers almost always mark passive sentences as questionable. This does not always mean that you should rewrite them in the active voice. Sometimes the passive voice is more appropriate. You will have to decide if your passive sentences are appropriate.

Sentences are in either the active or the passive voice. In active sentences, the subject *performs* the action of the verb. We want to emphasize the performer of the action, so we put the subject in front of the verb.

▶ **Michelangelo painted** the ceiling of the Sistine Chapel.

In passive sentences, the subject *receives* the action of the verb. We want to emphasize what happened, not who did it. The performer of the action is either unknown or unimportant, so the performer goes after the verb or is not mentioned at all.

▶ **Our house was painted** last year.

Passive verb forms

We form the passive voice with various tenses of *be* + a past participle.

SIMPLE TENSES		PERFECT TENSES	
Present	It **is written**	Present perfect	It **has been written**
Past	It **was written**	Past perfect	It **had been written**
Future	It **will be written** It **is going to be written**	Future perfect	It **will have been written**
PROGRESSIVE TENSES			
Present	It **is being written**		
Past	It **was being written**		

An object (direct or indirect) of an active sentence becomes the subject of a passive sentence. The subject of an active sentence becomes a phrase beginning with *by* or disappears entirely.

ACTIVE SENTENCES	PASSIVE SENTENCES
▸ Maria **wrote** the best essay.	▸ The best essay **was written** *by Maria*.
▸ People **speak** Portuguese in Brazil.	▸ Portuguese **is spoken** in Brazil (*by people*).[1]
▸ Someone **stole** my car yesterday.	▸ My car **was stolen** yesterday (*by someone*).[2]

[1] It was unnecessary to say *by people*, so it was omitted.
[2] It was unknown who stole my car, so *by someone* was omitted.

Both the direct object and the indirect object of an active sentence can become the subject of a passive sentence.

ACTIVE SENTENCES	PASSIVE SENTENCES
▸ My fiancé gave me **this ring**.	▸ **This ring** was given to me by my fiancé.
▸ My fiancé gave **me** this ring.	▸ **I** was given this ring by my fiancé.

You can make passive sentences only from transitive verbs because only transitive verbs can have objects. Therefore, you cannot write passive sentences with verbs such as *seem, happen, live, go, fall,* or *die.* For example, you cannot say *He was died* because *die* is an intransitive verb. You have to use *kill* to make a passive sentence: *He was killed.*

To make a passive sentence negative, put *not* after the first helping verb.

▶ Bananas **are *not* grown** in Alaska.

▶ This book **has *not* been translated** into English yet.

▶ Fish **should *not* be overcooked**.

ACTIVE VOICE	PASSIVE VOICE
Present tenses	
▶ Most people in the United States **eat** meat.	▶ Meat **is eaten** by most people in the United States.
▶ However, many Americans **are** now **eating** fish.	▶ However, fish **is** now **being eaten** by many Americans.
▶ People living near the sea **have** always **eaten** fish.	▶ Fish **has** always **been eaten** by people living near the sea.
Past tenses	
▶ Someone **painted** our house before we moved in.	▶ Our house **was painted** before we moved in.
▶ The painters **were** still **painting** it on the day we moved in.	▶ It **was** still **being painted** on the day we moved in.
▶ No one **had painted** it for many years.	▶ It **hadn't been painted** for many years.
Future tenses	
▶ Our two daughters **will share** the largest bedroom.	▶ The largest bedroom **will be shared** by our two daughters.
▶ We **are going to organize** the kitchen first.	▶ The kitchen **is going to be organized** first.
▶ By tomorrow night, we **will have put** everything in its proper place.	▶ By tomorrow night, everything **will have been put** in its proper place.
Modals	
Present ▶ We **should send** change-of-address cards to our friends.	▶ Change-of-address cards **should be sent** to our friends.
Past ▶ We **should have sent** them before we moved.	▶ They **should have been sent** before we moved.

ACTIVE VOICE	PASSIVE VOICE
Infinitives	
Present ▶ Our neighbors **plan to welcome** us with a neighborhood barbecue party.	▶ We **hope to be welcomed** with a neighborhood barbecue party.
Gerunds	
Present ▶ I look forward to someone **offering** me a job.	▶ I look forward to **being offered** a job.

PRACTICE—Section 11e (1)

A. Rewrite the following active sentences as passive sentences. Keep the same verb tense. Do not use a *by*-phrase when the performer of the action is unknown or unimportant. One sentence cannot be changed.

EXAMPLE
Teachers and students alike enjoy class parties.

Class parties are enjoyed by teachers and students alike.

1. Mr. Randall's class has traditionally given a Halloween party every year.
2. They are planning a huge party this year.
3. They will invite all the teachers.
4. The students in other classes want to come, too.

B. Rewrite the following passive sentences as active sentences. Keep the same verb tense.

EXAMPLE
Delicious food is prepared by some of the students.

Some of the students prepare delicious food.

1. The cafeteria is decorated by other students.
2. A costume must be worn by everyone.
3. Last year, a prize for best costume was awarded by the planning committee.
4. A good time is always had by everyone at the party.

Uses of passive sentences

In most writing, we prefer the active voice because it is more direct. However, we prefer the passive voice in five specific situations.

1. We want to emphasize what happened, not who did it.

   ▶ Jack **was promoted** last month.

2. The performer of the action is unknown.

▶ The wheel **was invented** during the Bronze Age.

3. The performer of the action is unimportant.

▶ Smoking **is prohibited** in airplanes.

4. We want to be objective. For this reason, we often use the passive voice in scientific and technical reports.

▶ 3 ml of HCl **was added** to the test tube and **heated** to 37°C.

5. We want to be diplomatic; that is, we don't want to say who did something wrong or made an error.

▶ I believe a mistake **has been made** on our bill. (NOT *You have made a mistake.*)

 Special Tip

Don't shift unnecessarily between active and passive voice.

She told us

▶ **The teacher passed out pencils, test booklets, and answer sheets. ~~We were told~~ to write only on the answer sheets, not on the test booklets.**

PRACTICE—Section 11e (2)

A. Rewrite this paragraph. Change to the passive voice where possible. Use *by*-phrases where they are appropriate, and omit them where the performer of the action is unknown or unimportant.

EXAMPLE

A young woman was murdered in our neighborhood last night. . . .

Someone murdered a young woman in our neighborhood last night. A neighbor had seen the woman walking her dog about ten o'clock. About midnight, someone heard a scream. However, no one went outside to investigate. This morning, another neighbor found her body. Someone called the police right away. They are investigating the crime. They told us, "Don't worry. We will find the murderer."

B. Edit this paragraph for unnecessary shifts between active and passive voice.

They were named

X rays were discovered quite by accident. ~~The discoverer named them~~ "X rays" because "X" means "unknown" in mathematics and science. Indeed, the mysterious ray was unknown. When people first used X rays, the dangers of radiation were not recognized and people used X rays indiscriminately. Fifty years ago, even shoe stores had X ray machines. Now people use X rays more cautiously.

12 Special Situations with Verbs

12a Gerunds

Forms of gerunds

Gerunds and gerund phrases

A gerund is an *-ing* form of a verb that is used as a noun.

▶ **Cooking** is my aunt's hobby.

A gerund phrase consists of a gerund plus all of the following words that complete its meaning.

▶ He prefers **swimming in the ocean.**

Negative gerunds

Put *not* in front of a gerund to make it negative.

▶ We enjoyed **not going** to class today.
   (*We didn't go to class, and we enjoyed doing other things.*)

Compare:

▶ We **didn't enjoy going** to class today.
   (*We went to class, and we didn't enjoy it.*)

Past gerunds

The past gerund form (*having* + past participle) tells about an activity that happened before the time of the main verb. It is seldom used because you can use the simple *-ing* form instead.

▶ When it started raining, he regretted **having left** his raincoat at home.
▶ When it started raining, he regretted **leaving** his raincoat at home.

Passive gerunds

There are two passive gerunds: a present or general form (*being* + past participle) and a past form (*having been* + past participle).

▶ I appreciate **being offered** a job with your company.
▶ I appreciate **having been invited** to your party.

The past form is used to emphasize that the action of the gerund took place before the action of the main verb. It is seldom used because you can use the general form instead.

▶ John was surprised at **having been elected** class president.

▶ John was surprised at **being elected** class president.

Noun/pronoun + gerund

The meaning changes when you put a noun or pronoun in front of a gerund.

▶ We were happy about **winning** the prize. (*We won the prize.*)

▶ We were happy about *your* (or *you*) **winning** the prize. (*You won the prize.*)

▶ We were happy about *Mark's* (or **Mark**) winning the prize. (*Mark won the prize.*)

In formal English, we use possessive nouns and pronouns in front of a gerund. In informal English, we often use object forms instead.

Formal ▶ I appreciate *your* **giving** me a ride.

      ▶ I understand *Ann's* **not wanting** to sing in front of the class.

Informal ▶ I appreciate *you* **giving** me a ride.

      ▶ I understand *Ann* **not wanting** to sing in front of the class.

Uses of gerunds

Gerunds are nouns, so they can be subjects, subject complements, or objects.

▶ <u>subject</u>
Playing golf is my uncle's favorite pastime.

▶ What he loves best is <u>subject complement</u>
playing in tournaments.

▶ He loves <u>direct object</u>
winning.

▶ He dreams *about* <u>object of preposition</u>
playing with Tiger Woods.

Gerunds as subjects

Gerunds can be subjects. A single gerund takes a singular verb.

▶ *Gardening* **is** my favorite weekend activity.

Two or more gerunds joined by *and* take a plural verb.

▶ *Sleeping, eating, and hanging out with friends* **are** a teenager's favorite weekend activities.

Gerunds as direct objects

Gerunds can be direct objects after these verbs.

admit	continue*	finish	mention	recall
appreciate	defer	forgive	mind	recommend
attempt*	delay	give up	miss	resent
avoid	deny	hate*	postpone	resist
begin*	detest	imagine	practice	risk
can't bear*	discuss	intend*	prefer*	start*
can't help	enjoy	keep (on)	prevent	suggest
can't stand*	escape	like*	put off	tolerate
consider	excuse	love*	quit	understand

*You can also use infinitives after these verbs. See *Section 12c.*

▶ He **admits** *watching* Saturday morning cartoons with his children.
▶ The suspect **denied** *knowing* the victim.

PRACTICE—Section 12a (1)

A. Combine the sentences in each pair. Change the underlined words in first sentence into a gerund or gerund phrase and make it the subject of the second sentence. Delete the words in parentheses.

EXAMPLE
(Young people should learn to) <u>manage money</u>. (This) is an important life skill.

Managing money is an important life skill.

1. (Companies) <u>advertise</u>. (This) encourages people to buy things.
2. (People) <u>buy things they don't need</u>. (This) can cause people to go into debt.
3. (It's a good idea to) <u>stay out of debt</u>. (This) should be everyone's goal.

B. Complete the sentences by using a gerund or gerund phrase as the direct object. Choose a verb from this list to form each gerund.

make   apply for   live   come home   work

EXAMPLE

John will graduate from college in June. He has been thinking about *applying for* a job with a big bank in New York.

1. John thinks he would enjoy _____ in New York.

2. However, John's father wants him to consider _____ and _____ for him.

3. John has decided to postpone _____ a decision for a while.

Gerunds as objects of a preposition

Preposition + gerund

Gerunds can follow prepositions.

▶ She gave no reason **for** *leaving* so suddenly.

▶ What are the advantages **of** *living* in a student dormitory?

Verb + preposition + gerund

A gerund can be the object of a preposition after certain verb + preposition combinations. Some of these verbs require a direct object; others do not. Verbs requiring a direct object are followed by the abbreviation *s.o.* (for *someone*) in parentheses in the following list.

accuse (s.o.) of	concentrate on	object to
adjust to	congratulate (s.o.) on	pay (s.o.) for
agree with	consist of	plan on
apologize for	deal with	prevent (s.o.) from
apologize to (s.o.) for	decide against	refer to
approve of/disapprove of	depend on	see about
argue about	devote (oneself, one's life) to	stop (s.o.) from
believe in	dream about	suspect (s.o.) of
blame (s.o.) for	feel like	talk about
care about	forget about	thank (s.o.) for
care for	forgive (s.o.) for	think about
comment on	insist on	warn (s.o.) about
complain about	look forward to	worry about

▶ They **are looking forward to** *going* on vacation.

┌ direct object ┐

▶ He **accused** his best friend **of** *lying*.

PRACTICE—Section 12a (2)

Complete the sentences by using a gerund or gerund phrase as the object of a preposition. Choose a word from this list. Add the correct preposition in front of the gerund.

    send   become   check on   stay in touch with

EXAMPLE

In the United States, young people look forward __to__ __becoming__ independent.

1. Parents worry _____ _____ their children out into the world alone.

2. That is why parents insist _____ _____ their children almost daily.

3. Young people object _____ their parents _____ them all the time.

Adjective + preposition + gerund

A gerund can be the object of a preposition after certain adjective + preposition combinations. These combinations often appear after the verbs *be, become, get* (when it means *become*), *seem, appear,* and *look.*

accustomed to	excited about	responsible for
afraid of	famous for	sorry about
angry at	good at	sure of/about
ashamed of	grateful to (s.o.) for	surprised at
capable of	incapable of	tired of
concerned about	interested in	used to
content with	lazy about	worried about
delighted at	proud of	

▶ The students got **tired of** *writing* essays.
▶ The teachers were **used to** *listening* to their complaints.

Used to + gerund vs. used to + base form

Used to + gerund means *accustomed to, it is not strange to me.* This "used to" needs a verb in front of it, usually *be, become,* or *get* (when it means *become*).

▶ I **am** not **used to** *living* in a cold climate.
                    gerund

▶ I **may** never **get used to** *being* cold all the time.
                        gerund

NOTE: You can also use a noun or pronoun after this "used to": *I am not used to the weather. I may never get used to it.*

Used to + base form of verb expresses a habit, activity, or situation that happened in the past but that no longer happens.

▶ I **used to** *live* in Bangkok, where it is always warm.
            base form

▶ When I lived there, we **used to** *go* to the beach as often as possible.
                    base form

PRACTICE—Section 12a (3)

Complete the sentences with any gerund that fits the meaning. There are many possible ways to complete the sentences. In one sentence, use the base form of a verb instead of a gerund form.

ADVISER: How are you, Henry? Are you getting used to *living* here in the United States?

HENRY: Yes, I'm slowly becoming used to _____ here, but I will never get used to
                                                   1.
      _____ American food. I miss my mother's cooking.
      2.

ADVISER:　How are your classes?

HENRY:　Well, to be honest, I'm a little tired of _____ homework. I'm a little lazy
　　　　　　　　　　　　　　　　　　　　　　　3.
　　　　about _____ it on time.
　　　　　　　　4.

ADVISER:　Didn't you use to _____ homework in your country?
　　　　　　　　　　　　　　5.

HENRY:　No, we didn't. We were responsible for _____ the material on our own.
　　　　　　　　　　　　　　　　　　　　　　6.

Special uses of gerunds and other *-ing* words

Go + gerund

Use *go* + gerund for sports and other recreational activities.

go bowling	go fishing	go jogging	go snowboarding
go camping	go hiking	go shopping	go swimming
go dancing	go in-line skating	go sightseeing	go waterskiing

▶ Tom **went** *scuba diving* in Cozumel last year.
▶ Let's **go** *shopping* this weekend.

Verbs of perception + *-ing* form or base form

You can usually use either an *-ing* form or the base form of a verb after certain verbs of perception with no difference in meaning.

feel	look at	see
hear	notice	smell
listen to	observe	watch

▶ We **heard** the dog *barking*.
▶ We **heard** the dog *bark*.

Special expressions + *-ing* form

Use the *-ing* form of the verb after these expressions.

have fun	have difficulty	spend time/money
have a good time	have a problem	waste time/money
have a hard time	have trouble	

▶ We **had fun** *shopping* in the city.
▶ Did you **have trouble** *finding* my house?
▶ Tina **spends most of her money** *buying* CDs.
▶ She **wastes a lot of time** *daydreaming*.

PRACTICE—Section 12a (4)

Complete each sentence with an *-ing* word or the base form of a verb chosen from this list. There is more than one correct answer for two sentences.

> *sing*   *get along with*   *dance*   *sew*   *search*

EXAMPLE
Would you like to go _dancing_ with me tonight?

1. My mother likes to spend her free time _____ clothes for my sister's baby.

2. I am having a problem _____ my roommate at the moment.

3. Every morning, I hear him _____ in the shower, and he sings off-key.

4. Yesterday morning, I noticed him _____ my closet for something to wear.

12b Infinitives

Forms of infinitives

Infinitives and infinitive phrases
The most common form of an infinitive is *to* + the base form of a verb.

▶ Children like **to play**.

An infinitive phrase is an infinitive plus all the words that complete its meaning.

▶ We waited **to cross the street**.

Negative infinitives
Put *not* in front of an infinitive to make it negative.

▶ We decided **not to buy** a new car this year.

Present, passive, progressive, and past infinitives
The different forms of infinitives are present, passive, progressive, and past.
A progressive infinitive tells about an activity in progress at the time of the main verb. A past infinitive tells about an activity before the time of the main verb.

Present / general infinitive	▶ Children like **to play**.
Passive infinitive	▶ Children need **to be loved**.
Progressive infinitive	▶ The children pretended **to be sleeping**.
Past infinitive	▶ They seem **to have lost** their fear of the dark.

Question word + infinitive

We can, and often do, insert words between the main verb and an infinitive. In fact, we often insert a question word such as *who, when, where,* or *how.*

▶ Bob and Mary have finally decided **when to get** married.
▶ However, they still can't agree on **where to get** married.
▶ Would you teach me **how to make** good guacamole?

 Special Tip

Never insert a word between *to* and the verb. This error is called a split infinitive.

▶ She began to (carefully) spell the word *syzygy.*

PRACTICE—Section 12b (1)

Complete each sentence with an appropriate infinitive form of the verb in parentheses. Use each of the four forms (present, passive, progressive, past) once.

EXAMPLE
I am eager _to go_ (*go*) home after graduation in June.

1. I am happy _____ (*complete*) all of my graduation requirements.

2. I decided _____ (*not go*) graduate school right away.

3. Right now, I would like _____ (*lie*) on a beach.

4. Next year, I hope _____ (*employ*).

Uses of infinitives

Infinitives as subjects

Infinitives and infinitive phrases can be subjects or subject complements.

┌──────── subject ────────┐
▶ **To find a rich husband** is her main goal in life.

┌ subject complement ┐
▶ His main goal is **to find a rich wife.**

It + *be* + adjective + infinitive

We often begin a sentence with *it* and move an infinitive subject to the end, especially when the sentence has the verb *be* + an adjective such as *important, easy, wrong, embarrassing,* or *exciting.*

┌─── subject ───┐
▶ **It is important** *to study hard.*

┌─────────── subject ───────────┐
▶ **It is embarrassing** *to forget your own telephone number.*

Adjective + *for/of/to* + noun/pronoun + infinitive

When you want to say *who* performs the action of the infinitive, use *for, of,* or *to* + an object noun or pronoun. After some adjectives, use only *for.* After other adjectives, use only *of.* After some adjectives, you can use either *for* or *of.* After *-ing* adjectives, use *for* or *to.*

▶ It is important **for parents** *to love* their children.
▶ It was kind **of you** *to send* me a card.
▶ It was wrong **for (of) him** *to say* that.
▶ It was surprising **for (to) me** *to see* how much the children had grown.

ADJECTIVES FOLLOWED BY *FOR*	ADJECTIVES FOLLOWED BY *OF*	ADJECTIVES FOLLOWED BY *FOR* OR *OF*	ADJECTIVES FOLLOWED BY *FOR* OR *TO*
advisable	considerate,	courteous,	amazing
beneficial	inconsiderate	discourteous	annoying
difficult	generous	foolish	disappointing
easy	good *(kind)*	polite, impolite	embarrassing
essential	intelligent	right	exciting
fatal	loyal, disloyal	rude	fascinating
good *(beneficial)*	nice	silly	interesting
hard		strange	puzzling
hopeless		stupid	satisfying
important		wise, unwise	shocking
necessary		wrong	surprising
normal			terrifying
possible,			
impossible			
preferable			
useful, useless			

PRACTICE—Section 12b (2)

Rewrite each sentence with *it* and an infinitive phrase. Add the noun or pronoun in parentheses (if one is given) and an appropriate preposition (*for, of,* or *to*) in front of the infinitive phrase.

EXAMPLE
Learning about social customs in different countries is fascinating. (*me*)

It is fascinating to me to learn about social customs in different countries.

1. Bringing your hostess a gift of flowers is courteous in Germany.
2. Giving an odd number of flowers is essential. (*Odd numbers are 3, 5, 7, 9, etc.*)
3. Not knowing this custom was embarrassing when I was in Berlin. (*me*)
4. Arriving late at a party is normal in many countries. (*guests*)
5. In contrast, being late is rude in the United States.

Infinitives as objects

Infinitives can be objects of verbs. There are different patterns depending on the verb.

Verb + infinitive

(can) afford*	come	hate**	neglect	remember
agree	continue**	hope	offer	seem
appear	decide	intend**	plan	start**
arrange	demand	learn	prefer**	threaten
attempt**	desire	like**	prepare	wait
begin**	fail	love**	pretend	
can't bear**	forget	manage	promise	
can't stand**	happen	mean	prove	
care	hesitate	need	refuse	

*Always use *afford* with a form of *can* or *be able to*: We can't afford a vacation this year. They are able to afford a new car every year.
**You can also use a gerund after these verbs with no difference in meaning: *He attempted to drive. He attempted driving.* See Section 12c.

▶ We **decided** *to leave* the party early.
▶ The protesters **demanded** *to speak* to the prime minister.

Verb + noun / pronoun + infinitive

advise*	convince	help**	persuade	tempt
allow*	direct	hire	remind	urge
appoint	enable	instruct	request	warn
cause	encourage	invite	require	
caution	forbid*	motivate	show ... how	
challenge	force	order	teach	
command	get (*cause*)	permit*	tell	

*You can also use a gerund after these verbs, but without a noun/pronoun. See Section 12c.
**You can also use the base form after *help* with no difference in meaning. *We'll help you to move. We'll help you move.* See Section 11c.

▶ The teacher **told the class** *to be* quiet.
▶ The teacher **told us** *to be* quiet.

Verb + infinitive OR Verb + noun / pronoun + infinitive

These verbs can have either pattern, but the meaning is different.

ask	dare	prefer*	would like
beg	expect	promise**	
choose	need	want	

Prefer can also be followed by a gerund. See *Section 12c.*
The meaning doesn't change with *promise*. *She promised to call* = *She promised **me to call*.

▶ I wanted *to leave.* ▶ I wanted them *to leave.*

▶ I expected *to win.* ▶ I expected my opponent *to win.*

PRACTICE—Section 12b (3)

A. Complete each sentence with the infinitive of any appropriate verb.

   EXAMPLE
   When I left home for the first time, my father offered <u>to pay my expenses for</u>
   <u>one year</u> .

   1. My mother said, "I can't bear _____."

   2. My friends promised _____.

   3. I prepared myself _____.

B. Complete each sentence with any appropriate noun or pronoun and infinitive.

   EXAMPLE
   During my second year away from home, my father warned <u>me to stay out</u>
   <u>of trouble</u> .

   1. My mother told _____ _____.

   2. I asked _____ _____.

   3. My friends urged _____ _____.

C. Complete each sentence with any appropriate infinitive. Add a noun or pronoun if
   one is necessary.

   EXAMPLE
   I told my adviser, "My parents expect <u>me to study business</u> ."

   1. He asked, "What have you decided _____?"

   2. I answered, "If my parents permit _____, I will be very happy."

   3. "But if they force _____, I will be very sad."

Infinitives following adjectives

Infinitives can follow certain adjectives. Most of these adjectives describe feelings.

afraid	content	fortunate	pleased	sorry
amazed	delighted	glad	prepared	shocked
angry	determined	happy	proud	stunned
anxious	disappointed	hesitant	ready	surprised
ashamed	disgusted	horrified	relieved	upset
astonished	disturbed	lucky	reluctant	willing
careful	eager	motivated	sad	

- ▶ Sean's parents were **proud *to announce*** their son's promotion.
- ▶ We were **surprised *to hear*** of his success.
- ▶ We thought he was **lucky *to have gotten*** a job.

Infinitives following nouns

We sometimes use an infinitive to give more information about a noun. In this pattern, the infinitive follows the noun. We often use an infinitive after *the first* . . . , *the second* . . . , *the next* . . . , *the last* . . . , and so on.

- ▶ She has **a plan *to start*** her own business.
- ▶ I admire **his ability *to make*** people relax.
- ▶ Tom is always **the first person *to arrive*** at a party and **the last person *to leave*.**

Infinitives of purpose

Use an infinitive to express a purpose. You can also use *in order to* + verb to express purpose with no difference in meaning.

- ▶ They live with her parents **to save** money.
- ▶ They live with her parents **in order to save** money.

 Special Tips

1. Don't use *for* + verb to express a purpose. Use an infinitive or *in order to* + verb.
   (in order) to buy
   - ▶ My sister went to the post office ~~for buy~~ stamps.
   (in order) to buy
   - ▶ My sister went to the post office ~~for buying~~ stamps.

2. You may use *for* + noun to express a purpose.
   ┌─ noun ─┐
   - ▶ My sister went to the post office **for stamps.**

PRACTICE—Section 12b (4)

A. Complete each sentence with the adjective or noun + the infinitive form of the verb in parentheses.

HENRY: Do you have <u>a few minutes to give</u> (*a few minutes/give*) me some advice?

TEACHER: Of course. I am always _____ (*glad/help*) you.
1.

HENRY: Can you tell me _____ (*an easy way/learn English*)?
2.

TEACHER: Hmm. I am _____ (*sorry/inform*) you that there is no easy way.
3.

B. Use these ideas to write sentences telling Henry how to improve his English. Each sentence should contain an infinitive of purpose. Use *in order to* or *to* as you wish.

EXAMPLE
watch television talk shows

<u>Henry, you could watch television talk shows in order to improve your</u>

<u>listening ability.</u>

1. write an essay every week
2. write sentences using new words
3. get an American friend

C. Edit the following paragraph for errors within infinitives.

Because of increased security at airports, you need to arrive at least two hours before your departure time for pass through all of the checkpoints. For saving time, don't go to the check-in counters for checking in your luggage; instead, use the skycap service. For a small fee, you can save yourself the trouble of standing in line. Even better, don't check luggage at all. If you pack carefully, you might be able to traveling with only a carry-on bag.

Infinitives with *too* and *enough*

We often add an infinitive to complete the meaning of an expression with *too* and *enough*. Notice the different word order. *Too* comes before adjectives and adverbs. *Enough* comes after adjectives and adverbs but before nouns.

▶ My 92-year-old grandfather is **too old** *to drive* a car.
(adjective)

▶ He drives **too slowly** *to pass* the test.
(adverb)

▶ My 15-year-old son isn't **old enough** *to get* a driver's license.
(adjective)

▶ He drives **well enough** *to pass* the test.
(adverb)

▶ He doesn't have **enough money** *to buy* a car.
(noun)

! *Special Tips*

The meanings of *very, too,* and *enough* are different.

1. *Very* intensifies (makes stronger) the meaning of an adjective.

▶ The test was *very* **difficult.** (*The test was difficult, but you could pass it.*)
▶ The coffee is *very* **hot.** (*The coffee is hot, but you can still drink it.*)
▶ I am *very* **pleased** to meet you.

2. *Too* signals a negative result.

▶ The test was *too* **difficult** to pass. (*No one could pass it.*)
▶ The coffee is *too* **hot** to drink. (*You can't drink it.*)

3. *Enough* means "sufficient / sufficiently."

▶ There wasn't *enough* **time** to finish the test.
▶ The coffee is finally **cool** *enough* to drink.

PRACTICE—Section 12b (5)

A young couple is moving into their new apartment.

A. Complete each sentence with *very, too,* or *enough* and the word in parentheses.

EXAMPLE
I really like the new mirror you bought. It's ___very beautiful___ (*beautiful*).

1. However, I think you have hung it _____ (*low*). Please hang it a little higher.

2. Is it _____ (*high*) now? I moved it up six inches.

3. Do you think you can move the piano by yourself? It's _____ (*heavy*).

4. It's _____ (*heavy*) for one person to move. I'll get someone to help me.

5. Is there _____ (*space*) in the den for the piano, or should we put it in the living room?

6. We've worked _____ (*long*). Let's stop and get something to eat.

B. Read each situation. Then complete the sentence with *too, enough,* an adjective or noun, and an infinitive that completes the meaning.

EXAMPLE
I'm glad we washed the windows. They were so dirty that we couldn't see through them.

The windows were ___too dirty to see through___.

1. The refrigerator is still in the street. The kitchen doorway wasn't wide. We couldn't get the refrigerator through it.

   The kitchen doorway wasn't _____.

2. Let's go out for dinner tonight. After moving all day, I'm tired. I can't cook.

   I'm _____.

3. No, let's eat at home. I don't have any energy. I don't want to go out.

   I don't have _____.

12c Gerunds vs. infinitives

No difference in meaning

Either a gerund or an infinitive can be the direct object after these verbs with no difference in meaning.

attempt	can't stand	intend	prefer
begin	continue	like	start
can't bear	hate	love	

▶ The baby **began** *breathing* after the doctor tickled her feet.
▶ The baby **began** *to breathe* after the doctor tickled her feet.

You can use either a gerund or an infinitive after the following verbs with no difference in meaning, but when you use an infinitive, you must give the verb a noun or pronoun object.

advise	allow	forbid	permit

▶ Some airlines **don't permit** *smoking*.
▶ My parents **don't permit** *me to smoke*.

Difference in meaning

Either a gerund or an infinitive can be the direct object after these verbs with a difference in meaning.

forget	regret	remember	stop	try

▶ She **forgot** *to buy* milk yesterday. (*She didn't remember to buy milk.*)
▶ She **forgot** *buying* milk yesterday. (*She didn't remember that she had bought milk yesterday.*)

▶ I **regret *to tell*** you that you did not get the job. (*I am sorry that I have to report bad news.*)

▶ I **regret *telling*** that lie. (*I am sorry about something that I did in the past.*)

▶ John always **remembers *to send*** his mother flowers on Mother's Day. (*John remembers to do something before he does it.*)

▶ John **remembers *sending*** roses last year. (*John remembers doing something after he did it.*)

▶ My neighbor **stopped *to say*** hello. (*My neighbor stopped on the street and said hello.*)

▶ My neighbor **stopped *saying*** hello. (*My neighbor doesn't say hello any more.*)

▶ I have been **trying *to call*** long distance all morning, but my calls don't go through. (*I have attempted to call.*)

▶ **Try *dialing*** "1" before you dial the area code and number. (*Use a different strategy.*)

PRACTICE—Section 12c

Complete each sentence with either the gerund or the infinitive form of the verb in parentheses. In some sentences, you can use either a gerund or an infinitive. In other sentences, you can use only one form or the other.

EXAMPLE
Michelle forgot ___to pay___ (*pay*) her electric bill again, so the company sent her a warning notice.

1. The company allows customers _____ (*make*) a late payment once in a while, but not three months in a row.

2. I hate _____ (*pay*) interest charges, so I always try _____ (*make*) all payments early.

3. Sometimes I forget _____ (*make*) a payment and pay the same bill twice.

4. Last month, for example, I didn't remember _____ (*pay*) my phone bill, so I paid it twice.

5. My father advised _____ (*write*) "paid" and the date on each bill to help me remember.

6. When I remember _____ (*do*) this, I don't have a problem.

7. When did you stop _____ (*smoke*)?

8. Let's stop _____ (*buy*) some flowers for our host on our way to the party.

9. Does this college allow students _____ (*take*) classes on a pass/fail basis?

10. Does this college allow _____ (*take*) classes for no credit?

12d Phrasal verbs

We can, and often do, change the meaning of a verb by adding a short word (sometimes two words) to it. These verbs are called phrasal verbs or two-word verbs. They are very common in spoken English, and their meanings are idiomatic. *Section 48* at the back of the book lists many of them.

Like regular verbs, phrasal verbs can be transitive (T) or intransitive (I). Intransitive verbs do not have objects. Transitive verbs have objects.

VERB	MEANING	EXAMPLE
look up (I)	*get better, improve*	▶ The economy **is looking up** this year.
look s.t. or s.o. **up** (T)	*1. search for information in a book or on the Internet*	▶ How many words do you **look up** in your dictionary every day?
	2. search for and meet with someone after a long separation	▶ I **looked up** several old friends when I visited my hometown last month.

Transitive phrasal verbs are either separable or inseparable.

Separable

When phrasal verbs are separable, you can separate the parts with a noun or pronoun object.

noun object
▶ Look *new words* up.

pronoun object
▶ Look *them* up.

Noun objects can go either before or after the second part of a phrasal verb. Pronoun objects must go between the two parts.

noun object
▶ Try *the shoes* on.

pronoun object
▶ Try *them* on.

▶ Try on *the shoes*.

▶ Try on *them*.

Inseparable

When phrasal verbs are inseparable, you cannot separate the parts.

noun object
▶ He **looks after** *his brothers.*

pronoun object
▶ He **looks after** *them.*

Phrasal verbs with three words such as *look forward to* are always inseparable.

▶ I **look forward to** my next birthday.

▶ I **look forward to** it.

PRACTICE—Section 12d

Refer to the list of phrasal verbs in *Section 48* at the back of the book to do this exercise. Complete the conversation with a phrasal verb in an appropriate tense. Choose a verb that matches the meaning given in parentheses, and include the underlined words.

JULIE: I wish I could _cheer Sally up / cheer up Sally_ (*make* Sally *feel happier*). She's really depressed these days.

ANDREA: What's wrong? What's bothering her?

JULIE: I can't _____ (*understand after thinking about it*). I'm not sure, but I know
          _{1.}
          that she and her roommate _____ (*not have a good relationship*).
                                    _{2.}

ANDREA: Why doesn't Sally _____ (*get into a sitting position*) with her roommate and
                            _{3.}
          _____ (*discuss it*)?
          _{4.}

JULIE: She plans to do that, but she keeps _____ (*postpone it*). I think she's afraid
                                              _{5.}
          of getting into a fight with her roommate.

ANDREA: Well, I guess she will just have to _____ (*tolerate her*) then.
                                              _{6.}

JULIE: If they would just _____ (*meet*) and talk, I am sure they could _____
                             _{7.}   _{8.}
          (*resolve their problems*).

ANDREA: I hope so. Thanks for giving me a ride home. Oh, I almost forgot. I have to
          _____ (*collect, gather something*) from the drugstore. Would you mind
          _{9.}
          _____ (*allowing me to leave the vehicle*) at the next corner?
          _{10.}

13   Subject-Verb Agreement

 Computer Note

Grammar checkers find some, but not all, errors in subject-verb agreement. For example, a grammar checker might mark the sentence *It is important that he is on time* as correct because it does not recognize the need for the base form of a verb after a clause like *It is important that.* Also, sometimes grammar checkers identify the wrong word as the subject.

Verbs must agree with their subjects in number (singular or plural) and person (*I, you, he, they,* and so on). A singular subject (one person or thing) has a singular verb. A plural subject (two or more people or things) has a plural verb.

Some subject-verb agreement errors happen when the subject is third-person singular (*he, she,* or *it*). Remember to use the *-s* form in the simple present tense. Also remember to use the *-s* form of the helping verbs *do* and *have.*

	ANY VERB—PRESENT TENSE			
	Singular		**Plural**	
First person	I	**work**	we	**work**
Second person	you	**work**	you	**work**
Third person	he she it	**works**	they	**work**

	DO—PRESENT TENSE				HAVE—PRESENT TENSE			
	Singular		**Plural**		**Singular**		**Plural**	
First person	I	**do**	we	**do**	I	**have**	we	**have**
Second person	you	**do**	you	**do**	you	**have**	you	**have**
Third person	he she it	**does**	they	**do**	he she it	**has**	they	**have**

The verb *be* is irregular, using different forms for first- and third-person singular in both present and past tense.

	BE—PRESENT TENSE				BE—PAST TENSE			
	Singular		**Plural**		**Singular**		**Plural**	
First person	I	**am**	we	**are**	I	**was**	we	**were**
Second person	you	**are**	you	**are**	you	**were**	you	**were**
Third person	he she it	**is**	they	**are**	he she it	**was**	they	**were**

13a Singular subjects

These subjects are always singular.

he, she, or **it**	▶ **It** *is* raining.
a singular noun	▶ **This rose bush** *hasn't* bloomed for three years.
a noncount noun	▶ **The coffee** *isn't* hot.
a single gerund or gerund phrase	▶ **Making trouble** *is* her hobby.
an amount of time, money, or weight (*Even though the word is plural in form, it is considered one unit.*)	▶ **Three years** *is* a long time to wait for a visa.
	▶ **Sixty dollars** *is* too much for that shirt.
	▶ **Thirty-two pounds** *is* the average weight gain during pregnancy.

These indefinite pronouns are always singular.

-one words	*-body* words	*-thing* words	
anyone	**anybody**	**anything**	▶ *Is* **anyone** at home?
			▶ *Has* **anybody** *seen* my car keys?
everyone	**everybody**	**everything**	▶ **Everyone** *likes* Chinese food.
			▶ **Everybody** *has* an equal opportunity.
someone	**somebody**	**something**	▶ **Someone** *has borrowed* my pen.
no one	**nobody**	**nothing**	▶ **Nothing** *satisfies* her.
			▶ **Nobody** *knows* how to solve this problem.
one			▶ **One** *has* a right to disagree with the government.

These indefinite pronouns are also always singular.

each	**either**	**neither**	
			▶ **Each** of their children *has had* a good education.
			▶ *Does* **either** of your parents speak English?
			▶ No, **neither** *does.*

13b Singular or plural subjects

The following indefinite pronouns and quantity expressions can be singular or plural.

all	**a lot of**	**most**	**one-half, two-thirds, etc.**
any	**none**	**some**	

They are singular when they refer to a singular or noncount noun or pronoun.

▶ **All** of his *money was* stolen.

They are plural when they refer to a plural noun or pronoun.

▶ **All** of his *books were* stolen.

▶ *Does* **any** of the *food* need heating?

▶ *Do* **any** of the *desserts* need refrigerating?

▶ **Some** of the *snow has* melted.

▶ **Some** of the *trees have* lost their leaves.

▶ **One-half** of his *face was* painted green.

▶ **One-half** of the *students were* from Asia.

▶ **None** of the *money was* missing.

▶ **None*** of the *questions were* easy.

*None is always singular in formal English. In informal English, *none* can be singular or plural.
▶ **None** of the students *is* here. (*formal*)   ▶ **None** of the students *are* here. (*informal*)

13c Plural subjects

These subjects are always plural.

they

▶ **They** *are* best friends.

a plural noun

▶ **The trees** *don't* have any leaves.

both

▶ **Both** of my parents *speak* English.

two or more subjects joined by *and*

▶ **John, Chris, and Anna** *are* in the same class.

EXCEPTIONS

1. When the subjects joined by *and* refer to a single unit or to the same person or thing, the subject is singular.

    ▶ **A hamburger and fries *is*** my favorite snack. (*The writer considers hamburger and fries as one unit.*)

    ▶ **My best friend and wisest counselor *is*** a dog. (*The two subjects refer to the same animal.*)

2. When the subjects joined by *and* have the word *each* or *every* in front of them, they are considered one unit and take a singular verb.

    ▶ **Each passenger and crew member *was*** questioned.

    ▶ **Every man, woman, and child in the country *knows*** who Elvis Presley was.

13d Confusing situations

Subject-verb agreement is sometimes confusing in the following situations.

Subject and verb separated by other words

Often a prepositional phrase or a clause comes between the subject and its verb. Words between a subject and verb do not change subject-verb agreement. You should mentally cross them out when deciding whether to use a singular or a plural verb.

▶ **Many varieties** of rice **are** grown around the world. (*The subject is* varieties, *not* rice.)

▶ The **color** of her eyes **changes** depending on the color of her clothes. (*The subject is* color, *not* eyes.)

▶ The **list** of students who have been admitted to the university but haven't yet registered for classes **is** posted outside the registrar's office. (*The subject is* list.)

Reference: Review how to find the subject of a sentence in *Section 4a.*

Subjects joined by *or, nor, either . . . or,* and *neither . . . nor*

Singular subjects joined by *or, nor, either . . . or,* and *neither . . . nor* take a singular verb.

▶ **A passport** *or* **other photo ID** *is* required at check-in.

Plural subjects take a plural verb.

▶ *Neither* **my parents** *nor* **my brothers and sisters** *know* that I am coming home.

When one of the subjects is singular and the other is plural, the verb agrees with the nearer subject.

▶ *Either* **the students** *or* **the teacher** *is* right.

▶ *Either* **the teacher** *or* **the students** *are* right.

Collective nouns

A collective noun names a group of people. These are collective nouns.

band	couple	family	majority	pair
class	crew	group	minority	staff
committee	crowd	jury	orchestra	team

A collective noun takes a singular verb when the group acts as a unit.

▶ **My family** *lives* together in one big house. (*acting as a unit*)

A collective noun takes a plural verb when the members of the group act individually.

▶ **My family** *take* separate vacations. (*acting individually*)

NOTE: British English prefers a plural verb in both situations.

You can avoid the issue by adding the word *members,* which becomes the (plural) subject.

▶ The **members** of my family *live* together in one big house.

▶ The **members** of my family *take* separate vacations.

Inverted word order

Changing the order of the subject and the verb does not change subject-verb agreement.

▶ There *is* **a large, angry elephant** running loose in the street.

▶ There *are* **several angry farmers** chasing it.

Sentences with a subject complement

When a sentence has a subject complement, the verb agrees with the subject, not with the subject complement. (A subject complement is a noun, often following the verb *be,* that renames the subject.)

▶ Her main **topic** of conversation *is* hairstyles.
(subject / subject complement)

▶ **Hairstyles** *are* her main topic of conversation.
(subject / subject complement)

Nouns ending in -s and other irregular nouns

A few nouns that look plural are singular, and other nouns that look singular are plural. A few examples of these exceptional nouns are listed here. For more complete information, see Irregular Plural Nouns in *Section 38c*.

A few nouns ending in *-s* are singular.

economics	▶ **Economics** *is* my hardest class.
the United States	▶ **The United States** *is* a relatively young country.
news	▶ The best **news** *is* sometimes no news.

A few nouns not ending in *-s* are plural.

men	▶ The **men** *were* waiting outside.
people	▶ **People** *want* peace and security.
police	▶ The **police** *have* arrived.
teeth	▶ Her **teeth** *are* very white.

A few nouns have the same singular and plural form.

data	▶ The **data** *shows* . . . The **data** *show* . . .
fish	▶ This **fish** *is* . . . These **fish** *are* . . .
species	▶ A **species** *has* . . . Several **species** *have* . . .

After *who, which,* and *that*

The verb after the relative pronouns *who, which,* and *that* agrees with its antecedent. An antecedent is the noun to which the relative pronoun refers.

singular antecedent
▶ Children may not see **a film** that *has* an X-rating.

plural antecedent
▶ Children may not see **films** that *have* an X-rating.

The number of / a number of

The number of takes a singular verb. *A number of,* which means *several,* takes a plural verb.

▶ **The number of** volunteers *was* surprising. (*The number was surprising, not the volunteers.*)

▶ **A number of** students *were* absent. (*Several students were absent.*)

PRACTICE—Section 13

Choose the correct form of the verb by circling it.

EXAMPLE

Rice cook/<u>cooks</u> best in an electric rice cooker.

1. Some of the cookies <u>were/was</u> eaten.
2. Some of the food <u>were/was</u> eaten.
3. Everything <u>are/is</u> wet from the rain.
4. The cost of textbooks <u>is/are</u> sky-high.
5. Buying clothes for four growing children <u>cost/costs</u> a lot of money.
6. There <u>weren't/wasn't</u> many people at the meeting.
7. There <u>weren't/wasn't</u> much water in the pool.
8. Four years <u>are/is</u> the average amount of time that it <u>take/takes</u> to earn a college degree.
9. Your information <u>are/is</u> incorrect.
10. The main idea of Professor Smith's last three articles, which <u>have/has</u> been published in many financial magazines, <u>are/is</u> that the government should lower taxes.
11. Each of the students <u>receive/receives</u> a special prize on the last day of school.
12. Neither of my children <u>are/is</u> interested in sports.
13. Either chemistry or physics <u>satisfy/satisfies</u> the physical science requirement.
14. Either the grass or the pine trees <u>are/is</u> making me sneeze.
15. Either the pine trees or the grass <u>are/is</u> making me sneeze.

14   Nouns: Count and Noncount

 Computer Note

Grammar checkers can sometimes (but not always) tell you when you have incorrectly added an *-s* to a noncount noun. For example, a grammar checker might mark *musics* and *knowledges* as errors but not *advices* or *sceneries*. Also, grammar checkers cannot know if you are using a noun such as *gas* in its count or noncount meaning.

English has proper nouns and common nouns. A common noun names a person, place, or thing: *queen, lake, building*. A proper noun names a particular person, place, or thing: *Queen Elizabeth, Lake Titicaca, Buckingham Palace*. Proper nouns begin with capital letters; common nouns do not.

Reference: Learn more about proper nouns in *Section 33c.*

In front of common nouns, we often use an article (*a, an,* or *the*), quantity expression (*much, many, a lot of, a few*), or pronoun (*this, these, his, my*). We sometimes, but not always, use *the* in front of proper nouns. (See *Section 15* for information about using articles.)

Common nouns in English are either count or noncount. Many languages have count and noncount nouns, but the words classified as count or noncount may be different. For example, the word *information* is a count noun in some languages, but in English, it is noncount.

14a Count nouns

Count nouns name people, places, and things that you can count (*one penny, two pennies, three pennies,* and so on). Count nouns can be singular or plural, and you can use an indefinite article (*a* or *an*) with singular count nouns.

SINGULAR	PLURAL
a penny, **the** penny	(**some**) pennies, **the** pennies

! Special Tip

Never leave a singular count noun standing alone. You *must* use an article (*a, an,* or *the*), the word *one*, or a pronoun (*his, her, my, this, that, each, every,* and so on) in front of every singular count noun.

▶ When you are ^*a* guest in someone's home, take ^*a* small gift to show your appreciation.

▶ ^*An* Appropriate gift for ^*your* host is ^*a* small bouquet of flowers or ^*a* box of candy.

▶ You should also send ^*a* handwritten thank-you note ^*a* day or two after your visit.

14b Noncount nouns

Noncount nouns name things that you cannot count. For example, you cannot count *sunshine, oxygen,* or *cotton*. Noncount nouns are never plural, and you cannot use *a* or *an* with them.

SINGULAR	PLURAL
(**some**) cotton, **the** cotton	—

The following chart shows some groups of noncount nouns. There are many others not listed here. A good ESL dictionary such as the *Longman Advanced American Dictionary* will tell you whether a noun is count or noncount.

Abstractions (*things that we cannot touch, that exist only in our minds*)	advice, beauty, confidence, courage, education, energy, entertainment, fun, happiness, health, help, honesty, hospitality, hunger, importance, information, justice, kindness, knowledge, laughter, liberty, love, luck, music, nature, peace, pollution, poverty, progress, recreation, strength, time, trouble, truth, violence, wealth, wisdom, work, youth
Liquids	water, coffee, tea, milk, juice, oil, gasoline, ink
Foods	bread, butter, cabbage, candy, cheese, chicken, chocolate, fish, fruit, ice cream, lettuce, meat, mayonnaise, spinach
Materials	chalk, wood, lumber, iron, gold, silver, glass, paper, silk, cotton, wool, coal, soap
Gases	air, oxygen, smoke, smog, steam
Weather and other natural forces	rain, snow, fog, ice, lightening, thunder, sunshine, fire, electricity, magnetism
Particles	dust, dirt, sand, salt, pepper, sugar, rice, flour, wheat, corn, grass, hair
Sports and other activities (*including all gerunds*)	baseball, soccer, tennis, motocross, chess, swimming, fishing, skydiving, shopping, traveling, working, studying, thinking
Fields of study	architecture, economics, engineering, mathematics, physics, psychology, science
Whole groups (*made up of similar items*)	clothing, furniture, equipment, machinery, makeup, jewelry, money, food, change, scenery, traffic, luggage, baggage, garbage, trash, literature, poetry, junk, mail, postage, homework, news, research, television

14c Count or noncount nouns

Many nouns have both count and noncount meanings.

▶ My car is out of **gas**. (*noncount*)

▶ Oxygen, hydrogen, and nitrogen are **gases**. (*count*)

▶ Her **hair** was black last week. This week it is blond. (*noncount*)
▶ There's a **hair** in my soup. (*count*)

▶ My family eats a lot of **fish**. (*noncount*)
▶ He caught a **fish** this morning. (*count*)

▶ Do you have **time** to help me? (*noncount*)
▶ She read the instructions several **times**. (*count*)

PRACTICE—Sections 14a–c

Which underlined part of these sentences is correct? Cross out the incorrect part. Sometimes both parts are correct.

EXAMPLE
We had ~~enjoyable evening~~/an enjoyable evening yesterday.

1. First, we ate a delicious Chinese food/some delicious Chinese food.
2. We went to restaurant/to a restaurant in our neighborhood.
3. We ordered steamed rice/some steamed rice, vegetables/a vegetables, a fish/fish, and a green tea/some green tea.
4. It was healthy meal/a healthy meal.
5. For dessert, we had some ice cream/an ice cream.
6. After dinner, we went home and watched popular new TV show/a popular new TV show.
7. We don't often watch a television/television, but friends had recommended this show.
8. My daughter and I had an argument/some argument last night.
9. She had asked me to help her with a difficult math homework/some difficult math homework.
10. The homework was a take-home test/take-home test, which she was supposed to complete without a help/help.
11. I sternly lectured her about the importance of an honesty/honesty and an independence/independence.

14d Expressing quantity

With noncount nouns

Use a counting expression.

To express quantity ("how much?") with noncount nouns, you can sometimes add a counting expression such as *a cup of* or *a piece of*.

cups of	a piece of	pieces of
▶ two ~~coffees~~	▶ ~~informations~~	▶ several ~~advices~~

This chart shows some common counting expressions used with noncount nouns.

a bottle of	milk, soda, water
a bowl of	cereal, soup
a can of	soda, soup
a carton of	milk, orange juice
a cup of	coffee, tea, flour, sugar
an ear of	corn
a gallon of	gas
a glass of	juice, milk, water
a head of	lettuce, cabbage
a jar of	jam, jelly, mayonnaise, mustard, peanut butter
a loaf of	bread
a piece of	advice, cake, candy, chicken, clothing, furniture, information, jewelry, junk, mail, money, luggage, lumber, meat, paper, pie, wood
a pound of	butter, bacon, hamburger, meat
a quart of	milk, ice cream, oil
a scoop of	ice cream
a serving of	applesauce, mashed potatoes, pasta, spinach
a sheet of	paper
a slice of	bread, bacon, cheese, ham, salami, tomato
a stick of	butter (ALSO a pat of butter)

Add or use another noun.

With other noncount nouns, you have to add another noun.

       assignments   *stamps*
▶ two homeworks   ▶ three postages

Sometimes you can substitute a different word.

                songs
▶ The radio station played great ~~musics~~ all night.
              views
▶ There are many beautiful ~~sceneries~~ from the top of the hill.
          skills
▶ A teacher has many special ~~knowledges~~.
              kind deeds
▶ My uncle was known for doing many ~~kindnesses~~ for the people in our village.

With count nouns and noncount nouns

The following chart shows the quantity expressions that you can use with count and noncount nouns in positive sentences, negative sentences, and questions.

QUANTITY EXPRESSIONS	COUNT NOUNS	NONCOUNT NOUNS
POSITIVE AND NEGATIVE SENTENCES AND QUESTIONS		
a, an	He bought **a** book and **an** apple.	Ø
	Did he buy **a** book?	Ø
	He didn't buy **a** book.	Ø
one	He bought **one** book.	Ø
each	He bought **each** book.	Ø
every	He bought **every** book.	Ø
two, three, etc.	He bought **two** books.	Ø
a couple of	He bought **a couple of** books.	Ø
both	He bought **both** books.	Ø
several	He bought **several** books.	Ø
a few	He bought **a few** books.	Ø
a number of	He bought **a number of** books.	Ø
a great deal of	Ø	He has **a great deal of** money.
	Ø	Does he have **a great deal of** money?
	Ø	He doesn't have **a great deal of** money.
most	**Most** students take math.	**Most** rice is white.
all	**All** students take English.	**All** ice is cold.
a lot of, lots of	He bought **a lot of/lots of** books.	He has **a lot of/lots of** money.
plenty of	He bought **plenty of** books.	He has **plenty of** money.
enough	He bought **enough** books.	He has **enough** money.
POSITIVE SENTENCES		
some	He bought **some** books.	He has **some** money.
few	He has **few** friends. *(He has almost no friends.)*	Ø
a few	He has **a few** friends. *(He has some friends.)*	Ø
little	Ø	He has **little** money. *(He has almost no money; he is very poor.)*
a little	Ø	He has **a little** money. *(He has some money—not a lot, but enough.)*

QUANTITY EXPRESSIONS	COUNT NOUNS	NONCOUNT NOUNS
NEGATIVE SENTENCES AND QUESTIONS		
many	He didn't buy **many** books. Did he buy **many** books?	∅ ∅
much	∅ ∅	He doesn't have **much** money. Does he have **much** money?
any	He didn't buy **any** books. Did he buy **any** books?	He doesn't have **any** money. Does he have **any** money?

! *Special Tips*

Should you write *most students* or *most of the students*? It depends on whether the word *students* refers to a group of real students or students in general.

A concrete noun refers to a real, concrete person, place, or thing. A generic noun is a symbol, representing all of its group. Learn more about concrete and generic nouns in *Section 15*.

Concrete ▶ **The Americans** who live across the street from us are friendly.

Generic ▶ **Americans** are friendly.

1. Use *of the* after words like *most, all, some, a few, a little, much,* and *many* when a concrete noun follows them.

   ▶ *Most of the* **people** in the room were new students.
   The phrase *in the room* makes the noun *people* real and concrete.

   ▶ *Most of the* **homework** that our teacher assigns is boring.
   The clause *that our teacher assigns* makes the noun *homework* real and concrete.

2. Don't use *of the* when the noun is generic.

   ▶ *Most* **people** like Chinese food.
   The writer means people in general, not a real, concrete group of people.

   ▶ *Most* **homework** is boring.
   Homework in general is boring.

   Note how the writer's choice of words shows the nature of the noun. Compare:

   ▶ *Most* **students** work hard.   ▶ *Most* **of the students** work hard.

   In the sentence on the left, the writer wants to say that students in general work hard. In the sentence on the right, the writer wants to say that a real group of students (perhaps the students in his or her class or school) work hard.

3. Never use *of* without *the* or another modifier in quantity expressions.

        the   *their*
   ▶ Most of students were absent yesterday.   ▶ All of money was stolen.

PRACTICE—Section 14d

Cross out all of the expressions that cannot complete the sentences.

EXAMPLE

Last year _____ (*several, a few, a̶, some, a number of, a̶ g̶r̶e̶a̶t̶ d̶e̶a̶l̶ o̶f̶*) friends and I spent a week camping in the mountains.

1. We didn't take _____ (*any, much, many, a great deal of, a lot of*) food except _____ (*a, some, a few, a little, a lot of*) dried apples.

2. Also, we brought _____ (*a few, little, one or two, a couple of, some*) equipment with us because we wanted to test our survival skills.

3. _____ (*Each, Every, All, Most, Several*) person carried only a small backpack with personal items.

4. On the first day, we spent _____ (*much, many, several, a couple of, two, a number of, a great deal of*) hours building a shelter.

5. We also collected _____ (*much, some, several, a lot of*) wood to build a fire.

15 Articles

Articles give information about a noun. They tell the reader whether a noun is generic, indefinite, or definite.

Definite and indefinite articles

There are two kinds of articles: definite and indefinite. The definite article is *the*. The indefinite articles are *a* and *an*. We use *a* with words and abbreviations that begin with a consonant sound: *a book, a hole, a university, a VCR*. We use *an* with words and abbreviations that begin with a vowel sound: *an egg, an octopus, an honest person, an MBA degree*. Sometimes we use no article at all.

Generic and concrete nouns

To decide which article to use or whether to use an article at all, you must first know whether a noun is generic or concrete.

In the following sentence, the word *coffee* is a generic noun. It is a symbol for coffee in general. It does not refer to real coffee that you can smell and taste.

As a generic noncount noun, the word *coffee* requires Ø article (*Section 15a*).

▶ Do you like **coffee**?

In the next two sentences, the word *coffee* is concrete. It refers to real coffee that you can smell and taste.

▶ You look tired. Would you like *some* **coffee**.

▶ *The* **coffee** is very strong. (*The coffee that I am drinking right now is strong.*)

The coffee in the first sentence is real coffee, but not any particular real coffee. As a concrete but indefinite noncount noun, the word *coffee* requires *some* (*Section 15b*). The coffee in the second sentence is a particular coffee, so the word *coffee* is definite and requires the definite article *the* (*Section 15c*).

15a Articles for generic nouns: *a, an,* or no article (Ø)

A generic noun is a symbol. It represents a whole group of people, places, or things and means *any* and *all* members of the group. The sentences in the following chart mean "*Any* dog is a loyal companion," "*All* dogs are loyal companions," and "*All* milk is good for you."

Use *a, an* or no article (Ø) with generic nouns.

	Singular	Plural
Count nouns	**A dog** is a loyal companion.	Ø **Dogs** are loyal companions.
Noncount nouns	Ø **Milk** is good for you.	

We use generic nouns to make generalizations.

▶ **Americans** are generally friendly.
▶ **A student** who sits in the front learns better than **a student** who sits in the back.
▶ **Students** who sit in the front learn better than **students** who sit in the back.

EXCEPTION: Occasionally, *the* is used with generic singular count nouns, especially with animal species and inventions.

▶ **The giant panda** is an endangered species.
▶ Do you know who invented **the microwave oven**?

PRACTICE—Section 15a

Write *G* (generic) in the blank spaces in front of generic nouns. Write *NG* (not generic) in front of concrete nouns.

EXAMPLE

The contestants on __NG__ the television show *Survivor* soon got tired of eating __G__ rice every day.

1. They started dreaming about _____ chocolate and _____ pizza.

2. One day, the television show's helicopter brought them _____ chocolate and _____ a slice of pizza.

3. The people had _____ contest to see who could win _____ chocolate and _____ pizza.

4. They had _____ contests on _____ show every few days.

15b Articles for indefinite nouns: *a, an,* or *some*

Use *a, an,* or *some* with indefinite nouns. An indefinite noun names real (not symbolic) people, places, and things, but it does not point out a particular person, place, or thing.

	Singular	Plural
Count nouns	▶ We want to get *a* **dog**.	▶ We saw *some* **puppies** for sale.
Noncount nouns	▶ Would you like *some* **coffee**.	—

Nouns are indefinite in the following cases.

1. When you don't have a specific person, place, or thing in mind

▶ Let's call *a* **friend**, make *some* **sandwiches**, buy *some* **fruit** and *some* **cold drinks**, and have *a* **picnic**.

2. When the person, place, or thing is unknown to the reader, perhaps because the noun appears for the first time

▶ My wife and I bought *a* **new house** last year.

▶ It has *a* **small yard**, so we planted *some* **grass** and *some* **flowers**.

You can also use *a* or *an* in the following cases.

3. When you mean "one"

4. When you want to identify or define a person, place, or thing (in singular only)

▶ I came here *a* **year** ago.

▶ He's *an* **American**. (BUT They're Americans.)

▶ She's *a* **doctor**. (BUT They're doctors.)

▶ Houston is *a* **city** in Texas. (BUT Houston and San Antonio are cities in Texas.)

▶ What's this? It's *a* **coffee grinder**. (BUT They're coffee grinders.)

 Special Tip

You can often omit *some* or substitute other quantity expressions.

▶ It has a small yard, so we planted Ø grass and Ø flowers.

▶ Let's call a friend, make *a few* sandwiches, buy *a little* fruit and *a couple of* cold drinks, and have a picnic.

15c Articles for definite nouns: *the*

Use *the* with nouns that name a specific person, place, or thing.

The with specific nouns

	Singular	Plural
Count nouns	▶ Let's ask *the* teacher.	▶ *The* sandwiches from Sam's Delicatessen are cheap and delicious.
Noncount nouns	▶ *The* milk that I just bought is sour.	—

Specific nouns are known to the reader. They can be known to the reader for any of the following reasons.

1. The noun names a unique person, place, or thing. (*Unique = There is only one.*)

- ▶ The crowd waited for hours to see *the* president.
- ▶ You can't see many stars in *the* sky.
- ▶ *The* moon is full tonight.

2. The noun is a superlative.

- ▶ John is *the* smartest student in our class.
- ▶ Venus is *the* brightest star in the sky.
- ▶ I had *the* worst cold in my life last winter.

3. You mention a noun for the second time.

- ▶ We bought *a house*. *The* house has a small yard.
- ▶ *The* yard has a lot of grass and a few trees.
- ▶ We planted *some flowers*, but *the* flowers haven't bloomed yet.

4. The reader knows the person, place, or thing because the writer and reader share common experiences or a common environment.

- ▶ *The* teacher chose my essay to read out loud.
- ▶ *The* class seemed to like it.
- ▶ John went to *the* library to study.

  The writer and reader are in the same school. They both know which teacher, which class, and which library are meant.

5. Sometimes (but not always) other words in the sentence identify the noun for the reader.

> ▶ *The* **red car** is mine.
>
> The adjective *red* tells us which car.

> ▶ *The* **sandwiches from Sam's Delicatessen** are cheap and delicious.
>
> From *Sam's Delicatessen* tells us which sandwiches.

> ▶ *The* **milk that I just bought** is sour.
>
> *That I just bought* tells us which milk.

An adjective, a phrase, or a clause does not always identify a noun, however. Sometimes it simply describes the noun but doesn't identify it for the reader.

> ▶ I want to buy **a red car.**
>
> *Red* tells only what color car I want to buy. It doesn't identify a specific car.

> ▶ Last night I dreamed about **a girl with green eyes.**
>
> *With green eyes* only describes. It doesn't identify a specific girl.

> ▶ John likes **steaks that are thick and juicy.**
>
> *That are thick and juicy* only tells what kind of steaks John likes. It doesn't identify a specific steak.

Special uses of *the*

Use *the* before the following kinds of common nouns.

1. Time periods

> ▶ in *the* **morning,** in *the* **afternoon,** in *the* **evening**
> BUT **at noon, at night, at midnight**

> ▶ *the* **past,** *the* **present,** *the* **future**

> ▶ *the* **beginning,** *the* **middle,** *the* **end**

> ▶ *the* **spring,** *the* **summer,** *the* **fall,** *the* **autumn,** *the* **winter**

> ▶ *the* **twentieth century,** *the* **second millennium**

2. Parts of the body in a prepositional phrase

> ▶ He cut himself on **the** leg. (ALSO on **his** leg)
> BUT He injured **his** leg. He broke **his** leg.
>
> These are not prepositional phrases.

3. Certain nouns that name different social and economic classes and some other special groups

the **middle class**
the **clergy**
the **public**

the **government**
the **media**
the **press**

4. Nouns made from adjectives that mean "a group of people who are ..." (rich, young, unemployed, etc.)

the **rich**
the **poor**
the **young**

the **unemployed**
the **disabled**
the **homeless**

PRACTICE—Section 15c

Cross out the incorrect article in each pair.

EXAMPLE

We watched ~~the~~/a TV show last night called *Survivor*.

1. It was similar to the/a European show that was popular in the/Ø nineties.
2. The/A European show was also about people living together on the/an island.
3. The/A main idea of both programs was to see who could survive the/a longest time in the/a hostile place.
4. Every few days, the/some contestants voted to send one person off the/an island.
5. The/A last remaining person would win the/a million dollars.
6. The/A biggest challenge was not to survive nature but to make friends with the other contestants so that they would not vote against you.
7. One man caught the/Ø fish almost every day, so he had lots of friends.
8. In fact, he was the/a winner of the/a million dollars.

The with certain proper nouns

Most proper nouns do not have articles. We say *Prince Charles, Friday, January, Mexico, Asia, Main Street,* and so on. The following kinds of proper nouns use *the*. For a more complete list, see *Section 51*.

1. All proper nouns that contain an *of*-phrase

▶ *the* **United States of America**

▶ *the* **University of Texas**

2. Certain geographic names

• Geographic names that contain the word *kingdom, republic,* or *union*

▶ *the* **United Kingdom**

▶ *the* **Dominican Republic**

• Plural geographic names (except waterfalls)

▶ *the* **United Arab Emirates**

▶ *the* **Philippines**
BUT **Niagara Falls**

• Bodies of water (except lakes and bays)

▶ *the* **Pacific (Ocean)**

▶ *the* **Amazon (River)**
BUT **Lake Victoria**

- • Regions
  - ▸ *the* **Middle East**
  - ▸ *the* **South**
- • Points on the globe
  - ▸ *the* **North Pole**
  - ▸ *the* **Equator**
- • Deserts and forests
  - ▸ *the* **Sahara (Desert)**
  - ▸ *the* **Black Forest**

3. Buildings, bridges, named roads, tunnels, towers, monuments (but not dams)
   - ▸ *the* **Empire State Building**
   - ▸ *the* **Chunnel**

4. Hotels, theaters, movie theaters, libraries, and museums
   - ▸ *the* **Hilton (Hotel)**
   - ▸ *the* **Louvre**

5. Historical periods and events
   - ▸ *the* **Tang Dynasty**
   - ▸ *the* **Russian Revolution**

6. Names of organizations, departments of government, and political parties
   - ▸ *the* **United Nations**
   - ▸ *the* **Red Cross**

7. Names of historical documents
   - ▸ *the* **Constitution**
   - ▸ *the* **Magna Carta**

8. Names of newspapers (Capitalize *the* if the newspaper uses it as part of its name.)
   - ▸ *The New York Times*
   - ▸ *the San Francisco Chronicle*

9. Plural family names (used to refer to all members of a family)
   - ▸ *the* **Smiths**
   - ▸ *the* **Bushes**

10. Adjectives naming nationalities that mean "the people from this country"
    - ▸ *the* **British**
    - ▸ *the* **Swiss**

11. Titles that refer to a unique person
    - ▸ *the* **Pope**
    - ▸ *the* **Dalai Lama**

12. Electronic sources
    - ▸ *the* **Internet**
    - ▸ *the* **World Wide Web**

13. Ships and trains
    - ▸ *the Titanic*
    - ▸ *the* **Shanghai Express**

Reference: Learn about capitalizing proper nouns in *Section 33.*

15d Idiomatic uses of articles

With *the*

Use *the* in these phrases even though the noun is not specific.

▶ go to *the* bank, *the* post office, *the* store, *the* bathroom
▶ go to *the* theater, *the* movies
▶ go to *the* doctor, *the* dentist, *the* hospital (BRITISH ENGLISH: go to hospital)
▶ be in *the* hospital (BRITISH ENGLISH: be in hospital)
▶ call *the* police, *the* fire department, *the* highway patrol
▶ live in *the* city, *the* country, *the* suburbs
▶ listen to *the* radio BUT listen to music
▶ turn off *the* television (= television set) BUT watch television (= the medium)
▶ play *the* piano, *the* violin, *the* guitar
▶ on *the* ground, in *the* sky BUT in space

Without *the*

Don't use an article in these expressions.

▶ on campus, off campus
▶ on foot
▶ by bus, by train, by car, by taxi, by plane, by subway
▶ go home, get home, arrive home, stay (at) home
▶ go to work, be at work, start work, finish work
▶ go to school, be in school, be at school
▶ go to college, be in college, be at college BUT go to *the* university
  (BRITISH ENGLISH: go to university, be at university)
▶ go to church, be at church
▶ go to class, be in class
▶ go to prison/jail, be in prison/jail
▶ go to bed, be in bed, stay in bed

Without *a/an*

Don't use *a* or *an* with the names of meals unless there is an adjective before the name of the meal.

▶ eat breakfast BUT eat *a* big breakfast
▶ after dinner BUT after *a* delicious dinner
▶ have lunch BUT have *a* quick lunch

15e Choosing the right article

Although this chart does not cover every situation, it may help you choose the right article most of the time. First, ask this question: Is the noun a proper noun (capitalized) or a common noun? Then follow the arrows.

PROPER *Is it listed in Section 51?*			COMMON	
Not listed	*No article*	I live in Ø New York City.	*Is it used as a generic (symbolic) noun?*	
Listed	*Use the.*	I live in **the** city of New York.		

GENERIC			NOT GENERIC	
	Singular	**Plural**		
Count noun	**A** dog is a loyal companion.	Ø Dogs are loyal companions.	*Does the noun name something known or unknown to the reader?*	
Noncount noun	Ø Milk is good for you.	—		

UNKNOWN			KNOWN	
	Singular	**Plural**	**Singular**	**Plural**
Count noun	We want to get **a** dog.	We saw **some** puppies for sale.	Let's ask **the** teacher.	**The** eggs were delicious.
Noncount noun	Would you like **some** coffee?	—	**The** milk I bought is sour.	—

PRACTICE—Section 15

Complete the paragraphs with appropriate articles. Sometimes no article (Ø) is necessary.

A.   _Ø_ Astronauts who make _____ long trips into _____ outer space can learn
1.   2.
from _____ contestants on _____ TV show *Survivor*. They can learn how to get
3.   4.

along with each other for _____ long periods of _____ time in _____ dangerous
                              5.   6.   7.
environments. _____ Trip to _____ Mars will last approximately three years: nine
                    8.   9.
months each way and approximately _____ year and _____ half on _____ surface
                                         10.   11.   12.
of _____ Mars. Spending _____ nine months in _____ small, enclosed spaceship
     13.   14.   15.
with _____ strangers will be difficult.
      16.

B.   _____ Spaceship that travels to _____ Mars will probably be larger than _____
       1.   2.   3.
car but smaller than _____ airplane. Mark Shepanek, who is _____ psychologist for
                      4.   5.
_____ National Aeronautics and Space Administration, said, "Imagine taking _____
 6.   7.
car trip with your family. Imagine that _____ trip lasts for months. Now imagine
                                          8.
that you can't open _____ windows. Imagine that you can't get out of _____ car.
                     9.   10.
Imagine that _____ bathroom and _____ meals are in _____ car with you. Do you
              11.   12.   13.
think you might have _____ problem getting along with each other?"
                      14.

16   Pronouns

A pronoun replaces a noun. (*He* asked *her* to dance.) Some pronouns can also
be adjectives when they modify a noun (*my book, that* problem). Learn more
about pronouns in *Section 1b.*

16a Subject, object, and possessive forms

Personal pronouns, interrogative pronouns, and relative pronouns change their
form to show their function in a sentence.

Subject forms
Subject forms are for subjects and subject complements.

▶ **She** had a car accident. (*subject*)
▶ **Who** called the police? (*subject*)
▶ It was **he.** (*subject complement*)

Object forms
Object forms are for objects.

▶ **Whom** did you see at the party? (*direct object*)
▶ The teacher wrote **me** a long note about my essay. (*indirect object*)
▶ A tall person sat in front of **me.** (*object of preposition*)

Possessive forms

Possessive forms show ownership.

▶ **Whose** backpack is this?

▶ This is **my** backpack. It's **mine**.

▶ We felt sorry for the student **whose** backpack was missing.

	SUBJECT FORM	OBJECT FORM	POSSESSIVE FORMS	
			Adjectives	Pronouns
Personal pronouns	I	me	my	mine
	you	you	your	yours
	he	him	his	his
	she	her	her	hers
	it	it	its	its
	we	us	our	ours
	they	them	their	theirs
Relative pronouns and interrogative pronouns	who which that	whom which that	whose + *noun*	

! *Special Tip*

Be consistent in your use of noun/pronoun combinations. Don't change from *you* to *he* or from *he* to *they* without a reason. Also, don't mix singular and plural nouns unnecessarily. In the following paragraph, the writer begins with a plural noun, *athletes*, so he should continue using plural nouns and pronouns.

```
                                                            they
Olympic athletes must be strong both physically and mentally. First of
     they
all, if y̶o̶u̶ hope to compete in an Olympic sport, y̶o̶u̶ must train hard.
  Athletes
A̶n̶ ̶a̶t̶h̶l̶e̶t̶e̶ in some sports trains several hours a day, five or six days a
                                                            they
week, for ten or more years. In addition to being in top shape, y̶o̶u̶ must
be mentally tough. This means that athletes are totally dedicated to their
sports, often giving up normal school, family, and social life.
```

16b Special situations

Be careful to use correct pronoun forms in the following special situations.

After *than* and *as*

To decide which pronoun to use after *than* or *as* in comparisons, finish the comparison in your mind.

▶ My brother is taller **than *I*** (am).

▶ I study as hard **as *he*** (studies), but my grades aren't as good **as *his*** (grades are).

NOTE: People say *He is taller than me* in informal conversation. However, *I* is correct and should be used in written English.

Who or whom?

To choose between *who* and *whom* in a question, decide whether the question word is a subject or an object.

Direct questions   ▶ **Who** won the contest? (Who *is the subject of* won.)

             ▶ **Whom** did they give the prize to? (Whom *is the object of* to.)

Indirect questions   ▶ I don't know **who** is going to win. (Who *is the subject of* going to win.)

             ▶ Let's decide **whom** to vote for. (Whom *is the object of* for.)

To choose between *who* and *whom* in an adjective clause, decide whether the relative pronoun is a subject or an object in its own clause.

     ┌─── adjective clause ───┐

▶ The man ***who* wrote that book** lives in London. (Who *is the subject of* wrote.)

     ┌─── adjective clause ───┐

▶ The man ***whom* she married** is a musician. (Whom *is the object of* married.)

NOTE: People say *who* instead of *whom* in informal conversation. It is acceptable in spoken English, but *whom* is preferred in written English.

❗ *Special Tips*

To test for *who* or *whom*, rewrite the question or the adjective clause as a sentence, replacing *who* or *whom* with the form of *he, she,* or *they* that sounds correct.

   (*Who?/Whom?*) ordered a pizza with mushrooms?

   He ordered a pizza with mushrooms.

▶ **Who** ordered a pizza with mushrooms?

   Where's the office of the adviser (*who?/whom?*) we have an appointment with?

   We have an appointment with **him.**

▶ Where's the office of the adviser **whom** we have an appointment with?

Don't let expressions such as *I think* and *he says* confuse you when they come between the subject *who* and its verb.

▶ Betty is the student **who** I think **wrote the best paper.** (Who *is the subject of* wrote, *not the object of* think.)

Reference: See *Section 23* for more information about *who* and *whom*.

PRACTICE—Sections 16a–b

A. Complete the sentences with appropriate pronouns.

1. When our parents celebrated their fiftieth wedding anniversary, my sisters and I wanted to give _____ a party.

2. All of _____ wanted to have the party at _____ own houses.

3. My sister Graciela has the biggest house, so we agreed to let _____ have the party at _____ house.

B. Cross out the incorrect pronoun.

1. Graciela is older than I/me.
2. I have a smaller house than she/her.
3. My sister Alicia and I/me wrote the invitations together.
4. We asked our parents who/whom they wanted to invite.
5. Many of the guests who/whom came to the party had attended their wedding fifty years ago.
6. At the party, my parents sat between my sisters and I/me.

16c *Myself, ourselves*

The following pronouns are called reflexive pronouns.

SINGULAR	PLURAL
myself	ourselves
yourself	yourselves
himself herself itself	themselves

Use reflexive pronouns in the following situations.

1. When the subject and an object are the same

   ▶ **The boy** hurt *himself* while skateboarding.
   ▶ Please make *yourselves* at home. (*The subject is* you *plural.*)
   ▶ Please help *yourself*. (*The subject is* you *singular. The meaning is "Don't wait for someone to serve you."*)
   ▶ **We** enjoyed *ourselves* at the game.
   ▶ **She** bought a house for *herself* and her three children.
   ▶ **I** often sing to *myself* when no one can hear me.

2. To emphasize a noun or pronoun

▶ The fire burned the roof, but **the house *itself*** was saved.

▶ **They *themselves*** were responsible for the fire.

3. With the preposition *by* to mean "alone"

▶ John lives **by *himself*.**

▶ It's not wise to walk in this area **by *yourself*** at night.

4. With or without the preposition *by* to mean "without any help"

▶ My two-year-old always says, "I want to do it **(by) *myself*!**"

▶ They changed the flat tire **(by) *themselves*.**

5. With the verb *be* to mean "act naturally, act as you normally do"

▶ In a job interview, just **be *yourself*.**

▶ He **hasn't been *himself*** since his wife died.

16d *Each other* and *one another*

The pronouns *each other* and *one another* are called reciprocal pronouns. They express two-way relationships. *One another* is more formal than *each other*.

▶ **My sister and I** call ***each other*** every night. (*I call my sister or my sister calls me.*)

▶ **Students** can help ***one another*** in many ways.

PRACTICE—Sections 16c–d

A. Cross out the incorrect pronoun.

    1. At the party, my parents talked to everyone, but they danced only with <u>each other/themselves</u>.

    2. We were happy to see our parents enjoying <u>them/themselves</u>.

    3. In their wedding ceremony, a bride and groom promise to love, honor, and cherish <u>themselves/one another</u> forever.

B. Add an appropriate reflexive pronoun.

    1. Some students like to work in groups, and others prefer to work by _____.

    2. My husband suggested that we paint the house _____ in order to save money.

    3. When my uncle spends too much time alone, he starts talking to _____.

    4. Put the knife down! You'll cut _____!

    5. Antonio taught _____ to play the piano by listening to CDs.

    6. Would you please help me move my piano into the corner? I can't do it _____.

17   Pronoun Agreement

A pronoun agrees in number (singular or plural) with the noun or nouns it replaces, not with the word it modifies. The replaced noun is called an antecedent.

▶ The **boy** left *his* books in the classroom.

▶ The **boys** left *their* books in the classroom.

A pronoun in English also agrees in gender (masculine, feminine, or neuter) with its antecedent, not with the word it modifies.

▶ **Linda** called *her* **son** last night and spoke to *him* for an hour.
  (NOT Linda called *his* son last night . . .)

Take special care to make pronouns agree with their antecedents in the following situations.

17a   Pronoun agreement with indefinite pronouns: *someone, everybody*

Singular

The following indefinite pronouns are always singular, so any other pronoun that refers to them must also be singular.

anyone	anybody	each
everyone	everybody	either
someone	somebody	neither
no one		
one		

▶ **Neither** of the brothers has *his* own bedroom.

▶ **Each** of the students has *his* or *her* own desk.

In very formal English, *one* is used to mean people in general. Nowadays, *you* is more common.

▶ **One** should be careful when buying a used car. (*very formal*)

▶ **You** should be careful when buying a used car. (*more common*)

Singular or plural

All, none, most, and *some* can be singular or plural depending on the noun after the word *of.*

▶ **Some** of the soda lost *its* fizz.

▶ **Some** of the trees lost *their* leaves.

Reference: Learn about subject-verb agreement with indefinite pronouns in *Section 13a.*

17b Pronoun agreement with generic nouns: *a student, an employee*

A generic noun represents an entire group, so it seems plural in meaning. However, a singular generic noun requires singular pronouns.

▶ **A student** should buy *his* or *her* books before the first day of class.

▶ **A teacher** has several responsibilities. First, *he* or *she* should know *his* or *her* subject well.

Reference: Learn more about generic nouns in *Section 15.*

! Special Tip

Most writers feel that using *he or she, him or her,* and *his or her* is not good style. There are two ways to avoid this problem.

1. Make the sentence plural.

    Students   *their*
▶ A ~~student~~ should buy ~~his or her~~ books before the first day of class.

2. Revise the sentence to eliminate the pronoun.

▶ A student should buy ~~his or her~~ books before the first day of class.

                              a
▶ Each of the students has ~~his or her own~~ desk. OR Each student has a desk. OR Every student has a desk.

Reference: See *Section 10c* on avoiding sexist language for more examples.

17c Pronoun agreement with collective nouns: *team, class*

In American English, a collective noun such as *band, committee, family, team, class, couple, crowd,* and *audience* is singular when the group acts as a unit and plural when the members of the group act individually. In British English, collective nouns are plural.

▶ The **band** played *its* biggest hit at the end of the concert. (*acting as a unit*)

▶ The **band** packed up *their* instruments and left. (*acting individually*)

Reference: Learn more about collective nouns in *Section 13d.*

17d Pronoun agreement with *either* . . . *or* and *neither* . . . *nor*

Singular subjects joined by *either . . . or* and *neither . . . nor* take singular pronouns, and plural subjects take plural pronouns.

▶ **Either** John **or** John's friend forgot *his* keys when he left the party.

▶ **Neither** the teachers **nor** the students remembered what *they* were supposed to do during an earthquake drill.

When one subject is singular and the other is plural, pronouns agree with the nearer subject. However, the resulting sentences can be awkward.

▶ **Either** John **or** his parents forgot *their* jacket.

▶ **Either** John's parents **or** John forgot *his* jacket.

Try to rewrite the sentences to avoid using a pronoun.

▶ **Either** John **or** his parents forgot *a* jacket.

Reference: Learn about subject-verb agreement with *either . . . or* and *neither . . . nor* in *Section 13d.*

PRACTICE—Section 17

A. Cross out the incorrect pronoun in each pair.

    1. The team won its/their final game of the season.
    2. The team ripped up its/their uniforms at the end of the game.
    3. The staff must have its/their timesheets signed by its/their supervisors.
    4. The staff turned its/their lunchroom into a daycare center for children.
    5. The audience jumped out of its/their seats and applauded loudly.

B. Revise the following paragraph to correct errors in pronoun agreement. One sentence is correct.

                    its

    Our class had ~~their~~ end-of-semester party last Friday afternoon. Everyone came, and some students brought his children to join in the fun. Maria brought his son, and Omar brought her two daughters. At the beginning of the party, a few students provided entertainment. One student played the guitar and sang a song in English. Mr. Wolfe and his class performed a skit that it had written themselves. Everyone was a little embarrassed because neither Mr. Wolfe nor the students remembered his lines, but the audience applauded anyway.

18 Pronouns: Unclear Reference

A sentence is confusing when there is no word that a pronoun refers to or when a pronoun refers to more than one word.

Unclear	Revised
▶ Charlie was upset when **they** failed him on his driving test. (*Who failed Charlie?*)	▶ Charlie was upset when **the examiner** failed him on his driving test.
▶ Charlie complained that **it** wasn't fair. (*What wasn't fair?*)	▶ Charlie complained that **the test** wasn't fair.
▶ Charlie's father said that **this** often happened on the first attempt. (*What does the pronoun* this *refer to? Unfair driving tests or failing them?*)	▶ Charlie's father said that **young people often failed the driving test** on their first attempt.
▶ Charlie's father told him that **he** was a good driver. (*Who was a good driver? Charlie or his father?*)	▶ Charlie's father told him, "**You're** a good driver."

Make sure that every pronoun has a specific antecedent.

- Don't use *it* or *they* to refer to unnamed things or persons.
- Make sure that *he* or *she* refers to only one person.
- Don't use *this* or *that* to refer to an entire idea or action. Revise the preceding sentence to give *this* and *that* a specific antecedent (a specific person, place, or thing), or replace *this* and *that* with specific words.

PRACTICE—Section 18

A. Edit the following sentences to correct errors in pronoun reference. There may be more than one possible way to make the corrections.

EXAMPLE

the window
When the ladder fell against the window, ~~it~~ broke.

1. Everyone in the class failed the test. When they realized this, they complained.
2. My father told my brother that he was a lucky man to have found such a wonderful wife.

B. Revise the following paragraph to correct errors in pronoun reference. One sentence has no errors, and one sentence has three.

The president
Recently, the government decided to raise taxes. ~~They~~ said that a tax increase was necessary. Most citizens didn't believe this. It said in the newspaper that most people's taxes would rise twenty percent. My uncle told my father that it was his fault because he had voted for the wrong political party in the last election.

19 Adjectives and Adverbs: Position

19a Position of adjectives

Adjective + noun

Adjectives usually come before nouns, not after them.

▶ a **big** house NOT a house big

Exceptions

Cardinal numbers used as adjectives follow nouns. (Cardinal numbers are numbers such as *one, two, three* that identify or name rather than count.)

▶ page **two**, chapter **five**, section **three**
BUT the **second** page, the **fifth** chapter, the **third** section
Second, fifth, and *third* are ordinal numbers. As adjectives, they precede nouns.

Adjectives follow measurements of space, age, and time.

▶ The Grand Canyon is **one mile** *deep.*
▶ The snake was at least **ten feet** *long.*
▶ The child is **two years** *old.*
▶ We came here **six months** *ago.*

Adjectives can follow certain indefinite pronouns.

▶ A bride traditionally wears **something** *old*, **something** *new*, **something** *borrowed*, and **something** *blue.*
▶ He said that his date wasn't ***anyone* special**, but we didn't believe him.

Adjectives can also follow linking verbs. The most common linking verbs are *be, become, appear, seem, look, feel, taste,* and *smell.*

▶ He **is** *happy.*   ▶ Candy **tastes** *sweet.*   ▶ The baby **became** *sleepy.*
▶ You **seem** *angry.*   ▶ That **smells** *good.*   ▶ The moon **appears** *full.*
▶ She **looks** *tired.*   ▶ Silk **feels** *smooth.*

19b Position of adverbs

Placing adverbs correctly in a sentence can be troublesome because adverbs can move around in a sentence more than any other kind of word in English. This section gives very general guidelines for adverb placement. There are many possible variations.

Adverb + adjective/adverb

Adverbs that modify adjectives and other adverbs go directly before the words they modify.

adjective
▶ She is **always** late.

adverb
▶ She is **almost** always late.

Adverbs modifying verbs

Adverbs that modify verbs can go in several different places in a sentence.

• At the beginning of their clause (usually followed by a comma)	▶ **Slowly,** we opened the door
• At the end of their clause	▶ We opened the door **slowly**.
	▶ She measures ingredients **carefully** when she cooks.
• Before a verb that is only one word	▶ We *slowly* **opened** the door.
	▶ Flights *often* **arrive** late in bad weather.
• After the first helping verb when the verb has one or more helping verbs	▶ The trees **are** *slowly* **dying**.
	▶ This flight **has** *never* **been late**.
	▶ We **should** *probably* **have left** earlier.

Adverbs used with *be*

Only a few adverbs can appear in a sentence when the main verb is a form of *be*. They are the adverbs of frequency and a few others. Put these adverbs after *am, are, is, was,* and *were*.

ADVERBS OF FREQUENCY		OTHER ADVERBS	EXAMPLES
always	rarely	already	▶ Flights **are** *often* late in bad weather.
usually	hardly ever	ever	
often	seldom	finally	▶ They **were** *already* there when we arrived.
frequently	never	generally	
sometimes	not ever	just	▶ The plane **is** *probably* late.
occasionally		probably	

EXCEPTION: Put *probably* before a negative.

▶ He *probably* **isn't** as sick as he pretends to be.

> ## *!* **Special Tip**
>
> Never put an adverb between a verb and a direct object.
>
> ▶ We opened (slowly) the door.

PRACTICE—Section 19

Edit the sentences for errors in word order. Three sentences are correct.

EXAMPLE

I find (always) my glasses on top of my head.

1. The children are playing outside in the snow.
2. They are building excitedly a snowman.
3. It often is foggy in London.
4. It sometimes rains in the winter months.
5. The boring lecture finally was over.
6. The boring lecture finally ended.

20 Special Situations with Adjectives

20a Agreement of adjectives

Adjectives are always singular. Never add *-s* to an adjective, and never use a plural word as an adjective.

▶ **big** feet   NOT ~~bigs feet~~
▶ **terrible** memories   NOT ~~terribles memories~~

Be especially careful when a compound adjective containing a number comes *before* a noun.

▶ a **five-dollar** bill   NOT ~~a five-dollars bill~~
▶ a **two-year-old** child   NOT ~~a two-years-old child~~
                               BUT The child is **two years old**.
▶ a **ten-kilometer** race   NOT ~~a ten-kilometers race~~
                               BUT The race is **ten kilometers long**.

In *The children are two years old* and *The race is ten kilometers long*, the adjectives come *after* the nouns. Their modifiers (*two years* and *ten kilometers*) can be plural, and they do not have hyphens. (See also *Section 19a*, the second exception.)

20b Order of adjectives

When you write several adjectives in a row, sometimes you must put them in a particular order, and sometimes you can choose your own order depending on the kind of adjective. One kind is called cumulative adjectives, and the other kind is called coordinate adjectives.

CUMULATIVE ADJECTIVES	COORDINATE ADJECTIVES
The **poor little black** dog	The **cold, wet,** and **hungry** dog The **wet, cold,** and **hungry** dog The **hungry, cold,** and **wet** dog

Cumulative adjectives

Cumulative adjectives are not separated by commas, and you must write them in a specific order. For example, you cannot write *the little poor dog*; you must write *the poor little dog*. The following chart lists the order of cumulative adjectives. Notice that some categories, such as "appearance," have subcategories.

OPINION	APPEARANCE	AGE/COLOR	ORIGIN	MATERIAL	NOUN USED AS ADJECTIVE
poor beautiful interesting cheerful expensive	**Size** big little small **Shape/length** long short round square **Condition** rusty broken	**Age** old new young **Color** black white red blue	**Nationality** English Italian Chinese **Religion** Buddhist Christian Jewish Muslim	silk gold metal wood(en)	fashion wedding baseball

▶ My friend is a model for **a well-known Italian fashion** designer.
▶ She wore **a beautiful white silk wedding** dress.
▶ The child drew a **large uneven** circle in the center of the paper.
▶ For his birthday, the boy received a **new wooden baseball** bat and a **soft leather** glove.

Coordinate adjectives

Any adjective that is not cumulative is a coordinate adjective. You do not have to write coordinate adjectives in a specific order, and you can put the word *and* between them (*hungry* and *wet* and *cold*). Separate coordinate adjectives from each other (but not from the following noun) with commas.

▶ The people want a **smart, independent, experienced, honest** leader.

▶ The **hungry, frightened** refugees ran when they saw soldiers.

PRACTICE—Section 20b

Edit the sentences for errors in word order and comma use.

1. She baked a chocolate delicious cake for his birthday.
2. She also gave him several presents very expensive.
3. They were tired of the cold rainy weather.
4. They asked their travel agent to find them a warm sunny vacation spot.
5. The travel agent recommended the Caribbean, which has many sandy white beautiful beaches.

20c Participial adjectives: *boring* or *bored?*

We often use participles as adjectives. There are two kinds of participles. One kind is the *-ing* form of a verb: *crying* baby, *speeding* car, *working* mother. This kind of participle has an active meaning: A baby cries, a car speeds, a mother works. The other kind is the past participle form of a verb: *dried* fruit, *recorded* music, *spoken* English, *hurt* feelings. This kind of participle has a passive meaning: Fruit was dried, music was recorded, English is spoken, feelings were hurt.

With certain pairs of participial adjectives that describe feelings and reactions, it is sometimes difficult to decide which one to use. Was the speaker *boring* or *bored?* Was the audience *interesting* or *interested?*

The *-ing* form describes a person or thing that <u>causes</u> a feeling or reaction.

▶ The movie's special effects were **amazing.**

▶ The teacher was **boring.**

The *-ed* form describes a person who <u>experiences</u> a feeling or reaction.

▶ We were **amazed** by the movie's special effects.

▶ The students were **bored.**

Reference: For a list of participial adjective pairs, turn to *Section 50* at the back of the book.

PRACTICE—Section 20c

Cross out the incorrect participial adjective in each underlined pair.

My old boyfriend Tom and I went out on a date last night. I was very

<u>surprising/surprised</u> when he asked me out. I didn't know he was still

1.

<u>interesting/interested</u> in me. Anyway, we went on a "double date." That means we

2.

went with another couple—his roommate Eric and Eric's date, a freshman named

Shanna. I was looking forward to an <u>exciting/excited</u> evening. However, the

3.

evening turned out to be very <u>disappointing/disappointed</u>. Eric was the most

4.

<u>boring/bored</u> person I have ever met! He talked about himself the whole evening.

5.

Shanna wasn't much fun either. She fell asleep during dinner.

21 Comparisons

We can compare the qualities of two, three, or more people, places, things, and actions. The three degrees of comparison are summarized in the chart.

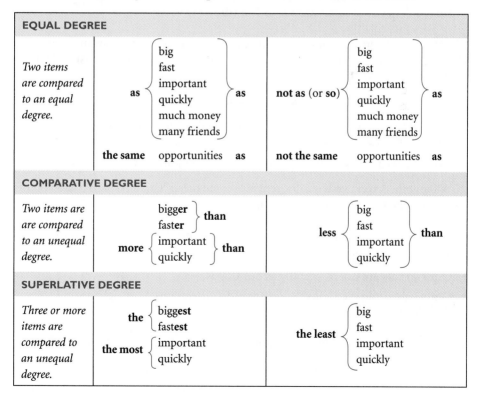

EQUAL DEGREE

Two items are compared to an equal degree.	**as** { big / fast / important / quickly / much money / many friends } **as**	**not as** (or **so**) { big / fast / important / quickly / much money / many friends } **as**
	the same opportunities **as**	**not the same** opportunities **as**

COMPARATIVE DEGREE

Two items are are compared to an unequal degree.	**bigger** } **than** / **faster** } / **more** { **important** } **than** / **quickly** }	**less** { big / fast / important / quickly } **than**

SUPERLATIVE DEGREE

Three or more items are compared to an unequal degree.	**the** { **biggest** / **fastest** } / **the most** { **important** / **quickly** }	**the least** { big / fast / important / quickly }

21a Equal degree: *as big as, the same size as*

Use *as* + adjective or adverb + *as* to say that two things are equal.

▶ John is *as* **smart** *as* his older brother Jim (is).
▶ He learns *as* **quickly** *as* Jim (does).

Use *not as . . . as* or *not so . . . as* to say that two things are not equal.

▶ John's grades are*n't* **as good** *as* Jim's (are).
▶ He does*n't* work **as hard** in school *as* Jim (does).
▶ John's grades are*n't* **so good** *as* Jim's.
▶ He is*n't* **so studious** as Jim.

We can also use *as much/many* + noun + *as*.

▶ John doesn't spend *as much* **time** studying *as* Jim (does).
▶ He takes *as many* **classes** *as* Jim (does).

When comparing nouns, use *the same* + noun + *as*.

▶ John had *the same* **opportunity** *as* Jim (did).
▶ He didn't have *the same* **success** *as* Jim (did).

When the meaning is clear, we usually omit the second verb, as in the examples above. However, we must keep the second verb when the meaning isn't clear, as in the examples below.

▶ Our son **doesn't** visit us as often as our daughter **does**.

   Without the second verb *does*, the sentence could mean "Our son doesn't visit us as often as he visits our daughter."

▶ Grandpa **liked** a good bottle of wine more than Grandma **did**.

   Without the second verb *did*, the sentence could mean "Grandpa liked a good bottle of wine more than he liked Grandma."

We also keep the second verb when it differs in number or tense from the first verb, as in the examples below.

▶ Our two cats **are** not as friendly as our dog **is**.
▶ Our neighbors in the United States **are** just as friendly as our neighbors in El Salvador **were**.

Reference: See *Section 16b* for more information about what pronouns to use after *as* and *than*.

21b Comparative and superlative degrees: *bigger than, the biggest; more difficult than, the most difficult*

Comparative vs. superlative

We use comparative forms to compare two people, places, things, and actions. We use superlative forms to compare three or more people, places, and things.

Comparative forms ▶ Flying is **faster** but ***more* expensive *than*** taking a train.

▶ Renting a car is ***less* easy** and ***less* relaxing *than*** taking a bus.

▶ You can travel ***more* economically** but ***less* comfortably** if you stay in youth hostels ***than*** if you stay in hotels.

Superlative forms ▶ Hiking and bicycling are ***the* cheapest** and ***the most* interesting** ways to travel.

▶ Flying is ***the least* cheap** and ***the least* interesting** way to see a country.

▶ You can travel ***the most* economically** but ***the least* comfortably** if you stay in campgrounds.

After comparative forms, add *than* if you name the second person, place, or thing. You may omit the *than*-phrase when it is clear who or what you are comparing.

▶ Jim works harder **than his brother**.
▶ John is smart, but Jim is smarter.

Superlatives always need *the,* and we often add an expression with *of* or *in* or a clause with *ever*.

▶ Their sister is **the** smartest **of all**.
▶ She is **the** best student **in her class**.
▶ This is **the** best book **that I have ever read**.

Comparative and superlative forms

Notice that there are two ways to form comparatives and superlatives that mean "more than" and "the most" depending on the number of syllables in the adjective or adverb. (A syllable is each part of a word that contains a vowel sound. For example, the word *small* has one syllable. The word *accurate* has three syllables: ac·cu·rate.)

One-syllable adjectives/adverbs

Use *-er* and *the -est* with all one-syllable adjectives and adverbs. Read about possible spelling changes when you add *-er* and *-est* in *Section 38b*.

small, smaller, the smallest
▶ Monaco is **smaller than** San Marino, and Vatican City is **the smallest** country in the world.

fast, faster, the fastest
▶ A jet flies **faster than** a propeller plane, and the supersonic Concorde flies **the fastest** of all.

sweet, less sweet, the least sweet
▶ A grapefruit is **less sweet than** an orange, and lemons and limes are **the least sweet** of all citrus fruits.

hard, less hard, the least hard
▶ Farmers work **less hard** in the summer **than** in the spring and fall, and they work **the least hard** in the winter.

Three-or-more-syllable adjectives/adverbs

Use *more/the most* and *less/the least* with all adjectives and adverbs of three or more syllables.

accurate, more/less accurate, the most/the least accurate
▶ An electric clock is **more accurate than** a sundial.

▶ An atomic clock is **the most accurate** clock of all.

accurately, more/less accurately, the most/the least accurately
▶ An adding machine calculates **less accurately than** a computer.

▶ A human calculates **the least accurately**.

Two-syllable adjectives/adverbs

When a word has two syllables, there are several possibilities.

I. Use *more/the most* and *less/the least* with most two-syllable adjectives and adverbs.

selfish, more/less selfish, the most/the least selfish
▶ Dogs are a lot **less selfish than** cats.

▶ My cat Violet is **the most selfish** cat that I have ever owned.

often, more/less often, the most/the least often
▶ Our daughter visits us **more often than** our son does.

▶ We see our grandchildren **the least often**.

2. A few two-syllable adjectives and adverbs ending in *-y* and *-ly* use *-er* and *the -est.*

early, earlier, the earliest

▶ I always get up **earlier** *than* my husband.

noisy, noisier, the noisiest

▶ Mrs. White has **the noisiest** children in the neighborhood.

3. Some two-syllable adjectives and adverbs can use either form.

common	handsome	lonely	pleasant	shallow
cruel	likely	lovely	polite	sincere
deadly	lively	narrow	quiet	stupid

friendly, friendlier, the friendliest

▶ Suburban people are often **friendl***ier* *than* city people.

OR

▶ People in the country are usually *the* **friendl***iest* of all.

friendly, more/less friendly, the most/the least friendly

▶ Suburban people are often *more* **friendly** *than* city people.

▶ People in the country are usually *the most* **friendly** of all.

4. Three adjectives and adverbs have irregular forms.

ADJECTIVE	ADVERB	COMPARATIVE	SUPERLATIVE
good	well	better	the best
bad	badly	worse	the worst
far	far	farther, further	the farthest, the furthest

21c Parallel forms with comparisons

When you make comparisons, make sure that the items you are comparing are parallel in form, that is, that they are the same kind of word or phrase.

Gerunds

▶ **Taking** a class on a pass/fail basis is sometimes better than ~~to get~~ *getting* a grade of C.

Possessives

▶ **My friend's TOEFL score** was higher than ~~the score I got~~ *mine.*

Noun phrases

▶ **The grammar section** of the TOEFL isn't as easy for me as ~~the~~ listening and reading *sections*.

Reference: Learn more about parallel forms in *Section 6d.*

PRACTICE—Section 21

A. In the following paragraph, write the correct forms of the words in parentheses. Add any other necessary words such as *more, less, than,* and *the.*

My family recently moved. Our new apartment is a lot __larger__ (*large*) and ___more comfortable than___ (*comfortable*) our previous one. In fact, it is _____ (*big*)
1.

and _____ (*luxurious*) apartment that we have ever lived in. It has four bedrooms.
2.

My bedroom is _____ (*small*) of the four, but it has _____ (*good*) view of the park
3.   4.

across the street. My older sister's bedroom is next to mine. It is _____ (*same size*)
5.

her bedroom in our old place. She chose it because it is _____ (*close*) to the
6.

bathroom of all the bedrooms. She thinks she is going to be first in the bathroom

during the morning rush. No way! She spends a half hour making herself beautiful,

which is _____ (*long*) the rest of the family combined, and we hardly have time to
7.

brush our teeth. In our new apartment, I guess I will have to get up _____ (*early*)
8.

my sister if I want to get to school on time.

B. Edit the following sentences for errors in comparisons. Look for mistakes in forms, missing words, and items that are not parallel. Some sentences have two mistakes.

EXAMPLE

                      than

Little boys are usually more active ~~as~~ little girls.

1. Both highest and lowest points in the continental United States are in California.
2. Does it rain oftener in the winter or in the summer in your country?
3. Most people like using e-mail because it is more faster and convenient than the postal service.
4. Jane and Joan are twins, but Jane's personality is quieter than Joan.
5. Because she is more shyer, Jane makes friends less easily as Joan.

C. Edit the following paragraph for errors in comparisons. Look for the same kinds of mistakes as you looked for in the sentences in Practice B above.

                               I do for

    I know I work as hard as ~~for~~ my English teacher as my computer teacher, but I consistently get A's in computer science and C's in English. I often go to the writing center when I have a big assignment, but the tutors there don't help me as much as my roommate. My roommate doesn't have same problems with writing as I do. He is just naturally a better writer than me, so he doesn't have to work as hard or rewrite assignments as many times as me.

22 Negatives

22a No vs. not

No

Use the word *no* to answer a question.

▶ A: Did you call John?
B: **No**, I didn't call him.

Use *no* (or *not any*) with nouns and pronouns. Do not use *not* alone.

▶ There's **no** food in the refrigerator. OR There is **not any** food in the refrigerator.

▶ I have **no** classes this morning. OR I do **not** have **any** classes this morning.

▶ **No** one came to my party.

Not

Use *not* to make a verb negative. Do not use *no*.

        is not
▶ My father ~~no is~~ here.
  does not have
▶ He ~~no has~~ a job.

Use *not* with adjectives and adverbs. Do not use *no*.

▶ He's **not** old enough to go to school. OR He **isn't** old enough to go to school.

▶ You're **not** always right. OR You **aren't** always right.

22b Double negatives

English allows only one negative word in a sentence. Therefore, you can't use a negative word like *never* or *no one* in the same sentence with *not*.

        ever   *s*
▶ She doesn't ~~never~~ admit that she is wrong. OR She ~~doesn't~~ never admit that she is wrong.

The words *seldom, rarely, hardly, scarcely,* and *barely* are negative words. Don't use them in the same sentence with another negative such as *not* or *no one*.

        s
▶ He ~~doesn't~~ seldom see his old friends.

▶ The children were so tired that they ~~couldn't~~ hardly keep their eyes open.

EXCEPTION: English allows sentences like *They weren't unhappy.* The meaning is "*They were happy*" (*not unhappy = happy*).

Reference: You can begin a sentence or a clause with a negative word such as *never* and *nowhere.* Doing so changes the word order. Learn more about beginning a sentence with a negative word in *Section 9b.*

PRACTICE—Section 22

Edit the following sentences for errors in the use of negative words. One sentence is correct.

EXAMPLE

When I first moved here, I had ~~not~~ friends. OR *I didn't have any friends.*

(no above "not")

1. My new sister-in-law no is a good cook.
2. In fact, she cannot hardly pour milk and cereal in a bowl and serve it.
3. Since she and my brother returned from their honeymoon, she hasn't cooked nothing.
4. She says she has not time to learn.
5. My brother doesn't mind, though, because he likes to cook.

23 Adjective Clauses

We make sentences with adjective clauses by combining two sentences.

Tonight's game is sold out. + Tonight's game will decide the championship.

┌— antecedent —┐ ┌———————— adjective clause ————————┐
　　　　　　　　　RP

▶ Tonight's game, **which** will decide the championship, is sold out.

Do you know anyone? + Someone has an extra ticket.

　　　　　　　　　┌——— adjective clause ———┐
antecedent　RP

▶ Do you know anyone **who** has an extra ticket?

Adjective clauses are sometimes called relative clauses. They begin with a relative pronoun (RP) or relative adverb. Like adjectives, adjective clauses modify (give more information about) nouns or pronouns. The modified noun or pronoun is called the antecedent.

When you make an adjective clause, choose an appropriate relative pronoun or relative adverb.

23a Subject pronouns: *who, which, that*

When a relative pronoun is the subject of an adjective clause, choose a subject pronoun: *who, which,* or *that.*

- *Who* is used for people.
- *Which* is used for things.
- *That* is used for people and things. Using *that* for people is informal.
- Use *that* in necessary clauses only. (Learn more about necessary clauses in *Section 23e.*)

                      S   V   S   V

  I like people. + ***They** are friendly.*   *I like classes.* + ***They** are challenging.*

                S   V   S   V

- ▶ I like people **who** are friendly.   I like classes **which** are challenging.
- ▶ I like people **that** are friendly.   I like classes **that** are challenging.

23b Object pronouns: *whom, which, that,* Ø (no pronoun)

When the relative pronoun is the object in an adjective clause, choose an object pronoun: *whom, which,* or *that.* Notice that an object pronoun is placed at the beginning of the adjective clause, before the subject.

- *Whom* is used for people in formal English. Informally, *who* is used instead of *whom.*
- *Which* is used for things.
- *That* is used for people and things. Using *that* for people is informal.
- *That* is used in necessary clauses only.
- You may omit an object relative pronoun in necessary clauses.

                                 S   V   O

  The man is my teacher. + *We saw **him**.*

                          O   S   V

- ▶ The man **whom** we saw is my teacher.
- ▶ The man **that** we saw is my teacher.
- ▶ The man Ø we saw is my teacher.

                           S   V   O

  I enjoyed the movie. + *We saw **it** last night.*

                            O   S   V

- ▶ I enjoyed the movie **which** we saw last night.
- ▶ I enjoyed the movie **that** we saw last night.
- ▶ I enjoyed the movie Ø we saw last night.

Object of a preposition

Whom, which, and *that* can also be an object of a preposition. There are four possible patterns, listed in order of most formal to least formal.

                                      P   O

*The waiter was fired. + Customers had complained **about the waiter**.*

               P   O

▶ The waiter **about whom** customers had complained was fired.

               O   P

▶ The waiter **whom** customers had complained **about** was fired.

▶ The waiter **that** customers had complained **about** was fired.

▶ The waiter Ø customers had complained **about** was fired.

                                    P O

*The address was wrong. + We had sent the letter **to it**.*

               P   O

▶ The address **to which** we had sent the letter was wrong.

               O   P

▶ The address **which** we had sent the letter **to** was wrong.

▶ The address **that** we had sent the letter **to** was wrong.

▶ The address Ø we had sent the letter **to** was wrong.

23c Possessive pronoun: *whose*

When the relative pronoun replaces a possessive word, use *whose*.

• *Whose* usually refers to people (a student, the poet) but may also be used for things (a business).

• Always write *whose* together with a noun: *whose essay, whose poems, whose prices,* and place *whose* + noun at the beginning of the adjective clause.

Subject

Whose + noun can be the subject of the adjective clause. Notice that when *whose* + noun is the subject of the adjective clause, the verb agrees with that noun, not with the antecedent.

                                 — S —   V

*She takes care of two children. + **Their mother** is dead.*

                                  — S —   V

▶ She takes care of two children **whose mother** is dead.

The verb *is* agrees with the singular subject *whose mother*.

                           — S —   V

*An orphan is a child. + **His or her parents** are dead.*

                           — S —   V

▶ An orphan is a child **whose parents** are dead.

The verb *are* agrees with the plural subject *whose parents*.

Object

Whose + noun can also be an object in its clause.

$$\text{S} \qquad \text{V} \qquad\qquad \llcorner\!-\text{O}\!-\!\lrcorner$$
*The poet visited our school. + We have been reading **her poems**.*

$$\llcorner\!-\text{O}\!-\!\lrcorner \;\; \text{S} \qquad \text{V}$$
▶ The poet **whose poems** we have been reading visited our school.

Whose poems is the direct object of the verb *have been reading*.

Object of a preposition

Whose + noun can also be an object of a preposition.

$$\text{S} \qquad\quad \text{V} \qquad \text{P} \;\; \llcorner\!-\text{O}\!-\!\lrcorner$$
*The cook was fired. + Customers had complained **about his cooking**.*

$$\llcorner\!-\text{O}\!-\!\lrcorner \quad \text{S} \qquad\qquad \text{V} \qquad\quad \text{P}$$
▶ The cook **whose cooking** customers had complained **about** was fired.

Whose cooking is the object of the preposition *about*.

$$\text{S} \quad \text{V} \qquad \text{P} \;\llcorner\!\text{O}\!\lrcorner$$
*It is difficult to work for a company. + You disagree **with its goals**.*

$$\llcorner\!-\text{O}\!-\!\lrcorner \qquad\qquad\qquad \llcorner\!\text{P}\!\lrcorner$$
▶ It is difficult to work for a company **whose goals** you disagree **with.**

Whose goals is the object of the preposition *with*.

23d Relative adverbs: *where* and *when*

When the relative word replaces a prepositional phrase of place, use *where*.
When the relative word replaces a prepositional phrase of time, use *when*.

$$\text{P} \quad\;\; \text{place}$$
*Let's walk to the park. + We can sit and relax for a while **in the park**.*

▶ Let's walk to the park, **where** we can sit and relax for a while.

$$\text{P} \quad\; \text{time}$$
*June is the month. + The most weddings take place **in June**.*

▶ June is the month **when** the most weddings take place.

Put *where* and *when* at the beginning of the adjective clause. Never use *where* or *when* with a preposition.

▶ Let's walk to the park, ~~in~~ **where** we can sit and relax for a while.
▶ June is the month **when** the most weddings take place ~~in~~.

With a preposition, use *which*.

▶ June is the month **in which** the most weddings take place.

23e Punctuation of adjective clauses

Sometimes you use commas with adjective clauses, and sometimes you don't.

Necessary clause: no commas

Don't use commas around an adjective clause that is necessary to identify its antecedent.

▶ Young adults **who were born after 1981** are called "Generation Y."

The clause *who were born after 1981* is needed to tell *which* young adults are called "Generation Y." Without this information, the main clause *Young adults are called "Generation Y"* is incorrect.

▶ Yesterday my brother crashed a car **that he had just bought**.

The clause *that he had just bought* is needed to tell *which* car my brother crashed.

▶ My mother remembers well the day **when I was born**.

The clause *when I was born* is necessary to identify *which* day my mother remembers well. The main clause *My mother remembers the day* doesn't make sense without the information in the adjective clause.

Unnecessary clause: commas

Use commas around an adjective clause that isn't necessary to identify its antecedent but merely gives extra information about it.

▶ Neil Howe, **who wrote a book describing Generation Y,** says that this generation is stronger and more positive than the preceding one.

The clause *who wrote a book describing Generation Y* is not needed to identify Neil Howe because his name identifies him. The fact that he wrote a book is merely extra information. The main clause *Neil Howe says that this generation is stronger and more positive than the preceding one* is correct without the extra information.

▶ Yesterday my brother crashed his new white Porsche 911 Turbo, **which he had just bought**.

The clause *which he had just bought* is not needed to identify which car my brother crashed because the words "his new white Porsche 911 Turbo" already tell us which one. The fact that he had just bought it is merely extra information about it.

▶ My mother remembers well March 2, 1980, **when I was born**.

In this sentence, the clause *when I was born* is not necessary to identify which day my mother remembers. The date *March 2, 1980* already identifies it.

Never use *that* in unnecessary clauses; use only *who, whom, which,* or *whose* + noun.

Reference: Read more about necessary and unnecessary clauses in *Section 25c*.

! *Special Tips*

1. Place an adjective clause after its antecedent and as close to it as possible to avoid confusion.

Not correct ✗ He left the car on the street that he had just bought.

It is not clear whether the adjective clause modifies *car* or *street*.

To correct ▶ He left the car on the street that he had just bought.

Move the adjective clause.

2. When a relative pronoun is the subject of the adjective clause, make the verb in the clause agree with its antecedent (except in clauses with *whose*).

Not correct ✗ A teacher who teach young children need a lot of patience.

The antecedent (*a teacher*) is singular, but the verbs *teach* and *need* are plural.

teaches   *needs*

To correct ▶ A teacher who ~~teach~~ young children ~~need~~ a lot of patience.

Make the verbs singular to agree with *a teacher*.

3. Don't use double pronouns.

Not correct ✗ Steven Jobs, who he is the president of Apple Computer, Inc., wears blue jeans and T-shirts to work.

✗ The movie that we saw it last night won an Oscar for best film of the year.

When you write an adjective clause, you don't add a pronoun; you replace one. You replace a personal pronoun (*he, she, it, they,* etc.) with a relative pronoun (*who, whom, which, that,* etc.)

To correct ▶ Steven Jobs, who ~~he~~ is the president of Apple Computer, Inc., wears blue jeans and T-shirts to work.

▶ The movie that we saw ~~it~~ last night won an Oscar for best film of the year.

Delete the personal pronoun.

4. Watch out for fragments.

Not correct ✗ Several hundred computer companies are located in Silicon Valley, California. Which is not really a valley.

To correct ▶ Several hundred computer companies are located in Silicon

, which

Valley, California. ~~Which~~ is not really a valley.

Connect the fragment to an independent clause.

PRACTICE—Section 23

A. Underline the adjective clauses, circle the relative pronoun or adverb, and draw an arrow to the antecedent of each.

EXAMPLE

The United States Census, (which) is a count of every person living in the country, takes place every ten years.

1. In the year 2000, when the last census happened, the government mailed a questionnaire to every home in the United States.
2. Everyone who received a questionnaire had to fill it out.
3. The questionnaire contained questions about the number and ages of all of the people who lived at each address on a certain day.

B. Edit the following sentences for adjective clause errors.

EXAMPLE

who
Census workers visited people ~~whom~~ didn't return the questionnaire.

1. The census information, which the government publishes it, is useful for planning.
2. For example, the number of people who is 65 years or older increased from three million in 1900 to over thirty-five million today.
3. The number of couples also increased who live together without being married.

C. Combine the sentences in each pair to make one sentence. Change the second sentence in each pair to an adjective clause. First, replace the underlined word with a relative pronoun or adverb. Then connect it to the first sentence. Finally, add commas around unnecessary clauses.

EXAMPLE

My best friend is already separated from her new husband. She just got married last month.

My best friend, who just got married last month, is already separated from her

new husband.

1. Her husband used to be her boss. She met him at work.
2. The company gave them a big party before their wedding. They worked there.
3. Then the company transferred her. This company has a rule against married couples working together.
4. Her new office is in a city. The city is 200 miles away.
5. Her husband has asked for a transfer too. He is no longer her boss.

This part explains the rules for using punctuation marks in American English. Punctuation rules in British English are a little different, so if you read publications from countries where British English is used, you will notice a few variations.

 Computer Note

Grammar checkers can find some, but not all, punctuation errors. They will tell you when you have forgotten an apostrophe in a contraction (*dont, isnt, hes*) or the second quotation mark of a pair. However, they can't find missing apostrophes in possessive nouns (*girl's, girls'*). Sometimes they will tell you to add a comma (before *which,* for example) or to delete a comma (before *that,* for example.) In general, however, computers are not good at punctuation, so you must check your own writing.

24 End Punctuation

Mark the end of every complete sentence with a period, a question mark, or an exclamation point.

24a Periods

1. Use a period at the end of statements and commands.

Statements	**Commands**
▶ It's Tuesday.	▶ Close the door.
▶ It isn't Wednesday.	▶ Don't be late.

2. Use a period as a decimal point in numbers.

   ▶ $\pi = 3.1416$ $10.65   7¼% = 0.0725

3. Use a period after initials in names.

   ▶ I. M. Pei   J. K. Rowling   B. F. Goodrich Company

   NOTE: British English does not use periods after initials in names.

4. Use a period after abbreviations of personal titles and after some abbreviations composed of small letters or ending in a small letter.

Mr.	Dr.	Jr.	Co.	St.	a.m. (ALSO A.M. OR AM)
Mrs.	Prof.	Esq.	Inc.	Ave.	p.m. (ALSO P.M. OR PM)
Ms.	Capt.		Ltd.	Apt.	i.e.

   NOTE: British English does not use periods after these abbreviations.

Abbreviations written in all capital letters do not need periods.

▶ NY   UN   NATO   ATM   UCLA

Reference: Learn more about abbreviations in *Section 36*.

24b Question marks

1. Use a question mark after direct questions, tag questions, and polite requests.

Direct questions	**Tag questions**	**Polite requests**
▶ Where do you live?	▶ It's a nice day, isn't it?	▶ Would you please leave?
▶ Are you cold?	▶ He isn't cold, is he?	▶ Could you help me?

2. Put a question mark after each question in a series of questions even when they are not complete sentences.

   ▶ I often think about my future. Will I become a teacher? A lab technician? A fashion designer?

! Special Tip

Don't put a question mark after indirect questions. An indirect question is a question that someone reports, not a question that someone asks directly.

▶ She wants to know where you live⊙   ▶ They asked if you were a teacher⊙

24c Exclamation points

Exclamation points show strong feeling. They are almost never used in formal academic and business writing.

▶ Ouch! That hurts!   ▶ Earthquake! Under your desks!

You may use exclamation points in certain kinds of writing, such as stories. However, don't use exclamation points too often, for they lose their effectiveness. In the following example, omitting the first three exclamation points makes the last one more powerful.

▶ We left the party about midnight and started walking home through the park. It was dark and quiet, and I felt a little nervous. Suddenly we heard footsteps behind us⊙ Two men were hurrying toward us⊙ As they came closer, I thought I saw guns in their hands⊙ We were going to be robbed!

PRACTICE—Section 24

Add or delete periods, question marks, and exclamation points.

EXAMPLE

We didn't know what to do⊙

1. Should we run, or should we just yell for help
2. I decided to yell
3. "Help Robbers" I yelled as loudly as I could
4. The two men looked embarrassed and asked us very politely where the nearest ATM was?
5. Who was embarrassed then

25 Commas

Using commas correctly is important because English depends on them to make meaning clear. Compare the very different meanings of these pairs of sentences.

▶ Stop, Bill! (*The speaker tells Bill to stop.*)

▶ Stop Bill! (*The speaker tells other people to stop Bill.*)

▶ All of the students who studied passed the test. (*Only some students passed the test.*)

▶ All of the students, who studied, passed the test. (*All students passed the test.*)

Commas also help readers by showing where there are breaks or separations within a sentence.

Confusing	Clear
▶ We ran for the bus was leaving.	▶ We ran, for the bus was leaving.
▶ The driver hadn't seen us yet he stopped.	▶ The driver hadn't seen us, yet he stopped.

25a Commas in compound sentences

Put a comma before coordinating conjunctions that join independent clauses in a compound sentence. (The coordinating conjunctions are *and, but, so, or, for, nor,* and *yet.*)

▶ My friend is a photographer, **and** his wife is a travel writer.

▶ Photography and writing are interesting and fun, **but** they don't provide much income.

▶ The young couple needs more money, **so** my friend also works in a bookstore.

There are two exceptions.

1. When the clauses are very short, a comma is not always necessary but is never wrong.

    ▸ The movie ended and we fell   OR   ▸ The movie ended, and we fell
    asleep.   asleep.

    ▸ Drive two blocks and turn left.   OR   ▸ Drive two blocks, and turn left.

2. Writers sometimes use a comma before the conjunction *but* even when it doesn't connect independent clauses.

    ▸ Shops are open Saturdays, **but** not every Saturday.

! Special Tips

1. Commas are used to separate parts of sentences. They are never used to separate sentences.

2. Put a comma before the conjunctions *and* and *or* <u>only</u> when they connect two independent clauses. Don't use a comma when they connect two other sentence parts such as two words or two phrases.

    Comma   **No comma**

    ▸ The park was dark, and it was empty.   ▸ The park was dark/ and empty.

    This sentence has two independent   This sentence has only one
    clauses. A comma is necessary.   independent clause. *And* connects
                                              two adjectives. A comma is incorrect.

    ▸ Did they want to kidnap us, or   ▸ Did they want to kidnap/ or just
    did they just want to rob us?   rob us?

    This sentence has two independent   This sentence has only one
    clauses. A comma is necessary.   independent clause. *Or* connects
                                              two verb phrases. A comma is
                                              incorrect.

3. Don't use too many commas. Don't throw commas into a sentence just because you think there should be a pause or because you think the sentence is too long and needs breaking up. Use commas only when there is a rule for doing so.

    ▸ Young people/ especially/ conform to a dress code that their parents may/ or may not/ approve of.

Reference: Learn more about compound sentences in the following sections: Independent clauses, *Section 3a*; Compound sentences with coordinating conjunctions, *Section 6a*.

PRACTICE—Section 25a

Edit the following sentences for the correct use of commas. One sentence is correct.

EXAMPLE

My name is Ricardo Gonzalez, but my American friends call me Rick.

1. I was born in a small town but my family moved to the capital when I was fourteen.
2. I attended a small elementary school in my hometown and transferred to a big city school in the ninth grade.
3. I was always good at sports so physical education was my favorite class.
4. My worst subjects were physics, and math.
5. I liked history, and geography, but not English.

25b Commas after introducers

Put a comma after introducers. An introducer is any element that comes in front of the first independent clause in a sentence. An introducer can be a single word, a phrase, or a dependent clause.

| Words | ▶ **Generally,** British and American people speak the same language and follow the same customs. |
| | ▶ **However,** there are a few differences. |

Phrases	▶ **For example,** a "biscuit" in Great Britain is a "cookie" in the United States.
	▶ **During my last trip to London,** I "hired" a car instead of "renting" one.
	▶ **While driving from Heathrow airport,** I almost had an accident.
	▶ **To tell the truth,** I was very tired from the long flight and wasn't paying attention.

| Dependent clauses | ▶ **Because Americans drive on the right side of the road,** they may have a problem driving in England. |
| | ▶ **Especially when American drivers make a turn,** they must remember to stay left. |

There are two exceptions:

I. A comma is not always necessary after a short introductory phrase but is never wrong.

▶ **Sooner or later** most drivers   OR   ▶ **Sooner or later,** most drivers
   learn to stay left.   learn to stay left.

2. The comma is usually omitted after a few short time words including *then, now, soon, today,* and *tomorrow.*

▶ **Then** the teacher asked us to close our books.

▶ **Now** we're going to have a quiz.

▶ **Today** the class began ten minutes late.

▶ **Tomorrow** there will be a test.

PRACTICE—Section 25b

Edit the following sentences for the correct use of commas. Three sentences are correct.

EXAMPLE

After graduating from high school, I worked in a veterinarian's office for two years.

1. Every morning, I fed the animals and gave them fresh water.
2. Then I cleaned their cages.
3. After three months I began to help the doctor with examinations.
4. In addition I sometimes watched her perform surgery.
5. Because I enjoyed this job a lot I have decided to become a veterinarian too.
6. It is not easy, to get into veterinary school.
7. First of all there aren't many colleges of veterinary medicine, so admission standards are high.
8. The United States has twenty-seven veterinary colleges, and Canada has four.
9. There are always more applicants, than the colleges have space for.

25c Commas around extra-information modifiers

Put commas around a modifier that gives extra information about the word it modifies but is not necessary to identify it.

▶ **Laughing and joking,** the students entered the library.

▶ The librarian, **a strict disciplinarian,** frowned and walked toward them.

▶ He stopped in front of poor Roberto, **who was making the most noise.**

Necessary vs. extra-information modifiers

Sometimes modifying words, phrases, or clauses are necessary to the meaning of a sentence because they identify the person, place, or thing that they modify. Other modifiers do not identify but just give extra information about the person, place, or thing. The technical name for necessary modifiers is "restrictive" modifiers, and the technical name for extra-information modifiers is "nonrestrictive" modifiers. In this handbook, we call them "necessary" and "extra-information" modifiers.

Separate extra-information modifiers from the rest of the sentence with commas; do not separate necessary modifiers.

Necessary (restrictive) modifiers

▶ A person **who speaks three languages** is trilingual.

In this sentence, the modifying clause *who speaks three languages* is necessary because it identifies who is trilingual. When you remove *who speaks three languages,* the remaining sentence doesn't make sense: *A person is trilingual.* Therefore, the clause is necessary and is not separated by commas.

Extra-information (nonrestrictive) modifiers

▶ Rogerio, **who speaks three languages,** is trilingual.

In this sentence, the clause *who speaks three languages* is not needed to identify who is trilingual. The name *Rogerio* already identifies this person. The clause *who speaks three languages* just adds extra information about him. If you remove the clause, the remaining sentence, *Rogerio is trilingual,* still makes sense. Therefore, the clause is extra information and is separated by commas.

Appositives, *-ing/-ed* phrases, and adjective clauses

There are three kinds of necessary and extra-information modifiers: appositives, *-ing/-ed* phrases, and adjective clauses.

Appositives

An appositive is a noun or noun phrase that renames another nearby noun.

Necessary   ▶ I have two brothers. My brother **Jerry** works in Hong Kong.

The appositive *Jerry* is necessary to identify which brother works in Hong Kong—my brother Jerry, not my brother Tim. As a necessary modifier, *Jerry* is not separated by commas.

Extra information ▶ Tim, **my other brother,** works in Sydney.

The appositive *my other brother* is not necessary to identify Tim because his name already identifies him. Since it is extra information, *my other brother* is separated from the rest of the sentence by commas.

Reference: Learn more about appositives in *Section 7b.*

-ing/-ed phrases

A phrase containing a present or past participle (*wearing, worn*) is sometimes called a participial phrase. It modifies a nearby noun.

Necessary ▶ The theater manager gave free popcorn to the customers **waiting in line outside the theater**.

The phrase *waiting in line* is necessary to identify which customers got free popcorn—those waiting in line outside the theater, not those already seated inside. It is not separated by commas.

Extra information ▶ A few customers, **tired of waiting,** had already left and didn't get any.

The phrase *tired of waiting* is not necessary to identify the customers who had already left. It merely provides extra information about them. It is separated by commas.

Reference: Learn more about *-ing* and *-ed* phrases in *Section 2e* and *Section 7c.*

Adjective clauses

An adjective clause is a dependent clause that acts like an adjective; that is, it modifies a noun. An adjective clause usually begins with a relative pronoun (*who, whom, which, whose, that*) or a relative adverb (*where, when*).

Necessary ▶ The customers **who had gone home** were angry, but the customers **who got free popcorn** were happy.

The adjective clauses *who had gone home* and *who got free popcorn* are necessary to identify which customers were angry and which ones were happy. They are not separated by commas.

Extra information ▶ The theater manager, **who had tried to be nice,** lost his job for giving away free popcorn.

The adjective clause *who had tried to be nice* is not necessary to identify the theater manager because there is only one manager. It merely provides extra information about him. It is separated by commas.

Reference: Learn more about adjective clauses in *Section 23.*

PRACTICE—Section 25c

Edit the following sentences for the correct use of commas. Four sentences are correct.

EXAMPLE

Susana, my best friend, will get married next year.
      ^   ^

1. My friend Alicia got married last year.
2. Planets that contain water, can support life.
3. Earth, our home planet, is two-thirds water.
4. You don't often see men or women, wearing hats these days.
5. Jennifer Lopez wearing an old sweatshirt and jeans was not recognized by the news photographers.
6. Airline companies that offer comfortable seats and good food are popular with frequent fliers.
7. Business travelers like to fly Magic Carpet Airlines which offers excellent food and gracious service.
8. My uncle John frequently flies to Asia on business.
9. Mary his wife sometimes accompanies him on these trips.

25d Commas with transition signals

Transition signals include conjunctive adverbs such as *therefore, however,* and *furthermore* and transition phrases such as *for example, in other words,* and *in fact.*

1. When you use a transition signal with only one independent clause, separate the transition signal from the clause with commas.

   Beginning of clause ▶ **Furthermore,** there are a few differences between British and American spelling.

   Middle of clause ▶ The words *honor* and *color,* **for example,** are spelled *honour* and *colour* in England.

   End of clause ▶ These spelling variations are not significant differences, **of course**.

2. Another way to punctuate transition signals is to use a semicolon and a comma.

   ▶ The pronunciation of English in Edinburgh, Scotland, is quite different from the pronunciation of English in New York City**; in fact,** a New Yorker might not be able to understand a person from Edinburgh.

Reference: Learn more about transition signals in the following sections: Compound sentences with transition signals, *Section 26b*; Unity and coherence, *Section 41c*; List of connecting words, *Section 52*; List of transition signals, *Section 53*.

PRACTICE—Section 25d

Edit the following sentences for the correct use of commas. One sentence is correct.

EXAMPLE

Also, British and American people use different expressions. Londoners, for
example, take the "underground," but New Yorkers take the "subway."

1. Some teachers give too much homework.
2. For example my English teacher gave us fifty pages to read in one night.
3. My math teacher on the other hand gives very little homework.
4. As a result I like math a lot better than I like English.
5. I'm not learning much math however.

25e Commas with direct quotations

Use commas to separate a direct quotation from expressions such as *he said*.
(A direct quotation is the exact words someone says or writes.) Notice the
location of commas: They are always to the left of a quotation mark.

▶ The librarian said, "Be quiet." ▶ "Be quiet," the librarian said.

! Special Tip

Don't use commas with indirect quotations. An indirect quotation is the
reported words of someone. Indirect quotations are also called reported
speech.

▶ The librarian said, that we should be quiet.

Reference: Learn more about punctuating direct quotations in *Section 29a*.

25f Commas with items in a series

Use commas to separate three or more items in a series. The items can be
single words, phrases, or clauses.

Words ▶ Would you like **coffee, tea, fruit juice, a soda,** or **nothing?**

Phrases ▶ Every morning I **get up, take a shower, eat breakfast, read the
newspaper, walk my dog,** and **fight with my wife.**

Clauses ▶ Her parents always want to know **where she is going, who she is going
with,** and **what time she will be home.**

! Special Tips

1. When there are only two items, never use a comma.

   ▶ **Red, and white** are the colors of the Japanese flag.

   ▶ We couldn't decide whether **to go, or to stay.**

2. When there are only three items, some writers omit the last comma, but sentences are usually clearer with it.

   Unclear ✗ The Olympic champion thanked **her coaches, her husband and her mother.**

   This sentence could mean that her husband and her mother are her coaches.

   Clear ▶ The Olympic champion thanked **her coaches, her husband, and her mother.**

3. When there are four or more items, you *must* keep the last comma.

   ▶ There are students from **Brazil, Japan, Ukraine, Bolivia, and Korea** in our class.

   NOTE: In British English, you never use a comma before *and* when connecting items in a series.

4. Don't put a comma after the last item in a series.

   ▶ Steve works out in the morning, at lunchtime, and in the afternoon, at the school gymnasium.

Coordinate and cumulative adjectives

Use commas with a series of coordinate adjectives but not cumulative adjectives.

Coordinate adjectives can appear in any order and can be connected by *and*.

▶ She saved the **cold, wet, tired,** and **hungry** dog.

    OR   **wet, cold, hungry,** and **tired**

    OR   **hungry, tired, wet,** and **cold**

Cumulative adjectives must appear in a specific order and cannot be connected by *and*.

▶ The bride wore a **beautiful long white satin** dress.

▶ He drove his **shiny new** car down the street and crashed it into a tree.

Reference: Learn more about coordinate and cumulative adjectives in *Section 20b*.

PRACTICE—Sections 25e–f

Edit the following sentences for the correct use of commas. One sentence is correct.

EXAMPLE

Graduating from school‸ leaving home‸ getting married‸ and having one's first child are four major events in a person's life.

1. When I left home to attend college, my father gave me some advice.
2. He said "Study hard respect your teachers and call home once a week."
3. "I will" I replied "but please call me too."
4. I think about home every morning, and every night.
5. I really miss my brother my sister my friends and my mother's cooking.

25g Other uses of commas

With personal names

Put a comma between a family name (surname) and a first (given) name to show that the order of a personal name is family name–first name. Do not use a comma when the order is first name–family name.

▶ **Mouse, Mickey**	OR	**Mickey Mouse**
▶ **Leong, Galen F.**	OR	**Galen F. Leong**
▶ **McMillan, Mary Jane Alger**	OR	**Mary Jane Alger McMillan**
▶ **García Marquez, Gabriel**	OR	**Gabriel García Marquez**
▶ **al-Saud, Abdul Aziz**	OR	**Abdul Aziz al-Saud**

! *Special Tip*

The normal order of names in Asian languages is family name–first name without a comma.

- ▶ **Kurosawa Noriaki**
- ▶ **Deng Xiao-peng**
- ▶ **Kim Dae Jung**
- ▶ **Ngo Dinh Diem**

However, when living or working in the West, Asian people often use the order first name–family name. If they do so, they should also add a comma when using the order family name–first name.

▶ **Kurosawa, Noriaki**	OR	**Noriaki Kurosawa**
▶ **Pak, Se Ri**	OR	**Se Ri Pak**
▶ **Pei, I. M.**	OR	**I. M. Pei**

With titles

Put a comma before titles that follow names. In sentences, put a comma after the title as well.

▶ Sigmund Freud, **MD**

▶ American leader Martin Luther King, **Jr.,** studied the nonviolent techniques of Gandhi.

▶ Dr. J. C. Combs, **Professor of Music,** will give a concert tonight at 8:00.

With place names and addresses

In sentences, put a comma after each part of a place name or address, including the last part.

▶ Nelson Mandela was born in **Umtata, South Africa,** as the son of a chief.

Do not put a comma between a state and a U.S. zip code.

▶ Please send the requested information to Linda Woodbury, **83 Park Place, Apt. 6B, Fairfax, Missouri 64446,** as soon as possible.

With dates

When the order of a date is month-day-year, put commas after the day and after the year.

▶ I was born on **March 2, 1980,** at exactly 3:36 p.m.

Commas are not necessary when the day is omitted or when the order is day-month-year.

▶ A human first left Earth's atmosphere in **November 1957** in the Russian spaceship *Sputnik 2.*

▶ A human first stepped on the moon on **20 July 1969** from the American spaceship *Apollo 11.*

With numbers

Use commas to separate large numbers into groups of three, starting from the right.

▶ He won **$64,000** on a television quiz game show.

▶ She always has **1,200,500** excuses but not one good reason.

▶ At least **150,000,000** ants came to our picnic.

A comma is optional in four-digit numbers.

▶ There are **2,537** (OR **2537**) students in the School of Engineering.

EXCEPTIONS: Do not use commas in telephone numbers, street numbers, zip codes, or years.

▶ My phone number is **(415) 884-8973.** (ALSO **415-884-8973**)

▶ I live at **7693** Amber Way.

▶ The zip code for the college is **94945.**

▶ My grandmother was born in **1910.**

With nouns of direct address

Separate a noun of direct address from its sentence with commas. (A noun of direct address is the noun, name, or other word you use when you speak directly to someone.)

▶ Please, **officer,** don't give me a ticket.

▶ **Dad,** I have something to tell you.

▶ Can I borrow some money, **Uncle Joe?**

With yes, no, and mild interjections

Put a comma after the words *yes* and *no* and after mild interjections like *oh* and *well* at the beginning of a sentence.

▶ **Yes,** I have a driver's license.

▶ **No,** I have never gotten a traffic ticket.

▶ **Oh,** was I speeding?

▶ **Well,** maybe I was going a little fast.

With tags

Put a comma before the tag part of a tag question.

▶ I wasn't speeding, **was I?**

▶ You aren't going to give me a ticket, **are you?**

In letters

Put a comma after the greeting in personal letters and after the closing in both business and personal letters. (Use a colon after the greeting in business letters.)

Personal letters	**Business letters**
▶ Dear Andrew,	▶ Dear Mr. Smith:
▶ Love,	▶ Very truly yours,

Reference: Learn more about business letters in *Section 44c.*

PRACTICE—Section 25g

Add and delete commas in the following sentences where necessary. One sentence is correct.

EXAMPLE

The world's population will be 9,500,000,000 by the year 2,100.
                             ^   ^   ^

1. Anyone can write to the U.S. president at this address: The President of the United States The White House 1600 Pennsylvania Avenue Washington DC 20500.
2. The United States declared its independence from England on July 4 1776 in Philadelphia Pennsylvania and started a war.
3. Can I borrow the car tonight Dad?
4. No you can't.
5. Well, can I have some money for the bus?
6. It's a nice day today isn't it?

26 Semicolons

A semicolon is more like a period than like a comma because it is used *between* independent clauses, not *within* them.

26a Semicolons in compound sentences

Use a semicolon between independent clauses when the relationship between them is clear without a connecting word. This kind of sentence is possible only when the two independent clauses are closely related in meaning.

▶ Some dogs love water; all cats hate it.

▶ My older brother is a senior in college; my younger brother is still in high school.

Reference: Learn more about compound sentences in *Section 6a.*

26b Semicolons in compound sentences with transition signals

Transition signals include conjunctive adverbs such as *therefore, however,* and *furthermore* and transition phrases such as *for example, in other words,* and *in fact.* When you use a transition signal between independent clauses to make a compound sentence, put a semicolon before and a comma after it.

▶ My roommate and I don't like to wash dishes**; therefore,** we always use paper plates and plastic cups.

▶ Many people want to learn English**; in fact,** there are more students of English in China than there are people in the United States.

Of course, you could also write the independent clauses as two separate sentences.

▶ My roommate and I don't like to wash dishes. **Therefore,** we always use paper plates and plastic cups.

Reference: Learn more about transition signals in the following sections: Compound sentences, *Section 6a*; Commas with transition signals, *Section 25d*; Unity and coherence, *Section 41c*; List of connecting words, *Section 52*; List of transition signals, *Section 53*.

26c Semicolons in a series containing commas

Use semicolons to separate items in a series when the items already have commas.

▶ Should we eat lunch today at the Chinese Kitchen, which has delicious dim sum**;** at Gino's, where the pizza is excellent**;** or at the student cafeteria, where the food is tasteless but cheap?

The example sentence could be confusing for the reader without semicolons. The semicolons keep the main items—*the Chinese Kitchen, Gino's,* and *the student cafeteria*—separate from their descriptions.

! *Special Tips*

1. Punctuate transition signals carefully. When you place a transition signal between two independent clauses, use either a semicolon and a comma, or a period, a capital letter, and a comma.

▶ Many state names in the United States are Spanish words**; for example,** Colorado means "red" or "reddish-colored," and Montana is from a Spanish word meaning "mountain."   OR

▶ Many state names in the United States are Spanish words. **For example,** Colorado means "red" or "reddish-colored," and Montana is from a Spanish word meaning "mountain."

When you place a transition signal in the middle of a single independent clause, use two commas.

▶ Many state names in the United States are Spanish words. Colorado, **for example,** means "red" or "reddish-colored," and Montana is from a Spanish word meaning "mountain."

(continued)

(*continued*)

2. Semicolons are a good way to add variety to your writing, but don't overuse them. Don't connect more than two clauses with a semicolon, and don't use more than one or two semicolons in a single paragraph.

Too many semicolons ✗ I am afraid of dogs; I had nightmares about dogs when

I was a child; a big dog bit me.

Revised ▶ I am afraid of dogs; I had nightmares about dogs
after
when I was a child; a big dog bit me.

PRACTICE—Section 26

Add semicolons and commas to the following sentences.

EXAMPLE

The *Oxford English Dictionary* lists 450,000 words; a large number of them have come from other languages.

1. English has always borrowed words from other languages for example we take siestas wear kimonos and eat croissants.
2. Spanish is spoken in more countries Chinese is spoken by more people.
3. Two hundred people came to his wedding three attended his funeral.
4. Albert Einstein was one of the last century's most brilliant thinkers however he did not do well in high school.
5. Students brought many delicious dishes to the class party: paella a Spanish seafood dish kim chee a mixture of pickled vegetables that is the national dish of Korea guacamole a Mexican dip made from mashed avocado lime juice and spices and sushi a Japanese favorite.
6. When the teacher does math problems on the blackboard they are easy when I do the same problems at home they are hard.

27 Colons

27a Colons in sentences

Using a colon at the end of an independent clause focuses attention on the words following the colon. After a colon, we often write lists, appositives, and direct quotations. Do not capitalize the first word after a colon unless it is a proper noun or the first word of another sentence.

Before a list

▶ Please bring the following to the final exam: **two pencils, an eraser, a blue book, and your brain.**

▶ The reading list for this class includes two German novels: *Death in Venice* **and** *The Trial.*

Before an appositive

▶ He had one great love in his life: **himself.**

▶ A doctor has two important abilities: **the ability to listen and the ability to analyze.**

Before a direct quotation

Use a colon to introduce a direct quotation when there is no reporting verb such as *he said.* Capitalize the first word of the quotation.

▶ The best advice I ever got from my mother was this: **"Remember that you are choosing not only a wife for yourself but also a mother for your children."**

▶ My father's advice was even better: **"Don't get married."**

Reference: Learn more about punctuating direct quotations in *Section 29a.*

! Special Tips

1. The information following a colon must refer to a word or phrase before the colon.

   ▶ I took four courses last semester: English, calculus, physics, and history.

   ▶ Hippocrates, the father of Western medicine, gave the first

   rule of medical practice: "First, do no harm."

   If the information does not refer to a word or phrase preceding, you cannot use a colon.

2. Don't use a colon after a preposition. Use a colon only at the end of an independent clause.

   ▶ After a long day at work, I look forward to enjoying a quiet dinner at home, playing with my children, and watching a little TV.

3. Don't use a colon after a verb unless you add words such as *the following, as follows, this,* or *these.*

   ▶ The two most important qualities of teachers are patience and enthusiasm. OR
   the following
   ▶ The two most important qualities of teachers are: patience and enthusiasm.

27b Other uses of colons

Before a subtitle

Use a colon between the main title and the subtitle of books, magazine articles, and plays.

▶ One of my favorite science fiction movies is *2001: A Space Odyssey.*

▶ Most of the information in her report came from a *Time* magazine article entitled "Teenage Pregnancy: The Facts."

To give a time

Use a colon between the hours and minutes when writing a time.

▶ 1:00 a.m.　　　12:45 p.m.

After business letter greetings

Put a colon after the greeting in business letters.

▶ Dear Professor Jones:

▶ Dear Customer Relations Department:

BUT

Use a comma after the greeting in personal letters.

▶ Dear Anna,　　▶ Dear Grandfather,

PRACTICE—Section 27

Edit the following sentences for the correct use of colons.

EXAMPLE

The dying woman had only one wish: to go home and die in her own bed.

1. Girls in my country look forward to an important event in their lives their fifteenth birthday.
2. The two causes of prejudice are: ignorance and fear.
3. The next bus leaves at 12.27 and arrives at 2.15.
4. Whenever you go hiking, you should take the following items a knife, a flashlight, a first aid kit, extra water, extra food, extra clothing, a map, a compass, matches or a lighter, and a whistle.
5. My strict parents didn't approve of: smoking, drinking, dancing, watching television, or playing cards on Sundays.
6. The title of this book is *The Essentials of English A Writer's Handbook.*

28 Apostrophes

Apostrophes have three main uses: to make nouns and indefinite pronouns possessive, to make contractions, and to make a few special plurals.

28a Apostrophes with possessives

Possessive words show ownership. In the phrase *John's car,* *John's* is a possessive noun showing that John is the owner of the car.

Possession with nouns

In English, we often (but not always) have a choice of ways to show possession with nouns. We can use *of the* and say *the courage of the firemen,* or we can use an apostrophe + *-s* and say *the firemen's courage.*

▸ the speed **of the runner** OR the **runner's** speed
▸ the condition **of the prisoners** OR the **prisoners'** condition
▸ the speech **of the president** OR the **president's** speech

We use an apostrophe or an apostrophe + *-s* more often when the owner is a living being, and we use the *of*-phrase more often when the owner is a nonliving thing. We prefer, for example, *the bird's wing* but *the wing of the airplane.* There are, however, many exceptions.

▸ the speed **of the car** OR the **car's** speed
▸ the warmth **of the sun** OR the **sun's** warmth
▸ a vacation **of two days** OR **two days'** vacation

When the owner's name is given, we don't have a choice. We must use an apostrophe or apostrophe + *-s.*

✗ ~~the car of John~~   ▸ **John's** car
✗ ~~the house of the Smiths~~   ▸ **the Smiths'** house

Possession with indefinite pronouns

Besides nouns, we also make indefinite pronouns possessive.

▸ **somebody's** book
▸ **anyone's** guess

Rules

Follow these rules for making nouns and indefinite pronouns possessive.

ADD APOSTROPHE + -*S*		
	Singular nouns	Plural nouns
1. To singular nouns and to plural nouns that don't end in -*s*	**child's** toy **boss's** office **Venus's** beauty **Mr. and Mrs. Smith's** house **Mr. and Mrs. Jones's** daughters	**children's** game **men's** ties **University Women's** Club **the media's** influence
2. To indefinite pronouns	**someone's** mistake **nobody's** fault	
3. To abbreviations	**NAFTA's** success **UNESCO's** budget	
ADD AN APOSTROPHE ALONE		
		Plural nouns
To plural nouns ending in -*s*		**students'** club **actresses'** costumes **the Smiths'** house **the Joneses'** daughters

Special situations

Compound nouns

In a compound noun and in groups of words functioning as one unit, make the last word possessive, not the first word.

▶ **my mother-in-law's** cooking
▶ **the Emperor of Japan's** palace
▶ **everyone else's** decision

Joint possession

When two or more people own something together, make only the second person's name possessive.

▶ **John and Mary's** wedding is next Saturday.

BUT When two or more people own things separately, make each owner's name possessive.

▶ **Mary's, Joan's,** and **Barbara's** husbands work for the same company.

PRACTICE—Section 28a

Change each item into a possessive phrase containing an apostrophe or an apostrophe + -*s.*

> **EXAMPLE**
> the girlfriend of Charles
> *Charles's girlfriend*

1. the brightness of the moon
2. the brightness of the stars
3. a delay of an hour
4. a delay of six weeks
5. the house of my aunt and uncle
6. the education of our son and daughter
7. the children of my sister-in-law
8. the safety of our children
9. the schedule of my boss

28b Apostrophes in contractions and in years

Contractions

In informal English, an apostrophe shows where letters are missing in a contraction.

▶ **isn't**	is not		▶ **it's**	it is
▶ **can't**	cannot		▶ **there's**	there is
▶ **he's**	he is OR he has		▶ **they're**	they are
▶ **he'd**	he had OR he would		▶ **I'll**	I will

Years

In informal English, an apostrophe sometimes replaces the first two numbers in a year or decade.

▶ He's a member of the class of **'04.**

▶ Jazz music first became popular in the **'20s.**

 Special Tip

We use contractions in conversation and in informal writing such as letters to friends. Avoid using them in formal academic and business writing.

28c Apostrophes with special plurals

Plurals of letters

Use an apostrophe + -*s* to make the plural of letters of the alphabet.

▶ There are four ***s*'s** and four ***i*'s** in the word *Mississippi.*

▶ The teacher gave two **A's** and ten **F's** last semester.

Plurals of abbreviations

You may use an apostrophe + -*s* to make the plural of abbreviations that have more than one period, such as M.D. and Ph.D. However, the modern style is to omit periods in these abbreviations. In this case, add -*s* without an apostrophe.

▶ My mother has two **Ph.D.'s:** one in English and one in philosophy.

OR

▶ My mother has two **PhDs:** one in English and one in philosophy. (*modern style*)

Reference: Learn more about special plurals in *Section 37c* and *Section 38c.*

 Special Tips

1. Don't confuse *it's* and *its.*

It's is a contraction of *it is. Its* is a possessive pronoun. Possessive pronouns (*my, your, our, his, her, its, their*) never have apostrophes.

▶ **It's** hot today.

▶ The book lost **its** cover.

2. Don't confuse the contraction of a noun + *is* and the possessive form of the noun.

  ▸ **John's** sick today. (*John is sick today.*)
  ▸ **John's** car is a Toyota. (*The car that belongs to John is a Toyota.*)

3. Don't use an apostrophe to make nouns plural.

  ▸ The Smith's have a new baby daughter.

PRACTICE—Section 28

Edit the following sentences for the correct use of apostrophes. Two sentences are correct.

EXAMPLE

My brother's wife is ten year's younger than he is.

1. Both of my aunts birthdays are the same day.
2. The womans purse was stolen.
3. The womens clothing department is on the third floor.
4. Let's go to Carlos's house to study.
5. The cat hurt its paw, so its licking it.
6. He has two PCs, one at his office and one at home.

29 Quotation Marks

Quotation marks are always in pairs. The form of quotation marks in English may differ from their form in your language. In English, both marks curve toward the quotation, and both marks are written at the top of a line. Quotation marks are mainly used to enclose direct quotations, but they have a few other uses as well.

29a Quotation marks with direct quotations

A direct quotation is someone's exact words (spoken or written) and is usually introduced by an expression such as *he said* or *she wrote*. Put quotation marks before and after the person's exact words.

  ▸ He said, "**I'm hungry.**"

Don't use quotation marks with indirect quotations. An indirect quotation is someone's reported words and is usually introduced by *that*.

  ▸ He said **that he was hungry.**

Rules for punctuating direct quotations

Follow these rules for punctuating direct quotations.

1. Separate a quoted sentence from a reporting expression with a comma.

▶ Tom said**,** "That woman in the water is waving at us."

▶ "Maybe she is just being friendly," his friend commented.

If there is no reporting verb, use a colon before the quotation.

▶ Tom remembered his swimming teacher's words**:** "Never put yourself in danger, even to save a life."

2. Begin each quoted sentence with a capital letter. When a quoted sentence is separated into two parts, begin the second part with a small letter.

▶ "**B**e quiet. **S**he's still waving," Tom said, "**a**nd she's also saying something."

3. Commas, periods, question marks, and exclamation points go *inside* the second quotation mark of a pair.

▶ "Hand me the binoculars**,**" his friend said. "Maybe she is in trouble**.**"

▶ "Help**!**" the woman screamed. "I can't swim**!**"

▶ "What did she say**?**" Tom asked.

BUT   A question mark goes outside the second quotation mark when the reporting expression is a question.

▶ **Did she say**, "I love to swim"**?**

4. Semicolons and colons go *outside* the second quotation mark.

▶ The woman yelled again, "I . . . swim"**;** her voice was weaker.

5. Use single quotation marks to enclose a quotation within a quotation.

▶ His friend replied, "I think she said **'I can't swim,'** but I'm not sure."

29b Other uses of quotation marks

With titles of short works

Put quotation marks around titles of newspaper and magazine articles, short stories, poems, chapters of books, songs, and episodes of television programs.

▶ *National Geographic*'s article **"Vanishing Cultures"** discusses three ancient cultures that are struggling to survive.

▶ In the poem **"Fire and Ice,"** the poet wonders how the world will end.

Titles of long works and names of magazines and newspapers are either italicized or underlined.

Reference: Learn more about underlining or italicizing titles in *Section 35a.*

With words with unusual meanings

Put quotation marks around words with unusual, especially ironic, meanings.

▶ The **"banquet"** consisted of a cheese sandwich and a soda.

▶ The little girl proudly showed her latest **"masterpiece"**: a crayon drawing of a flower.

Notice the location of the colon in the second example. Semicolons and colons go outside the second quotation mark (*Section 29a*).

Don't put quotation marks around slang.

▶ The final exam was "a piece of cake." (*a piece of cake = easy*)

With translations of foreign words

When you translate from another language into English, put foreign words in italics (or underline them), and enclose the English translation in both quotation marks and parentheses.

▶ German has many long words such as *Strassenbahnführersgeldtasche* ("streetcar conductor's money purse").

PRACTICE—Section 29

Edit the following sentences for the correct use of quotation marks. Change small letters to capital letters where necessary.

EXAMPLE

When I left home to go to school, my parents said take care of yourself and call us often.

(edits shown: , "Take ... often.")

1. My parents told me that "I should do my best."
2. My parents told me do your best, and you will be successful in life.
3. Do your best my parents told me and you will be successful in life.
4. The national song of the United States is The Star-Spangled Banner, and the national song of Great Britain is God Save the Queen.
5. People in many corners of the world use the Italian word *ciao* (hello and goodbye) in informal speech.
6. In his poem The Raven, poet Edgar Allen Poe repeats the phrase Quoth the Raven Nevermore at the end of several verses. (The verb *quoth* is an old form of the verb *quoted.* Also, this sentence has a quotation within a quotation.)

30 Parentheses

Parentheses have two uses.

Around nonessential information

Use parentheses to enclose information that is not essential but may be helpful for your reader to know.

▶ Parentheses (**singular: parenthesis**) have two uses.

▶ The Ming Dynasty (**1368–1644**) was an important period in Chinese history.

Around numbers and letters in a list

Use parentheses to enclose numbers and letters that label items in a list.

▶ Your final grade in this class will be based on (**1**) completion of all assignments, (**2**) tests, and (**3**) class participation.

▶ The company offered each employee the choice of (**a**) a $500 bonus or (**b**) one extra day's vacation.

Punctuation with parentheses

Periods and commas normally go *outside* the second parenthesis mark.

▶ In English, the same spelling may have different pronunciations (**through, although, tough**), and the same pronunciation may have different spellings (**sea, see**).

BUT   When you enclose a complete sentence in parentheses, put the end punctuation mark (period, exclamation point, or question mark) *inside* the final parenthesis.

▶ After her mother died, she decided to start a new life in another country. (**Her father had died ten years earlier.**)

31 Dashes

On a typewriter or computer word processor, use two hyphens to form a dash (--). If your word processor has an em dash (—), you may use it instead of two hyphens. Do not put a space before or after a dash.

Dashes are more informal than commas, so they are not used frequently in formal writing. However, they are useful in three situations.

For emphasis

Use a dash to separate nonessential information that you want to emphasize especially.

▶ We drank hot coffee—**very hot coffee**—with our meal.

▶ Everyone in the family—**from the youngest child to the oldest grandparent**—helps with household chores.

Around appositives containing commas

Use dashes to separate an appositive that already contains commas from the rest of the sentence.

▶ Sam—**my best friend, most loyal companion, and wisest counselor**—is a dog.

▶ Everyone in the college—**teachers, students, and administrators**—was shocked when the president quit.

Before dramatic shifts

When the mood or flow of ideas in a sentence dramatically changes direction, use a dash to mark the change.

▶ The little old lady entered the bank, stepped up to the counter, smiled sweetly at the teller—**and pulled out a gun.**

▶ The singer was young, beautiful, famous—**and addicted to drugs.**

PRACTICE—Sections 30–31

Add parentheses and dashes to the following sentences. In two sentences, replace commas.

EXAMPLE

My neighbors' children are very well behaved when they are asleep.

1. She entered the room, greeted everyone with a cheerful "good morning," sat down at her desk, and burst into tears.
2. The Norman Conquest of England 1066 changed the English language forever.
3. The language of the conquerors, French, became the language of the upper classes.
4. The different greetings Americans use *hello, hi, hiya, howdy,* and *how do you do* have different levels of formality.

32 Brackets and Ellipses

Brackets ([ ]) and ellipses (. . .) show additions and deletions to quotations. (See *Section 45e* for information.)

PART 5 Mechanics

In this part, you will find the answers to your questions about the mechanics of English: Which words begin with a capital letter? When should I write out numbers in words (*fifteen*) and when can I just write the number (*15*)? What words must I underline? Which abbreviations can I use? The last section of this part reviews the rules for spelling.

 Computer Note

If you write on a computer, always use your computer's spelling checker. Spelling checkers can find spelling mistakes and some problems in mechanics such as capitalization errors. However, spelling checkers cannot find all mistakes. For example, they cannot tell you if you type *ties* instead of *tries*, but they can tell you if you type *trys*. It's always a good idea to proofread your work for errors that a computer misses.

Grammar checkers can find some errors in mechanics. They can find most errors in capitalization and abbreviations, and they can find some missing hyphens. For example, if you write *december* without a capital *D*, the grammar checker will tell you. However, grammar checkers cannot always tell you how to write numbers, and they don't tell you what to underline.

33 Capital Letters

The use of capital letters differs in all languages. Some languages, such as German, use capital letters more often than English. Other languages, such as Spanish, use them less often. The following rules will help you decide when to capitalize words. Always consult a dictionary if you are not sure.

33a Pronoun *I*

Capitalize the pronoun *I*.

▶ My twin brother and **I** look exactly alike.

33b First word of a sentence

Capitalize the first word of a sentence.

▶ **O**ur personalities are identical, too.

Capitalize the first word of a quoted sentence.

▶ My father said, "**S**tudy hard, stay out of trouble, and call home once in a while."

Capitalize a series of questions after a colon (even when they are not complete sentences.)

▶ The children couldn't decide what to order: **A** cheeseburger or fried chicken? **French** fries or onion rings? **Lemonade** or milk?

BUT Don't capitalize single words or short phrases after a colon.

▶ Their mother finally told them what they could have: **a** plain hamburger, **french** fries, and **milk**.

33c Proper nouns and most proper adjectives

Proper nouns

English has two kinds of nouns: proper nouns and common nouns. A common noun names a person, place, or thing: *poet, country, bridge*. A proper noun names a specific person, place, or thing: *Shakespeare, Brazil, the Golden Gate Bridge.* Capitalize all proper nouns. Do not capitalize common nouns.

Specific people and their titles

▶ Madonna   Mother Teresa
▶ Tiger Woods   Professor Indiana Jones
▶ Mr. and Mrs. John Smith   Mom (*used as a name*)

Don't capitalize titles without names.

▶ An American-born woman is the former **q**ueen of Jordan.
▶ Who will the next **p**resident be?

BUT Capitalize a title when only one person holds the title.

▶ The **D**alai Lama and the **P**ope met in Rome last month.

Some writers also capitalize titles such as *president* and *prime minister* when they clearly refer to one person.

▶ The **P**resident (or **p**resident) will speak to the nation on television tonight.

Capitalize family words only when they are used as names.

▶ Our favorite aunt is **A**unt Anna.
▶ All her life, **M**other has loved to cook.

BUT All her life, my **m**other has loved to cook.

Nationalities, languages, ethnic groups, races

▶ Japanese   Asian
▶ Tanzanian   Hispanic
▶ Latin American   African American

BUT Don't capitalize the words *black* or *white* to describe a race.

▶ There are equal numbers of blacks, whites, Hispanics, and Asians in my daughter's class.

Names of God, religions and their followers, holy days, holy books

▶ God, Allah, Buddha   Buddhist, Hindu, Jew
▶ Islam, Judaism, Christianity   Easter, Ramadan, Tet, Passover
▶ Muslim/Moslem, Christian   the Bible, the Koran, the Veda

BUT Don't capitalize the word *god* when it is a common noun.

▶ Some religions have multiple gods; others have only one.

Specific places and geographic areas

▶ Djakarta   the Gulf of Mexico
▶ the North Pole   the Middle East
▶ the Andes   the South

BUT Don't capitalize compass directions.

▶ Drive two blocks west, and turn south.

Specific structures: buildings, bridges, roads, dams, monuments

▶ the White House   the Pan-American Highway
▶ the Suez Canal   the Washington Monument
▶ the Great Wall of China   Fifth Avenue

Specific times: days of the week, months of the year, holidays

Friday   New Year's Eve
September   Thanksgiving
Independence Day   Mother's Day

BUT Don't capitalize the names of the seasons.

▶ The four seasons of the year are summer, fall (autumn), winter, and spring.

Historical events, periods, documents

▶ the Vietnam War   the Tang Dynasty

▶ the Renaissance   the Declaration of Independence

BUT Don't capitalize newly named time periods, decades, movements, centuries, or millennia.

▶ the cold war   the twentieth century

▶ the age of technology   the second millennium

Organizations, government bodies, political parties, companies, schools, departments, sports teams, clubs

▶ the European Union   Microsoft Corporation

▶ the Red Cross   Moscow University

▶ the U.S. Senate   the Los Angeles Lakers

▶ the Social Democrats   the Student Nurses' Club

Titles of school courses

▶ Chemistry 410   Introduction to Computer Programming

BUT Don't capitalize the names of school subjects or fields of study except languages and names of nationalities, religions, and ethnic groups.

▶ algebra   English

▶ organic chemistry   Asian art

Don't capitalize names of academic degrees except as a title after a person's name.

▶ master of arts degree   Carolyn Moore, Master of Arts

Specific electronic sources

▶ the Internet, the Net   the World Wide Web, the Web

Trademarked names (names legally owned by a company)

▶ Coke   Levi's

▶ Scotch tape   Jell-O

Ships, airplanes, spacecraft, trains

▶ the *Titanic*   *Mir*

▶ the *Spirit of Saint Louis*   the *Shanghai Express*

Proper adjectives

Proper adjectives are formed from proper nouns. Most proper adjectives are capitalized.

▶ a **P**ersian rug   a **S**hakespearean play   **R**oman numerals

A few proper adjectives are not capitalized. Consult a dictionary when you are not sure.

▶ **f**rench fries   **v**enetian blinds   **b**russels sprouts

33d Titles and subtitles of works

Capitalize the first word, the last word, and all important words in titles and subtitles of books, magazines, films, poems, television programs, plays, and songs. Do not capitalize articles (*a, an, the*), prepositions (*of, to, with,* and so on), or coordinating conjunctions (*and, but, or*). Capitalize these words only when they are the first or last words or appear after a colon, semicolon, or dash.

▶ *Of Mice and Men*   *Classical Music: What to Listen For*
▶ *The Essentials of English: A Writer's*   *Around the World in Eighty Days*
  Handbook

33e Greetings and closings in letters

Capitalize the greeting and the first word of the closing in both personal and business letters.

Greetings	Closings
▶ **D**ear Mom,	▶ **L**ove always,
▶ **D**ear Sir or Madam:	▶ **S**incerely yours,

Reference: Learn more about business letters in *Section 44c.*

33f Certain abbreviations

Some abbreviations are capitalized; others are not. In general, capitalize abbreviations when the letters are the first letter of a word.

▶ **UN**   United Nations   **BA**   Bachelor of Arts
▶ **INS**   Immigration and   **TOEFL** Test of English as a Foreign
            Naturalization Service   Language

There are many exceptions. Learn more about abbreviations in *Section 36.*

! *Special Tips*

I. Never capitalize words just to make them seem more important.

       f   *d*

▶ The Faculty of our Department includes several Ph.D.'s.

2. The sciences have special rules for capitalizing scientific terminology.

▶ *Homo sapiens*   *Orcinus orca*

3. Some academic fields of study have different rules for capitalizing titles in research paper documentation. Ask your instructor or a librarian for guidance.

PRACTICE—Section 33

Edit the following letter for capitalization errors. There are forty-two errors.

          1619 grand avenue
          denver, colorado 80207
          january 1, 2002

mr. thomas b. jackson
jackson computer consultants
900 park avenue
new york, new york 10012

dear mr. jackson:

I will graduate from the university of denver in a few months and am looking for a position with a company such as yours. I will receive a Master's Degree in computer engineering in june.

recently, i saw one of your Company's advertisements in the *new york times* newspaper. I plan to visit the east during the week of april 11-18 during my School's easter vacation and would like to visit your offices then.

I will call your Human Resources director on monday, january 10, to arrange an appointment. Copies of my resume and college grades are enclosed.

          Very Truly Yours,

          Dmitri Popovich

34 Hyphens

Hyphens have two main uses in English: (1) to form some compound words and (2) to divide words that are too long to fit on a line.

34a Hyphens in compound words

 Computer Note

Spelling checkers and grammar checkers will notice some, but not all, hyphen errors in compound words. For example, if you type *selfcontrol,* they will suggest that you change it to *self-control.* However, if you type *self control,* a computer will recognize *self* and *control* as separate words and won't mark it as an error.

A compound word is a word made from two or more words that function together as one word, such as *bookstore* (*book + store*). Some compound words are spelled with hyphens; others are not. A dictionary will show you whether to write a compound word with a hyphen (*time-consuming*), without a hyphen (*timesaving*), or as two separate words (*time clock*).

Make sure that you are using a current dictionary because the rules for using hyphens in compound words are changing. Hyphens are used less often now than they used to be. For example, the word *on-line* is now more frequently written *online,* without a hyphen.

Basic rules

1. Some compound words always have hyphens.

   ▶ sister-in-law   part-time   left-handed
   ▶ attorney-at-law   old-fashioned   good-bye

2. Always use a hyphen to write fractions and numbers from twenty-one to ninety-nine.

   ▶ one-half   twenty-one   twenty-first

3. Always use a hyphen to connect these four prefixes to words: *all-, great-, self-,* and *ex-* when it means "former."

   ▶ all-star   great-grandmother   self-confidence   ex-president

4. We sometimes (but not always) use a hyphen to connect a single letter to a word, especially when the letter names a shape.

   ▶ U-turn   L-shaped   E-mail (ALSO **e-mail** OR **email**)

5. Use a hyphen to connect certain other prefixes to proper nouns and proper adjectives (but usually not to common nouns: *antiwar, postgraduate,* and *prehistory*).

 ▶ **anti-Semitism**   **post-World War II**   **pro-Arab**
 ▶ **Pan-African**   **pre-Columbian**   **un-American**

Compound adjectives

A compound adjective is two or more words that act as a single adjective.

1. Use a hyphen when a compound adjective comes in front of a noun.

 ▶ This is a very **well-written** paragraph.
 ▶ She has a **twelve-year-old** daughter.
 ▶ They built an **eight-foot** wall around their house.

 Notice that *year* and *foot* are singular. Compound adjectives in front of nouns are singular even when numbers are part of the compound. (Learn more about this rule in *Section 20a.*)

2. Do not use a hyphen when a compound adjective follows a noun or pronoun.

 ▶ This paragraph is **well written.**
 ▶ Her daughter is **twelve years old.**
 ▶ The wall around their house is **eight feet high.**

3. Do not use a hyphen in a compound adjective beginning with an adverb ending in *-ly,* even before a noun.

 ▶ a **newly married** couple
 ▶ **freshly baked** bread
 ▶ **recently discovered** cure

34b Hyphens dividing words at the end of a line

 Computer Note

Most word processing programs can automatically hyphenate words at the end of a line. Use automatic hyphenation programs with caution, however. Sometimes a program hyphenates words that should not be hyphenated, such as names of people. Also, sometimes it does not "unhyphenate" a word when it should.

When a word is too long to fit at the end of a line, use a hyphen to divide it and continue it on the next line.

American English and British English use different systems for dividing words. The American system uses pronunciation as a basis for dividing words. Americans divide words between syllables. The British system divides words into roots and affixes. This handbook gives the rules for dividing words according to the American system.

American English	British English
knowl-edge	**know-ledge**
democ-racy	**demo-cracy**

Basic rules

Try not to divide words. When you must divide them, however, these six rules will help you decide where to make the break.

1. Divide words between syllables. A dictionary shows syllable breaks with a dot.

  ▶ **foot•ball**   **u•ni•ver•si•ty**

2. Never divide one-syllable words.

  ▶ **foot**   **mouse**

3. Divide a word that already has a hyphen only at the hyphen, or don't divide it at all.

Incorrect	Correct
▶ **long-dis-**	**long-**
▶ **tance**	**distance**

4. Never leave just one letter at the end of a line or fewer than three letters at the beginning of a line.

Incorrect	Correct
▶ **u–**	**uni–**
niversity	**versity**
▶ **universi-**	**univer-**
ty	**sity**

5. Never divide contractions or people's names.

Incorrect	Correct
▶ **should-**	**shouldn't**
n't	
▶ **William Shake-**	**William**
speare	**Shakespeare**

6. Put the hyphen at the end of the first line, not at the beginning of the second line.

Incorrect	Correct
▶ **diction**	**diction-**
-ary	**ary**

PRACTICE—Section 34

Edit the following sentences for hyphen errors. Two sentences are correct.

EXAMPLE

full-time

John is a ~~full time~~ employee.

1. A well-known author was the graduation speaker.
2. The author of that book is well-known.
3. Our bank recently hired five Spanish-speaking tellers.
4. A large group of soldiers arrived and attacked the anti-Ameri-can demonstrators.
5. The recently-discovered mummy is more than two-thousand years old.
6. The twelve member jury decided that the defendant was guilty.
7. Our gas tank was two thirds full when we left.

35 Underlining and Italics

Italics, or italic type, *looks like this.* The letters are slanted. Underlining and italics have the same use. We use underlining when we write by hand or on a typewriter, and we use italics when we write on a computer.

▶ **The Wall Street Journal** publishes business and financial news.

▶ *The Wall Street Journal* publishes business and financial news.

35a Titles of long works

Italicize (or underline) titles of most long works.

Books

▶ *Harry Potter and the Sorcerer's Stone*   *War and Peace*

BUT Do not italicize (or underline) the titles of holy books or legal documents.

▶ **the Bible**   **the Constitution**

Newspapers, magazines, pamphlets

▶ *The New York Times*   *Ten Tips for Taking Tests*   *Newsweek*

BUT Do not italicize (or underline) titles of articles in magazines and newspapers. Put quotation marks around them instead.

▶ An article in *National Geographic* entitled **"Vanishing Cultures"** tells about three cultures that are struggling to survive in the modern world.

Long poems, long musical works, record albums, CDs

▶ Milton's **Paradise Lost**   the Beatles' **Abbey Road**

▶ Beethoven's **Symphony No. 5**   Michael Jackson's **Thriller**

BUT Do not italicize (or underline) the titles of short poems or individual songs. Put quotation marks around them instead.

▶ "The Road Not Taken"   "Jingle Bells"

Plays, musicals, operas, films, television and radio programs

▶ *Romeo and Juliet*   *Star Wars*

▶ *The Phantom of the Opera*   *Sesame Street*

▶ *Madame Butterfly*   *CBS News at Noon*

Paintings and sculptures

▶ Picasso's **Guernica**   Rodin's **The Thinker**

Computer software and Web sites

▶ Microsoft **Word**   *toefl.org*

▶ *Encarta 2000 Encyclopedia*   *calpoly.edu*

Ships, airplanes, spacecraft, trains

▶ the *Titanic*   *Mir*

▶ the *Spirit of Saint Louis*   the *Shanghai Express*

NOTE: Some academic fields do not require either underlining or italicizing in research paper documentation. Always ask your instructor or a librarian before using italics and underlining in research paper citations and works cited lists.

35b Foreign words

Italicize (or underline) a foreign word or phrase that your reader might not know.

▶ *quinceaños*   *Galgenhumor*   *feng shui*

Do not italicize foreign words that are commonly used in English, such as "salsa" and "sushi." When you are not sure about a particular word or phrase, check a dictionary.

▶ They settled the problem *mano a mano.*

    BUT

▶ Every Friday, the entire office goes out for **sushi.**

When you add an English translation of a foreign word or phrase, enclose the translation in both quotations marks and parentheses.

▶ My Hawaiian neighbors made me feel like a member of their *ohana* (**"family"**).

Always italicize Latin scientific names.

▶ *Homo sapiens*   *Ursus horribilis*   *Rosa caroliniana*

35c Numbers, letters, and words used as words

Italicize (or underline) numbers, letters, and words used as words.

▶ The number *13* is an unlucky number in many cultures.
▶ The *b* in the words *doubt* and *debt* is not pronounced in English.

❗ *Special Tips*

1. Don't underline words just to make them seem more important. Choose stronger words instead.

   deafening.
   ▶ The music was ~~really loud~~.

2. If you underline two or more words in a row, underline the space between the words, too.

   ▶ Crime Statistics: The Misuse of Numbers

PRACTICE—Section 35

Underline words where necessary in the following sentences. (Use a dictionary for this exercise if you wish.)

EXAMPLE
Have you read the latest issue of <u>Time</u> magazine?

1. Hemingway's novel The Old Man and the Sea takes place in Cuba.
2. She spent the entire day preparing hors d'oeuvres for her guests.
3. Humuhumunukunukuapua'a is the very long Hawaiian name for a very small Hawaiian fish. Its Latin scientific name is even longer: Rhinecanthus rectangulus.
4. I always forget to put two n's in the word millennium.
5. Two-year-old Mark can't pronounce the letter y, so he can't say the word yes; instead, he says "ess."
6. Did you read today's front-page story in the Los Angeles Times?
7. She subscribes to three news magazines: Time, Newsweek, and U.S. News & World Report.

36　Abbreviations

 Computer Note

Spelling checkers and grammar checkers can find some abbreviation errors, such as *Mon.* (for "Monday") and *econ* (for "economics"), but they will not find all problems. Always check your own writing. Consult a dictionary if you are not sure.

In general, we do not use abbreviations in formal writing except those listed here in *Sections 36a–c.* In scientific and technical writing, on the other hand, many more abbreviations are allowed. If you are writing in these fields, ask your instructor for guidance.

The punctuation and capitalization of abbreviations vary widely because they frequently change. For example, you can find the abbreviation for *electronic mail* written in three ways: *email, E-mail,* and *e-mail.* Furthermore, British and American English differ in the use of periods with names and titles of people.

American English	British English
▶ **Mr. R. W. Henderson**	**Mr R W Henderson**

In general, the modern trend is to write abbreviations without periods, but it is acceptable to write many abbreviations both ways.

▶ **PhD** OR **Ph.D.**	**BA** OR **B.A.**
▶ **USA** OR **U.S.A.**	**AM** OR **A.M.** OR **a.m.**

In general, abbreviations composed of all capital letters do not have periods or spaces between letters.

▶ **UN**	**NY**
▶ **CD-ROM**	**ATM**

In general, abbreviations composed of small letters or ending in a small letter have periods and no spaces between letters.

▶ **etc.**	**Mr.**
▶ **Ave.**	**Inc.**

But there are many exceptions.

▶ **mph**	**cm**
▶ **km**	**cc**

The rules and examples in this handbook are general guidelines. There are many variations and exceptions. When there are several possible ways to abbreviate (for example, *A.M., AM,* or *a.m.*), be consistent. Don't write *6:00 A.M.* and then *6:00 a.m.* later on.

36a Titles of people

Abbreviate titles used before and after people's names.

Titles before names	Titles after names
▶ **Mr.** Cesar Chavez	Karen J. McClain, **RN** (OR **R.N.**)
▶ **Mrs.** Cesar Chavez	Ingrid S. Kassler, **MA** (OR **M.A.**)
▶ **Ms.** Gloria Steinem	Stanley Hing, **CPA** (OR **C.P.A.**)
▶ **Miss** Soon Li	Robert W. Henderson, **Esq.**
▶ **Prof.** Indiana Jones	
▶ **Rev.** Jesse Jackson	

NOTE: *Miss* is not followed by a period because *Miss* is not an abbreviation. It is included here for reference.

Doctors (medical doctors, dentists, PhDs, and EdDs) can use a title either before or after their names.

▶ **Dr.** Margaret Hsu	OR	Margaret Hsu, **MD** (OR **M.D.**)
▶ **Dr.** Marta Rodriguez	OR	Marta Rodriguez, **DDS** (OR **D.D.S.**)
▶ **Dr.** Walter Seuss	OR	Walter Seuss, **PhD** (OR **Ph.D.**)

! Special Tips

1. Don't abbreviate a title without a name.

         professor
  ▶ Dr. Seuss is a ~~prof.~~ of Hispanic literature.

2. Don't use a title both before and after a name.

  ▶ ~~Dr.~~ Margaret Hsu, MD   OR   Dr. Margaret Hsu, ~~MD~~

36b Dates and times

Use the following abbreviations with these kinds of dates and times.

▶ 44 **BC** (OR **B.C.**)	"before Christ"; before the beginning of Western calendar time; place it after numbers
▶ **AD** (OR **A.D.**) 1492	*anno Domini,* "in the year of our Lord"; after the beginning of Western calendar time; place it before numbers
▶ 11:26 **a.m.** (OR **AM** OR **A.M.**)	*ante meridiem,* "before midday"
▶ 8:00 **p.m.** (OR **PM** OR **P.M.**)	*post meridiem,* "after midday"

> **!** *Special Tip*

Don't use a.m. and p.m. without numbers.

                    morning

▶ Most of my classes are in the a.~~m.~~

36c Familiar abbreviations

You may use some kinds of abbreviations as long as they are familiar to your readers. Particular abbreviations are familiar to particular groups of people. If your readers might not know an abbreviation, write out the complete name the first time you use it and show its abbreviation in parentheses. After that, use the abbreviation.

▶ **The Information Technology Department** (IT) will give free classes for employees. Contact **IT** for information and schedules.

Abbreviations familiar to English speakers in the United States and Canada include the following.

Universities	▶ UCLA, NYU, MIT
Corporations	▶ IBM, BBC, UPS
Organizations	▶ YMCA, EU, UN, OPEC
Government agencies	▶ FBI, CIA, INS, IRS
Products and machines	▶ TV, VCR, CD, VW, ATM, MRI, PC
Tests	▶ SAT, GRE
Countries	▶ USA, UK
Acronyms*	▶ AIDS, RAM, ROM, NATO, SALT, NAFTA, TOEFL

*Acronyms are abbreviations pronounced as words.

> **!** *Special Tips*

1. Don't write names of countries in all capital letters. Capitalize only the first letters of the main words. We write USA in capital letters because it is an abbreviation of "United States of America." ROK is an abbreviation for "Republic of Korea." "Japan" and "Saudi Arabia" are not abbreviations.

           Japan   *Saudi Arabia*

  ▶ I am from ~~JAPAN~~.   ▶ ~~SAUDI ARABIA~~ is my native country.

2. Don't abbreviate names of countries in sentences. Write out the name in words.

                    United Kingdom

  ▶ My family immigrated to the ~~U.K.~~ in 1998.

EXCEPTION: You may use the abbreviation U.S. (with periods) as an adjective, but not as a noun.

▶ She became a U.S. citizen two years ago. BUT

                United States
▶ She has lived in the U.S. for ten years.

36d Postal codes

Use the two-letter abbreviations for the states of the United States and the provinces of Canada. They are written in capital letters without periods or spaces. Use these abbreviations in addresses only. In sentences, write out the names in full.

▶ **NY** (New York)   **CA** (California)   **ON** (Ontario)   **BC** (British Columbia)

36e Latin abbreviations

In general, don't use Latin abbreviations. Always write out the English meaning. A few common Latin abbreviations are listed here for reference only.

▶ **ca.**	*circa,* "approximately"	**etc.**	*et cetera,* "and so on"
▶ **cf.**	*confer,* "compare"	**i.e.**	*id est,* "that is"
▶ **e.g.**	*exempli gratia,* "for example"	**NB**	*nota bene,* "note well"
▶ **et al.**	*et alii,* "and others"	**vs.**	*versus,* "against, opposing"

36f Words usually not abbreviated

Don't abbreviate these kinds of words in formal writing.

	miles *kilometers*
Units of measurement	▶ A marathon race is 26 mi. or 41.3 km.
	Street *Massachusetts*
Geographical names and parts of addresses	▶ She lives at 358 State St., Boston, MA.
	Monday *September*
Names of days, months, holidays	▶ Classes begin on Mon. morning, Sept. 21.
	Department *Corporation*
Parts of a business name and divisions of a business	▶ Her job is in the Marketing Dept. of Starex Corp.
	Junior
Parts of the name of a school and names of academic subjects	▶ She graduated from Santa Rosa Jr. College, where
	political science
	she studied poly sci.

> **!** ***Special Tip***

Never use abbreviations to save time or space.

         minutes   *appointment*   *professor*

▶ I was ten ~~mins.~~ early for my ~~appt.~~ with the ~~prof.~~

PRACTICE—Section 36

Edit the following sentences to correct errors in abbreviations.

EXAMPLE

           miles   *hours*

We drove 500 ~~mi.~~ in six ~~hrs.~~

1. In the U.S., Thanksgiving is always on the fourth Thurs. in Nov.
2. Our chem instructor will not hold office hrs tomorrow p.m.
3. My aunt is an assistant mgr. at Coca-Cola Co.
4. She works from 8:30 a.m. until 4:30 PM Mon. through Fri.
5. Please send information about your health plan to Dr. William J. Bryan, Ph.D.
6. My address is 3015 Ninth Ave., NY, NY 10021.

37 Numbers

> **Computer Note**
>
> A grammar checker can find some errors in writing numbers. For example, it will tell you if you begin a sentence with numerals. However, it will not notice all errors, so always proofread your writing.

This section explains when to write out numbers as words (*fifteen*) and when to write them as numerals (*15*). These general rules may differ from the rules in your field of study, especially if you study a science or technical field. Ask your instructor for guidance when you write scientific or technical papers.

37a Numbers written as words

  I. Write out numbers that are one or two words long.

    ▶ I have **five** brothers and sisters.

    ▶ I spent **two hundred** hours on my art class project.

  Use numerals for numbers of three or more words.

                         175

    ▶ My aunt owns **~~one hundred seventy-five~~** pairs of shoes.

2. Write out all numbers that begin a sentence.

> *One million*
> ▶ ~~1,000,000~~ people died in a hurricane in Bangladesh in 1970.

> *Sixty*
> ▶ ~~60~~ percent of the class received a passing grade.

> *Five*
> ▶ ~~5~~ of our classmates have dropped out.

When the number is more than two words, rewrite the sentence.

> An earthquake killed 750,000 people in China in 1976.
> ▶ **Seven hundred fifty thousand** ~~people died in an earthquake in China in 1976.~~

3. Write out people's ages and simple fractions. (Simple fractions are *one-fourth, two-thirds, one-half, fifteen-sixteenths,* and so on.)

> ▶ My youngest sister is **five**, and my oldest sister is **twenty-three**.
> ▶ I spend **one-third** of my salary on rent.

Write out in word the age of a person over one hundred.

> ▶ The oldest person in our town died at the age of 123.

4. When numbers are in a series, do not mix words and numerals.

> *50*
> ▶ My aunt owns **175** pairs of shoes, ~~fifty~~ pairs of boots, and **35** pairs of sandals.

5. When two numbers are together, write one number in words and the other number in numerals.

> *$20*
> ▶ The ATM machine gave me **five** ~~twenty-dollar~~ bills.

> *fifty-three*
> ▶ There are ~~53~~ **14,000-foot** mountains in Colorado.

> *89*
> ▶ My mother at ~~eighty-nine~~, and her brother at 103.

6. Use a combination of numerals and words for round numbers larger than one million. (Round numbers are numbers that are reduced to the nearest convenient decimal.)

> ▶ The storm caused **$1.2 million** in damage.
> ▶ In 1998, there were **2.5 million** refugees in the world.

7. Do not combine symbols (%, $, ¢, ¥, ', ") or abbreviations (lb, oz, km, KB, a.m.) and numbers written as words. In general, avoid using symbols and abbreviations in formal writing (except in scientific and technical fields).

> ▶ **Sixty percent** (BUT **60%**)
> ▶ **Two hundred** dollars (BUT **$200**)
> ▶ **Five** feet **six** inches (BUT **5'6"**)
> ▶ **Twenty-five** pounds (BUT **25 lb**)
> ▶ **Eight** centimeters (BUT **8 cm**)

37b Numbers written as numerals

The following kinds of numbers are usually written as numerals.

Numbers of three or more words	▶ **650,000**
Dates	▶ **60** BC (OR B.C.)
	▶ December **31, 1999**
	▶ **12/31/99**
Addresses	▶ **1630** Main Street, Apt. **16**-C
	▶ **2458** West **109**th Avenue
	▶ **1501** Tenth Street
Time of day	▶ **6:30** p.m. (OR P.M. OR PM)

EXCEPTION: Write the time in words with *o'clock, in the morning, in the afternoon, in the evening, at night, noon,* and *midnight.*

> ▶ **six o'clock** in the evening

> ▶ **twelve** noon

> ▶ **twelve** midnight

Decimals	▶ **3.345 0.334**
Fractions with a whole number	▶ **3⅜ 1½**
Exact amounts of money	▶ **$1.25 $212.32**

NOTE: You may write round amounts of money as words or numerals.

> ▶ **two hundred dollars** OR **$200**

Statistics and sports scores	▶ a ratio of **3 to 1**
	▶ a final score of **2–0**
Divisions of books and plays	▶ volume **56**, chapter **2**, pages **33–34**
	▶ act **4**, scene **3**, line **256**

NOTE: Act and scene numbers of plays are often written in Roman numerals.

> ▶ act **IV**, scene **iii**, line 256

37c Forming plural numbers

Add *-s* to make a numeral plural.

▶ So far, John has received one 100, two **95s,** and three **85s** on his weekly math tests.

Numbers written as words follow normal spelling rules.

▸ There were **hundreds** of young people at the concert.

▸ My mother is in her **eighties.**

▸ How fast can you count by **sixes**? (*6, 12, 18, 24, and so on*)

! Special Tips

The way of writing numbers in your language may differ from the way of writing numbers in English on these four points.

1. Use commas, not periods, in large numbers.

▸ A mile is **1,609** meters.

▸ His medical bills were more than **$300,000** last year.

2. Use periods, not commas, in decimals.

▸ A mile is **1.6** kilometers.

▸ π = **3.1416**

3. Write the parts of a date in month-day-year order.

▸ **11/19/82**   NOT   19/11/82

4. The words *hundred, million,* and *billion* are singular even after numbers like *five* and after the word *several.* Use the plural forms *hundreds, millions,* and *billions* only when there is no number.

▸ five **hundred** fish   BUT   **hundreds** of fish

▸ fifty **thousand** dollars   BUT   **thousands** of dollars

▸ several **billion** stars   BUT   **billions** of stars

PRACTICE—Section 37

Edit the following sentences to correct errors in writing numbers.

EXAMPLE

         March 15, 1988   two

I was born on ~~3/15/88~~, and my sister was born exactly ~~2~~ years later.

1. 3 classes were canceled last week.
2. The war cost several millions dollars.
3. The U.S. flag has 13 stripes and fifty stars.
4. Nearly ½ of the class has the flu.
5. They invited more than 100 people to their wedding.
6. The company lost more than 1,750,000 million dollars last year.

38 Spelling

> ### Computer Note
>
> Spelling checkers in word processing programs are a great help to writers who use computers. If you write on a computer, by all means use the spelling checker! It can find most spelling and typing mistakes. However, do not depend on it to catch all errors. Spelling checkers can tell you if you type *changable* instead of *changeable,* but they can't tell if you type *form* instead of *from* since both are English words. In order to catch this kind of error, always proofread your writing even after you use a spelling checker.

Unlike the spelling of other languages, English spelling is not very regular or predictable. You cannot always predict how to spell a word from its pronunciation or how to pronounce it from its spelling. There are a few spelling rules that you can learn. However, the rules have exceptions. It is always best to consult a dictionary when you are not sure about a specific word.

38a *ei* or *ie* rule

Every schoolchild memorizes the following rhyme to learn how to spell words with *ie* or *ei*: "*I* before *e* except after *c* and when sounded like 'ay' as in *neighbor* and *weigh*."

I BEFORE *E*	*E* BEFORE *I*	"AY" SOUND
bel**ie**ve	rec**ei**ve	**ei**ght
p**ie**ce	rec**ei**pt	w**ei**ght

EXCEPTIONS: **foreign, either, height, leisure, seize, weird**

38b Adding suffixes

Suffixes are word parts that you add to the end of words. Sometimes you add suffixes like *-ed* to change a verb from present to past tense. Sometimes you add suffixes to change a word's part of speech—to change a verb to a noun or an adjective to an adverb, for example.

Words ending in -e

When you add suffixes to words ending in *-e*, sometimes you drop the *e* and sometimes you keep it. Here are the rules.

1. Drop the final *-e* before suffixes beginning with a vowel.

   mov̶e + ing = **mov**ing   lov̶e + able = **lov**able

   us̶e + ual = **us**ual   sincer̶e + ity = **sincer**ity

   nic̶e + er = **nic**er   saf̶e + est = **saf**est

   EXCEPTIONS: Words ending in soft *g* and *c* sounds keep the *e*.

   courage + ous = **courage**ous   change + able = **change**able

   advantage + ous = **advantage**ous   notice + able = **notice**able

2. Keep final *-e* before suffixes beginning with a consonant.

   move + ment = **move**ment   love + ly = **love**ly

   nine + ty = **nine**ty   sincere + ly = **sincere**ly

   EXCEPTIONS:

   judg̶e + ment = **judg**ment   tru̶e + ly = **tru**ly

   argu̶e + ment = **argu**ment   tru̶e + th = **tru**th

   aw̶e + ful = **aw**ful   nin̶e + th = **nin**th

Words ending in -y

When you add suffixes to words ending in *-y*, sometimes you drop the *y* and sometimes you keep it.

1. When there is a vowel before final *-y*, keep the *y*.

   play + ed = **play**ed   key + s = **key**s

   say + ing = **say**ing   boy + ish = **boy**ish

2. When there is a consonant before final *-y*, change the *y* to *i*.

   tr̶y + ed = **tri**ed   tr̶y + es = **tri**es

   rely + able = **reli**able   happy + ness = **happi**ness

   marry + age = **marri**age   library + es = **librari**es

   friendly + er = **friendli**er   busy + est = **busi**est

   EXCEPTIONS:

   - Don't change *y* to *i* when you add *-ing*.

     try + ing = **try**ing   rely + ing = **rely**ing

   - Don't change proper names when you add *-s* to make them plural.

     one Mary, two **Mary**s

Doubling rule

When you add a suffix that begins with a vowel to a word that ends in a single vowel and a single consonant, sometimes you double the final consonant.

1. Double the final consonant when the word is one syllable.

tip + ing = **tipp**ing

bit + en = **bitt**en

EXCEPTIONS:

fax + es = **fax**es

box + ing = **box**ing

2. Double the final consonant when the word ends in a stressed syllable.

omit + ed = **omitt**ed

forget + ing = **forgett**ing

regret + able = **regrett**able

38c Forming plurals

Regular plural nouns

Add -s

We form the plural of most nouns in English by adding -*s*.

Common nouns		Proper nouns	
book	books	one Mary	two Marys
apple	apples	one Simpson	two Simpsons

Add -es

We form the plural of nouns ending in -*s*, -*sh*, -*ch*, -*x*, or -*z* by adding -*es*.

Common nouns		Proper nouns	
business	businesses	Gonzales	the Gonzaleses
wish	wishes	Fox	the Foxes
church	churches	Williams	the Williamses
fax	faxes		
quiz	quizzes (*Note the double z.*)		

EXCEPTIONS: monarchs, stomachs (*because here* ch *is pronounced* /k/)

Nouns ending in -y

We form the plural of nouns ending in *-y* in two ways:

Vowel before –y: + -s		Consonant before -y: *i* + -es	
attorney	attorneys	city	cities
boy	boys	country	countries
key	keys	lady	ladies
ray	rays	memory	memories
valley	valleys	story	stories

Nouns ending in -f

For nouns ending in *-f* and *-fe,* we change *f* to *v* and add *-es.*

calf	calves	loaf	loaves
half	halves	self	selves
knife	knives	thief	thieves
leaf	leaves	wife	wives
life	lives	wolf	wolves

EXCEPTIONS: beliefs, roofs, chiefs

We can form the plural of a few words either way.

scarf	scarfs OR scarves
hoof	hoofs OR hooves
wharf	wharfs OR wharves

Nouns ending in -o

Nouns ending in *-o* sometimes add *-s* and sometimes *-es.*

Add -s		Add -es	
auto	autos	echo	echoes
kilo	kilos	hero	heroes
memo	memos	potato	potatoes
photo	photos	tomato	tomatoes
piano	pianos		
radio	radios	Add -s or -es	
solo	solos	cargo	cargos OR cargoes
soprano	sopranos	mango	mangos OR mangoes
studio	studios	motto	mottos OR mottoes
tattoo	tattoos	volcano	volcanos OR volcanoes
video	videos	zero	zeros OR zeroes
zoo	zoos		

Irregular plural nouns

Irregular plurals

A few nouns are completely irregular.

man	**men**	foot	**feet**	person	**people**
woman	**women**	tooth	**teeth**	mouse	**mice**
child	**children**	goose	**geese**		

Plural same as singular

A few nouns have the same singular and plural forms.

deer	**deer**	means	**means**
fish	**fish**	series	**series**
sheep	**sheep**	species	**species**

No singular

A few nouns have no singular.

▶ The **police** *are* investigating the crime.

cattle	clothes	(eye)glasses
police	jeans	scissors
	pajamas	
	pants	
	shorts	
	trousers	

Jeans, pajamas, scissors, (eye)glasses, and others are plural even though they refer to a single item. To make them singular, you can add *pair of.*

▶ My new **jeans** *are* too small.   ▶ My new **pair** of jeans *is* too small.

Singular

A few nouns that end in *-s* are singular.

economics	news	the Netherlands
mathematics	athletics	the Philippines
physics	gymnastics	the United Nations
statistics	measles	the United States
	mumps	

▶ **Gymnastics** *is* a popular Olympic sport.
▶ **The Philippines** *is* a nation of 7,000 islands.

Plural foreign nouns

English plural

Some foreign nouns that have become part of the English language now have English plural forms.

gymnasium	gymnasiums	index	index**es**
memorandum	memorandums	thesaurus	thesaurus**es**
kindergarten	kindergartens		

Foreign plural

Other foreign nouns have the plural form of the original language.

datum	data*	alumnus	alumn**i**
bacterium	bacteria*	nucleus	nucle**i**
medium	media*	alumna	alumn**ae**
millennium	millenn**ia**	analysis	analys**es**
criterion	criteria	basis	bas**es**
phenomenon	phenomena	crisis	cris**es**
		thesis	thes**es**

*These words are used mainly as plural nouns.

Special plurals

Compound nouns

Compound nouns add -s to the main noun, not to the end of the whole word.

sister-in-law	sisters-in-law (NOT sister-in-law~~s~~)
passerby	passersby (NOT passerby~~s~~)

Abbreviations

Make the plurals of abbreviations, numbers, and words used as words by adding -s.

CD**s**	MD**s**	1990**s**	*ands*
TV**s**	PhD**s**	two 9.8**s**	*buts*

▶ I borrowed several **CDs** for my party.
▶ The gymnast received eight perfect **10s** and two **9.8s**.
▶ Don't use too many ***ands*** and ***buts*** in one sentence.

However, in two situations, add apostrophe + -s.

1. Use an apostrophe + -s to make the plural of letters of the alphabet.

   ▶ There are four **s's** and four **i's** in the word *Mississippi.*
   ▶ The teacher gave two **A's** and ten **F's** last semester.

2. Use an apostrophe + -s to make the plural of abbreviations that have more than one period, such as *M.D.* and *Ph.D.* However, the modern style is to omit the periods from these abbreviations. In this case, add -s without an apostrophe.

   ▶ My mother has two **Ph.D.'s**: one in English and one in philosophy. OR
   ▶ My mother has two **PhDs**: one in English and one in philosophy. (*modern style*)

Whenever you are not sure about how to form a plural, consult a dictionary. If you wish to use a plural foreign noun that you cannot find in a dictionary, use the plural form of the original language.

PRACTICE—Sections 38a–c

Write the plural form of the following nouns.

1. hand	7. scissors	13. belief
2. eye	8. day	14. tooth
3. glass	9. daisy	15. crisis
4. box	10. potato	16. 100
5. brother-in-law	11. video	17. CD-ROM
6. fish	12. knife	18. X

38d British and American spelling

Following are some common differences in British and American spelling.

American spelling	British spelling
-ll-	*-l-*
fulfill, skillful	fulfil, skilful
fulfillment, enrollment, installment	fulfilment, enrolment, instalment
-led, -ling	*-lled, -lling*
canceled, canceling	cancelled, cancelling
traveled, traveling	travelled, travelling
-er	*-re*
center, theater, fiber, meter	centre, theatre, fibre, metre

American spelling	British spelling
-or	-our
color, labor, honor	colour, labour, honour
neighbor, behavior	neighbour, behaviour
-ection	-exion
connection, reflection	connexion, reflexion
-ense	-ence
defense, offense, license	defence, offence, licence
-e-	-ae-
encyclopedia, medieval	encyclopaedia, mediaeval
-ed	-t
burned, learned, leaped,	burnt, learnt, leapt,
smelled, spelled, spoiled	smelt, spelt, spoilt
-ment	-ement
judgment, argument,	judgement, arguement,
acknowledgment	acknowledgement
-ize, -ization	-ise, -isation
realize, realization	realise, realisation
civilize, civilization	civilise, civilisation
memorize, memorization	memorise, memorisation
industrialize, industrialization	industrialise, industrialisation

39 Writing in English

Good writing in English is very different from good writing in other languages, such as Arabic or Japanese or Spanish. Everyone expects differences in grammar, but there is another difference that is equally important. This difference is the way writers organize and express their ideas.

English writing: direct and linear

In contrast to some other languages, English writing is *direct;* you state your thoughts in a straightforward and forceful manner when you write in English. You do not present your ideas delicately or subtly, as good writing in some languages requires. English writing is also *linear;* ideas flow in a straight line. You stay on one topic from beginning to end without making any "detours," as some languages allow. You don't add new ideas, even if they are interesting and are somewhat related to the main topic.

Other languages: different ways

The direct and linear style of English writing comes from Anglo-European cultural patterns. Other cultures and languages have developed different styles. Here are some examples:

Arabic and Persian speakers write in a parallel style. In parallel style, important ideas are often repeated. The repetitions are connected with coordinating words, such as *and* and *but.* In English, style is often judged by the degree of subordination rather than by the degree of coordination. Therefore, the Arabic and Persian styles of writing, with their emphasis on coordination, seem awkward to an English reader.

Some Asian writers, on the other hand, use an indirect approach. In Asian writing, the topic is viewed from several angles. The topic is never analyzed directly; it is referred to only indirectly. This indirect style is unnecessarily vague to an English reader. English readers want writers to state the main point right at the beginning and to explain it openly and clearly.

Spanish writing style differs from English style in another way. In English writing, every sentence in a paragraph follows a straight line from beginning to end, but a Spanish-speaking writer makes detours. A Spanish paragraph may begin and end on the same topic, but the writer often takes the reader on interesting side trips that are not directly related to the main point. This style breaks one of the important rules of English writing—the rule of paragraph unity.

Direct, linear writing may seem unsophisticated to people who are good writers in another language, and they may become frustrated while learning this new way of thinking and writing. Remember that no way of writing is either better or worse than other ways—the styles are just different.

English organizational patterns

Good writing in English requires that you organize your thoughts in ways that are familiar to native speakers. Native speakers are accustomed to seeing a long piece of writing divided into paragraphs, each paragraph discussing a single idea. They also expect to find a sentence near the beginning of each paragraph that states that paragraph's main point. Finally, they are used to having information presented in a certain order, such as time order or order of importance.

Sections 41 and *42* of this handbook explain the structure of English paragraphs and essays and the different patterns of organization that native speakers of English commonly use.

40   The Writing Process

Writing is a process of creating, organizing, writing, and polishing. In the first step of the process, you create ideas. In the second step, you organize the ideas. In the third step, you write a rough draft. In the final step, you polish your rough draft by editing it and making revisions.

40a   Creating

The first step in the writing process is to choose a topic and collect information about it. This step is often called *prewriting* because you do the step *before* you start writing.

Choosing a topic

For some writing assignments, you do not choose your own topic because your teacher or your boss tells you what to write about. When you do choose your own topic, however, here are two tips for making a good choice.

Topic should interest you

Choose a topic that interests you. It is always easier to write about a subject that you enjoy. If you aren't sure what you are interested in, pay attention to what kinds of newspaper and magazine articles you read. Do your eyes stop at stories about new discoveries in science? Do you turn immediately to the travel or entertainment sections of the newspaper? If you spend time watching television or exploring the Internet, what captures your interest when you are flipping through TV channels or surfing the Net? Paying attention to your habits may help you discover good topics to write about.

Topic size should fit assignment

Choose a topic small enough for the assignment. A common mistake of beginning writers is to choose a topic that is too big. When you choose a topic that is too big, you aren't able to explain it completely. You are only able to discuss it very generally, without the details that make writing informative and interesting to readers.

- If your assignment is to write a one-page paragraph, don't choose "Sports" as your topic. Don't even choose "Basketball" or "NBA Basketball Stars" or "Shaquille O'Neal." For a one-page paragraph, you might write about one aspect of Shaq's game, such as his early difficulty making free throws.

- If your assignment is to write a 1500-word essay (about four double-spaced typewritten pages), you might write about two or three aspects of Shaq's basketball skills and his effect on the game.

- If your assignment is to write a 15-page research paper, you could write even more about Shaq. You could write about his childhood, family life, basketball training, business interests, and so on.

- If your assignment is to write a 300-page book, you could write about the history of basketball!

Collecting information and developing ideas

There are several ways to collect information and develop ideas. For some writing tasks, you will need to go to outside sources such as newspapers, magazines, library books, or the Internet. For other assignments, you can interview friends, classmates, and neighbors to get their ideas and opinions. For still other writing tasks, you can search your own brain and life experiences for ideas. Four useful techniques for exploring within yourself are:

- Journal writing
- Freewriting
- Listing
- Clustering

Journal writing

Journal writing is one way to get and develop ideas. A journal is a collection of personal writing. In a journal, you can record your daily experiences. You can write down quotations that are meaningful to you. You might write about a dream that you had. You can write one sentence or several pages. The advantage of writing a journal is that you are writing only for yourself. You can write your thoughts and explore ideas without worrying what other people will think. A personal journal can be a very rich source of ideas.

November 15, 2002

10:30 p.m.

Today was a good day. I think I made a new friend. An American girl in my art class started talking to me. She just talked about what we were doing in class, how I liked the class and the teacher, and things like that. She DIDN'T ask me "foreigner" questions the way most people here do. Americans always want to know where I am from and how long I've been here and what language I speak etc., etc., etc. I get tired of answering the same questions all the time. Maybe they (Americans) are really interested, or maybe they are just trying to be friendly, but questions about my background make me feel that I'll always be a stranger here. Anyway, that girl was very nice and I can practice speaking English with her.

Freewriting

Freewriting is a technique in which you write on one topic nonstop for a specified period of time. Write sentences about whatever ideas come into your mind while you are thinking about the topic. Don't stop to think about grammar or spelling. Just keep moving your pencil across the page or your fingers on the computer keyboard. At the end of the specified time, stop. Read what you have written and mark any key words or phrases that might spark more ideas. Then begin freewriting again about these key words. You may have to practice this technique a few times before ideas flow easily, but with practice, it will happen. You may be surprised at the number of ideas that will pour out.

> *I have to freewrite for ten minutes about my favorite possession. I don't*
>
> *know what to write about. Maybe my ⬚photo⬚ album. No, that's not good.*
>
> *Maybe I should write about something from my childhood, like my favorite toy.*
>
> *No. Favorite what? Maybe my favorite possession is not a thing. Maybe it's*
>
> *something like ⬚my family,⬚ or my mother's empanadas. Well, I am stuck. I need*
>
> *to keep writing. Favorite possession. Does it have to be a thing? I don't think*
>
> *things are very important. We didn't have a lot of things when I was younger.*
>
> *Maybe that's why I can't think of anything. What keeps coming into my mind*
>
> *is my family. To me, that is more important than any thing. My parents*
>
> *showed each other and us children so much love. That is certainly my favorite*
>
> *"possession"—⬚my family's love.⬚ Well, that doesn't mean that we never had*
>
> *fights. Of course my brothers and sisters and I fought with each other. A lot.*
>
> *But we always supported each other. I remember one time when I was*

By the end of the ten minutes, this writer had found something to write about:
her family's love. Since her teacher wanted her to write about a favorite
possession, she then decided that her favorite possession was a photograph of
her family. She could then freewrite further to develop more ideas about her
family and their love for one another. Soon, she had enough material for a
thoughtful and interesting paragraph or essay.

Listing

Listing is a technique in which you think about a topic and quickly make a list
of whatever words or phrases come into your mind. You shouldn't write
complete sentences. Just write words and phrases. The goal is to list as many
ideas as possible without worrying about correct spelling or relevance of ideas.
In the following example, a student was asked to write about his job.

"My Job"

waiter in a restaurant	polished shoes
busy	tips—sharing
hard work—on feet all the time	learning the job was hard
rush hours—lunch and dinner	computer system difficult at first
have to work fast	manager sometimes hard to get along with
have to be friendly	*biggest mistake—forgot to put order for
sometimes make mistakes*	an entire table into computer
kitchen staff also make mistakes	can work nights, have free time during day
head chef forgot to put sugar in pie	holidays—sometimes have to work
personal appearance important	free food
hair—short, clean, no wild hairstyles	some customers nice, others rude and
clean fingernails especially important	demanding
uniform clean and ironed	some customers in a hurry, others take
have to get along with buspersons and	3 hours to eat
host/hostess	

After listing these ideas, the writer reviewed his list. He identified four main ideas, which he underlined and numbered. Next, he put each of the other ideas into one of the four main groups. He crossed out ideas that didn't fit into a group and added new ones. He now has material for at least four paragraphs about his topic.

"My Job"

waiter in a restaurant	④ polished shoes
busy	~~tips—sharing~~
① <u>hard work</u>—on feet all the time	③ <u>learning the job</u> was hard
① rush hours—lunch and dinner	③ computer system difficult at first
① have to work fast	② manager sometimes hard to get along with
② <u>have to be friendly</u>	③ *biggest mistake—forgot to put order for
③ sometimes make mistakes*	an entire table into computer
~~kitchen staff also make mistakes~~	~~can work nights, have free time during day~~
~~head chef forgot to put sugar in pie~~	~~holidays—sometimes have to work~~
④ <u>personal appearance</u> important	~~free food~~
④ hair—short, clean, no wild hairstyles	② some customers nice, others rude and
④ clean fingernails especially important	demanding
④ uniform clean and ironed	② some customers in a hurry, others take
② have to get along with buspersons and	3 hours to eat
host/hostess	

Clustering

Clustering is another way to get ideas. In this technique, you write the main topic inside a circle at the center of a piece of paper. Then you write words and phrases in smaller circles around the main circle. As you get more ideas, you write them in still smaller circles. When you are finished, you have groups of connected circles. These groups of connected circles are called clusters. There are enough ideas in each cluster of circles in the diagram for a paragraph.

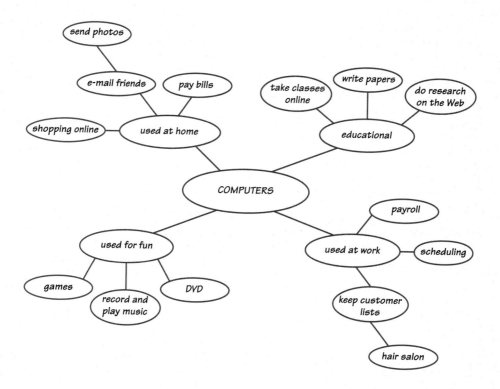

PRACTICE—Section 40a

Practice freewriting, listing, and clustering for ten minutes each on one of the following topics. You may practice all three prewriting methods on one topic, or you may choose a different topic for each method. Your goal is to choose a topic and collect ideas for a 750-word essay (about two double-spaced typewritten pages).

- A good or bad high school experience
- A childhood memory
- A favorite relative
- Marriage
- Music
- Your hobby or favorite sport

40b Organizing

The next step in the writing process is to organize your ideas. Many writers do this by making an outline. Making an outline forces you to put your ideas into logical order. In addition, having an outline in front of you while you are writing keeps you "on target." You don't have to worry about running out of ideas or about which point comes next—it's all right there in your outline.

Paragraph outline

An outline can be informal or formal (see below). An informal outline is just a main idea and a list of supporting points. A formal outline has a system of numbers, letters, and indenting. The main idea appears at the top, and supporting points and supporting details appear indented (moved to the right) under the main idea. Equal ideas have the same kind of letter or number. That is, all supporting points have capital letters (A, B, C, and so on), and all details have numbers (1, 2, 3). Notice that there is no number next to the third detail in the formal outline. In a formal outline, we do not number single items.

Informal paragraph outline

```
Main idea

  • Supporting point
  • Supporting point
  • Supporting point
  • Supporting point
  • Supporting point

Conclusion
```

Formal paragraph outline

```
Main idea

  A. Supporting point 1
     1. Detail
     2. Detail

  B. Supporting point 2
     Detail

Conclusion
```

Here is a sample outline for a paragraph about using fingerprint scanners to identify people.

```
                    Fingerprint Scanners
```

Main idea

```
Fingerprints have several advantages over PINs* and
passwords as a means of personal identification.

  A. Problems with PINs and passwords
     1. People forget them.
     2. Others can steal them.

  B. Advantages
     1. Each person's fingerprints are unique.
     2. They can't be forgotten, stolen, lost, or copied.
     3. They are always with a person.
```

Conclusion

```
This new technology will become more common as software
for its use is developed.
```

*PINs = Personal Identification Numbers: numbers people use to access bank accounts, e-mail, and so on

Essay outline

An outline for an essay with several paragraphs might look like one of the following. The advantage of a formal outline is that you can more easily separate supporting points from details. Also, you can see where you need to add, delete, or rearrange. For example, in the formal outline below, the writer can easily see that there are no details for supporting point IIB and add some.

Informal essay outline

```
Introduction
-Central idea of essay

Main idea
  ● Supporting point
  ● Supporting point


Main idea

  ● Supporting point
  ● Supporting point
  ● Supporting point    Body
  ● Supporting point




Main idea
  ● Supporting point
  ● Supporting point
  ● Supporting point

Conclusion
```

Formal essay outline

```
  I. Introduction
     -Thesis statement

 II. Main idea
     A. Supporting point
        1. Detail
        2. Detail
     B. Supporting point

III. Main idea

     A. Supporting point
        1. Detail
        2. Detail
        3. Detail          Body
     B. Supporting point
        1. Detail
        2. Detail

 IV. Main idea
     A. Supporting point
        1. Detail
        2. Detail
     B. Supporting point
        Detail

  V. Conclusion
```

Here is a sample outline for an essay about culture shock. (To read part of the finished essay, turn to pages 317–318 in *Section 44a.*)

```
                    Culture Shock
  I. Introduction
     Thesis Statement: Although not everyone experiences culture shock in
     exactly the same way, many experts agree that it has roughly five
     stages.

 II. In the first stage, you are excited by your new environment.
     A. Simple difficulties—quickly overcome
        1. Telephone
        2. Public transportation
     B. Positive feelings
        1. Eager to meet people
        2. Eager to try new foods
```

III. Second stage: Differences in behavior and customs become more noticeable.
   A. Don't know social customs—difficult to make friends, "small talk"
   B. Often understand words but don't understand meaning
     Sometimes wonder why people are laughing
   C. Shopping a problem
     1. Self-service store or not?
     2. Can you exchange purchases?

IV. In the third stage, you no longer have positive feelings about the new culture.
   A. Feel that you have made a mistake in coming here
   B. Feel lonely and isolated
   C. Want to be with familiar people
     Begin to spend most of free time with people from your home country
   D. Want to eat familiar food
     1. Eat in native restaurants
     2. Food becomes an obsession

V. You know that you are in the fourth stage of culture shock when you have negative feelings about almost everything.
   A. Actively reject new culture
   B. Become critical, suspicious, and irritable
     1. Believe people are unfriendly
     2. Believe landlord is trying to cheat you
     3. Believe teachers don't like you
     4. Believe food is making you sick

VI. Finally, you reach the fifth stage.
   A. Language skills improve, self-confidence grows
     1. Able to meet people and make "small talk"
     2. Able to negotiate in business situations
   B. Begin to accept differences and tolerate them
     1. Food
     2. Clothes
     3. Behavior

VII. Conclusion

PRACTICE—Section 40b

Practice making an outline. Complete the outline that follows by filling in the blank lines with an appropriate word or group of words. There are many possible ways to complete the outline.

Television: An Educational Tool

  I. Introduction
    Thesis: Television is an educational tool for people of many different ages and interests.

  II. Television keeps you informed about news and current events.
    A. Daily news programs
      1. *CBS Nightly News*
      2. _____

    B. Weekly news programs

        1. _____

        2. _____

III. _____

      1. *Sesame Street*

      2. *Mr. Rogers' Neighborhood*

IV. There are many home improvement and repair programs.

      _____

V. _____

      1. *Cook the Italian Way*

      2. *The French Chef*

      3. *Chinese Cooking for Beginners*

VI. Television also has many good programs about nature and science.

      1. _____

      2. _____

VII. Conclusion

40c Writing

After organizing your ideas, the next step is to begin writing. The first copy is called the first or "rough" draft. *Rough* means not smooth, not polished, and a *draft* is a copy of a document.

First draft

It is a good idea to write your first draft quickly, without a lot of stops and starts. Write it all at one sitting, if possible. Your writing will be much smoother. Keep your outline in front of you and follow it. Don't worry about correct grammar, punctuation, or spelling in the first draft. You can always make corrections later. Just get the first sentence down on paper and keep going.

Topic sentence or thesis statement

If your assignment is to write a paragraph, begin with your topic sentence (the sentence that states the central idea of a paragraph) and continue. If your assignment is to write a long essay, write your thesis statement (the sentence that states the central idea of an essay) at the top of the paper. Doing so may help you stay focused on your thesis. Then you have a choice. Some writers write the introductory paragraph first. Other writers find it easier to start with a body paragraph (a paragraph in the middle of an essay) and write the introduction later. It doesn't matter where you begin as long as you keep the words flowing and stay focused on your thesis. Of course, always follow your outline if you are using one.

The examples in the next few pages show how a student writer followed the steps in the writing process. The assigned topic was "An Exciting Experience."

First, the student freewrote until he found his topic: living in the United States. Next, he made this informal outline.

An Exciting Experience

Main idea

My most exciting experience is living in the United States.

- I am living away from home for the first time.
- I miss my family and friends back home.
- I am having a lot of new experiences.
- I am learning about different cultures.

Then he wrote a first draft.

DRAFT 1

An Exciting Experience

Topic sentence

Supporting point 1

Supporting point 2

Living in the U.S. for the past six months is a great experience for me. Because being so far from my family and my friends makes me realize how much I've been missing them. Staying away from my relatives and friends helps me to recognize how much important they are to me. When we're away from all the persons and things that we appreciate we recognize the worth or importance that they have.

Supporting point 3

Supporting point 4

I am having a lot of new experiences. Traveling give us the chance to know different places, different people, and their customs. As a result of that we learn about them and they about us, too. And we can understand what similarities and what difference we have.

Reference: For more information about paragraphs, see *Section 41*. For more information about essays, see *Section 42*.

40d Polishing

The fourth and final step in the writing process is to polish what you have written. This step is also called revising and editing. Polishing is most successful if you do it in two stages. First, attack the big issues of content and organization (revising). Then work on the smaller issues of grammar and punctuation (editing).

Checklists are helpful during the polishing step. In this section are two checklists that you can use, or you can design your own checklists to fit your own special needs and writing habits.

! *Special Tip*

Your school may have a writing center or tutoring office where you can get help with your writing. Find out where to go, what services are available, and how to make an appointment. Some centers offer help on a "drop-in" basis, so you may not need an appointment.

Revising

Check your first draft and look for ways to improve the paragraph or essay as a whole. You may find that you need to change the order of some sentences or even move entire paragraphs. You may need to add more details or delete sentences that are off the topic. You may need to state your thesis more clearly. You may need to add transition signals. You may need to add a conclusion. Finally, check the format. Some questions to ask yourself are listed in the following checklist. Then write a second draft.

Revising Checklist

Content

- Is my topic interesting to my readers?
- Can my readers understand my ideas?
- Did I stay on topic throughout the entire paper?
- Did I omit any important points?

Organization

- Does each paragraph discuss only one main idea?
- Did I state the main idea clearly in one sentence?
- Are all the sentences directly related to the main idea?
- Are my supporting points in logical order?
- Did I prove each point with at least one specific detail (an example, a statistic, a quotation)?
- Does my introductory paragraph catch the reader's interest?
- Does my introductory paragraph have a clear thesis statement?
- Are the paragraphs arranged in logical order?
- Does my concluding paragraph reinforce my central idea effectively?

Coherence

- Does each sentence flow smoothly and logically into the next?
- Does each paragraph flow smoothly and logically into the next?
- Did I use transition signals effectively?

Format

- Did I use black or dark blue ink on white paper?
- Did I leave margins on both sides of the page?
- Did I indent the first line of each paragraph?
- Did I double space (if my instructor requires it)?
- Does my paragraph, essay, or report have a title?

Here is the first draft of our student writer, with the revisions he made after checking his draft with the help of the Revising Checklist. (The numbered notes at the left refer to the numbered sentences at the right.)

DRAFT 1

Change the title.	*Coming to the U.S.* ~~An Exciting Experience~~
¹Make topic sentence more specific.	¹Living in the U.S. for the past six months is a great 　　　　　　*for two reasons* experience for me. ²Because being so far from my family and my friends makes me realize how much I've been missing
³Repeats same idea as sentence 4. Delete. ⁴Add an example. ⁵Boring topic sentence. Delete.	them. ³~~Staying away from my relatives and friends helps me~~ ~~to recognize how much important they are to me.~~ ⁴When we're away from all the persons and things that we appreciate we recognize the worth or importance that they have. *For example, when I lived at home I always fight with my older brother but now I miss him and wish I could ask him for advice about various things like how to buy a car.*
⁶Start new paragraph and add a transition. ⁷Correct transition phrase. ⁸Add a specific example. Add a concluding sentence.	*In addition, traveling* ⁵~~I am having a lot of new experiences.~~ ⁶~~Traveling~~ give us the chance to know different places, different people, and their customs. ⁷As a result ~~of that~~ we learn about them and they about us, too. ⁸And we can understand what similarities and what difference we have. *For instance, I was surprised to learn how similar my friend Juan's large and happy family is to mine even though we grew up on different continents. He is as close to his brothers and sisters as I am to mine. For these two reasons—appreciating my family more and getting to know a different culture—my time in the U.S. has been a great experience for me.*

The student wrote a second draft based on these revisions.

Editing

Now edit your second draft for sentence structure, grammar, punctuation, mechanics, spelling, and word choice.

Writers usually know what their own weaknesses are. For example, if you know that you sometimes use the wrong verb tense, check each and every verb carefully. If you sometimes write sentence fragments, look for this error. Use an editing checklist—the one that follows or one that you custom-design for yourself.

Then write a third draft.

Editing Checklist

Sentence structure
- No fragments or run-together sentences
- No choppy writing or overuse of *and*
- No mistakes in parallel form
- Varied sentence length and types
- Varied sentence openings

Grammar
Check for errors in
- Verb tenses and verb forms
- Articles
- Subject-verb agreement
- Pronoun reference
- Word order

Punctuation
- Period (or question mark or exclamation point) after every sentence
- Commas
- Apostrophes
- Quotation marks

Mechanics and spelling
- Spelling
- Capital letters

Word choice
Look for
- Repetition of the same word
- Overused words such as *good, bad,* and *thing*
- Errors in word form

Here is the second draft of the student writer showing his editing corrections. (The numbered notes at the left refer to the numbered sentences at the right.)

DRAFT 2

Coming to the U.S.

> *has been*
> ¹Living in the U.S. for the past six months ~~is~~ a great

¹Correct verb tense.

> *Being*
> experience for me for two reasons. ²~~Because being~~ so far

²Fragment. Delete *because*.

> from my family and my friends makes me realize how much
> I've been missing them. ³When we're away from ~~all the~~

³Unclear— rewrite.

> *familiar people and places* *their*
> ~~persons and things that we appreciate~~ we recognize ~~the~~
> *to us*
> worth or importance ~~that they have~~. ⁴For example, when I

⁴Correct verb tense.

> *fought*
> lived at home, I always ~~fight~~ with my older brother, but
> now I miss him and wish I could ask him for advice about
> various things like how to buy a car.

> *s*
> ⁵In addition, traveling give͜ us the chance to know
> different places, different people, and their customs. ⁶As

⁵Correct subject-verb agreement.

⁶Add comma.

6, 7Combine sentences.

> *and*
> a result, we learn about them and they about us, ~~too. ⁷And~~
> *s*
> we can understand what similarities and what difference͜ we

⁷Correct singular/plural error.

> have. For instance, I was surprised to learn how similar
> my friend Juan's large and happy family is to mine even
> though we grew up on different continents. He is as close
> to his brothers and sisters as I am to mine. For these two
> reasons—appreciating my family more and getting to know a
> different culture—my time in the U.S. has been a great
> experience for me.

The student writer wrote a third draft incorporating these editing corrections.

Final check

After completing the third draft, give it a final check. When the student writer read his paper again, he found several ways to improve it.

DRAFT 3

> *United States*
> Coming to the ~~U.S.~~

¹Don't abbreviate United States.

> *United States*
> ¹Living in the ~~U.S.~~ for the past six months has been a
> *First of all, being*
> great experience for me for two reasons. ²~~Being~~ so far

²Add transition.

> from my family and my friends makes me realize how much

²Correct verb
tense error.

³No
contractions.

⁹Revise
conclusion. It's
too similar to
the topic
sentence.

miss
I've been missing them. ³When we're *we are* away from familiar
people and places, we recognize their worth or importance
to us. ⁴For example, when I lived at home, I always fought
with my older brother, but now I miss him and wish I could
ask him for advice about various things like how to buy
a car.

⁵In addition, traveling gives us the chance to know
different places, different people, and their customs. ⁶As
a result, we learn about them and they about us, and we
can understand what similarities and what differences we
have. ⁷For instance, I was surprised to learn how similar
my friend Juan's large and happy family is to mine even
though we grew up on different continents. ⁸He is as close
to his brothers and sisters as I am to mine. ⁹For these
two reasons—appreciating my family more and getting to
know a different culture—my time in the U.S. *United States* has been
a great *good learning* experience for me.

This is the student's final draft.

FINAL DRAFT

Coming to the United States

Living in the United States for the past six months has
been a great experience for me for two reasons. First of
all, being so far from my family and my friends makes me
realize how much I miss them. When we are away from familiar
people and places, we recognize their worth or importance to
us. For example, when I lived at home, I always fought with
my older brother, but now I miss him and wish I could ask
him for advice about various things like how to buy a car.

In addition, traveling gives us the chance to know
different places, different people, and their customs.
As a result, we learn about them and they about us, and
we can understand what similarities and what differences we
have. For instance, I was surprised to learn how similar
my friend Juan's large and happy family is to mine even
though we grew up on different continents. He is as close
to his brothers and sisters as I am to mine. For these two
reasons—appreciating my family more and getting to know
a different culture—my time in the United States has been
a good learning experience for me.

PRACTICE—Section 40

A. Use the Revising Checklist on pages 266–267 to suggest revisions to this student's first draft, which discusses three main differences between high schools in the student's country and high schools in the United States. You can add, delete, or rearrange information. Hints:

1. Decide what the three main differences are.
2. Move sentences so that all the sentences about one main point are together.
3. Delete the two sentences that do not support any of the main ideas.
4. Add the following transition signals one time each. Put each one in front of an appropriate sentence: *First, Second, Third, For example,* and *For instance,.*

School Differences

High school in my country is very different from high school in the United States. The classroom atmosphere is very different. American classrooms are very informal. Students can wear jeans and T-shirts to school. The teachers dress casually too. Discipline is different. American high school students talk during class and sometimes they don't pay attention. In my country, high school students wear uniforms, and teachers wear business clothes. Students in my country have to study harder. I think that in the U. S., activities like sports teams, clubs, community service projects, and dating seem more important than schoolwork. American high school students go out on dates. We take a difficult exam at the end of high school that covers all the subjects we have studied. In the United States, there are a lot of tests during the year, but there is not a big test at the end of high school. In my high school, we stand up when the teacher enters the room, and no one talks while the teacher is talking. We have to study more subjects. We take science classes for four years, but most Americans take only two years of science. Our math classes are more advanced, too. Students in my country reach the level of calculus. Our teachers are very strict.

B. Use the Editing Checklist on page 268 to help you find and correct seventeen errors in another student's second draft.

Driving Habits

Driving in my country is completely different from driving in United States. Our death rate from car accidents is the highest in world. Almost 8,000 people a year. In my country, driving is really dangerous no one pays attention to driving rules. In this country, drivers usually obey it. They stopping at stop signs and red lights. By contrast, when drivers in my country see a traffic light turning yellow they are driving even faster! Also, everyone here wear seat belts. In my country is not "macho," so no one puts them on, until they see a policeman. American drivers usually very polite and will let other drivers change lanes, make turns, and take a parking space when its their turn. In my country on the other hand people is totally selfish behind the wheel of a car. They steal parking spaces, refuse to let other driver into their lane, and honk when the car in front is too slowly. Pedestrians are not safe, either. I once saw a car cut across six lanes in heavy traffics and drive onto a sidewalk because the driver wanted to greet a friend who is walking there. In conclusion, when you visit my country, be prepared to run for your life!

41   Paragraphs

A paragraph is a group of related sentences that discuss one (and usually only one) main idea.

We mark a paragraph by indenting the first word. (To indent means to start writing about ½ inch—five spaces on a typewriter or computer—to the right.)

Xxxxxxxxxxxxxxxxxxx
xxxxxxxxxxxxxxxxxxxxx
xxxxxxxxxxxxxxxxxxxxx
xxxxxxxxxxxxxxxxxxxxx
xxxxxxxxxxxxx .

A paragraph has three parts.

The three parts of a paragraph are the topic sentence, the supporting sentences, and the concluding sentence. (Not all paragraphs have a concluding sentence.)

1. The topic sentence tells what topic the paragraph is going to discuss.

2. The supporting sentences give details about the topic.

3. The concluding sentence summarizes the main points and perhaps makes a final comment.

A paragraph is like a sandwich. The topic sentence and concluding sentence are the two pieces of "bread" enclosing the "meat"—the supporting sentences. A diagram of a paragraph looks like this:

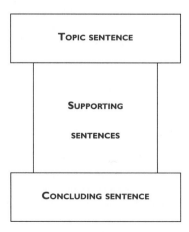

TOPIC SENTENCE

SUPPORTING

SENTENCES

CONCLUDING SENTENCE

Color Words in English

¹Topic sentence

^{2–5}Supporting sentences

⁶Concluding sentence

¹In English, there are several idioms with color words that describe emotions. ²When a person feels sad, he/she is feeling blue. ³A person in a black mood feels even worse: He/she is either angry or depressed. ⁴A person turns red with embarrassment, white with fear, green with envy, and purple with rage. ⁵When you say that someone is yellow, you mean that he/she is cowardly. ⁶It is interesting that English has many color-word idioms to describe anger, jealousy, and fear but doesn't have any to describe happiness, contentment, or peace.

41a Topic sentence

The topic sentence states the topic + controlling idea.

The topic sentence announces the main idea of a paragraph. The topic sentence names the topic and also tells what the paragraph will say about the topic. In the example paragraph at the beginning of this section, the topic sentence names the topic: *idioms with color words*. It also explains what the paragraph will explain about color-word idioms: They *describe emotions*. This part of the topic sentence is called the controlling idea because it controls or limits the topic to a very specific area.

The topic sentence is neither too general nor too specific.

A topic sentence such as *I have a roommate* is too general because there is no controlling idea. A topic sentence such as *My roommate always leaves his dirty socks in the bathroom* is too specific because it gives a detail—in this case, an example. A good topic sentence gives the reader a hint about the contents of the paragraph but none of the details: *My roommate is a messy person.*

Here are some examples of topic sentences.

```
        ┌──── topic ────┐   ┌ controlling idea ┐
```
▶ My roommate is a messy person.
```
        ┌──────── topic ────────┐    ┌ controlling idea ┐
```
▶ My roommate and I are very different.
```
        ┌──────── topic ────────┐    ┌──── controlling idea ────┐
```
▶ A good roommate has three basic qualities.

The topic sentence is usually the first sentence of a paragraph.

Experienced writers sometimes put topic sentences in other locations such as at the end, but the best spot is usually right at the beginning of a paragraph. Readers who are used to English writing want to know what they will read about as they begin. Knowing in advance what you will read about helps you understand it better.

PRACTICE—Section 41a

Read the following paragraph. Then choose the best topic sentence for it from the choices listed below.

_____. First of all, it is a beautiful city. From the top of its hills, the views of the sparkling blue water of San Francisco Bay and the green hills beyond are spectacular. Second, San Francisco has many excellent restaurants. With hundreds of restaurants serving delicious food from every part of the world, the city is truly a food-lover's paradise. San Francisco is also fun. Riding a cable car down one of the city's steep hills, eating a seafood cocktail at Fisherman's Wharf, window-shopping in Chinatown, or walking across the famous Golden Gate Bridge are just a few of the activities on every visitor's "must-do" list.

Possible topic sentences

1. San Francisco is one of the most beautiful cities in the world.
2. San Francisco is the perfect place to spend a vacation.
3. San Francisco has many tourist attractions.
4. San Francisco is a great place to visit, but it is expensive.

41b Supporting sentences

Supporting sentences explain or prove the topic sentence. The example paragraph about color-word idioms has four supporting sentences. Each one proves the truth of the topic sentence by giving one or more examples of a color-word idiom describing an emotion.

Use facts, not opinions, for support.

Facts are objective statements of truth. Opinions are subjective statements based on a person's beliefs or feelings.

Facts	▶ One inch equals 2.54 centimeters.
	▶ Young male drivers have more fatal automobile accidents than any other group.
Opinions	▶ The metric system of measurement is easier to use than the English system.
	▶ Men are better drivers than women.

It is certainly acceptable to express opinions in academic and business writing. Teachers and bosses usually want you to express your own ideas. However, you must support your opinions with facts. In academic and business writing, even statements that most people consider to be facts need further support. They need specific supporting details such as examples, statistics, or quotations to be convincing.

Unsupported "fact"	▶ Young male drivers have more fatal automobile accidents than any other group.
Specific supporting details	▶ Car crashes are the leading cause of death for American teenagers.
	▶ Young people ages 15–20 make up 6.7% of the total driving population in the United States but are involved in 14% of all fatal crashes.
	▶ Two out of three teenagers killed in car crashes are male.
	▶ Male drivers between the ages of 15 and 24 have 48.2 auto-related deaths per 100,000 population, a rate 2 times the national average.
Unsupported "fact"	▶ The English system of measurement has an interesting history.
Specific supporting details	▶ An acre was traditionally an area of farmland that a team of oxen could plow in one morning without getting tired.
	▶ A pound was originally the weight of 7,000 grains of barley.
	▶ An inch was originally the width of a man's thumb, and a foot was the length of a man's foot.
	▶ A yard was the distance between King Henry I's (1068–1135) nose and the tip of his outstretched arm.

Use examples, statistics, and quotations as specific supporting details.

Keep in mind that supporting sentences are the "meat" of a paragraph. Make your supporting sentences as specific and detailed as possible; they make your paragraph rich and interesting.

Notice the difference between paragraphs 1 and 2 that follow. Both paragraphs begin with the same topic sentence, but the supporting sentences in paragraph 2 are more specific than those in paragraph 1. They give statistics, specific names, a specific example, and a quotation from an authority. As a result, paragraph 2 is not just longer; it is also livelier and more convincing.

Paragraph 1

```
                        Giant Pandas

     Giant pandas are an endangered species. There are not
many pandas still living in the wild. The area in China
where they live is quite small, and they do not reproduce
in zoos easily. There has been only one panda baby born in
a zoo in the United States. Experts say that pandas in
zoos don't reproduce well enough to maintain the species.
```

Paragraph 2

Statistics

Specific names

Example

Quotation

Giant Pandas

    Giant pandas are an endangered species. Only about 1,000 giant pandas still live in the wild, occupying six small forest fragments totaling 5,400 square miles in the provinces of Sichuan, Gansu, and Shaanxi in southwestern China. Not only is their natural habitat limited, but they also do not reproduce easily in zoos. In 1999, Bai Yun and Shi Shi, two pandas in the San Diego zoo, produced the first zoo-born baby panda outside China in ten years. According to the San Diego Zoo's Center for Reproduction of Endangered Species, "Captive pandas are not reproducing well enough to maintain the species."

Use support that is both appropriate and relevant.

Make sure that your support is appropriate. For instance, if you want to prove that men are better automobile drivers than women, don't use famous race car drivers as examples.

Use supporting quotations from appropriate sources. A quotation about global warming from a tabloid newspaper (the kind of newspaper sold at supermarket checkout stands) is not appropriate for an academic paper. On the other hand, a college classmate is an appropriate source for a quotation about the cost of textbooks.

Second, make sure that your support is relevant. If you want to prove that smoking is harmful to health, don't use the fact that many airlines now ban in-flight smoking as support. The airline ban may be indirectly related to health issues, but there is no direct connection. You cannot say, "Airlines don't allow smoking. This proves that smoking is harmful to health."

PRACTICE—Section 41b

Read the topic sentence. Then place a check mark (✓) next to sentences that provide good support. Put an X next to sentences that provide poor support because they are not facts, because they are not appropriate, or because they are not relevant. You should check five sentences.

Topic sentence: Japan is a nation of workaholics.

Possible supporting sentences

_____ 1. Japan has more national holidays than the United States or Germany.

_____ 2. The average worker in Japan gets eighteen days of paid vacation every year.

_____ 3. The average worker uses only nine of his or her eighteen days of paid vacation every year.

_____ 4. Many Japanese are uncomfortable taking vacation days when their coworkers have to be at work, according to Japanese sociologists who have studied the problem.

_____ 5. "I wish I could take more than a week," said office worker Masako Tanaka, "but the environment at work doesn't really let you do that."

_____ 6. Americans who work for Japanese companies quickly learn to put in the same long hours as their Japanese colleagues.

_____ 7. Japanese schoolchildren go to school every other Saturday, and they spend most evenings, weekends, and holidays attending study clubs or cram schools.

_____ 8. The Japanese government wants workers to take more time off because people spend more money on vacation, which would help the Japanese economy.

_____ 9. Many Japanese enjoy hard work and long hours; if they didn't, they wouldn't do it.

_____ 10. Japanese get used to working long hours when they are schoolchildren.

41c Paragraph unity

Make sure that all sentences discuss the main idea.

Unity means that a paragraph discusses one main idea from beginning to end. Give a paragraph unity by making sure that each sentence is directly related to that main idea.

The example paragraph on page 273 has unity because it discusses only one main idea: color-word idioms that describe emotions. Every supporting sentence is directly related to this idea. There are no other ideas and no sentences that are off the topic.

The following paragraph has been edited for unity. Sentences that are off the topic are crossed out.

My Best Teacher

Mrs. Smith was the best teacher I have ever had. Until I took her Spanish class in my third year of high school, I had been just an average student who studied an average amount of time and earned average grades, but Mrs. Smith changed that. The only class I got good grades in was math. For some reason, math has always been easy for me. Mrs. Smith was not an easy teacher. On the contrary, her class was one of the hardest in my entire four years of high school. Her homework assignments were always interesting and challenging. I usually did her homework first. We went shopping in Spanish food stores and prepared Spanish food. We wrote e-mails to students in Spanish-speaking countries around the world. In addition, Mrs. Smith's classes were always lively and fun. We watched Spanish soap operas on TV. We wrote and performed puppet shows in Spanish. We sang Spanish songs. She ended each class by telling a joke in Spanish. My first-year Spanish teacher never told jokes, and in my second year class, we just studied grammar. In short, Mrs. Smith was a great teacher because she made learning so much fun.

PRACTICE—Section 41c

Edit the following paragraph for unity. Cross out two sentences that are "off the topic."

How to Meet People

In a recent experiment, two British psychologists proved that walking a dog will help you meet people. One of the psychologists walked a dog to work for five days. She lives near the university where she works. Sixty-five strangers either talked to her or smiled at her when the dog was with her, but only three strangers did so when she was dogless. The psychologists believe that the presence of a dog may remove people's fear of talking to strangers. The scientists didn't use cats or other pets in the experiment. Moreover, the dog's appearance didn't matter. Strangers were friendly whether the dog wore a fashionable matching collar and leash or an ugly leather collar and an old piece of rope. Therefore, if you want to meet people, get a dog and don't worry about how it's dressed.

41d Paragraph coherence

When a paragraph has coherence, it is easy to read and understand. Each sentence flows smoothly into the next one. There are no sudden jumps, and the reader can often predict what might come next.

Use transition signals.

One of the main ways to achieve coherence is to use transition signals. Transition signals tell the reader how one idea relates to another idea. They are like traffic signs; they tell the reader when to go ahead, where to make a U-turn, and when to stop. For example:

- *and* and *in addition* tell the reader to go ahead (expect a similar idea)
- *but* and *however* tell the reader to make a U-turn (expect a different idea)
- *to sum up* and *in conclusion* say "stop"

Notice how the addition of transition signals helps the reader follow the flow of ideas in the following paragraph.

Paragraph *without* transition signals

```
    My morning routine never changes. My alarm clock rings
for the third time. I get up. I sleepwalk to the shower. I
stand in the shower for ten minutes. I am finally awake. I
get dressed. I go to the kitchen, make a cup of tea, and
put a slice of bread in the toaster. I eat breakfast and
feed my cat. I put her outside. I am ready to face the
world. I get on the bus and go to school. My first class
begins. I go back to sleep.
```

Paragraph *with* transition signals	My morning routine never changes. **When** the alarm clock rings for the third time, I get up and sleepwalk to the shower. I stand in the shower for ten minutes **until** I am finally awake. **Then** I get dressed. **Next,** I go to the kitchen, make a cup of tea, and put a slice of bread in the toaster. **After** I eat breakfast and feed my cat, I put her outside. **Finally,** I am ready to face the world, **so** I get on the bus and go to school. **As soon as** my first class begins, I go back to sleep.

Decide which transition signals to use.

There are different kinds of transition signals. A few of them are listed in the following chart. You will find a more complete list in *Section 53* at the back of the book.

TRANSITION WORDS AND PHRASES AND CONJUNCTIVE ADVERBS	COORDINATING CONJUNCTIONS	SUBORDINATING CONJUNCTIONS	OTHERS (ADJECTIVES, PREPOSITIONS, VERBS)
To list ideas in order of time			
First, Second, Third, Next, Then After that, Meanwhile, Now Soon		before after until when while as soon as	The first (reason, cause, step, etc.) An additional ... The second ... Another ... The final ...
To list ideas in order of importance			
First, First of all, Second, More important, Most important, Above all, Most of all,			The first (reason, cause, step, etc.) An additional ... The second ... Another ... A more important (reason, cause, step, etc.) The most important ...

(continued)

(continued)

TRANSITION WORDS AND PHRASES AND CONJUNCTIVE ADVERBS	COORDINATING CONJUNCTIONS	SUBORDINATING CONJUNCTIONS	OTHERS (ADJECTIVES, PREPOSITIONS, VERBS)
To add a similar or equal idea			
Also, Furthermore, In addition, Moreover,	and		too as well as as well
To add an opposite idea			
However, On the other hand, Nevertheless,	but	although	in spite of
To give an example			
For example,			such as like
To give a reason			
For this reason,		because	because of
To give a result			
Therefore, As a result, Consequently,	so		to result (in) to cause
To add a conclusion			
Finally, In brief, In conclusion, To conclude, In short, To sum up,			
To emphasize			
Most important, Above all,			the most important . . . the most significant . . .

Locate and punctuate transition signals carefully.

Each kind of transition signal has different rules for position in a sentence and for punctuation.

Transition signals and conjunctive adverbs

1. Most words and phrases in this group can appear at the beginning, in the middle, or at the end of a sentence and are usually separated by commas.

   My roommates and I decided to paint our apartment last weekend.

   ▶ **First,** we went to buy the paint.
   ▶ One of our roommates, **however,** is allergic to paint.
   ▶ He couldn't help us with the actual painting, **therefore.**

   EXCEPTIONS:

   We often use time words such as *then, now,* and *soon* without commas.

   ▶ **Then** we had to clean the walls.
   ▶ We **soon** got tired of cleaning and sanding.
   ▶ We cleaned up **afterward.**

   Don't use a comma with *also* in the middle of a clause.

   ▶ We **also** had to use sandpaper to make the walls smooth.

2. Transition signals can also connect two independent clauses. In this case, we use them with a semicolon and a comma.

   ▶ One of our roommates was allergic to paint; **therefore,** he couldn't help us with the painting.

Coordinating conjunctions

Coordinating conjunctions (*and, but, so, or, for, nor, yet*) may or may not have commas.

1. When they connect two words or phrases, don't use a comma.

   ▶ We were excited about our project **and** eager to get started.

2. When they connect two independent clauses, use a comma.

   ▶ We started to work, **but** I soon got tired of cleaning and sanding.

Subordinating conjunctions

A subordinating conjunction is the first word in a dependent clause. A dependent clause is always connected to an independent clause to make a sentence. If the dependent clause comes first, put a comma after it. If the dependent clause comes second, don't put a comma before it.

▶ **Because** one of our roommates is allergic to paint, he couldn't help us with the painting.

▶ One of our roommates couldn't help us with the painting **because** he is allergic to paint.

EXCEPTION: Clauses of contrast beginning with *whereas* and *while* are always separated with a comma, even when they follow an independent clause.

▶ One of my roommates worked all day, **while** the other two quit after lunch.

Adjectives, prepositions, and verbs

This group doesn't require special punctuation.

▶ One roommate couldn't paint **because of** his allergies.

▶ The **final** step in a painting project is cleaning up.

Reference: Learn more about transition signals in the following sections: Compound sentences with transition signals, 11, *Section 25d*; List of connecting words, 11, *Section 52*; List of transition signals, 11, *Section 53*.

PRACTICE—Section 41d

Improve the coherence of this paragraph by adding appropriate transition signals. Choose from the transition signals in parentheses. Sometimes the punctuation before or after a blank will help you choose. Circle your choice.

Making your first scuba dive can be a stressful experience because there are so many things to remember. You have to move slowly and think about each step.

_____ (*The first step* / First of all/ For example) is to check your equipment before you enter the water. Make sure that everything is securely in place. _____,
1.
(Also/ However/ Therefore) make sure that your air is turned on, that your regulator is working, and that there is a little air in your vest. _____ (Then/ On
2.
the other hand/ In conclusion) check your dive buddy's equipment. At last, you are ready to enter the water. Put your regulator in your mouth, hold it in place with one hand, hold your mask in place with your other hand, and jump or roll into the water. After you are in the water, take a moment to recheck both your and your buddy's equipment. _____ (While/ As soon as/ Until) both of you are
3.
ready, give the OK signal, let the air out of your vest, and begin to go down. _____ (While/ As soon as/ Until) you are going down, clear your ears every few
4.
feet by pinching your nose and blowing. If you begin to feel pain in your ears, go back up a few feet, clear your ears, and try to go down again. _____, (On the
5.
other hand/ Therefore/ Most important) keep breathing. Take deep, slow breaths. When you and your buddy reach your agreed-on depth, stop for a moment, and give each other the OK signal. Congratulations! You are now scuba diving!

41e Concluding sentence

A concluding sentence signals the end of the paragraph and reminds the reader of the main idea. Not all paragraphs need a concluding sentence. When a paragraph is very long or when it stands alone as a piece of writing, it is helpful to your reader to add a concluding sentence. Paragraphs that are part of longer pieces of writing don't always need concluding sentences.

When you write a concluding sentence, here are some hints to help you write a good one.

Start with a transition signal.

I. You can use a "conclusion" transition signal, followed by a comma.

All in all,	**In summary,**
In brief,	**It is clear that** . . . (*without a comma*)
In conclusion,	**To conclude,**
Indeed,	**To summarize,**
In short,	**To sum up,**

2. However, if the paragraph gives reasons, you may choose one of these "reason" or "result" transition signals.

As a result,	**For these reasons,**
Consequently,	**Therefore,**

Do not copy the topic sentence.

I. You can repeat the idea in the topic sentence, but use different words.

> **Topic sentence:** Japan is a nation of workaholics.

▸ It is clear that workers in Japan are dedicated employees—perhaps too dedicated for their own health and happiness.

2. You can also summarize the main point or points of the paragraph.

▸ In short, peer pressure and training during the school years have combined to produce a nation of extremely dedicated workers.

▸ To summarize, the Japanese worked long hours as children at school, and group pressure in the workplace causes them to continue this practice as adults.

Do not introduce a new idea.

Never end a paragraph by introducing a new idea

✗ In conclusion, Japanese employees spend so much time working that family life suffers as a result.

PRACTICE—Section 41e

Read the following paragraph. Then choose the best concluding sentence from the choices listed below.

Giant Pandas

Giant pandas are an endangered species. Only about 1,000 giant pandas still live in the wild, occupying six small forest fragments totaling 5,400 square miles in the provinces of Sichuan, Gansu, and Shaanxi in southwestern China. Not only is their natural habitat limited, but they also do not reproduce easily in zoos. In 1999, Bai Yun and Shi Shi, two pandas in the San Diego zoo, produced the first zoo-born baby panda outside China in ten years. According to the San Diego Zoo's Center for Reproduction of Endangered Species, "Captive pandas are not reproducing well enough to maintain the species." _____.

Possible concluding sentences

1. In conclusion, giant pandas are an endangered species and may soon disappear from Earth.
2. In short, zoos must acquire more pandas, or this much-loved species may soon disappear from Earth.
3. It is clear that zoos must find ways to help pandas reproduce, or this much-loved species may soon disappear from Earth.

41f Patterns of paragraph organization

Writers use certain typical patterns to organize ideas. The pattern you use depends on your topic and your purpose for writing. For example, to explain the procedure for an experiment in a laboratory report, you would use the time-order pattern. To explain the differences between two economic theories on an economics test, you would use the comparison-and-contrast pattern.

This handbook contains examples of five patterns of organization: (1) description, (2) time order, (3) logical division of ideas, (4) order of importance, and (5) comparison and contrast.

Note three keys to using any particular pattern of organization:

- Write a topic sentence that suggests which pattern you will use.
- Arrange the points in an order that is appropriate for the pattern.
- Use transition signals appropriate for the pattern.

Description

A description is a "word picture." A writer of a good description is like an artist who paints a picture that can be "seen" in the mind of the reader.

Descriptive writing appeals to the senses, so it tells how something looks, feels, smells, tastes, and sounds.

Looks   **shiny black** hair   **Smells**   **smoky** air   **Sounds**   **howling** wind

Feels   **soft, silky** skin   **Tastes**   **sweet** apple juice

Just as an artist plans where to place each object in a painting, a writer plans where to put each detail in a "word painting." One of the ways to organize the details is to use spatial order. Spatial order is the arrangement of items in order by space. Things can be described from

- left to right OR right to left
- front to back OR back to front
- near to far OR far to near
- top to bottom OR bottom to top

For example, to describe the view from your window, you might begin with objects close to the window and end with objects in the distance. To describe a person, you might begin with a description of the whole person and then zoom in on a detail such as eyes.

The following paragraph is a description of a sand dollar, which is the skeleton of a kind of sea urchin found on beaches around the world. Notice that the topic sentence names the object to be described—a skeleton. Notice also the order of the description: outside, outer edge, top, bottom, inside. The writer also uses many sensory words so that the reader can feel, see, smell, and hear the sand dollar.

A Beach Treasure

The topic sentence names the object.

    The *fragile white* skeleton lay half-buried in the sand at my feet. I stopped, picked it up, and brushed away the *fine* sand clinging to its *rough, dry* **surface.** I was holding a *flat, round* disk in my hand. Because the disk was dry and hollow, it weighed almost nothing. It wasn't perfectly round, however. Four V-shaped notches were equally spaced **around its outer edge,** making it look like a fat cross. **On the top of the disk,** nature had punched hundreds of tiny holes in the shape of a *beautiful* flower with five petals. The petals were *long* ovals outlined by two *dark* stripes. The outer stripe was about one-fourth inch wide, and the inner stripe was no wider than a line of dots made by a sharp pencil. No artist could have drawn the petals more evenly or more delicately. I turned the disk over. Compared to the top, **the bottom** was rather plain. There was only a small hole in the center, from which dry sand trickled. I held it up to my nose and sniffed the *salty, seaweedy* smell of the ocean. As I brought the disk toward my face, I heard what sounded like the *rattle* of tiny bones coming **from inside,** and, in fact, I was holding a skeleton—the skeleton of a sea urchin. For people like me who love the sea, finding a perfect sand dollar is a joy of the simplest yet most profound kind.

Spatial order is outside, top, bottom, inside (see boldface italic words).

Sensory words: *fragile, white, fine, rough, dry, flat, round, beautiful, long, dark, salty, seaweedy, rattle*

Time order

Time order is the arrangement of ideas in the order of their occurrence.

Process paragraph

We often use time order to explain how to do or make something. This kind of paragraph is called a process paragraph. When you use time order to explain a process such as cooking rice or learning a new dance, separate the process into steps: *put four cups . . . , add four cups . . . , cover it . . . , turn down the heat . . . ,* and so on. Show the order of the steps by using time-order transition signals: *first, next, then, until, as soon as,* and so on. Notice that the words *if you follow these simple steps* in the topic sentence indicate time order.

	Making Sushi Rice
The topic sentence shows time order.	Making Japanese sushi rice is easy if you follow these simple steps. **First,** put four cups of short-grain rice into a large, heavy pan. **Next,** add four cups of water and four teaspoons of sugar, and soak the rice for two hours.
The steps are in order by time.	**Then** cover it with a lid and bring it to a boil on high heat **until** the water begins to come out from under the lid. **Immediately** turn the heat down to low and cook it for twelve minutes. **Then** remove the pot from the heat and let it stand for ten minutes. Do not lift the lid during the
Transition words (boldface italic) show the order of the steps.	cooking or standing time. **Meanwhile,** combine one-half cup white vinegar, six tablespoons sugar, and four teaspoons salt in a small pan. Heat this mixture just **until** the sugar dissolves. **Finally,** empty the rice from the pot into a large bowl and fold in the vinegar mixture. **While** folding in the vinegar, cool the rice quickly with a fan. **As soon as** the rice is cool, you can make sushi with it.

Narrative paragraph

In addition to explaining a process, we also use time order to write about an event or series of events such as a wedding, a birthday celebration, a vacation, a frightening experience, a happy occasion, a person's life story, and so on. This kind of paragraph is called a narration or a narrative paragraph.

A narrative paragraph might begin with a topic sentence like one of the following:

▶ **A camping trip with my family** is always a lot of fun.

▶ **Our last vacation** was one disaster after another.

▶ In my country, we celebrate **a girl's fifteenth birthday** in a special way.

In addition to transition words and phrases such as *first, next, after that, then, meanwhile,* and *finally,* narrative paragraphs also use time phrases such as *during the morning, after lunch,* and *while waiting* and time clauses such as *while we were waiting* and *after we finished lunch* to show the order of events.

An Unforgettable Experience

The topic sentence suggests that this paragraph will tell a story.	On my twelfth birthday, a fishing trip almost turned into a tragedy. It was almost eight o'clock in the morning **when** we finally left the dock in my uncle's boat. My cousin and I sat next to each other in the middle of the small boat **while** my uncle steered the boat from the back. We were looking forward to a day of fishing. The sun was shining, but there was a strong wind blowing, which made the water a little rough. The boat bounced up and down in
Time-order words show the order of events.	the waves **as** we got closer to the narrow channel that would lead us to the open sea. **All of a sudden**, I was in the water. **Then** I was under the water, and everything was black. I couldn't see anything. **After a few seconds**, my head popped up out of the water, but it was still dark around me. It took me **a few seconds** to realize that I was trapped under the boat, which was floating upside down on top of me. Fortunately, there was a pocket of air trapped with me under the boat, so I could breathe, but I couldn't get out. My life jacket, which had caused me to rise to the surface, now kept me from swimming down and out. **Just as** I was about to panic, I felt a person's leg kicking at me. I grabbed the leg, and **then** the person attached to the leg reached under the boat and pulled me out. My rescuer was a surfer who had seen the accident and had immediately paddled over to help. **Afterward**, I learned that a huge wave had hit us and flipped the boat upside down, throwing all of us into the water. The boat had come down right on top
The last sentence summarizes the experience.	of me. Miraculously, no one had been seriously hurt, but we had had an adventure that none of us would soon forget!

Logical division of ideas

Another typical pattern of organizing the ideas in a paragraph is logical division of ideas. In this pattern, you divide the topic into different points and discuss each point separately.

A paragraph using the logical division pattern might begin with a topic sentence that indicates that the topic is divided, such as one of the following:

▸ Architects must be **both artists and engineers.**

▸ In my job, I have **several responsibilities.**

▸ There are basically **three kinds of shoppers** who come to the store where I work.

Transition words that show the divisions are words and phrases like *first of all, second, in addition, the third kind, the final reason,* and so on.

Architecture

The topic sentence indicates two divisions.	Architects must be both artists and engineers. *First of all,* they must have an artist's sense of space, proportion, and mass. They must also have an artist's strong visual
Artistic side is discussed first, then engineering.	sense so that they can visualize what a building or house or bridge will look like after it is built. Of course, they should have a talent for drawing. *In addition,* architects should know about colors and textures in order to select beautiful materials to finish their buildings.
Transition signals show the two divisions: *first of all, second.*	*Second,* architects must be engineers with strong mathematical skills. Even if they hire consultants, they should have enough knowledge of structural engineering to design a strong building. *Besides* structural engineering,
The conclusion rephrases the topic sentence.	architects must study geological, mechanical, and electrical engineering. They need to know about earthquake zones and types of soils, **and** they need to understand the complex mechanical and electrical systems of a building. Indeed, the profession of architecture requires a combination of seemingly opposite talents: art and math.

Order of importance

A variation of the logical-division-of-ideas pattern is order of importance. In the order-of-importance pattern, you discuss the most important point either first or last. Transition signals like *the first and most important . . .* and *the second most important . . .* make it clear that you are discussing the most important point first. On the other hand, a transition signal like *the final and most important . . .* or *the last and most significant . . .* shows that you are discussing the most important point last.

An order-of-importance paragraph might begin as follows:

▸ There are many factors to consider when choosing a career. **The most important factor** is . . .

Comparison and contrast

In the comparison-and-contrast pattern, you explain the similarities and differences between two items such as two characters in a book or play, two political parties, or two computer operating systems. There are two ways to organize the points in a comparison-and-contrast paragraph. One way is called block organization, and the other way is called point-by-point organization.

Block organization

You can group all the similarities together and all the differences together and write about each group. This is called block organization because all the similarities are in one block and all the differences are in another block. The writer of the example paragraph about film and digital cameras below uses block organization.

If there are many similarities and many differences, make each block a separate paragraph.

All similarities
All differences

Point-by-point organization

The other way to organize a comparison-and-contrast topic is to write about similarities and differences by subtopic. For example, if you are comparing and contrasting the menus at two restaurants, your subtopics might be breakfast, lunch, and dinner. You would probably write three separate paragraphs and mix comparison and contrast in each one. This is sometimes called point-by-point organization.

Breakfast   (similarities and differences)
Lunch   (similarities and differences)
Dinner   (similarities and differences)

In the paragraph that follows, notice the words and phrases that show comparison and contrast. They make it very clear to the reader what is similar and what is different about the two kinds of cameras. Notice also that the topic sentence not only names the subjects of the comparison (film cameras and digital cameras) but also indicates comparison-and-contrast organization.

Film or Digital?

The topic sentence names two items to be compared and contrasted.

> If you are shopping for a new camera, you now have a choice between a traditional film camera and one of the new digital cameras, so you should know a little bit about their similarities and differences. With **both kinds** of cameras, you take pictures **the same way:** You point the camera at something and push a button. **Both** digital and

Block
organization:
similarities first,
then differences

film cameras offer **similar** features, such as autofocus,
automatic exposure control, and zoom lenses.

However, what happens after you push the button is
quite **different.** With a film camera, you take your roll of
film to a store for processing. The store develops the
film and prints your pictures. You get back the negatives
and positive copies of all of the pictures, even the bad
ones like the one showing Uncle Ed with his mouth open. If
you want more copies, you have to take the negatives back
to the store. Also, the negatives are permanent. You can't

Transitions signals
point out the
similarities and
differences.

adjust the color or delete Uncle Ed. With a digital
camera, **in contrast,** there is no film. Pictures are stored
on a memory card and can be transferred to your home
computer. Also, **unlike** pictures on film, you can process
your own digital photos. You can adjust colors and
borders, and you can print as many copies as you want.
Furthermore, you can choose which pictures to print and

The paragraph
ends with a
recommendation.

which to delete (Uncle Ed). **Another difference** between
digital and film cameras is their cost. You can buy a good
point-and-click film camera for less than $100, **whereas**
you have to pay at least $300 for a basic digital camera.
In conclusion, if you want simplicity and low cost, stick
with film, **but** if you want to edit, e-mail, and print your
own photos, go for digital.

Combination paragraphs

Most paragraphs are not "pure" time order or "pure" comparison and contrast.
Writers often combine patterns like logical division of ideas or order of
importance with other patterns. For example, the writer of the paragraph
about sushi rice could emphasize the importance of the last step by adding an
order-of-importance transition signal: *The last and most important step in
making sushi rice is to cool it quickly while adding the vinegar mixture.*

First-borns vs. Last-borns

Psychologists note distinct personality differences
between the first- and last-born child in a family.
Probably the most important difference is due to the fact
that first-born children receive most of their parents'

The paragraph
combines
comparison-
contrast and
order of
importance.

attention. **In contrast,** the youngest child is generally
left to explore the world on his or her own. **Less
important but still influential** is the fact that first-
borns are given more responsibility as children, often
being placed in charge of younger siblings. The youngest
child, **on the other hand,** is the "baby" of the family and
may be pampered by everyone. As a result, first-borns
typically become super-achieving adults, meeting or even
exceeding their parents' expectations, **whereas** last-borns
are typically more fun-loving and relaxed as adults.

42 Essays

An essay is a group of paragraphs about one topic. It has three main parts: an introduction (or introductory paragraph), a body, and a conclusion (or concluding paragraph).

1. The introduction introduces the topic of the essay and arouses the reader's interest. It always contains one sentence that clearly states the main idea of the whole essay. This sentence is called the thesis statement.

2. The body of an essay is made up of one or more paragraphs. Each body paragraph explains or develops one part of the essay topic. The body paragraphs are arranged according to a pattern of organization such as time order or comparison and contrast.

3. The conclusion is the last paragraph. It summarizes the main points of the essay.

Reference: To write an essay, follow the steps of creating, organizing, writing, and polishing described in *Section 40*.

! *Special Tip*

Because an essay is longer than a paragraph, it is especially helpful to make and follow an outline in order to keep good organization. To see an example of an essay outline, go to *Section 40b*, pages 262–263.

42a Introduction

An introduction, or introductory paragraph, is the first paragraph of an essay. It has two purposes: It introduces your topic, and it catches your reader's attention. There are several kinds of introductions.

"Funnel" introduction

In academic and business writing, a typical introductory paragraph is a "funnel" introduction. A funnel introduction begins with one or two very general sentences about the topic. Each subsequent sentence becomes increasingly focused on the subject until the last sentence, which states very specifically what you are going to write about. Writing a funnel introduction is like focusing a camera with a telephoto lens. You start with a wide picture and gradually narrow the focus so that just one object appears in your viewfinder: your thesis statement. The thesis statement is usually the last sentence in an introductory paragraph. (In each of the following examples of introductions, the thesis statement is in boldface type.)

Any person who has lived in the twentieth century has seen a lot of changes take place, and the twenty-first century will bring even greater changes. Some people are excited by the challenges that these changes offer; others worry about their consequences. *The twenty-first century will bring certain advantages such as faster communication and a higher standard of living, but it will also bring some disadvantages such as increased pollution and the depersonalization of human relationships.*

Present surprising statistics, facts, or examples

The following kinds of introductions show different ways to catch your reader's attention.

Describe a dramatic event.

First, the windows began to rattle. Then the floor beneath our feet began to move. A moment later, the light fixture above the dining table began to swing back and forth, and we heard glass breaking, walls cracking, and books and other objects falling to the floor. We had just experienced a 6.1 earthquake. It had lasted less than a minute, but the damage was terrible. *This earthquake made it clear to our family that we needed to prepare better for the next one.*

Present surprising statistics, facts, or examples.

On average, a male college graduate earns $800,000 more during his lifetime than a male high school graduate, and a female college graduate earns about $600,000 more than a female high school graduate. What's more, high school graduates are twice as likely as college graduates to become unemployed. It is clear that a college education brings significant financial rewards, but there are other benefits as well. *A college education is a good investment for four reasons.*

Give historical background.

The Pilgrims who arrived in Massachusetts in 1620 came to find religious freedom. In the seventeenth and eighteenth centuries, large numbers of African men and women were brought as slaves to work on plantations in the South. Immigrants from northern and southern Europe came in the early nineteenth century to escape poor economic conditions. Later in the same century, the first immigrants from China came as contract laborers to build the railroads connecting East and West. In the century just past, political and economic refugees arrived from Vietnam, Eastern Europe, and Latin America. Indeed, immigrants have come to the United States from many different parts of the world, and they have come for many different reasons. *Their ability to adjust to life in their adopted land has depended on several factors.*

Tell an entertaining story.

I was five years old and still believed in Santa Claus. One Christmas Eve, I carefully poured a glass of milk and arranged two peanut butter cookies on a small plate. I placed them on a table near the fireplace, where Santa would see them when he came to deliver our presents. Imagine my concern the next morning when I discovered both cookies, soggy and uneaten, floating in the bathroom toilet. *I slowly began to suspect that the world was not exactly as I had pictured it.*

> ## ! *Special Tip*
>
> Writing a good introduction is not always easy. If you find writing an introduction difficult, try writing it later, after you have written the body paragraphs. Some writers even write the introduction last.

Thesis statement

The most important part of an introduction is the thesis statement. A thesis statement is a sentence that specifically states what the essay is going to be about. It usually appears at the end of the introductory paragraph and gives the reader an idea of what he or she is going to read. Just as a diner at a restaurant can predict the approximate contents of a salad from the words "potato salad" or "mixed green salad," a reader should be able to predict the approximate contents of your essay from reading your thesis statement.

States topic and subtopics

The thesis statement always states the main topic and often lists the subtopics as well.

Main topic
▶ Young people in my culture have less freedom than young people in the United States in making three of life's major decisions.

Main topic + subtopics
▶ Young people in my culture have less freedom than young people in the United States in their choice of where they live, whom they marry, and what their job is.

Shows the pattern of organization

The pattern of organization often shows in the thesis statement. These are examples of thesis statements for various patterns.

Time order	▶ Beginning in World War II and continuing through the period of rapid economic growth, the status of women in my country has changed.
Logical division of ideas	▶ The status of women in my country has changed in recent years in the areas of economic independence, political rights, educational opportunities, and social status.
Comparison and contrast	▶ Although the status of women in my country has improved in recent years, it is still very low when compared to the status of women in industrialized countries.
Cause and effect	▶ The status of women in my country has changed in recent years due to increased educational opportunities and changes in the laws.

Reference: Learn more about patterns of essay organization in *Section 42d.*

! Special Tips

The thesis statement is the most important sentence in your essay, so write it with special thought and care. Avoid these common problems.

1. The thesis is too general.

Too general	✗ A college education is a good investment.
Improved	▶ A college education is a good investment for four reasons.
Too general	✗ Lasers are very useful.
Improved	▶ Lasers have several applications in industry and medicine.

2. The thesis makes an announcement.

Announcement	✗ I am going to teach you how to make a flower lei.
Improved	▶ Making a flower lei is not difficult if you follow these instructions.

3. The thesis states an obvious fact.

Obvious fact	✗ The Internet is a communication superhighway.
Improved	▶ The explosion of the Internet has had both positive and negative consequences.
Obvious fact	✗ I had to adjust to a new culture when I moved here.
Improved	▶ Adjusting to a new culture was a challenging experience in more than one way.

PRACTICE—Section 42a

The sentences in the following introductory paragraph are in scrambled order. Put the sentences in the correct order. Place the thesis statement last.

> Although there was a smoke detector in his home, the man's hearing was so poor that he couldn't hear its warning signal. In the same week, a ninety-year-old man burned to death in his home. He had left a pot on the stove, which had started a fire. Experts who have studied the problem have proposed three possible programs. With an increasing population of elderly people, this country needs to find better ways to take care of them. Last month, an ambulance rushed an eighty-nine-year-old woman to the emergency room. A neighbor had found her on her living room floor, where she had been lying for two days after falling.

42b Body

The body of an essay is made up of one or more paragraphs. Each body paragraph has a topic sentence, supporting sentences, and sometimes a concluding sentence. Each body paragraph explains in detail one subtopic mentioned in the thesis statement, so the number of body paragraphs will vary according to the number of subtopics.

Depending on your topic and your purpose, the pattern of organization of body paragraphs can be time order, comparison and contrast, logical division of ideas, and so on (see *Section 42d*).

Transitions between paragraphs

It is helpful to use transitions between paragraphs to show how one paragraph is related to another. Transitions can tell your reader if the topic of the next paragraph follows the same line of thought or reverses direction.

Follows the same line of thought	▶ **Besides** industrial uses, lasers also have many medical applications.
Reverses direction	▶ **On the other hand,** lasers can be used as weapons of war.

Notice how transitions link body paragraphs.

Introduction	Xxxxxxxxxxxxxxxxxxxxxxxxxxxxxxxxxxxxxxxxxxxxxxxxxxxxxxx xxxxxxxxxxxxxxxxxxxxxxxxxxxxxxxxxxxxxxxxxxxxxxxxxxxxxxxx xxxxxxxxxxxxxxxxxxxxxxxxxxxxxxxxxxxxxxxxxxxxxxxxxxxxxxxx xxxxxxxxxxxxxxxxxxxxxxxxxxxxx
Body	*The first reason* a college education is a good investment is financial. Statistics show that men and women with college degrees earn a lot more money than those with only high school diplomas. Xxxxxxxxxxxxxxxxxxx xxxxxxxxxxxxxxxxxxxxxxxxxxxxxxxxxxxxxxxxxxxxxxxxxxxxxxx xxxxxxxxxxxxxxxxxxxxxxxxxxxxxxxxxxxxxxxxxxxxxxxxxxxxxxxx xxxxxxxxxxxxxxxxxxxxxxxxx.

In addition to earning more money, college graduates have a wider choice of jobs, and their jobs are likely to be more interesting. Xxxxxxxxxxxxxxxxxxxxxxxxxxxxxxxxxxxxx xxxxxxxxxxxxxxxxxxxxxxxxxxxxxxxxxxxxxxxxxxxxxxxxxxxxxxxxxxx xxxxxxxxxxxxxxxxxxxxxxxxxxxxxxxxxxxxxxxxxxxxx.

A college education leads *not only* to more interesting and better-paying jobs, *but* it may *also* lead you to discover new interests and uncover unknown talents. Xxxxx xxxxxxxxxxxxxxxxxxxxxxxxxxxxxxxxxxxxxxxxxxxxxxxxxxxxxxxxxx xxxxxxxxxxxxxxxxxxxxxxxxxxxxxxxxxxxxxxxxxxxxxxxxxxxxxxxxxxx xxxxxxxxxxxxxxxxxxxxxxxxxxxxxxxxxxxxxxxxxxxxxxxxxxxxxxxxxxx.

The final reason a college education is a good investment is the personal contacts you make while in college. Xxxxxxxxxxxxxxxxxxxxxxxxxxxxxxxxxxxxxxxxxxxxxxxxxx xxxxxxxxxxxxxxxxxxxxxxxxxxxxxxxxxxxxxxxxxxxxxxxxxxxxxxxxxxx xxxxxxxxxxxxxxxxxxxxxxxxxxxxxxxxxxxxxxxxxxxxxxxxxxxxxxxxxxx xxxxxxxxxxxxxxxxxxx.

Conclusion   Xxxxxxxxxxxxxxxxxxxxxxxxxxxxxxxxxxxxxxxxxxxxxxxxxxxxxxxxxxx xxxxxxxxxxxxxxxxxxxxxxxxxxxxxxxxxxxxxxxxxxxxxxxxxxxxxxxxxxx xxxxxxxxxxxxxxxxxxxxxxxxxxxxxxxxxxxxxxxxxxxxxxxxxxxxxxxxxxx xxxxxxxxxxxxxxxxxxx.

42c Conclusion

The conclusion is the last paragraph of an essay. It has three purposes:

1. It signals the end of the essay.

2. It reminds the reader of your main points.

3. It leaves the reader with your final thoughts on the topic. Notice how the writer accomplishes these three purposes in the following conclusion.

> To sum up, a college education provides at least four main benefits. College graduates enjoy greater financial rewards, and they also have more choices in choosing a career. In addition, taking college classes in different fields may reveal hidden interests and talents that enrich one's personal life as well as providing opportunities for social contacts. Indeed, a college education is well worth investing time and money in now in order to have a better future.

- The transition phrase *To sum up* signals the end of the essay.
- It summarizes the main points: the four benefits of a college education.
- It gives a final comment: investing now will bring a better future.

Begin your conclusion with a conclusion transition signal. (See *Section 41e,* page 283, for a list of transition signals.)

Special Tips

1. Don't use the exact same words in your conclusion that you used in your thesis statement or topic sentences. Find different ways to express the same points.

2. Don't introduce a new idea in the conclusion. Compare these two conclusions:

New idea	To sum up, laser technology is bringing great benefits to humankind. There are hundreds of uses for lasers in industry, and more are discovered every day. Also, medical science is developing new ways to use lasers. On the negative side, lasers have the potential to become terrible weapons of destruction. *We owe it to our children and grandchildren to make sure that lasers are used for peaceful purposes only. Therefore, the government should cancel the "Star Wars" system of space weapons.*
Revised	To sum up, laser technology is bringing great benefits to humankind. There are hundreds of uses for lasers in industry, and more are discovered every day. Also, medical science is developing new ways to use lasers. On the negative side, lasers have the potential to become terrible weapons of destruction. *The future direction of this new technology is in our hands.*

You could use the first conclusion for a different kind of essay—one in which you argue against the use of lasers as weapons. However, it is not a good conclusion for an essay in which you only explain the different uses of lasers.

PRACTICE—Section 42c

Read the following introduction. Then choose the best conclusion from the choices listed.

Introduction

When two countries come into contact over a period of time, there is usually a cultural exchange. Countries import and export words, products, food, and even values. Sometimes cultural imports benefit the importing country. Sometimes they are neither good nor bad. Sometimes, however, imports harm the importing culture. My own country has been influenced by other countries in all three ways.

Possible conclusions

1. In conclusion, other countries have influenced my country in many areas. Our citizens buy Japanese electronics, which have clearly benefited our society. Our young people wear blue jeans and drink Coca-Cola, which are relatively harmless imports from the United States. However, many of our young people have also adopted the values that they see in Hollywood movies. It is unfortunate that countries can't just import the good and keep the bad out.

2. In conclusion, my country has been influenced by other countries in many ways. We have benefited from some and been harmed by others. Other imports have been neither especially helpful nor harmful. Some people in my country would like to stop harmful cultural imports. For example, they want to ban Hollywood movies and even the use of English. In my opinion, you can't—and shouldn't—stop the flow of ideas between countries. It is unfortunate that countries can't just import the good and keep the bad out.

3. In conclusion, my country has Japanese electronics, American blue jeans, and French perfume. As a result, we are culturally richer. It is unfortunate that countries can't just import the good and keep the bad out.

42d Patterns of essay organization

Like paragraphs, essays in English often have typical patterns of organization. The pattern you choose depends on your topic and your purpose. For example, to explain how to celebrate a special holiday, you might use a time-order pattern of organization. To discuss a problem such as homelessness or teenage gangs, you might use a cause-and-effect pattern.

Following are examples of five patterns of essay organization: (1) time order, (2) logical division of ideas, (3) comparison and contrast, (4) cause and effect, and (5) argumentation.

Time order

Use time order for process essays (essays that explain how to do or make something) and for narrative essays (essays that tell a story or relate an event). (See pages 286–287 in *Section 41f* for more information about time order.)

Topics for time-order essays are similar to the following.

Process topics

- How to cook a special dish
- How to give a surprise birthday party
- How to dance the *lambada*
- How we celebrate New Year's in my country
- How to take a perfect vacation in my country
- How to paint a house/car/room
- How to prepare for an earthquake

Narrative topics

- A learning experience
- Leaving home
- A frightening event
- An unforgettable day in my life
- A typical day in my future life
- The day I learned the meaning of _____ . (*fear, love, courage, compassion, frustration, relief, regret, anger, kindness, generosity, mean-spiritedness, incompetence,* etc.)

Transition signals for time order include the following words and phrases.

TRANSITION WORDS AND PHRASES	TIME PHRASES	TIME CLAUSES
first **second** **next** **then** **after that** **meanwhile**	**every evening** **the next day** **in the morning** **during lunch** **before the war** **while waiting**	**while** we were waiting for our visas **when** we first arrived in this country **as soon as** we heard the news **before** we left our country **until** I had this experience **since** we have lived here

A Learning Experience

Introduction

People say that animals can sense danger better than humans can. For example, if your dog growls at a stranger who is standing at your front door, be careful. There is probably something dangerous about the stranger. If, on the other hand, your dog seems relaxed and wags his tail,

Thesis statement

the stranger probably intends no harm. The wisdom of trusting an animal's sense of danger became very clear to me during a recent camping trip.

Body

Last spring, my host family's son Ben invited me to go camping with him and a couple of his friends during a school break. We were going to Yosemite National Park, a very famous and beautiful park about five hours' drive from Ben's home. During the day, we planned to hike. At night we planned to cook our dinner over a campfire. We intended to sleep in tents, but we could also sleep in Ben's family's van if it started to rain. Ben was going to bring his dog, a big black Labrador named Tim. It sounded like a lot of fun.

Time-order transitions show the order of events.

We left *after breakfast* on a Wednesday morning and arrived at the park *about two o'clock in the afternoon. As soon as* we arrived, we drove to our assigned campsite, parked, and unloaded the food and equipment. Tim, the dog, stayed in the van *while* we set up the tents and organized the campsite. We had to put all our food into a big metal container called a "bear box." The park rangers had told us that there were bears in the campground. The bears were very smart and could smell food anywhere, even food wrapped in plastic. The rangers had also told us that bears often broke into tents and cars to get food. Yosemite's bears were so smart, in fact, that they could find food hidden in the trunk of a car under a blanket!

After putting everything in the bear box, we went for a walk. Ben snapped a leash on Tim and said, "Come, Tim. We're going for a walk." Tim, however, refused to get out of the van. He whined and looked very unhappy, so we left without him. *An hour later,* we returned to our campsite and cooked dinner. Tim *still* refused to get out of the van. Instead, he crawled under an old blanket in the very back and began to shiver. Ben started to worry. "Maybe he's sick," he said.

After dinner, we sat around the campfire joking about snakes, bears, mountain lions, and other wild creatures. We tried to scare one another with predictions of how snakes would crawl into our sleeping bags or how bears would rip open our tents. Certainly, none of us really believed that there were bears around. Ben checked Tim again, who was ***still*** shivering in the van. ***Now*** Ben was really worried. He said, "Hey, guys. Maybe we should go home. Tim never acts like this. He must be really sick." We started teasing Ben, saying that his big, tough dog was just scared of the dark.

Just at that moment, we heard scratching noises in the darkness a few feet away. ***Then*** we heard a low growl. ***In the next moment,*** we saw a very large mother bear and her two cubs climbing down a tree right behind us. ***In a flash,*** all four of us were inside the van, shivering along with Tim. The mother bear came over, put her front paws against the van, and tried to push it over. Were we scared? No, we weren't scared—we were terrified!

Finally, the bears left, and we ***eventually*** calmed down enough to go to sleep—safely inside the van, of course. In the morning, the bears were gone and Tim had miraculously recovered from his "illness." ***Then*** we realized the reason for Tim's behavior: He hadn't been sick at all—he had just known that there were bears nearby.

Conclusion | From this experience, I gained respect for an animal's superior sense of danger. I also learned that animals are sometimes smarter than humans, so in the future, I will pay closer attention to the signals that they try to send.

Logical division of ideas or order of importance

Use logical division of ideas or order of importance to explain topics that you can divide into subtopics. (See pages 287–288 in *Section 41f* for more information about these patterns.)

Suitable topics for logical division or order of importance include the following.

- Kinds of students (subdivided by study habits, clothing or hair styles, and so on)
- Kinds of shoppers, automobile drivers, dancers, bosses, jobs
- The influence of television on children
- The advantages of being an only child
- The disadvantages of being an only child

- Qualities of a good marriage partner
- Causes of teenage rebellion, poverty, bad behavior in children, racial intolerance, and so on
- Why I want to be an _____
- Lessons my parents taught me
- Lessons I had to learn on my own
- Accomplishments I am proud of

Transition signals for these two patterns include the following.

LOGICAL DIVISION OF IDEAS		ORDER OF IMPORTANCE
first	besides	more important, more importantly
second	furthermore	the most important, most
third	in addition	importantly
also	in addition to	more significant, more significantly
as well as	moreover	the most significant, most
		significantly
		the best, the worst
		first and foremost

My Worst Teacher

Introduction

Students have many teachers during their school years. Mrs. Bucco, my fifth-grade teacher, was lovely, enthusiastic, kind, and dedicated. I learned a lot that year. My sixth-grade teacher, on the other hand, was terrible. I spent the entire year hating school. He wasn't my worst teacher, however. My worst teacher was Ms. Smith, my English teacher in my first year of high school. She had four of the worst qualities a teacher can possibly have.

The thesis statement shows the number of subtopics.

Body

First of all, Ms. Smith was always late to class. Of course, the students had to be on time, but Ms. Smith apparently felt that she could stroll in at any time. Sometimes she didn't appear at all. The school secretary would leave a note on the door stating "CLASS CANCELED" with no further explanation. I calculated that we missed at least 40 percent of the class hours. At first, the students were delighted when Ms. Smith was absent. We had a whole hour to do nothing except gossip (girls) and horse around (boys). As the year progressed, however, we realized that we would be in serious trouble at exam time because we weren't learning anything. Our parents, of course, were totally unaware of the situation.

Logical division transition signals introduce each subtopic.

In addition to being absent a lot, Ms. Smith never did any work when she was there. Of course she assigned homework—lots of it, in fact—but then weeks would go by before she looked at it. Once I waited six weeks for her to return an essay that I had labored over for days. *Moreover,* her corrections were a joke. She wrote the same comment on everyone's paper—"NEEDS WORK. REWRITE"—but she never told us what was wrong. In a way, her class was easy. You could write anything. Brilliant writing and trash all received the same comment. We considered buying her a gift, a rubber stamp that said "NEEDS WORK. REWRITE" or maybe just "NWR," to save her the effort of writing it out twenty-five times each week.

Third, Ms. Smith was the most boring teacher in our school. Sitting through a whole hour of her class was as exciting as watching laundry dry. Her voice level never changed, **and** she never made eye contact. **Furthermore,** her lessons consisted of students' standing up and reading out loud, sentence by sentence, from the book. Then she would ask us stupid questions about grammar and punctuation. She never asked about the meaning of what we read. It was really hard to stay awake most of the time.

Order-of-importance transition signal

A lot of teachers are boring, but not many are also incompetent. Ms. Smith's **worst quality** as a teacher was her shocking lack of knowledge. She was never prepared for class and sometimes didn't even remember what book we were reading at the moment. She gave such vague answers to our questions that we wondered if she had even read the book. She **also** didn't seem to know much about English grammar. Any question more complicated than "What is the plural of *book*?" completely confused her.

The first part of the conclusion reviews the four topics.

In short, Ms. Smith had several qualities of a poor teacher. She was irresponsible, lazy, boring, and incompetent. I didn't learn much about English that year, but I did learn other useful skills: how to sleep during class without being noticed, how to rewrite an assignment without making changes but still get a better grade, and how to avoid being called on. I have a feeling, however, that these are not the skills that my parents thought I was learning.

Comparison and contrast

In the comparison-and-contrast pattern, you explain the similarities and differences between two items such as two characters in a book or play, two restaurants, or two computer operating systems.

Topics suitable for comparison and contrast include the following.

- Two relatives, friends, or teachers
- Two styles of music or two musicians
- Two cars, computers, or other products
- Two airlines or restaurants
- Two cities or places to go on vacation
- Two periods in history
- Dating and marriage customs in two cultures
- Family relationships in two cultures
- Two school systems (public/private, high school/college, United States/your country)
- Your lifestyle now and at an earlier time
- Two jobs you have had
- Your life and your mother's (or father's) life

When you compare and contrast, do not simply write a description of the first item and then a description of the other item. You must show the reader what is the same and what is different by using transition signals that make the similarities and differences clear.

Transition signals for comparison and contrast include the following.

COMPARISON		CONTRAST	
also	as	however	though
likewise	just as	in contrast	while
similarly	as ... as	instead	whereas
too	like	in/by	unlike
and	just like	comparison	compared
both ... and	similar to	on the other	to/with
not only ... but	be like, be alike	hand	be different
also	be similar	but	(from)
neither ... nor		yet	differ (from)
		although	be dissimilar
		even though	be unlike

You can organize a comparison and contrast essay in two ways. One way is called block organization, and the other way is called point-by-point organization.

Block organization

In block organization, you discuss all the similarities together in a block (which can be one paragraph or several paragraphs). Then you discuss all the differences together in a block. It doesn't matter which block comes first.

It is helpful to the reader if you put a transition between the two blocks, telling the reader, "I am finished talking about similarities. Now I am going to discuss differences." In the model essay that follows, notice the transition sentence at the beginning of the third paragraph: *Although my friends had similar backgrounds, they were as different as two children can be.*

Ingrid and Rafael

Introduction	When I was ten years old and lived with my parents in Djakarta, Indonesia, I had two good friends, Ingrid and Rafael. I divided my time between them carefully, playing
The thesis statement suggests comparison-and-contrast organization.	at Rafael's house one day and at Ingrid's the next. **Both** Rafael and Ingrid had moved to Indonesia because of their fathers' jobs; **however,** that was the closest they ever came to having anything in common. Rafael and Ingrid were almost total **opposites** in almost every other way.

The body starts with a paragraph of similarities.

Transition signals point out the similarities.

Transition sentence

The body continues with two paragraphs of differences.

Transition signals point out the differences.

Conclusion

As I mentioned, Rafael and Ingrid had a few *similarities*. ***Both*** of them were from foreign countries. Rafael was from Mexico, but he could speak English fluently, ***just as*** Ingrid, who was from Sweden, could. Therefore, it was easy for us to communicate with each other. Another *similarity* was their family background. **Both** of their fathers were businessmen who traveled a lot. As a result, Ingrid had moved often and had lived in several other countries, ***just as*** Rafael had. Finally, ***both*** of my friends lived in my neighborhood.

Although my friends had similar backgrounds, they were as *different* as two children can be. First of all, they were completely *dissimilar* in appearance. Rafael had charcoal black hair, ***while*** Ingrid had shiny blond hair. Rafael's beautiful white teeth were perfect ***compared to*** Ingrid's, which were so crooked that she had to wear braces. ***On the other hand,*** Ingrid always dressed up and looked pretty in her pink dresses, ***whereas*** Rafael liked to wear torn jeans and untied black shoes. Ingrid's face, with its sunkissed, freckled nose, was soft and feminine; ***in contrast,*** Rafael's face, with its lively black eyes and sharp nose, was definitely masculine.

Another difference between my two childhood friends was in the activities we did together. When I played with Ingrid, I always came home clean, **but** when I played with Rafael, I usually came home covered with dirt and with scratched arms and legs. Ingrid and I usually did the things girls do. For example, when we went to the beach in the summer, we spent the day collecting seashells and building sand castles. ***In contrast to*** Ingrid's and my quiet activities at the beach, Rafael's and my games were noisy. Sometimes we tied strings onto locusts' wings and flew them around our heads like motorized model airplanes. We shouted and ran and threw sand at each other. In addition, ***while*** Ingrid and I could play for hours and hours without arguing, Rafael and I often fought. He would hold my arms and get his brother Armando to hit me in the stomach. One day, I got mad and punched Rafael right on his nose. I didn't play with Rafael for a while after that.

To summarize, my two childhood friends were as *different* as two children could be. Ingrid was quiet, soft, and well-behaved; ***in contrast,*** Rafael was noisy, rough, and mischievous. ***However,*** I had fun with each of them and cried for days when they moved away.

Point-by-point organization

Point-by-point organization combines comparison and contrast with logical division of ideas or order of importance. In this pattern, you compare and contrast items by subtopic. Each subtopic is one paragraph, and you can mix comparison and contrast in the same paragraph. For example, if you were comparing and contrasting two restaurants, your subtopics might be food, service, interior decor, and prices. In your paragraph about food, there might be similarities—both restaurants serve typical American dishes such as fried chicken and steak—as well as differences—one restaurant serves Mexican dishes but the other doesn't.

A partial outline for a point-by-point essay comparing and contrasting two restaurants might look like this.

Two Restaurants

Thesis statement	I. Joe's Diner and Pepe's Grill are similar in many ways, but they have a few differences that might influence your decision to eat at one or the other.

Body	II. Food
	   A. Both serve American food. (*similarity*)
	      Fried chicken, steak, baked potatoes, french fries, hamburgers, hot dogs, apple pie
	   B. Pepe's serves a few Mexican dishes. (*difference*)
	      Enchiladas, chicken in mole sauce, tamales, burritos, quesadillas, chile verde
	   C. The food is good in both places. (*similarity*)
	      1. The fried chicken at Joe's was crisp, not greasy.
	      2. The chicken enchiladas at Pepe's were perfect.
	
	III. Service
	   A. Both restaurants hire college students. (*similarity*)
	   B. The servers are friendly at both places. (*similarity*)
	      Both hosts greeted us and seated us at a nice table.
	   C. They are a little more formal at Pepe's. (*difference*)
	      1. Servers wore uniforms at Pepe's. Our server did not tell us his name.
	      2. No uniforms at Joe's. Server told us his name and wore a name tag.
	   D. The service was just as efficient at one restaurant as at the other. (*similarity*)

Conclusion	IV. I recommend both restaurants, depending on the occasion.

Choosing one organization or the other will depend on your topic. It is easier to use block organization for some topics and point-by-point organization for others. You will probably discover which organization works better for your topic when you make an outline.

Cause and effect

In a cause-and-effect essay, you discuss the causes or reasons for some problem or event, and then you discuss the effects or results.

Topics suitable for a cause-and-effect essay include the following.

- Pollution
- Crime
- Teenage gangs
- Teenage rebellion
- Divorce
- Bad schools

- Violence at sports events
- A particular disease such as lung cancer or heart disease
- Drug abuse
- A particular war, revolution, or social movement

Transition signals showing the relationship between causes and effects include the following.

CAUSE (REASONS)		EFFECTS (RESULTS)	
because	due to	so	to result in
since	because of	as a result	to cause
as	the effect of	as a consequence	to have an effect
to result from	the consequence of	therefore	on
to be the result of	as a result of	thus	to affect
	as a consequence of	consequently	the cause of
		hence	the reason for

You can use block organization, in which you discuss the causes as a block and the effects as a block, or you can use chain organization.

Chain organization

Chain organization often works better for cause-and-effect topics when the causes and effects happen like a chain reaction. One event (a cause) causes a second event (an effect), but then the second event becomes a cause of a third event, and the third event causes a fourth, and so on. The example essay that follows uses chain organization.

Global Warming

Introduction

The government of the island nation of Tuvalu in the South Pacific wants to buy land in another country because it believes that rising ocean levels will force its ten thousand citizens to leave. The danger is very real, not just to Tuvalu and other Pacific islands but also to river deltas in Bangladesh and cities such as Venice, London, New York, Boston, and Miami. Why is this happening? As we will see,

Thesis statement

rising sea levels are **the result of** a long chain of events.

Body	The Earth has an insulating blanket of gases surrounding it. This blanket allows heat from the Sun to enter the Earth's atmosphere. It also allows some heat to escape back into space, but it traps enough to keep our planet at an average temperature of 16 degrees Celsius (60 degrees Fahrenheit). However, growth in industry, agriculture, and transportation since the Industrial Revolution has produced larger amounts of the gases that form the
The first three body paragraphs describe one step in the chain reaction.	blanket. *As a result,* the blanket has become thicker, and *because* the blanket is thicker, it traps more heat under it. More trapped heat, in turn, *causes* higher air temperatures. In fact, the decade of the 1990s produced six of the hottest years ever recorded. Estimates for future temperature increases range from 4 to 20 degrees in the next one hundred years.
	Because of higher temperatures, ice near the North and South Poles has begun to melt at a faster rate. For example, the Arctic ice cap has shrunk 40 percent. The average thickness was ten feet in 1958–1976, but by 1993–1997, it was just six feet. Hundreds of glaciers in Alaska are melting, and the largest glacier in Europe has retreated five miles.
Transition signals make the cause and effect relationships clear.	The water produced by the rapidly melting ice *has resulted in* a rise in sea level of several inches. Joseph Kono, a native of Chuuk, an island in Micronesia, said the rising water of the western Pacific Ocean *has caused* the disappearance of thirty feet of a beach where he used to swim and fish as a boy. Scientists predict a rise of at least ten to eighteen inches as more glaciers and snow masses melt away. *Consequently,* the citizens of Tuvalu have good reason to worry.
The last body paragraph describes other effects of global warming.	Other *effects* of global warming include climate changes, more frequent tropical storms, changes in agriculture, the spread of tropical diseases, and the extinction of species *due to* the disappearance of their habitats. For example, coral reefs, which are sensitive to temperature changes, are dying. The death of coral reefs, in turn, threatens hundreds of species of fish.
Conclusion	In conclusion, it is clear that global warming is not just a threat; it is a reality. The nations of the world must take action soon, or the Earth will suffer these and possibly other *consequences* that we have not yet noticed.

Argumentation

Argumentation is a kind of essay in which you try to persuade your reader to agree with your opinion about a controversial topic. We state an opinion in the thesis statement (*In my opinion, the sale of handguns to ordinary people should be illegal,* or *I believe that smokers have rights, too*) and then support our opinion with reasons.

Topics suitable for an argumentation essay include the following.

- Gun control laws
- Capital punishment
- Antismoking laws
- Arranged marriage

- School uniforms
- Required attendance and homework in college
- Grades in college

State the opposite point of view first.

We often begin an argumentation essay by mentioning the opposing point of view. We do this early in the essay (either in the introduction or first body paragraph) because we want our readers to know that we have considered all sides of the issue. When we show that we are reasonable and open-minded, our readers are more likely to listen to our point of view.

One way to give the opposite opinion is to briefly mention it in the thesis statement.

▶ Although the Constitution of the United States says that all citizens have the right to own guns, I believe that the sale of handguns to ordinary people should be illegal.

To discuss the opposite opinion in more detail, write an entire paragraph. The paragraph can be either the introductory paragraph or the first body paragraph.

▶   Since the first immigrants arrived in North America, guns have been part of American culture. The newcomers from Europe clearly needed guns for survival. They needed them to hunt for food and to defend themselves against attacks by hostile Indians. Later, as people moved west, they faced all of the dangers of living alone in a wild land. Again, guns were necessary for survival. In the "Wild West," settlers faced wild animals, angry Indians, and violent criminals. There was little or no law enforcement, and if someone wanted to steal your horse or your cow, there was no police department to call, no court, no judge, and no jail. People were truly on their own to defend their family and their property. Therefore, everyone had a gun, and gun ownership became as much a part of American culture as hot dogs and blue jeans. It is therefore not surprising that the writers of the U.S. Constitution gave every citizen the right to own guns.

State your own opinion and give your reasons.

After you have given the opposite point of view, state your own opinion:

▶ However, we no longer live in the "Wild West," and we no longer need guns for survival.

In the rest of the essay, explain the reasons you believe your opinion is the correct one and support your reasons with specific facts, examples, statistics, and/or quotations.

In the following sample essay, the writer mentions in the thesis statement that there is a different opinion. Then, in the first body paragraph, he briefly summarizes three of the opposing arguments. In the remaining body paragraphs, he both answers the opposing arguments and gives his own reasons in favor of genetic engineering.

Designer Babies

Introduction

The young husband and wife fill out the order form together: male, blue eyes, blond hair, 6'2" tall, 20/20 vision, muscular body build, athletic ability, IQ of 130+, quick wit, pleasing personality. They give the completed form to their doctor, who sends it to the laboratory. The lab prepares the correct mixture of genes and sends it back to the doctor, who injects it into the freshly fertilized egg that will become the couple's first child. Science fiction? No, according to some scientists. They say that the time is coming when parents will be able to choose their children's physical and mental characteristics as well as their sex. The question is no longer <u>can</u> we make designer babies. Now the question is

Thesis statement

<u>should</u> we. Although there are certainly reasons to be cautious with this or any new technology, I believe the benefits of genetic engineering far outweigh the dangers.

Opposite point of view: three points mentioned

Opponents of genetic engineering say that it is wrong to tamper with nature. They fear that allowing parents to choose their children's sex will cause a disastrous imbalance in the ratio of men to women in certain areas. Others fear that genetic engineering will lead to the creation of "gene stores" where people can buy and sell genes. Even worse, they predict that children will become manufactured objects, like automobiles or dishwashers.

Argument against first opposing point

In response to the first argument, I say that human beings are constantly tampering with nature—from cesarean sections to heart transplants and laser surgery. If it isn't wrong to save lives by transplanting hearts, why is it wrong to save lives by transplanting genes? For example, it is known that a gene named apO-A1 increases a person's level of HDL, the good cholesterol, and therefore reduces the risk of heart disease. Would it be wrong to transplant this gene to help a child in a family with a history of early death from heart disease? To give another example, it is also known that having two copies of the gene CCR5 provides immunity to the AIDS virus. Would it be wrong to use this technology to prevent the deaths of

Own opinion

millions? Since genetic engineering can eliminate fatal genetically transmitted diseases such as cystic fibrosis and Tay-Sachs disease, why shouldn't we use it?

Argument against second opposing point

The ability to select the sex of children will not cause a disastrous imbalance in the world. According to social scientists, worldwide imbalances in the ratio of men to women have happened throughout history due to differences in mortality rates between men and women, catastrophes such as wars and epidemics, and other factors. Such imbalances are not necessarily harmful. In fact, they may be helpful. According to Dr. Malcolm Potts, a professor of public health at the University of California, "If there is a prolonged decrease of one sex over the other, that sex is likely to become more valued by society. We now see this in the case of younger generations of women in Korea and Japan."

Own opinion

On the contrary, the ability to choose the sex of children will benefit the world because it will reduce overpopulation and decrease the number of unwanted children. We are currently experiencing a world crisis in overpopulation. Studies show that if couples strongly want a boy or a girl, they are likely to keep having children until they succeed. In Western societies, this trend is producing larger families than people desire or would produce if given more control. Internationally, preference for a son leads to larger families in countries like

Another support for own opinion

Bangladesh, Nepal, Egypt, Sierra Leone, and Pakistan. In countries where there are legal restrictions on family size, preference for sons leads to abortion or the killing and/or abandonment of girl babies. Professor Dolly Arora of the University of Delhi, for instance, reports that an estimated 200,000 female fetuses are aborted each year in India. Allowing these parents to choose their child's sex would eliminate this practice.

Argument against third opposing point

Own opinion

Finally, I don't believe that genetic engineering will lead to designer babies in the bad meaning of the phrase. I believe that after a period of discussion and experimentation, humankind will develop responsible practices for genetic engineering, just as it is developing responsible practices for other innovations of technology such as atomic energy and the Internet. As psychologist Joshua Coleman, Ph.D., stated in a recent article on the subject, "Most people have responded to each breakthrough in the evolution of human reproduction technology in a balanced manner." There is no reason to think that they will not continue to do so.

Conclusion

In conclusion, although I agree that we should be cautious in using this powerful new technology, I believe that genetic engineering will lead to the elimination of diseases, the reduction of overpopulation, and improved conditions for females. It will not produce a generation of look-alike supermodels with genius IQs, as some people fear.

PART 7 Formats

43 Writing on a Computer

Computers are wonderful tools for writers because they make it easier to research, write, edit, and format writing assignments.

One advantage of a computer is that it lets you experiment and make changes easily. You can move words, sentences, and even whole paragraphs from one location to another and then back again if you don't like the new location. You don't have to recopy or retype entire pages.

Also, you can format papers and reports with the help of computer word processing programs. You can use **bold type** for titles and for headings to divide long papers into sections. You can use *italic type* or <u>underlining</u> when they are required. You can use different fonts (type styles) in different sizes. You can include photographs, drawings, and charts. You can print in color. If your major is science, engineering, or technology, you can write complex mathematical formulas using scientific symbols, which you cannot do on an ordinary typewriter.

In short, a computer is a useful tool that makes the process of writing easier and even fun. If you use a computer, here is a short list of DO's and DON'Ts.

DO	DON'T
Use the spelling and grammar check programs. They can find some, but not all, errors. They are especially good at finding mistakes in spelling and capitalization. For example, they will tell you if you typed *september* instead of *September*.	**Don't depend on spelling and grammar checkers for 100% accuracy.** Consider the information they give you, but realize that their information is not always correct. For example, they might not tell you if you typed *He want to go* instead of *He wants to go*.
Use the formatting capabilities of your computer. • Use **bold type** for titles and for headings to divide long papers into sections. • Use *italic type* or <u>underlining</u> when they are required.	**Don't overformat your papers and reports.** • Don't use formatting just for decoration. • Never use a font that looks like handwriting. Use only standard fonts. Standard fonts look like the print in newspapers and magazines. • Never use underlining, italics, or capital letters to make words or sentences appear important. • Don't use color printing except for pictures, charts, and graphs. Use only black ink for words.

DO	DON'T
Use the computer for research. If you have access to the Internet, you can get a lot of information online. **Reference:** For information about using online sources for research, see *Section 45d–f.*	**Don't use information from the Internet without evaluating it.** Just as there is a lot of "junk" information on television and in tabloid newspapers, there is also a lot of "junk" information on the Internet.

44 Document Formats

The word *format* means the way a piece of writing looks on a page. It includes spacing, margins, indenting, ink color, type style and size, and so on. College professors expect your papers to look a certain way, and companies expect business letters and reports to have a certain appearance. Using an appropriate format may mean the difference between a good grade and an average grade on a school assignment or between getting an interview and not getting one when you send your résumé to a prospective employer.

44a Academic papers (MLA style)

Most college and university instructors have specific format requirements for written assignments. Different fields of study have different format requirements, so if you write a paper for a psychology class, one for a biology class, and one for an English class, the required formats will be different. Always check with your instructor.

MLA style

For English and other language classes, use the format recommended by the Modern Language Association, an association of college teachers. It is called "MLA style." All the guidelines and sample papers in this section follow this style (except the lab report). For complete information about MLA style, consult the latest edition of the *MLA Handbook for Writers of Research Papers* published by the Modern Language Association.

Paper and ink

1. For typed or computer-printed papers, use plain white 8½-inch by 11-inch paper of good quality.

2. For handwritten papers, use lined 8½-inch by 11-inch notebook paper with three holes. Never use odd-sized paper or paper torn out of a notebook.

3. With continuous-feed computer paper, separate the pages and tear away the narrow strips from both sides of the paper.

4. Use only black ink for printed or typed papers and black or dark blue ink for handwritten papers. Never use pencil or colored ink.

5. In a handwritten paper, never cross out mistakes. If you make a mistake, recopy the page or paint over the mistake with a correction liquid designed for the purpose.

6. Type, print, or handwrite on one side of the paper only.

! *Special Tip*

Be sure to write on the correct side of three-hole notebook paper. The holes go to the left.

Font and spacing

1. Use a standard 10- or 12-point font. Standard fonts look like the printing in books, newspapers, and magazines. Never use a font that looks like handwriting.

2. Leave 1-inch margins on all sides of the paper.

3. Double-space; that is, leave a blank line between each line of typing or writing.

4. Indent the first line of each paragraph five spaces (½ inch in handwritten papers).

5. If your paper has a title, center it at the top of the first page. Don't underline the title or put quotation marks around it.

Page numbers

1. Put your full name, the instructor's name, the course number, and the date the assignment is due in the upper left corner of the first page. Place this information ½ inch below the top. Write the date in the order *day month year* without punctuation.

2. Put your last name and the page number in the upper right corner of all pages. Put this information ½ inch below the top. Use Arabic numerals (1, 2, 3, and so on). Do not put a period after the number or enclose it in parentheses. If you have a separate title page, do not number it or include it in your page count.

Spaces after punctuation marks

1. When typing, put one space after commas, semicolons, and colons. Also put one space between words and between the dots in ellipsis marks.

2. Put two spaces after periods, question marks, and exclamation points.

When you handwrite a paper, make it look like this.

Your name
Instructor
Course no.
Due date

Center title

Indent ½ inch

Skip lines

Indent ½ inch

Ricardo Hernandez   Hernandez 1
Mr. Smith
ESL 065
1 April 2002   1-inch
                                                           margin
                        Christmas in Peru

    Christmas in Peru reminds me of July 4th in the United

States because we use a lot of fireworks. In the weeks before Christ-

mas, we spend many hours shopping for just the right fireworks

and helping our parents prepare food for this special holiday. We

also shop for gifts, which we wrap and put under the Christmas tree.

    When everything is ready on the afternoon of Christmas Eve,

we go outside with our friends to talk about how and where we are

going to shoot off the fireworks. When I say "friends," that includes

neighbors of many different ages. For me, this is the best part of

Christmas in my country, when grandparents, parents, children,

aunts, uncles, cousins, neighbors, and friends all come together

to share the fun. At exactly midnight, the fireworks begin. Everyone

is outside watching the sky, and "oohing" and "aahing" with each

explosion.

    After the fireworks are over, we go to our homes to eat the food

that we have prepared and to open our gifts. The food is different

The second and all later pages should look like this.

Last name and
page number

Hernandez 2

1-inch
margin

in each family. In my family, we always have chicken prepared

by our mother in a special way. There are lots of sweet cakes and

cookies too.

Indent ½ inch

The next morning, we go to church, and then we spend the

rest of the day visiting friends and admiring everyone's gifts.

There is always something delicious to eat at every house we visit.

Indeed, Christmas is a special time for families and friends to be

together in my country. There is a happy spirit of sharing. To me,

Christmas is the best holiday we have.

! Special Tip

Always check with your teacher before handwriting or typing the final copy of a paper. He or she may have different format requirements.

Sample academic paper—typewritten

When you use a typewriter or computer, make your paper look like this.

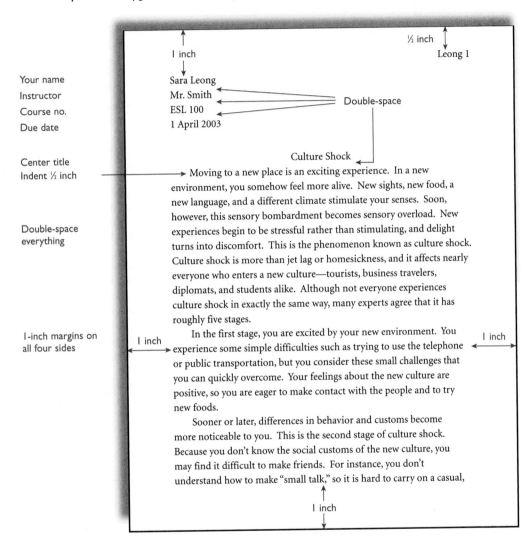

½ inch

1 inch

Leong 1

Your name
Instructor
Course no.
Due date

Sara Leong
Mr. Smith
ESL 100
1 April 2003

Double-space

Center title
Indent ½ inch

Culture Shock

Moving to a new place is an exciting experience. In a new environment, you somehow feel more alive. New sights, new food, a new language, and a different climate stimulate your senses. Soon, however, this sensory bombardment becomes sensory overload. New experiences begin to be stressful rather than stimulating, and delight turns into discomfort. This is the phenomenon known as culture shock. Culture shock is more than jet lag or homesickness, and it affects nearly everyone who enters a new culture—tourists, business travelers, diplomats, and students alike. Although not everyone experiences culture shock in exactly the same way, many experts agree that it has roughly five stages.

Double-space
everything

1-inch margins on
all four sides

1 inch

In the first stage, you are excited by your new environment. You experience some simple difficulties such as trying to use the telephone or public transportation, but you consider these small challenges that you can quickly overcome. Your feelings about the new culture are positive, so you are eager to make contact with the people and to try new foods.

1 inch

Sooner or later, differences in behavior and customs become more noticeable to you. This is the second stage of culture shock. Because you don't know the social customs of the new culture, you may find it difficult to make friends. For instance, you don't understand how to make "small talk," so it is hard to carry on a casual,

1 inch

The second and all later pages should look like this.

½ inch
Leong 2

1 inch

1-inch margins on all four sides

get-acquainted conversation. One day in the school cafeteria, you overhear a conversation. You understand all the words, but you don't understand the meaning. Why is everyone laughing? Are they laughing at you or at some joke that you didn't understand? Also, you aren't always sure how to act while shopping. Is this store self-service, or should you wait for a clerk to assist you? If you buy a sweater in the wrong size, can you exchange it? These are not minor challenges; these are major frustrations.

In the third stage, you no longer have positive feelings about the new culture. You feel that you have made a mistake in coming here. Making friends hasn't been easy, so you begin to feel lonely and isolated. Now you want to be with familiar people and eat familiar food. You begin to spend most of your free time with students from your home country, and you eat in restaurants that serve your native food. In fact, food becomes an obsession, and you spend a lot of time shopping for and cooking food from home.

You are in the fourth stage of culture shock when you have negative feelings about almost everything. In this stage, you actively reject the new culture. You become critical, suspicious, and irritable. You believe that people are unfriendly, that your landlord is trying to cheat you, that your teachers don't like you, and that the food is making you sick. In fact, you may actually develop stomachaches, headaches, sleeplessness, lethargy, or other physical symptoms.

Finally, you reach the fifth stage. As your language skills improve, your self-confidence grows. You begin to have some success in meeting people and in negotiating situations. You are able to exchange the sweater that was too small, and you can successfully chat about the weather with a stranger on the bus. After realizing that

1 inch

44b Lab reports

Most laboratory classes in science and engineering require written reports in which you explain experiments that you have performed in the lab. Lab instructors sometimes have specific requirements for the format of a lab report, so always check with each instructor.

A lab report usually has a title page and several pages of text, and it may have drawings, charts, graphs, or tables of data. The following is a sample lab report from a chemistry class.

Sample lab report

The title page shows the course number, instructor's name, number and title of the experiment, date the report is due, and the student's name. Center all of this information on the page.

Name and
number of the
lab class
Instructor's name

Chemistry 101

Prof. Duncan

Number and title
of the experiment

Experiment D-2

**Sodium Hydroxide and
Hydrochloric Acid**

Due date

2 June 2002

Students' names
(Two students
worked together
on the sample
report.)

Jacob Bien
Erin Pallas

The next and all other pages should look like this.

Purpose of the experiment

1-inch margins on all four sides

Description of the steps in the experiment

Notice the passive voice verbs

Double-space the text, and type headings in boldface type

Calculations from data

---

1 inch

Bien/Pallas 1

Purpose

Hess's law of constant heat summation states that the amount of heat produced by a chemical reaction is the same whether the reaction takes place in one step or in several steps. The purpose of this lab was to determine if the observed change in enthalpy (heat content) in the reaction between solid sodium hydroxide and aqueous hydrochloric acid is predicted by Hess's law.

Procedure

In the first part of the experiment, the temperature of 100 mL of distilled water was measured for 3 minutes, and then 3.43 grams of solid sodium hydroxide was dissolved in it. The temperature of the solution was recorded at 30-second intervals for an additional 5 minutes.

In the second part of the experiment, the temperature of 100 mL of 1.5 moles of hydrochloric acid was measured for 3 minutes, and then 4.0 grams of solid sodium hydroxide was added. The temperature of this solution was recorded at 30-second intervals for an additional 5 minutes. The pH of the final solution was tested.

In the third part of the experiment, the temperature of 50 mL of 1.5 moles of hydrochloric acid was measured for 2 minutes, and then 50.0 mL of the sodium hydroxide solution created in the first reaction was stirred into it. The temperature of this solution was recorded at 30-second intervals for an additional 3 minutes. The pH of the final solution was tested.

Calculations

Heat Q is found by the equation $Q = CM\Delta T$, where C is approximately 4.184 joules/g°C and M is the mass of water:

Reaction	ΔT Observed	Heat Q Calculated
1	−7.0°C	−34 kJ per mole NaOH
2	−21.5°C	−90 kJ per mole NaOH
3	−6.0°C	−58 kJ per mole NaOH

$$NaOH(s) \longrightarrow \cancel{NaOH(aq)} \qquad \Delta H = -34 \text{ kJ}$$
$$\cancel{NaOH(aq)} + HCl(aq) \quad H_2O(l) + NaCl(aq) \qquad \Delta H = -58 \text{ kJ}$$
$$NaOH(s) + HCl(aq) \longrightarrow H_2O(l) + NaCl(aq) \qquad \Delta H = -90 \text{ kJ}$$

The change in enthalpy of reaction 2 is −90 kJ, whereas the sum of reactions 1 and 2 would have predicted −92 kJ. The 2-kJ discrepancy is probably a result of a systematic error.

1 inch

Bien/Pallas 2

Explanation of all
data and of the
results

Discussion

   In each reaction, the temperature of the solution increased. The change in temperature of reaction 1 was 7.0°C. The change in temperature of reaction 2 was 21.5°C. This temperature increase occurred very rapidly. The limiting reagent of this reaction was sodium hydroxide as there were 2.81 moles of hydrochloric acid and only 0.100 moles of sodium hydroxide. In addition, the solution was very acidic at the conclusion of the reaction; it had a pH of 1.

   The change in temperature of reaction 3 was 6.0°C and was much more gradual than that of reaction 2. The reaction produced a water and sodium chloride solution. The limiting reagent in this solution was therefore the sodium hydroxide solution as there were 1.4 moles of sodium chloride and only .043 moles of sodium hydroxide.

   The resulting graphs of these three reactions vary. The first graph has a gradual temperature-versus-time curve, the curve of the second is much steeper, and the third shows that the change in temperature occurred in a very brief period of time. These differences can be attributed to the different states, concentrations, and combinations of the reactants. The second graph shows that the reaction between sodium hydroxide and hydrochloric acid produces a lot of exothermic heat. The sodium hydroxide and water solution was not as exothermic, nor was the diluted amount of sodium hydroxide in the third reaction.

Summary of the
results and
discussion of their
significance

Conclusion

   The experiment produced results predicted by Hess's law. Hess's law predicts that the enthalpy change of reaction 2 can be predicted by adding the enthalpy changes of reactions 1 and 3. The sum of the observed enthalpy changes per mole of reactions 1 and 3 is close to the enthalpy change of reaction 2, as Hess's law predicts: "The overall change in enthalpy for a reaction is the same whether a reaction takes place in a single step or a series of steps." In this experiment, reactions 1 and 3 are essentially the "series of steps" that end up having the same enthalpy change as reaction 2.

Tables, graphs, or
charts of all data
from the
experiment

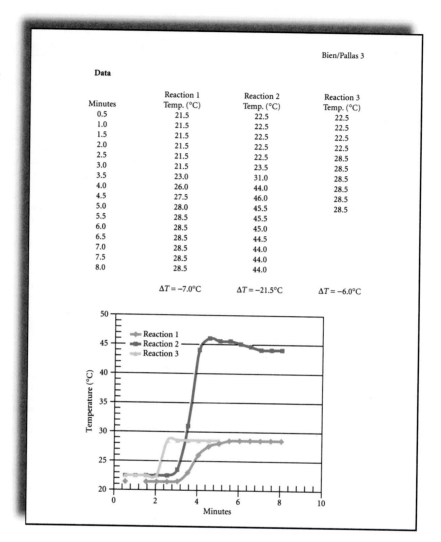

Bien/Pallas 3

Data

Minutes	Reaction 1 Temp. (°C)	Reaction 2 Temp. (°C)	Reaction 3 Temp. (°C)
0.5	21.5	22.5	22.5
1.0	21.5	22.5	22.5
1.5	21.5	22.5	22.5
2.0	21.5	22.5	22.5
2.5	21.5	22.5	28.5
3.0	21.5	23.5	28.5
3.5	23.0	31.0	28.5
4.0	26.0	44.0	28.5
4.5	27.5	46.0	28.5
5.0	28.0	45.5	28.5
5.5	28.5	45.5	
6.0	28.5	45.0	
6.5	28.5	44.5	
7.0	28.5	44.0	
7.5	28.5	44.0	
8.0	28.5	44.0	

$\Delta T = -7.0°C$ $\Delta T = -21.5°C$ $\Delta T = -6.0°C$

44c Business documents

For business documents, use white 8½-inch by 11-inch paper of good quality, black ink, and a standard 10- or 12-point font. Never use lined, colored, or odd-sized paper, and never use a font that looks like handwriting. You may, of course, use letterhead stationery, which is stationery preprinted with a company's name, address, and telephone/fax/e-mail information. Never use personal social stationery for business documents.

Business letters

The format of a business letter depends on whether you will use plain paper or letterhead stationery. Use the format of the sample letter on page 328, which is called *modified block format*, when writing a business letter on plain paper. When writing a business letter on letterhead stationery, use the format of the sample letter on page 329 (*full block format*).

You may write business letters by hand. Use the same format as you would if you were typing, and write or print legibly in black or dark blue ink.

Spacing

1. Write or type each letter so that everything is centered in the middle of the first page. This means that if your letter is very short, you should adjust the spacing so that the typing isn't all at the top of the first page. If your letter has a second page, you don't need to worry about centering it. Just be sure to leave a one-inch margin at the top of the second and all later pages.

2. Single-space both the writer's and the recipient's address and the date. Single-space each paragraph.

3. Double-space between paragraphs and between all other parts of the letter, *except* item (4) that follows.

4. Quadruple-space (four lines down) between the date and the recipient's address and between the closing and the writer's typed name.

Margins and indenting

1. Leave a minimum of 1½-inch margins on all four sides.

2. Indent the writer's address and the date, the closing, and the writer's typed name so that each one begins at the center of the page.

3. Don't indent the first sentence of each paragraph.

Writer's address and date

1. Use the U.S. Postal Service two-letter abbreviations for the states of the United States and the provinces of Canada. Write them in capital letters, and do not use periods.

2. Write the name of a foreign country on a separate line below the city and state or province.

3. Put commas between all parts of an address that appear together on one line *except* between a two-letter state/province abbreviation and a zip code. Don't put commas at the end of lines.

4. Don't abbreviate such words as *Avenue, Boulevard, Road,* and *Street.* Write them out.

5. Write the date in the order *month day year.* Don't abbreviate the names of the months. Write them out. Put a comma between the day and the year.

Recipient's name and address

1. Put a comma between the recipient's name and job title. If the job title is very long, write it on the next line.

2. Don't use *Mr., Mrs., Miss,* or *Ms.* in the address.

Greeting

1. Use a colon after the greeting.

2. Address your letter to a person if at all possible.

   If you do not know the name of a person to write to, call the business or school and ask.

   Address it to a job title, a department, or a company when you cannot find out a name of a person.

   ▶ Dear Marketing Manager:
   ▶ Dear Human Resources Department:
   ▶ Dear Telephone Company:

   Use the title *Ms.* for a woman if you do not know whether she is married or single, or if you know that she prefers it.

Body

1. Use formal English. Don't use contractions or abbreviations.

2. Be direct, polite, and brief. State your main point quickly and courteously. Don't include comments about the weather, questions about the recipient's health, or compliments about the recipient's company. Such comments and questions are customary in some cultures, but not in American culture.

3. State the reason for your letter right at the beginning.

   ▶ In response to your advertisement in the *Kansas City Star*, I am applying for the job of . . .

   ▶ I am writing to call your attention to an error . . .

   ▶ I am writing to request information about . . .

4. In the middle part of the letter, include information that will help the recipient respond appropriately.

   • In a job application letter, tell why you want the job and why you would be a good employee. Don't repeat information that is on your résumé.

   • In a complaint letter, explain briefly what your problem is.

   • In a request letter, be specific about what information or item you want. For example, if you want an application form for a school, say specifically which school or which program.

5. At the end of the letter, give instructions.

   • In a job application letter, tell the recipient how to contact you and when you are available for an interview.

   • In a complaint letter, state specifically what you want (a refund, a credit, a replacement, an apology, and so on).

   • In a request letter, tell where to send the information or item.

6. End the letter with a positive statement.

   ▶ I look forward to hearing from you.

   ▶ I look forward to hearing from you at your earliest convenience. (*stronger, but polite*)

   ▶ Thank you very much.

   ▶ Thank you for your assistance with this matter.

   ▶ Thank you for your prompt attention to this matter. (*stronger, but polite*)

Closing

1. Start the closing two lines below the body and in the center of the page, aligned with your address and the date.

2. Use a standard closing word or phrase. Notice that a comma follows the closing and that its first word is capitalized.

   ▶ Yours truly,   ▶ Very truly yours,

   ▶ Sincerely,   ▶ Sincerely yours,

   ▶ Cordially,   ▶ Respectfully, (*the most formal*)

3. Use an informal closing such as *Best regards* or *Best wishes* only if you know the recipient well.

Name and signature

1. Type your name (or print it clearly in a handwritten letter) four lines below the closing.

2. Put a job or professional title, if you have one, after your name.

   ▶ William Smith, MD 　　▶ John Knight
   　　　　　　　　　　　　　　　 Accounts Payable

3. Don't use a title (*Mr., Mrs., Miss, Ms., Dr., Pres.,* and so on) in front of your own name. (For exceptions, see Special Tips on page 327.)

4. Write your signature in the space between the closing and your typed or printed name.

Enclosures and copies

1. Indicate when you include something inside the envelope with a letter. The "something" is called an enclosure. With a job application letter, enclose your résumé. With a complaint letter about an error in a bill, enclose a copy of the bill.

2. Type the word *Enclosure(s)* or the abbreviation *Enc.* (with a period) at the left margin, two lines below your typed name. If you wish, you can state what the enclosures are or indicate how many there are, but it is not necessary to do so. The five options are

   ▶ Enc.　　　　　　　　　▶ Enc. (3)

   ▶ Enclosure　　　　　　　▶ Enclosures

   ▶ Enclosure: résumé

3. Indicate when you send copies of your letter to additional people. Put the abbreviation *cc:* at the left margin, two lines below your typed name or one line below the abbreviation *Enc.* Use small letters (*cc:,* not *CC:*) followed by a colon. Then list the names vertically.

   ▶ cc: Susan Smith
   　　 Richard Tyson

Envelope

1. Use a standard-sized, plain white envelope.

2. Type or print the recipient's name, title, and address exactly as it appears in your letter. Position it in the low center of the envelope.

   NOTE: The U.S. Postal Service prefers but does not require printing on envelopes to be all capital letters. Capital letters make machine-reading easier.

3. Type or print your own name and address in the upper left corner.

Second page

If your letter is longer than one page, type the following information 1 inch below the top left corner of the second and all other pages.

▶ Thomas E. Brown (*recipient's name*)
October 3, 2002 (*date of letter*)
Page 2 (*page number*)

! *Special Tips*

1. The normal order for names in English is first name/middle name (or middle initial)/family name. Therefore, you may want to use this order even if you use a different order in your language. Doing so makes it easier for an English-speaking person to know whether to reply to *Mr. Chang* or *Mr. Kee* after receiving a letter signed *Chang Fook Kee*.

2. You may want to put *Mr., Miss, Mrs.,* or *Ms.* in parentheses in front of your typed name if—and only if—an English-speaking person might not recognize from your name whether you are male or female. It is usually not correct to give yourself a title. In this case, however, it helps the recipient of your letter to know how to address the reply. Putting parentheses around the title shows that the title is for informational purposes only.

   ▶ **(Miss) Chun-Yi Sun**

Sample envelope

Writer's name
and address in
upper left corner

Chun-Yi Sun
6558 South Main Street, Apt. 6
Chicago, IL 42005

Center the
recipient's name
and address in the
lower half of the
envelope.

Thomas E. Brown
Department of English
Grandview College
6500 College Avenue
Houston, TX 77251

Sample business letter—modified block format

I½-inch margins
on all four sides

Writer's address
and the date

Skip four lines.

Recipient's name,
title, and address

6558 South Main Street, Apt. 6
Chicago, IL 42005
October 3, 2002

Start the address in
the center of the page

Thomas E. Brown
Professor, Department of English
Grandview College
6500 College Avenue
Houston, TX 77251

Skip one line

Greeting

Dear Professor Brown:

Reason for the
letter in first
sentence

I am writing to ask you for a letter of recommendation. I am applying for
admission to graduate school at three different universities and need a letter of
recommendation for each. The schools are the University of Chicago,
Northwestern University, and the University of Illinois.

Information to
identify the writer

I was a student in your English 400 class in the fall semester, 2002. You may
remember the research paper that I wrote for your class. It was a comparison of
teaching methods in my home country, Taiwan, and teaching methods in the
United States.

Specific request:
what, when,
where

If you are willing to write a recommendation for me, I would be very
appreciative. Enclosed are three stamped, preaddressed envelopes, one for each
school. The deadline for all applications, including the recommendations, is
November 30. Kindly send your letters to the addresses typed on each of the
three enclosed envelopes.

Final sentence

Thank you most sincerely.

Closing

Signature

Very truly yours,

Chun-Yi Sun

(Miss) Chun-Yi Sun

Align with writer's
address and the date

Skip four lines

Typed name

Enclosure
information

Enc. (3)

Sample business letter—full block format

The following business letter uses *full block* format. Full block format is the most formal format for business letters and is used on letterhead stationery. Full block and modified block are the same *except* for the following.

- It is not necessary to type the writer's address. Just type the date about two lines below the bottom of the printed address information.
- Lines are not indented. Every line begins at the left margin.

	Adventure Travel, Inc. **64 First Street, Newton, MA 02495** **(413) 222-2222** **FAX: (413) 222-2223** **E-mail: goforit.com**
Date	June 12, 2002
Recipient's name and address	Robert Webster Accounts Receivable Webster Printing Company 125 Second Street Newton, MA 02454
Greeting	Dear Mr. Webster:
Reason for letter	I am writing to call your attention to an error in your most recent statement to us.
Explanation of problem	Your statement dated June 1, 2002 (copy enclosed), shows a balance due of $1,356.19. However, we paid this bill on May 15, 2002. Enclosed is a copy of our canceled check 3509 for this amount as proof of payment.
Specific instructions	Kindly correct your records and credit our account. If you have any questions, please call me. I am generally available during normal business hours.
Final sentence	I look forward to your prompt attention to this matter.
Closing	Very truly yours,
Signature	*John Knight*
Typed name and job title	John Knight Accounts Payable
Enclosure information	Enclosures: Statement dated 6/1/02 Canceled check 3509 (front and back)

Résumés

A résumé is a summary of your qualifications for employment. The best résumés are short (one page, if possible), well-organized, attractive to look at, and easy to read.

A résumé usually contains the following information.

Name, address, telephone number

Type your name, address, telephone number, fax number, and e-mail address at the top of the page.

NOTE: It is illegal for employers to ask job applicants for certain personal information such as age, sex, marital status, race, and religion. Include this information only if doing so might help you get the job.

Employment objective

State in a few words what kind of job you are looking for.

Education

List each college or university you attended, the years attended, your field of study, the degree received, and any awards or special honors. Begin with the most recent college. You may list your high school, especially if you are applying for your first job.

Experience

List all the jobs you have had, beginning with the most recent one.

Give each job title, the name and location of each employer, the dates of employment, and a short description of your duties. Tell about promotions or any special recognition, but do not give salary information.

Special skills, activities, and interests

List any special skills, activities, and interests, such as computer or foreign language skills, club memberships, and community service. Include hobbies such as photography or model building if they are relevant to the job you are seeking or if you need to fill out an empty page.

References

You may say "Available on request" or you may list the name, address, and telephone number of people who are willing to recommend you. Always ask a person's permission before you list him or her as a reference.

Sample résumé

Name in
boldface type

Name and address
lines can be
centered or
aligned.

Headings in
boldface type
make them stand
out.

Most recent
experience first

Minimum
1½-inch margins
on all four sides

Emilia H. Richardson
2230 La Cienega Boulevard, Apt. 4
Los Angeles, CA 92222
(818) 566-7809

Objective   To obtain an entry-level position with an architectural firm.

Education   1996-2002
California State Polytechnic University, San Luis Obispo, California
- Bachelor of Architecture, June 2002
- G.P.A. 3.5 out of a possible 4.0
- Dean's List 12 out of 15 quarters
- Architecture Students' Honor Society

Summer 2000
University of Guadalajara, Guadalajara, Mexico
Summer Spanish language program, combined with study of
Spanish colonial architecture

Experience June 2002–present
Smith and Bell, Architects, San Luis Obispo
Junior draftsman. Drafted interior stairwell details using CAD for
large office building project

Summer 2001
Kobayashi Associates, Architects, San Francisco
Summer internship. Helped librarian organize catalogs and
material samples. Performed general office duties.

Summer 1999
Los Angeles School District
- Tutored math and science in a summer program for high
school students
- Mentored three girls from low-income families interested in
studying architecture

Skills and Fluent Spanish
Activities   Exhibitor, Los Angeles County Fair, model-building competition
- Blue ribbon, 1999
- Honorable mention, 1997 and 1998

References Available on request

 Special Tip

Some computer word processing programs have résumé formats. You simply type
in your information, and the program puts it in an attractive format for you.

Memorandums

A memorandum, or memo, is a form of written communication from one person to others in the same company. A memo is usually short and about one topic. It is a quick way to give information, to make a request, or to make a recommendation in writing.

Companies usually have their own format for memos, and they often have preprinted memo forms or a memo template on their computer system. The following lines normally appear at the top of a memo. Notice that each word is followed by a colon.

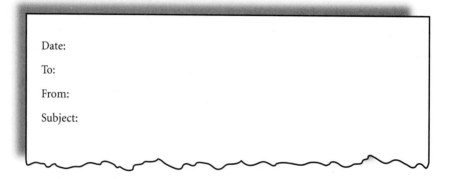

Date:

To:

From:

Subject:

List the names of people or departments who will receive the memo after the word *To*. Use the abbreviation *cc* to list names of any other people (besides the main recipients) who will get a copy. If the list of recipients is long, you may put it after the word *Distribution* at the bottom of the page, as in the sample memo on page 333.

Sometimes the word *Subject* is replaced by the abbreviation *Re*. Busy working people want to know immediately the topic of a memo, so the subject should stand out. Make it the last line before the body, and print it in bold type.

The body of the memo is very short and to the point. Since its purpose is to communicate information as efficiently as possible, state the main point right at the beginning, and make your explanations brief.

Sample memorandum

The subject is in **boldface** type.

The body of the memo is as concise as possible.

The list of recipients has other information beside each name, so it is at the bottom of the page.

HAWAIIAN PARADISE HOTELS AND RESORTS

MEMORANDUM

Date: October 4, 2002

From: Laura Montgomery

To: Distribution

Re: **Employee Name Badges**

Hawaiian Paradise Hotels and Resorts has purchased a name badge for each employee (full-time and part-time) as a security measure. Enclosed are badges for you and the employees in your department. Please give employees their badges with paychecks on October 6 and ask employees to begin wearing them as part of their daily uniform.

Distribution:

Matt Maheshwaran	Housekeeping
Faye Su	Front Desk
Ann Medeiros	Guest Activities
Charles Horner	Maintenance
John Nishikawa	Grounds
Silvia Fernandez	Accounting
Ed Blum	Security

44d E-mail

E-mail (electronic mail) has changed the way people communicate with each other. Like other forms of written communication, e-mail has customary rules for format and content.

Format

1. Always fill in the subject line with a short phrase that tells the topic of your message.

   ▶ Lab report due next week
   ▶ Meeting scheduled for 3/15/03

2. Begin with a greeting and end with a closing, just as you would in a letter. Use a formal greeting for people you don't know well. Use informal greetings and closings only with friends.

Formal	Informal
▶ Dear Mr. Duncan,	▶ Hi, Laura,
▶ Sincerely,	▶ Ciao,

3. Don't write in all capital letters or all small letters. Follow the rules for capitalizing in English.

4. If your message is too long to fit on one computer screen, it is helpful to your reader if you break the message into sections. Give each section a heading.

Content

1. As with other business correspondence, be brief, clear, and direct. State your main point right away—in the first sentence if possible.

2. Use formal English in business messages.

3. Always proofread a message before sending it. Use a spelling checker if your e-mail program has one.

Sample e-mail message

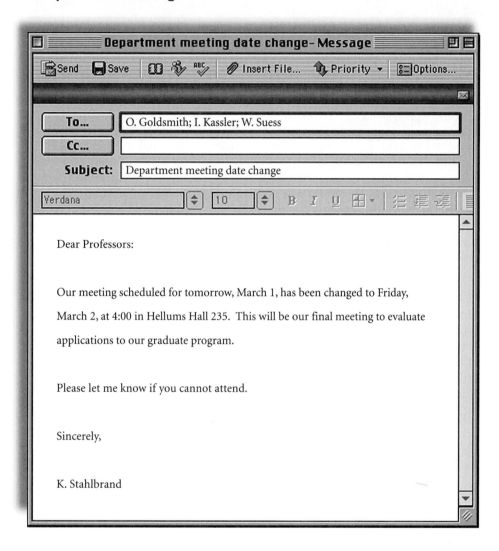

45 Research Papers

In many high school and college classes, writing a formal academic paper is a major part of the coursework. This paper is often called a "term paper" because students generally work on it for several weeks, completing it at or near the end of the school term. Teachers assign term papers to encourage independent thinking and to give students a chance to explore in depth a topic that interests them.

In American schools, teachers encourage students' original thinking and writing. Teachers in other cultures often value different intellectual skills. For example, teachers may ask students to display their mastery of a subject by explaining the ideas of others without evaluating them. In the American system, teachers ask students not only to evaluate others' ideas but also to develop their own thoughts on the subject. For students new to the American system, criticizing the works of scholars and developing their own ideas about a topic may feel strange and even uncomfortable. However, in American classrooms, students are expected to do so, and term papers and research papers are a part of the system.

Many term papers require research as well as independent thinking; these are called "research papers." For some research papers, you gather information about your topic from outside sources and present it as a kind of report. For others, you combine outside information with your own ideas to create a unique analysis of a topic. Make sure that you understand which kind of paper your instructor expects before you begin.

Although researching and writing an academic paper is a complex process with many guidelines for proper procedure and rules for correct form, it is also an exciting intellectual adventure. Try not to become overwhelmed by the mechanics of the process.

These are recommended steps in writing a research paper.

45a Making a schedule

The process of writing a research paper has many steps and takes a very long time, so the best advice is this: START EARLY! Especially if you have an entire semester to do the paper, it is tempting to put off starting for a few days—and then a few more days—and then a few more. However, don't procrastinate. On the day you receive the assignment, make a schedule and stick to it. Here is the schedule one student made for herself. She learned about the assignment on September 15. The due date was November 15.

Sample schedule

Task	Time Allowed	Finish by
Take a library tour.	1 day	9/16
Choose a topic.	2 days	9/18
Look for information.	2 weeks	10/2
Narrow the topic.	1 day	10/3
Read and take notes.	3 weeks	10/24
Plan the paper. (Make an outline.)	3 days	10/27
Write the first draft.	1 day	10/28
Visit the writing center to get suggestions for revisions.	1 day	10/29
Revise the paper. Do more research if necessary.	2 weeks	11/12
Prepare a works-cited list.	1 day	11/13
Type and proofread the final copy.	2 days	11/15

45b Taking a library tour

Take a tour of your school library to learn what research tools are available and how to use them. Find out how to locate encyclopedias, books, magazine and newspaper articles, maps, pictures, and anything else you might need for your research. Get to know the reference librarians. They are knowledgeable professionals who are always willing to help you find the information you need.

Also, find out if your school has a writing center or tutoring lab, what services it offers, and how to make an appointment. Then, if you run into problems, you will know where to get help.

45c　Choosing a topic

Choose a topic that interests you, and then narrow it to a specific area that you can cover thoroughly within the page limit of your assignment. If your topic is too broad, you will spend too much time doing research. "Education" is an example of a topic that is too broad. Imagine using "Education" as a keyword for an Internet search. You would undoubtedly have to check out thousands of Web sites to find usable information. "Bilingual education" would be a better choice, but even that keyword would give you several hundred Web sites to check out.

Also make sure that you can find information about your topic easily. If you choose a topic such as the diet of nomadic sheepherders in Outer Mongolia or medicinal plants of the Amazon rainforest, make sure you can find information without too much effort.

If you need help choosing and narrowing an appropriate topic, ask your instructor for advice. You can also get help from a reference librarian, the writing center, or the tutoring lab.

45d　Collecting information

In this step, do the actual research. Search the library and the Internet for information about your topic. Some sources are available both in the library and on the Internet. Others are available only in the library or only on the Internet.

Check different kinds of sources.

Reference books

Reference books include dictionaries, encyclopedias, atlases, and books of facts. There are general encyclopedias such as *The Encyclopedia Americana* and specialized encyclopedias such as *The Film Encyclopedia.* There are also general dictionaries and specialized dictionaries such as *A Dictionary of Botany.*

Reference books are in the reference room or reference area of the library. You cannot check them out and take them home; you must use them inside the library. Make photocopies of pages that you need.

 Special Tip

Although encyclopedias are a good place to get basic information about your topic, many college instructors will not allow them as sources in college research papers. Ask your instructor.

Books

Libraries today usually list all books in a computerized catalog. You can search for books by title, by author's last name, or by subject. Unless you know the name of an author or the title of a book, you will begin searching by subject. You may have to look under several subjects at first. To find books on IQ tests, for example, look under the subject "IQ tests." If there are no books listed, try looking under the subjects "intelligence testing" or "testing" and "intelligence" separately. Eventually you will find what you need.

When you find a book that you think might be useful, write down the title, the name of the author, and the book's call number. A call number is a book's "address" in the library. You must know this number to find the book on the library shelves.

 Special Tip

When researching your topic, look for books that have a bibliography in the back. A bibliography is a list of sources that the author consulted. Maybe he or she used sources you could also use for your paper. You can tell if a book has a bibliography if you see the abbreviation *bibliog.* in the catalog listing.

Articles in popular magazines and newspapers

Examples of popular magazines are *Psychology Today* and *Newsweek.* You can find magazine articles in two main ways. The first way is to search in an index. An index is a catalog of magazine and newspaper articles, and like a book catalog, it lists articles by title, author, and subject. Indexes are usually on CD-ROMs. There are different indexes for magazines, newspapers, and specialized subjects like psychology and business. Articles in popular magazines are indexed in the *Readers' Guide to Periodical Literature. The National News Index* lists articles from five major U.S. newspapers.

Listings are full of abbreviations, which makes them a little difficult to read at first. There is always a guide to abbreviations, usually in the first few pages. With a little practice, you will soon learn what each abbreviation means. Here is a sample listing from the *Readers' Guide.*

subject heading

illustrated (has pictures, photos, charts, etc.)

Intelligence Testing

title of article   author   name of magazine

New Research Questions Validity of IQ Tests. S. Watson. il *American Education*

date

33-37 N 3 '01

page numbers

Print out the pages listing articles on your topic and mark those that you think may be useful. Then locate the magazines containing the articles on the library shelves, find the articles, and make photocopies to take home to read.

A more convenient way to find magazine articles is to use an online computer search service such as *InfoTrac* or *Ebscohost*, which most libraries have. The process is the same as searching an index. However, these online services have an advantage: They allow you to print out articles directly from the computer terminal. This saves you the time and trouble of looking for the magazine on the library shelves.

 Special Tip

Be cautious about using information from popular magazines and newspapers. Some popular magazines and tabloid newspapers publish false or misleading information to increase their sales. Some Internet sources also may not be reliable. See "Evaluate your sources" on page 341.

Internet sources

Searching the Internet is a convenient way to do research, but it takes practice to do it efficiently. There are several ways to find information. One way is to type in keywords. Keywords are words that name your specific topic, such as *tattoos* or *poisonous snakes*. Search engines (search programs) such as Google and Yahoo search the Internet and display a list of Web sites containing your keywords. The more specific your keywords are, the more selective the search will be. For example, the keyword *snakes* will give an enormous number of sites to check out. The keywords *poisonous snakes* will give fewer, and *Central American poisonous snakes* will give the fewest.

Your own sources

Your instructor may allow you to gather information on your topic by performing an experiment, taking a survey, or interviewing people.

Scholarly journals

For students in graduate school who do advanced research, scholarly journals are important sources of information. Scholarly journals are magazines that print academic articles, usually about a specific field of study. They are also called periodicals or periodical journals. Examples of scholarly journals are *Journal of Educational Psychology* and *New England Journal of Medicine*. Instructors in undergraduate classes do not usually require students to use scholarly journals.

Evaluate your sources.

When you find a possible source, you should ask yourself two questions: (1) Is the information useful? (2) Is the information reliable?

Is the information useful?

Judging a source's usefulness is easier if you have a rough outline. Read a few paragraphs, or read the first sentence of each paragraph. Does the information seem relevant? Does it fit in your outline? If so, it is potentially useful.

Is the information reliable?

There is a lot of outdated, biased, and false information in print and on the Internet. Your sources should be reliable, which means that the information should be current, unbiased, and true. You can judge a source's reliability by doing the following.

1. Check the date. Your sources of information should be current unless your topic is a historical one. For example, if your topic is space exploration, a source dated before 1960 would probably not have very useful information.

2. Check the reputation of the author(s). What do you know about them? You should find out their occupations, at a minimum. A reliable author isn't necessarily famous; he or she just has to have special knowledge about your topic. For example, if your topic is the conditions in U.S. prisons, a letter or article written by a prisoner is reliable. However, the same prisoner might not be a reliable source on the topic of ballet dancing.

3. Check the reputation of the publisher. What company or organization published the information? Is it nationally or internationally known?

4. What is the purpose of the publication or Web site? Is it to sell a product, support one side of a controversy, promote a political point of view, or merely provide information?

5. Check the content. Is it mostly fact, opinion, or propaganda? Does it seem strongly biased? Are the ideas supported by reliable evidence?

6. Check the language. Does it seem well written? Is it free of emotional language? Do you notice any spelling errors?

7. Check the quality of the presentation. Is the quality of the printing good? Is the Web site well organized? Does it offer links to other sites? Check them out.

If you aren't sure about a source, ask your instructor or a reference librarian for help in evaluating it. There are also sites on the Internet that can help. Find them by searching the keywords "evaluating Internet information."

Print or make copies of useful pages.

When you find a useful and reliable source, print the pages or make photocopies. Then you can read and take notes in a quiet, unhurried way at home.

Keep good records of all of your sources.

One of the final steps in the research paper process is to prepare a list of all of the sources from which you borrowed words and ideas. The list gives complete and exact information about where to find each source in the library or on the Internet. It is a good idea to start this list at the very beginning so that you don't have to go back and find the book or article or Web site again. Carefully write down (or print out) the following information for each source.

Book

1. Author's full name (last name first)
2. Full title (including any subtitle)
3. Edition (if the book is a second or later edition)
4. Number of the volume and the total number of volumes (if the book is a multivolume work)
5. City of publication
6. Shortened name of the publishing company
7. Year of publication

Newspaper or magazine article

1. Author's name
2. Title of the article
3. Title of the newspaper or magazine
4. Date of publication
5. All page numbers on which the article appears

Internet source

1. Author's name
2. Title of the document
3. Date of electronic publication or latest update

4. Name of the institution or organization sponsoring or associated with the site

5. Date you accessed the source

6. Internet address or URL

In addition, you should copy down any other information that will help you find the source again if you need to. For example, copy down the call number of a book or the origin of a magazine reference (which magazine index or online search program).

PRACTICE—Section 45d

Check the sources that might be useful and reliable sources of information on the topic body art (body painting, tattooing, and piercing) in ancient and modern cultures.

Print sources

1. *Tattoo History: A Source Book* by Stephen G. Gilbert. Collection of historical writings on tattooing. Includes accounts of tattooing in the ancient world, Polynesia, Japan, the pre-Columbian Americas, nineteenth-century Europe and the United States. Published in 2001.
2. *The Rose Tattoo.* Play by Tennessee Williams, made into a movie starring Anna Magnani and Burt Lancaster. Story of a widow whose loyalty to her dead husband is tested by a handsome truck driver.
3. "Tattooing among the Maoris of New Zealand." Article by William Oldenburg in the June 1946 issue of *Journal of Cultural Anthropology.*
4. "Regulating the Body Art Industry." A doctor proposes laws to ensure the safe practice of tattooing and body piercing in the state of New York. Article written by Dr. Evan Whitman in the February 10, 2001, issue of *The New York Times.*
5. "Living Canvas." Article by Jerry Adler in the November 29, 1999, issue of *Newsweek.* Tattooing and body piercing, long fashionable with bikers and rebellious teens, are gaining popularity among the "beautiful people" of high society.
6. *Body Decoration: A World Survey of Body Art* by Karl Groning. A collection of photographs traces more than ten thousand years of body art, from the body painting of prehistoric people to the body piercing of modern punk. Published in 1998.

Internet sources

1. Tattoos.com. A Web site that provides information about tattooing and links to other sites.
2. "Tattoo." An article in the online *Encyclopedia Britannica* found at britannica.com.
3. Body Piercing Shop. A Web site offering titanium, surgical steel, silver, and gold body jewelry. Also semiprecious gemstones and Austrian crystal. Best prices.
4. "Body Marking." An article in the online *Columbia Encyclopedia* on body marking, painting, tattooing, or scarification (cutting and burning) of the body for ritual, aesthetic, medicinal, magic, or religious purposes.

5. Getting Pierced Safely. A Web site that explains health factors. All the facts you need if you are thinking of body piercing. Choosing a safe practitioner. Risks.
6. "The Human Canvas." A report on body art throughout history. *Discovery* Online, Expeditions series, produced in cooperation with the American Museum of Natural History.

45e Reading and taking notes

By now you have collected many pages of information on your topic. As you read your photocopied pages, mark important paragraphs or sentences with colored marking pens. While reading, you should also make notes. Some people handwrite notes on 4-inch by 6-inch cards or single sheets of paper and file them in a box, a divided three-ring binder, or several file folders. Other people write notes on a computer and keep them in separate files.

Develop a system for keeping your notes organized. A rough outline is a big help. At a minimum, make a list of subtopics that might become sections of your finished paper. For example, for a paper about bilingual education, you might have these subtopics: *definition, goals, laws about, problems, successes, failures, history of, future of, bilingual ed in other countries,* and so on. If you are not sure what your subtopics should be, the question words *who, what, where, when, why,* and *how* are good ones to start with. As you read and take notes, write a code on each note to identify its subtopic or place in your rough outline.

Also develop a system for keeping track of the source of each note. Write a code or abbreviation for the source and page number on each note card.

Three kinds of notes: quotation, summary, and paraphrase

There are three kinds of notes: quotation, summary, and paraphrase. For all three kinds, remember to keep track of the source so that you don't accidentally commit plagiarism. It is also helpful to write the subtopic on your note card, as in the three sample notes that follow.

Original

"U.S. English and other such groups maintain that linguistic divisions have caused unrest in several countries, such as Canada and Belgium—though they generally fail to note that the countries where strife and violence have been most pronounced, such as Spain, are the ones where minority languages have been most strenuously suppressed."

(Bill Bryson. <u>The Mother Tongue: English & How It Got That Way</u>. New York: Avon, 1990, page 240)

Quotation note

A quotation uses the exact words of the original.

(English-only movement)

Referring to U.S. English's claim that violence occurs in countries with linguistic divisions, Bill Bryson notes that "the countries where strife and violence have been most pronounced, such as Spain, are the ones where minority languages have been most strenuously suppressed."

(Bryson, page 240)

Summary note

A summary records only main ideas; therefore, a summary is shorter than the original.

(English-only movement)

The most violence between speakers of different languages occurs in countries where minority languages are the most strongly suppressed.

(Bryson, page 240)

Paraphrase note

A paraphrase includes main ideas and supporting details, so it is almost the same length as the original.

(English-only movement)

Referring to U.S. English's claim that having different languages in a country leads to strife, Bill Bryson notes that the most violence occurs in countries where minority languages are the most strongly suppressed, such as Spain—not in other dual-language countries such as Canada and Belgium.

(Bryson, page 240)

Quotations

Here are some hints on using quotations.

1. Identify the writer or the source of quotations. Identify people by name or by occupation. In the example quotation note, the speaker is identified by name. When the source of the quotation is a document or an organization, give the title of the document or the name of the organization.

   ▶ The **Bill of Rights** states, "The right of people to keep and bear arms shall not be infringed."
   ▶ The **National Rifle Association** says that . . .

2. You may use a reporting verb or reporting phrase to introduce a quotation, or you may include the quotation in one of your own sentences. See page 102 for a list of reporting verbs.

   Reporting verbs   ▶ Bryson **notes** that U.S. English . . .

   Reporting phrase   ▶ **According to** Bryson, "U.S. English . . . ."

   Quotation included   ▶ The belief that people have a right **"to keep and bear arms"** is not as appropriate in twenty-first-century America as it was 250 years ago.

3. It may be necessary to explain the context of the quotation. In the example quotation note on page 345, the words *Referring to U.S. English's claim that* . . . provides the context for Bryson's statement.

4. You may have to add or delete words from your original source.

- You may delete parts of quotations that are irrelevant to your point as long as you do not change the meaning of the original. Show a deletion with an ellipsis (three periods with a space between each) enclosed in square brackets.

  ▶ "U.S. English and other such groups maintain that linguistic divisions have caused unrest in several countries [...] though they generally fail to note that the countries where strife and violence have been most pronounced [...] are the ones where minority languages have been most strenuously suppressed."

  The student writer felt that the names of the countries in the original source were not important, so he deleted them and put ellipses and square brackets in their place.

- You may add letters or words to make the quotation grammatically correct. Enclose added material in brackets [ ].

  ▶ "U.S. English[...]maintain[s] that linguistic divisions have caused unrest ... "

- Another reason for adding words to a quotation is to explain or identify something in the quotation. For example, the name *U.S. English* may need identifying.

  ▶ Bryson notes, "U. S. English [**an organization that supports English as the only official language in the United States**] and other such groups ... "

  ▶ Bryson notes that "the countries where strife and violence have been most pronounced, such as Spain [**where the Basque and Catalan languages are minority languages**], are the ones where minority languages have been most strenuously suppressed.

5. Don't just drop a quotation into your paper. Make the connection between the quotation and your idea clear. For example, a student writing a paper on the topic of making Spanish an official language in the United States might use part of the quotation about U.S. English in his paper. However, he must connect his own idea to the quotation by adding a few sentences before and after it.

The first sentence states the writer's main point.	Making Spanish and English equal would erase barriers and promote harmony between the two cultures. Not everyone agrees, however. Bryson notes, "U.S. English [an
The second sentence connects his idea to the quotation.	organization that supports English as the only official language in the United States] and other such groups maintain that linguistic divisions have caused unrest in
The last two sentences explain the connection.	several countries, such as Canada and Belgium [. . .]" (Bryson 240). However, I believe that people are more likely to fight against the majority culture if their language is suppressed. If two languages are equal, there is no reason to fight.

6. You can use both direct and indirect quotations.

- Direct quotations are the exact words of a speaker or writer. They must be enclosed in quotation marks and introduced by a reporting verb or phrase such as *Bryson wrote . . .* or *According to Bryson. . . .*

- Indirect quotations are not enclosed in quotation marks and are introduced by a reporting verb and the word *that: Bryson wrote that. . . .* Indirect quotations are also called reported speech.

Quotations are the easiest kind of notes to make because you simply copy existing words. However, a research paper with only quotations is hard to read and doesn't require much creativity. For most of your paper, use your own words to summarize and paraphrase information from your reading. Use quotations only when they support an idea with especially appropriate or memorable language.

Reference: Learn more about quotations in the following sections: Quotation marks, *Section 29a;* Reported speech, *Section 11c.*

Summaries and paraphrases

When you summarize and paraphrase someone else's words, you tell them in your own words. A summary tells only the main points, so it is shorter than the original. A paraphrase includes both main points and details, so it is about the same length as the original. It is important to change the words and sentence structure when you write summary and paraphrase notes. If you do not, you commit plagiarism.

Summarizing and paraphrasing are not always easy for students whose first language is not English. Here is a technique to try.

I. Read the material until you understand it well. Then write short phrases for each idea from memory. Don't look at the original while you are writing. Don't write complete sentences, and use synonyms wherever possible. Here are rough notes from the original on page 344.

- ▶ U.S. English [group that wants English to be the only official U.S. language] says—unrest, violence in countries with diff. languages—BUT Bryson says— most violence occurs in countries (Spain) where minority lang. suppressed.

2. Write a summary or paraphrase note. Check your note against the original source to make sure that (a) you have not misrepresented any ideas, (b) you haven't forgotten any important ideas, and (c) you have not used the same words and sentence structure as the original source.

Plagiarism

In some cultures, students demonstrate their knowledge by repeating and/or explaining the ideas of others without necessarily naming the works the ideas came from. In the United States, however, you must *always* acknowledge the source of another person's words and ideas, even if your reader already knows where you got your information. If you do not, you risk committing plagiarism. Plagiarism is borrowing another person's work without saying so, and it is a serious form of cheating. Students who plagiarize receive punishment ranging from failure in the course to expulsion from school. Even when plagiarism happens accidentally, as when a student forgets to use quotation marks, the punishment can be severe.

Plagiarism is not just using someone's words without quotation marks. It is also using someone's ideas without acknowledging him or her as the source. Even if you change the words or summarize the ideas, you must give credit to the other person.

Here are two examples of plagiarism and ways to avoid it.

Example 1

Original ▶ There is little evidence to suggest that people are refusing to learn English. According to a 1985 study by the Rand Corporation, 95 percent of the children of Mexican immigrants can speak English. By the second generation more than half can speak *only* English. There is after all a huge inducement in terms of convenience, culture, and income to learn the prevailing language. (Bill Bryson, <u>The Mother Tongue: English & How It Got That Way.</u> New York: Avon, 1990, page 241)

Plagiarism ▶ It is clear that immigrants want to learn English. As Bill Bryson notes, there is after all a huge inducement in terms of convenience, culture, and income to learn the prevailing language (241).

Even though the student writer gives the author's name and a page number, the second sentence is plagiarism because it has exactly the same words as the original, and there are no quotation marks.

To correct ▶ It is clear that immigrants want to learn English. As Bill Bryson notes, "There is after all a huge inducement in terms of convenience, culture, and income to learn the prevailing language" (241).

The student can easily avoid plagiarism by adding quotation marks.

Example 2

Original ▸ U.S. English and other such groups maintain that linguistic divisions have caused unrest in several countries, such as Canada and Belgium—though they generally fail to note that the countries where strife and violence have been most pronounced, such as Spain, are the ones where minority languages have been most strenuously suppressed. It is interesting to speculate also whether the members of U.S. English would be so enthusiastic about language regulations if they were transferred to Quebec and found their own language effectively outlawed. (Bill Bryson, <u>The Mother Tongue: English & How It Got That Way.</u> New York: Avon, 1990, page 240)

Plagiarism ▸ Countries with more than one language, such as Canada and Belgium, suffer internal strife, according to organizations like U.S. English. However, they don't mention that countries where minority languages are suppressed, such as Spain, have the most violence. One wonders how supporters of these organizations would feel if they moved to Quebec, where the use of English is severely restricted.

This paraphrase doesn't use the same words or sentence structure as the original. However, it is plagiarism because it does not mention the source of the original.

To correct ▸ *Bill Bryson writes that countries*
~~Countries~~ with more than one language, such as Canada and Belgium, suffer internal strife, according to organizations like U.S. English. However, they don't mention that countries where minority languages are suppressed, such as Spain, have the most
Bryson
violence. ~~One~~ wonders how members of U.S. English would feel if they lived in Quebec, where the use of English is severely restricted *(240)*.

The student can avoid plagiarism by inserting the name of the author and adding a source citation at the end.

PRACTICE—Section 45e

Practice taking notes from the following original sources: (a) Read each one until you understand it well. (b) Make a rough note, using short phrases. (c) Write both a summary and a paraphrase note from your rough note.

1. Topic: Bilingual education in the United States
   Subtopic: Arguments against
   Source: Bryson, Bill. *The Mother Tongue: English & How It Got That Way.* New York: Avon, 1990 (page 240).
   Synonyms: matter = problem; provided = given; chaos = craziness; proficient = skilled, fluent; cossets = spoils, pampers; inducement = incentive, encouragement; move into the American mainstream = become part of American life

It is easy to understand the strength of feeling among many Americans on the matter. A California law requiring that bilingual education must be provided at schools where more than twenty pupils speak a language other than English sometimes led to chaos. At one Hollywood high school, on parents' night every speech had to be translated from English into Korean, Spanish, and Armenian. As of December 1986, California was employing 3,364 state workers proficient in Spanish in order to help non-English speakers in matters concerning courts, social services, and the like. All of this, critics maintain, cossets non-English speakers and provides them with little inducement to move into the American mainstream.

2. Topic: Globalization
   Subtopic: Negative effects on native cultures
   Source: Davis, Wade. "Vanishing Cultures." *National Geographic* Aug. 1999 (pages 64–65).
   Synonyms: indigenous = native; whirlwind of change = rapid change; Yanomami, Ogoni, Efe Pygmies = native people; decade = period of ten years; destitute = extremely poor; saturate = soak; delta = area of rich farm land where a river empties into a sea; impoverishing = making unproductive; fertile = able to produce food; ravaging = destroying

Worldwide some 300 million people, roughly 5 percent of the global population, still retain a strong identity as members of an indigenous culture, rooted in history and language and attached by myth and memory to a particular place. Yet increasingly their unique visions of life are being lost in a whirlwind of change.

In Brazil a gold rush brings disease to the Yanomami, killing a quarter of the population in a decade, leaving many of the 8,500 survivors hungry and destitute. In Nigeria pollutants from the oil industry saturate the delta of the Niger River, homeland of the Ogoni, impoverishing the once fertile soil. [. . .] And in the forests of the Congo [. . .] diseases [. . .] from the outside are ravaging the Efe Pygmies.

45f Writing and revising the paper

By now you have read widely and acquired a lot of information about your topic. You have done a lot of thinking and collected a lot of notes. You have probably formed an idea about the overall shape of your paper and the content of individual sections.

Write an outline.

The next step is to organize all your own ideas and all the information from outside sources into an outline. Some teachers require outlines; others do not. However, even if your teacher doesn't require one, an outline is helpful as a kind of road map to guide your thinking and writing. It will help you decide how each section of the paper relates to other sections. It will help you put the sections into logical order. It will help you figure out where to use various quotations and other notes to support your points. (See *Section 40b* for information about outlines.)

Choose a pattern of organization.

Organize a research paper just as you would organize a long essay. Depending on your topic, use one of the standard patterns of organization such as chronological order, cause and effect, comparison and contrast, or logical division of ideas. Begin with an introductory paragraph and end with a concluding paragraph.

Write a thesis statement.

Your thesis statement should clearly state the main point of your work. Look at the following examples.

▶ While bringing benefits to most of the world, globalization will cause irreversible damage to the few remaining indigenous cultures in the world.

▶ Bilingual education fails children in three ways.

▶ Spanish should become an official language in several regions of the United States.

▶ Eating disorders are a growing problem among young people. An understanding of their causes and effects may help lead to their prevention.

▶ Prepare your child for successful entry into first grade by following these suggestions.

Review your notes.

After you have a satisfactory thesis statement and outline, review your notes. You may find that some of your notes are irrelevant or don't support your arguments very well. Put these notes away. Resist the temptation to include every note just because of all the work you have done. Use only notes that really support your points.

Integrate your notes and your ideas.

How you integrate your notes with your own ideas is variable. Develop a system that works for you. One student marks on his outline where he will use each note. Another student lays all her note cards and scraps of paper with her own thoughts written on them on the floor. Then she matches each scrap of paper with note cards and tapes them together. A third student who has written all his notes on a computer uses the cut and paste functions to insert notes into his text.

Write and revise.

After you have done your organization, the actual writing should flow quickly. Write the first draft, if possible, at one sitting. The result will be smoother. Then write and revise and write and revise again until you are satisfied that you have communicated your ideas effectively. Visit the writing center or tutoring lab to get suggestions for revisions.

Format correctly.

When you prepare the final copy to hand in, format it correctly. Research papers, like other academic papers, have specific formatting requirements. Different fields of study use different format styles. For example, most of the social sciences use APA (American Psychological Association) style. Other fields of study use the Chicago and CBE (Council of Biology Editors) styles. Papers for English and other language classes usually use the MLA (Modern Language Association) style. Always ask your teacher which style you should use. (*Section 44a* and *Section 45g* give basic information about MLA style, and the sample research paper in *Section 45h* uses this style.)

45g Citing your sources (MLA style)

Whenever you use borrowed information, you must cite its source (tell where the information came from). There are two steps in citing a source.

1. Insert a short reference in the body of your paper. The short reference is called an in-text citation.

2. Prepare a list describing all your sources completely. This list is titled Works Cited and appears as the last page of your paper.

This handbook contains only basic guidelines for citing sources in the MLA style. It does not include all possible variations. If you need more examples, consult a comprehensive English handbook such as the *MLA Handbook for Writers of Research Papers.* You can find this book and others like it in the reference area of any library.

In-text citations

The purpose of an in-text citation is to refer the reader to the works-cited list at the end of your paper. In-text citations are also called parenthetical references because they are enclosed in parentheses. Place in-text citations immediately after the borrowed information, usually at the end of a sentence, before the final period.

Example of an in-text citation

▶ You can identify Americans anywhere in the world because of their behavior. Their identifiable characteristics are openness, friendliness, informality, optimism, creativity, loudness, and vitality **(Hall and Hall 140).**

The citation at the end of this sentence tells us that the information in the sentence came from page 140 of a work written by Hall and Hall.

Corresponding entry in works-cited list

If readers want more information about this source, they can turn to the works-cited list and find this information under the names Hall and Hall:

▶ Hall, Edward T., and Mildred Reed Hall. <u>Understanding Cultural Differences</u>. Yarmouth, ME: Intercultural, 1990.

This entry tells us that the authors are Edward Hall and Mildred Hall and that the title of their book is *Understanding Cultural Differences.* The book was published in Yarmouth, Maine, in 1990 by a company whose shortened name is Intercultural.

Common types of in-text citations

In-text citations are as short as possible. They contain only enough information to allow the reader to find the full reference in the list of works cited at the end of your paper. Here are some common types.

One author	▶ **(Davis 64–65)** Use the last name of the author and a page number (or numbers, if the borrowed information appears on more than one page). Use no punctuation.
Two or three authors	▶ **(Hall and Hall 140)** If there are two or three authors, give all their names.
Four or more authors	▶ **(Singleton et al. 345)** If there are four or more authors, use the first author's name and the Latin abbreviation *et al.* (shortened from *et alii,* "and others"). Note the period after the abbreviation *al.*
Entire article on one page	▶ **(Allen)** Leave out page numbers if the source is only one page long.
Author already mentioned	▶ **(140)** If you have already mentioned the author's name in the text, do not repeat the name in your citation. For example, if you introduced the borrowed information with a phrase such as *According to Davis* or *As Hall and Hall wrote,* give only the page number.

Same author, two different works	▶ (Tannen, <u>Gender</u> 220)
	▶ (Tannen, <u>You Just</u> 47)

When you use information in a paper from two different works by the same author, include a short name for each work to differentiate them. In the examples, an author named Tannen wrote two books. The title of the first book is shortened to *Gender,* and the title of the second book is shortened to *You Just.*

No author	▶ ("Earthquakes" 212)

If there is no author, use a short title in quotation marks.

Encyclopedia article	▶ ("Global Warming")

For an encyclopedia article, use the author's name if you know it. If you don't know it, use the title of the article in quotation marks. You do not need a page number since encyclopedia articles are arranged alphabetically and your reader will be able to find the source easily.

Electronic source	▶ (J&J "Credo" screen 2)

For an electronic source (online or CD-ROM), follow the same system as for print sources. If there are no page numbers, use whatever numbering system the source has—section number (abbreviated as "sec."), paragraph number (abbreviated as "par."), screen number—or use no number.

Works-cited list

The second step in citing sources is to list all the sources that you actually used in your paper. (Don't include sources that you read but didn't use.) List them alphabetically by last name of the author or, if there is no author, by the first word of the title (disregarding *A, An,* and *The*). Include information about each source as follows. Pay close attention to punctuation and capitalization, and indent the second line five spaces. For kinds of sources not included here, consult a more comprehensive English handbook.

Books

One author	┌── (1) ──┐ ┌────────── (2) ──────────┐
	▶ Bryson, Bill. <u>The Mother Tongue: English & How It Got That Way</u>.
	      ┌──── (3) ────┐
	      New York: Avon, 1991.

This is the form of a basic book reference. Divide the information into three parts: (1) name of the author, (2) title of the book, (3) publishing information. Put a period and one space after each part, and indent the second line.

(1) Write the author's last name first and put a comma after it. Do not include a person's titles.

(2) Put a colon between the title and subtitle, and underline or italicize both.

(3) Write the city of publication, a colon, the name of the publishing company, a comma, the year of publication, and a period. Get this information from the title page or the back of the title page inside the book, not from the book's cover. Use the first city listed if there are several. Include an abbreviation for a state or country if the city is unfamiliar or in any way unclear. Use the most recent year. Shorten the name of the publisher by omitting words such as *Press, Publishers, Books, Inc.,* and *Co.*

Two or three authors

▶ Hall, Edward T., and Mildred Reed Hall. Understanding Cultural Differences. Yarmouth, ME: Intercultural, 1990.

Use reverse order (last name, first name) for the first author's name, and then write all other authors' names in normal order. Put a comma after the last name of the first author and also between authors.

Four or more authors

▶ Quirk, Randolph, et al. A Comprehensive Grammar of the English Language. London: Longman, 1985.

OR

▶ Quirk, Randolph, Sidney Greenbaum, Geoffrey Leech, and Jan Svartvik. A Comprehensive Grammar of the English Language. London: Longman, 1985.

When there are four or more authors, you may either list the first name in reverse order and the Latin abbreviation *et al.* ("and others") or list them all. If you list them all, write only the first author's name in reverse order and the other names in normal order.

More than one edition

▶ Gibaldi, Joseph. MLA Handbook for Writers of Research Papers. 5th ed. New York: MLA, 1999.

Put the number and the abbreviation *ed.* (2nd ed., 3rd ed., 4th ed., and so on) after the title, followed by a period.

Same author, two different works

▶ Tannen, Deborah, ed. Gender and Conversational Interaction. New York: Oxford UP, 1993.

▶ ---. You Just Don't Understand: Women and Men in Conversation. New York: Morrow, 1990.

Type the author's name for the first work. For all other works, type three hyphens in place of the name. List the works in alphabetical order.

Deborah Tannen was the editor, not the author, of the first book, so a comma and the abbreviation *ed.* follow her name. (An editor is a person who prepares material written by others for publication.)

The abbreviation *UP* means *University Press.*

Articles

Encyclopedia article

▸ Kispert, Robert J. "Universal Language." <u>World Book Encyclopedia</u>. 1997 ed.

▸ "Intelligence Test." <u>The New Encyclopedia Britannica</u>: <u>Micropedia</u>. 15th ed.

Use the author's name if it is given. Sometimes the author's name appears at the end of an encyclopedia article and sometimes it doesn't. If there is no author, put the title of the article first. Enclose the title in quotation marks. Underline or italicize the title of the encyclopedia. Put the edition number if there is one; if there is none, use the year.

Magazine article

▸ Allen, Bill. "From the Editor." <u>National Geographic</u> Aug. 1999: 1.

▸ Dickinson, Amy. "Kindergrind." <u>Time</u> 8 Nov. 1999: 61–62.

Put the title of the article inside quotation marks. Underline or italicize the name of the magazine. Include the month and year of monthly magazines (the first example), followed by a colon and the page number or numbers on which the article appears. Include the day, month, and year for weekly magazines (the second example). Abbreviate the names of months except May, June, and July.

Newspaper article

▸ Dahlburg, John-Thor. "Global Warming Threat Real to Pacific Island: As World Debates, Some Prepare to Vacate." <u>San Francisco Chronicle</u> 25 Nov. 2000: C1.

This article appeared on page 1 of section C of the newspaper.

Other sources

Personal interview

CD-ROM

▸ Auld, Martha. Personal interview. 5 Dec. 2001.

▸ "Dam." Microsoft Encarta 97 Encyclopedia. CD-ROM. Redmond, WA: Microsoft, 1997.

Online

▸ "Global Warming." <u>The Columbia Encyclopedia</u>. 6th ed. New York: Columbia UP. 2001. 27 Feb. 2002 <http://www.bartleby.com/br/65.html>.

▸ International Rivers Network. "IRN's China Campaign: Three Gorges, Yangtze River." 2 Feb. 2001. 3 Mar. 2002 <http://irn.org/programs/threeg/>.

Citations for online sources need the same basic information as print sources: author, title, and date of publication. The date of publication for an online source is the date it was put online or the date it was last revised. If you cannot find an author or a publication date, just list whatever information you are able to find.

In addition, you need to give these two pieces of information for an online source:

1. Your date of access. Because online sources are often revised, you need to show exactly which version you used. Put the date you accessed (visited) the site just before the source's electronic address. Do not put a period after the access date.

2. The exact electronic address. Copy the address from the top of your computer screen and enclose it in angle brackets (< >). Copy the exact address of the page you used, not just the home page address. If you must divide an address because it is too long to fit on a line, divide it only at a slash mark (/) and don't use a hyphen.

The first example for an online source at the bottom of page 357 is for an article from an online encyclopedia. The second example is for an article from the Web site of a nonprofit organization. Notice that there are two dates in this citation. The first date is the date of the site's last revision, and the second date is the date the researcher accessed the site.

You can find further information about MLA style at the Modern Language Association's Web site: http://www.mla.org.

PRACTICE—Section 45g

Write the information about each of the following sources in MLA style for a list of works cited. Then put them in alphabetical order.

1. A magazine article entitled "Don't Eat Again Until You Read This" by Jeff Wheelwright on pages 36–43 of the March 2002 issue of *Discover.*
2. A book entitled *Frankenfood* by Robert Walker published by Ross & Selvidge in Pasadena in 2000.
3. A newspaper article entitled "Gene-Spliced Wheat Stirs Global Fears" on page A1 of the February 27, 2002, issue of *The Washington Post.* The author's name is Marc Kaufman.
4. A Web site entitled "Genetic Engineering of Our Food." The last update is October 12, 1999. The Internet address is http://www.argonet.co.uk/users/john.rose/. Use today's date as your date of access.
5. An article in an online encyclopedia. The title of the article is "Plant Disease." The site's address is www.britannica.com and the copyright date is 2000. Use today's date as your date of access.

45h Sample research paper

The following research paper was written by a student majoring in business at Northwestern University in Illinois. It uses MLA style.

Title page

MLA style does not require a title page or an outline; however, if your instructor asks for one or both, here are examples for you to use as models.

Put a colon between the title and subtitle (if there is one).

Center every line.

Double-space everything.

Crisis Management:
A Comparison of Two Companies

by
Patrick MacLeamy
Business and Social Responsibility
Professor Silver
15 March 2002

Outline

Center the word
Outline 1 inch
from the top.

Double-space
everything.

1-inch margins on
all four sides

Indent each kind
of number and
letter about ½
inch.

Outline

I. Thesis statement: A comparison of two companies' reactions to crises demonstrates the importance of these four strategies.

II. Acknowledge the problem quickly.

    A. J&J made the crisis public by the end of the first day.

    B. Exxon waited more than 24 hours to announce the disaster.

        1. Waited more than one week to express sympathy.

        2. Media had had almost two weeks to bombard the public.

III. Investigate the problem and try to solve it with as much energy as possible, publicizing the investigation and its progress.

    A. J&J moved within 24 hours.

        1. Recalled Tylenol, wrote letters, created Tylenol testing center.

        2. Publicized efforts to catch the person responsible for the poisonings.

    B. Exxon was slow to take action to contain the oil.

        1. Did not begin work for two days.

        2. Did not have the proper equipment.

        3. Conveyed an image of uncaring, uninterested corporation.

            a. Communicated poorly with media.

            b. Did not share details of investigation and cleanup with public.

IV. Select one person to be the company spokesperson.

    A. J&J chose company chairman, James E. Burke.

    B. Exxon had several different spokespersons.

        1. Second spokesperson undercut first spokesperson's statements.

        2. Multiple spokespersons were not a cohesive unit.

V. Maintain the company in a context larger than the crisis.

      A. J&J publicized its company credo and succeeded in shifting focus away from deaths to J&J's social responsibilities.

      B. Exxon did not refer to any company code of ethics, and media coverage focused only on effects of the oil spill.

VI. Conclusion: Companies must use the four strategies if they want to retain public goodwill after a crisis.

If your instructor doesn't require a title page, use the following first-page format.

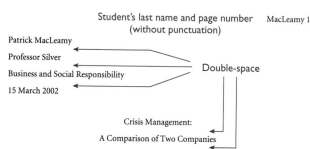

Student's last name and page number　　MacLeamy 1
(without punctuation)

Student's name

Teacher's name

Name of course

Due date

Patrick MacLeamy

Professor Silver

Business and Social Responsibility　　　Double-space

15 March 2002

Center the title.

Crisis Management:

A Comparison of Two Companies

When faced with a crisis, it is important that a company react correctly to

retain its image with the public. According to Marconi, a company should use four

specific strategies. (1) The company must publicly acknowledge the crisis as soon as

possible. (2) The company must actively investigate the crisis and at the same time

keep the media and public informed on the progress and results of its investigation.

(3) One person should be spokesperson for the company. This person should be the

sole voice in all contacts with the media so that conflicting statements are never issued.

(4) The company should present itself in a larger context than the crisis. This step is

necessary to shift focus from the crisis to the solution (Marconi 21–41). A comparison

of two companies' reactions to crises demonstrates the importance of these four

strategies. Johnson & Johnson (J&J) did an excellent job of saving the company's

image after the incident when several people died from consuming poisoned Tylenol

capsules in 1982; in contrast, Exxon created its own public relations disaster after its

ship *Valdez* ran aground in March 1989 and spilled over 1.25 million barrels of oil into

Prince William Sound, Alaska.

The first step in crisis management is to acknowledge the problem quickly. It is

extremely damaging if there is no response from the guilty company or if a response

is delayed for a long period of time. By issuing a statement quickly, the company takes

advantage of a fleeting chance to reach the public with a first impression of the crisis

Borrowed
information
introduced by
"According
to . . ."

Citation form:
author's name,
page numbers

Thesis statement

Abbreviation form:
the first time, write
out the company's
name and put its
abbreviation in
parentheses.
Thereafter, use the
abbreviation.

Each paragraph
begins with a
clear topic
sentence.

1-inch margins on
all four sides

½ inch

1 inch
MacLeamy 2

On every page,
type your last
name and a page
number (without
punctuation)
½ inch from the
top right corner.

Citation form: no
author

Quotation used
as part of
sentence
Citation form:
one author, one-
page article

Transition phrase
introduces the
next topic.

before the media creates a less favorable picture. In the Tylenol incident, J&J made

the crisis public by the end of the first day. It not only acknowledged the problem but

had already begun to solve it. In contrast, Exxon President Frank Iarossi didn't admit

the disaster for more than a day. He accepted "full financial responsibility" for the

disaster at 12:04 a.m. on March 25, more than 24 hours after the spill on March 24

("Largest" 212). Not until April 3—more than one week after the spill—did the

company finally publish full-page advertisements in major newspapers expressing the

company's sympathy toward residents, wildlife, and the environment. By this time,

television, radio, and newspapers had had almost two weeks to bombard the public

with words and images of the disaster. The April 3 statement that "Exxon has moved

swiftly and competently to minimize the effect this oil will have on the environment"

was an insult to the public because they had been watching the drama unfold since

March 24 (Rawl).

1 in. →

← 1 in. →

    In addition to publicly acknowledging a crisis, a company should investigate

the problem and try to solve it with as much energy as possible. Publicizing the

investigation and its progress is equally important. If people see that a company is

genuinely concerned and is taking steps to see that the problem does not happen

again, they will be more likely to forgive the company. In the poisoned Tylenol

incident, J&J again demonstrated competence by moving within 24 hours to ensure

that no more poisoned Tylenol would be consumed. It issued an immediate recall, it

wrote letters to at-risk individuals, and it created a Tylenol testing center. In addition,

J&J's well-publicized investigation to find the individual who had poisoned the

Tylenol won the public's goodwill and even pity for J&J. Exxon was the opposite of

J&J in its handling of the cleanup of Prince William Sound. Just as Exxon failed to

publicly acknowledge the *Valdez* oil spill quickly, the company was extremely slow in

taking action to contain the oil. Work did not begin for two days. "Efforts to

1 inch

This quotation appears on two pages.

Quotation within a quotation form: single quotation marks inside double quotation marks

The next three quotations are from the same source as the previous one, so only a page number is necessary.

Transition signal introduces new topic.

MacLeamy 3

contain the spill lagged from the start" and little was accomplished ("Largest" 212–213). Don Cornett of Exxon "conceded that it was impossible to contain the spill 'with the equipment we have available today'" (213). The lack of organization and proper equipment show that Exxon was slow to investigate and to initiate action to solve the crisis. In addition, media interviews and conversations with cleanup personnel conveyed an image of an uncaring, uninterested corporation. Good communication lines were not established between Exxon and the media from the outset. Meaningful, detailed descriptions of Exxon's cleanup and investigation procedure were not shared with the public, even in Exxon's full-page advertisement a week later. Because Exxon's public statements were late in coming, the media were already creating their own views of the situation. Alaska Lt. Governor McAlpine summarized the public's image of Exxon's cleanup effort as of March 28: "Despite all the statements to the contrary, I don't think they ever had a handle on it" (213). The benefits of a well-crafted and well-publicized investigation can sometimes overcome the negative publicity a company receives for a bad beginning.

Another key to successful media relations during a crisis is the selection of one person to be the company spokesperson. This person should be responsible for all press releases and outside contact. One spokesperson gives the company a united front and prevents employees from inadvertently giving out contradictory or harmful information. J&J presented their chairman, James E. Burke, as spokesperson. His openness with the media and detailed descriptions of company action created a positive image of J&J. In contrast, Exxon had several different spokespersons and suffered the consequences. The first spokesperson was Frank Iarossi, the President of Exxon Shipping. He accepted financial responsibility for the spill on March 25, 1989, and handled other press conferences throughout the

MacLeamy 4

crisis. However, on March 28, the coordinator for Exxon Shipping's Alaska operation, Don Cornett, admitted that the spill was impossible to contain with the available equipment. Cornett's admission undercut Iarossi's statement and damaged Exxon's chances of gaining the goodwill of the public for its cleanup effort. Then on March 29, an unnamed Exxon spokesperson announced that only 6,000 of the 1,260,000 barrel of spilled oil had been recovered and that the company didn't expect to recover many more (212–213). Finally, on April 3 a full-page advertisement apologizing for the spill appeared in major newspapers. L. G. Rawl, Exxon's chairman, was the spokesperson in this advertisement. It is clear that Exxon, with multiple spokespersons, did not organize itself into a cohesive unit in order to communicate with the media.

The last strategy for protecting a company's image in a crisis is maintaining the company in a context larger than the crisis. This strategy was utilized by J&J to take attention away from the deaths. The company publicized its company credo, or statement of values, which puts its responsibility to its customers first. The first sentence of the credo states, "We believe our first responsibility is to the doctors, nurses and patients, to mothers and fathers and all others who use our products and services" (J&J "Credo-United States"). In its Web site, the company says that J&J " [. . .] has drawn heavily on the strength of the credo for guidance through the years, and at no time was this more evident than during the Tylenol crises of 1982 and 1986, when [. . .] company managers and employees made countless decisions that were inspired by the philosophy embodied in the credo" (J&J "Credo" screen 2). J&J succeed in shifting the focus from the victims' deaths to J&J's social responsibilities. In contrast, Exxon failed to present itself in a similar light. Exxon did not make any reference to a company mission statement or code of ethics that might have helped portray the company in a larger context. As a result, media

Words omitted from the original quotations are replaced by ellipses and square brackets.

MacLeamy 5

coverage focused primarily on the effects of the oil spill and the failure of Exxon in the cleanup.

Conclusion, introduced by a transitional signal, reviews the four main topics.

To summarize, companies must react swiftly to crises. Public goodwill is almost impossible to retain if the four strategies of quick public acknowledgement, investigation plus announcement of the investigation, using one spokesperson, and presentation of the company in a larger context are ignored. J&J's handling of its Tylenol poisoning crisis was an example of good crisis management. From the start, J&J's chairman James E. Burke was the spokesperson and catalyst for the company rescue plan. By the end of the first day, the crisis was made public and J&J had taken extreme action to ensure that no more poisoned capsules would be consumed. It publicized its company credo and used its principles to guide company actions. In contrast, Exxon did not adequately begin cleanup of the oil spill until two days after the Exxon Valdez ran aground. Many people, rather than one person, spoke for the company. By the time Exxon printed advertisements in the papers admitting to the spill, the press had already had almost two weeks of speculation, observation, and revealing conversations with Exxon employees. Although Exxon claimed to have multiple allies—the US Coast Guard for the cleanup, federal courts for quick payment of damage fees, and even Alaska residents—individuals told a different story. As an Alaskan fisherman commented,

Quotation introduced by *As* + reporting verb.

Citation form: one author, page no.

"The resources are recovering. But the people still hurt" (Mitchell 98). In addition, the small fishing village of Cordova is still in court with Exxon, arguing over a $5 billion settlement, which is hardly an indication of public support. Exxon failed miserably in managing their oil crisis. The repercussions of their actions still haunt them years later as the tenth anniversary of the disastrous *Valdez* spill approaches.

MacLeamy 6

Center the title

Works Cited

Type the works-cited list on a separate page. Continue the page numbers.

Double-space everything.

List is in alphabetical order.

Indent the second line of a reference five spaces or ½ inch.

Johnson & Johnson. Credo. 3 Mar. 1999. <http://jnj.com/who_is_jnj/cr_index.html>.

—. Credo-United States. 3 Mar. 1999. <http://jnj.com/who_is_jnj/cr_usa.html>.

"Largest U.S. Oil Spill Fouls Alaska Marine Habitat." *Facts on File* 31 Mar. 1989: 212–213.

Marconi, Joe. *Crisis Marketing: When Bad Things Happen to Good Companies.* Chicago: Probus, 1992.

Mitchell, John G. "In the Wake of the Spill: Ten Years After." *National Geographic* Mar. 1999: 96–117.

Rawl, L. G. "An Open Letter to the Public." *New York Times* 3 Apr. 1989: A5.

PART 8   Reference Lists

This section lists most of the irregular verbs in English. When two forms are listed (*lit/lighted*), both forms are correct.

Base Form	Simple Past	Past Participle	Base Form	Simple Past	Past Participle
arise	arose	arisen	**forgive**	forgave	forgiven
awake	awoke	awoken	**freeze**	froze	frozen
be	was/were	been	**get**	got	gotten/got
beat	beat	beaten	**give**	gave	given
become	became	become	**go**	went	gone
begin	began	begun	**grind**	ground	ground
bend	bent	bent	**grow**	grew	grown
bet	bet	bet	**hang** (*suspend*)	hung	hung
bite	bit	bitten	**hang** (*execute*)	hanged	hanged
bleed	bled	bled	**have**	had	had
blow	blew	blown	**hear**	heard	heard
break	broke	broken	**hide**	hid	hidden
bring	brought	brought	**hit**	hit	hit
build	built	built	**hold**	held	held
burn	burned/burnt	burned/burnt	**hurt**	hurt	hurt
burst	burst	burst	**keep**	kept	kept
buy	bought	bought	**kneel**	knelt	knelt
catch	caught	caught	**knit**	knit/knitted	knit/knitted
choose	chose	chosen	**know**	knew	known
cling	clung	clung	**lay** (*put*)	laid	laid
come	came	come	**lead**	led	led
cost	cost	cost	**leap**	leapt	leapt
creep	crept	crept	**leave**	left	left
cut	cut	cut	**lend**	lent	lent
deal	dealt	dealt	**let**	let	let
dig	dug	dug	**lie** (*lie down*)	lay	lain
dive	dived/dove	dived	**light**	lit/lighted	lit/lighted
do	did	done	**lose**	lost	lost
draw	drew	drawn	**make**	made	made
dream	dreamed/dreamt	dreamed/dreamt	**mean**	meant	meant
drink	drank	drunk	**meet**	met	met
drive	drove	driven	**pay**	paid	paid
eat	ate	eaten	**prove**	proved	proved/proven
fall	fell	fallen			
feed	fed	fed	**put**	put	put
feel	felt	felt	**quit**	quit	quit
fight	fought	fought	**read**	read	read
find	found	found	**ride**	rode	ridden
fit	fit	fit	**ring**	rang	rung
flee	fled	fled	**rise**	rose	risen
fling	flung	flung	**run**	ran	run
fly	flew	flown	**say**	said	said
forbid	forbade/forbad	forbidden	**see**	saw	seen
forget	forgot	forgotten	**seek**	sought	sought

Base Form	Simple Past	Past Participle	Base Form	Simple Past	Past Participle
sell	sold	sold	stand	stood	stood
send	sent	sent	steal	stole	stolen
set	set	set	stick	stuck	stuck
sew	sewed	sewn / sewed	sting	stung	stung
shake	shook	shaken	stink	stank / stunk	stunk
shave	shaved	shaved / shaven	strike	struck	struck
shine	shone	shone	swear	swore	sworn
shoot	shot	shot	sweep	swept	swept
show	showed	shown	swim	swam	swum
shrink	shrank / shrunk	shrunk / shrunken	swing	swung	swung
shut	shut	shut	take	took	taken
sing	sang	sung	teach	taught	taught
sink	sank	sunk	tear	tore	torn
sit	sat	sat	tell	told	told
slay	slew	slain	think	thought	thought
sleep	slept	slept	throw	threw	thrown
slide	slid	slid	understand	understood	understood
speak	spoke	spoken	upset	upset	upset
speed	sped	sped	wake	woke	woken
spend	spent	spent	wear	wore	worn
spill	spilled / spilt	spilled / spilt	weave	wove	woven
spin	spun	spun	weep	wept	wept
spit	spit / spat	spat	win	won	won
split	split	split	wind	wound	wound
spread	spread	spread	withdraw	withdrew	withdrawn
spring	sprang	sprung	wring	wrung	wrung
			write	wrote	written

47 · Verb + Preposition Combinations

This section lists many common verb + preposition combinations. A good dictionary will give you information about other combinations not listed here. The abbreviation "s.o." stands for "someone"; "s.t." stands for "something."

accuse of
agree with s.o. about s.t.
apologize to s.o. for s.t.
appeal to
apply to / for
approve of
argue for / against
argue with s.o. about s.t.
arrive in / at
ask for
associate with

believe in
belong to
blame s.o. for s.t.
blame s.t. on s.o.

border on
borrow from

care about / for
collide with
comment on
compare to / with
complain to / about
concentrate on
confide in
congratulate s.o. on s.t.
consent to
consist of
contribute to
cooperate with
count on

cover with

decide on
demonstrate for / against
depend on
die of
differ from
differentiate from / between
disagree with s.o. about s.t.
disapprove of
distinguish from / between
dream of / about

escape from
excel at / in

(continued)

feel like	participate in	stare at
fight for/against	pay for	stop from
flee from	persist in	strive for
forget about	plot against	struggle against
forgive s.o. **for** s.t.	point at/to	subscribe to
frown at	pray for	substitute for
	prefer s.o./s.t. **to** s.o./s.t.	succeed in/at
glance at	prevent from	suffer from
grieve for s.o.	prohibit from	
grieve over or **about** s.t.	protect from	take advantage of
	provide with	take care of
happen to		talk to/with s.o. **about** s.t.
hear from/about/of	rebel at	thank for
hide from	recover from	think about/of
hope for	reign over	throw at
	rely on	throw to
insist on	remind about	transform into
interfere with	remind of	translate from ... to ...
	reply to	
knock on	rescue from	unite with
	respond to	
laugh at	result from	vote for/against
learn about	result in	
lecture on/about	retire from	wait for
listen to	rule over	warn about/against
live on		wink at
long for	search for	wish for
look after	shop for	withdraw from
look at	shout at	wonder about
look for	smile at	work for
look forward to	speak to/with s.o. **about** s.t.	
meet with	spend on	yield to
object to		

48　Phrasal Verbs

Phrasal verbs are verbs that consist of a verb and a preposition or adverb that gives the verb a special meaning. Many phrasal verbs have more than one meaning. The following list does not list all phrasal verbs, and it does not give all meanings of the verbs that are listed. Consult a good English learner's dictionary for other verbs and other meanings.

- Separable verbs are shown with the object between the verb and the particle (s.o. = someone; s.t. = something).

  ▶ **ask** s.o. **over**　　　We **asked** some friends **over** to watch a video.
  ▶ **fill** s.t. **out**　　　Please **fill** the application **out** in pencil.

You do not have to separate the two parts when the object is a noun. You can write either

  ▶ Please **fill out** the application in pencil. OR Please **fill** the application **out** in pencil.

BUT When the object is a pronoun, you *must* separate the two parts.

▶ Please **fill** it **out** (NOT ~~fill out it~~).

● You must always separate a very small number of verbs. These verbs are followed by an asterisk (*) in the list that follows.

    ▶ **talk** s.o. **into***   She **talked** her parents **into** letting her live alone.

● Inseparable verbs are shown in the list without an object.

    ▶ **call on**   The teacher **calls on** Paula every time she hasn't studied the lesson.

● When the same verb can be used both with and without an object, the object is in parentheses in the list.

    ▶ **break** (s.t.) **up**   The police **broke** the fight **up.**
                              The party **broke up** at midnight.

● When a verb has a different meaning with and without an object, there are two separate entries in the list.

    ▶ **give** s.t. **up**   *stop doing or having s.t.*   She **gave** her job **up** so that she could be at home when her children came home from school.

    ▶ **give up**   *stop trying*   I tried to call you but got the wrong number several times. I finally **gave up.**

● When the same verb has different meanings, the different meanings and examples are numbered in the list.

    ▶ **blow out**   1. *stop burning*   1. The candle **blew out.**
                        2. *burst*   2. The front tire **blew out.**

PHRASAL VERB	MEANING(S)	EXAMPLE(S)
ask s.o. **out**	*invite s.o. to go on a date*	Andy **asked** me **out** tonight. We're going to a movie.
ask s.o. **over**	*invite to one's home*	Prof. Smith **asked** some students **over** for coffee.
block s.t. **out**	*stop (light, noise, etc.) from passing through*	These heavy curtains help **block out** noise from the street.
blow s.t. **out**	*stop from burning by blowing*	The wind **blew** the fire **out.**
blow out	1. *stop burning* 2. *burst*	1. The candle **blew out.** 2. The front tire **blew out.**
blow s.t. **up**	*fill with air*	The children **blew up** the balloons.
blow (s.t.) **up**	*explode*	The terrorists **blew** the building **up.** My boss **blew up** in anger.

(continued)

PHRASAL VERB	MEANING(S)	EXAMPLE(S)
break down	1. *stop functioning (machines)* 2. *have an emotional reaction*	1. Their car **broke down** on the highway. 2. She **broke down** and cried during the funeral.
break out	1. *happen suddenly* 2. *escape from jail or prison*	1. War **broke out** after the peace talks failed. 2. Three murderers **broke out** of prison yesterday.
break up	*end a romance or marriage*	Mary and John **broke up** last week.
break (s.t.) **up**	1. *separate (into groups or pieces)* 2. *end (a fight, party, group meeting, etc.)*	1. The teacher **broke** the class **up** into groups. The class **broke up** into groups. 2. The police tried to **break** the fight **up.** The party **broke up** at midnight.
bring s.t. **back**	*make a person remember s.t.*	These photos **bring back** many memories.
bring s.o. **up**	*rear children*	They **brought up** six successful children.
bring s.t. **up**	*mention a topic*	He **brought up** the same topic again.
call (s.o.) **back**	*return a telephone call*	I'll **call** (you) **back** later.
call s.t. **off**	*cancel*	They **called off** the wedding at the last minute.
call on	1. *ask to speak in class* 2. *visit*	1. The teacher often **calls on** me. 2. An outside salesperson **calls on** customers in their workplaces.
call (s.o.) **up**	*call on the telephone*	Let's **call up** Kim. We **called up** twice yesterday.
carry s.t. **out**	*do, cause to happen*	They **carried out** their plan without any hesitation.
catch on	1. *become popular* 2. *understand*	1. Do you think miniskirts will **catch on** again? 2. He's very smart; he **catches on** quickly.
check in/into	*register at a hotel*	You can't **check in** until 3:00 p.m. You can't **check into** most hotels until 3:00 p.m.
check into	*investigate*	The company promised to **check into** the problem.

PHRASAL VERB	MEANING(S)	EXAMPLE(S)
check s.o./s.t. **out**	1. *take a book from a library* 2. *investigate* 3. *look at* (slang)	1. You can **check** six books **out** at one time. 2. The electric company promised to **check** it **out.** 3. Hey! **Check out** that new car!
check out (of)	*leave a hotel*	We must **check out** (of the hotel) by noon.
cheer (s.o.) **up**	*make (s.o.) feel happier*	Marta is depressed. Let's try to **cheer** her **up.** She will **cheer up** when she hears the good news.
clean (s.o./s.t.) **up**	*make neat and clean*	Please **clean up** your room. We always **clean up** before dinner.
clear s.t. **up**	*make neat and clean*	Let's **clear up** this messy kitchen.
clear (s.t.) **up**	*make or become clear*	Her explanation **cleared** my confusion **up.** The weather **will** probably **clear up** by noon.
come across	*meet or discover by chance*	I **came across** an old picture of our house recently.
come back	*return from a place*	When will you **come back** from your trip?
come from	*originate from a place or source*	He **comes from** China. Milk **comes from** cows.
come in	*enter a place*	The door is open. Please **come in.**
come off (s.t.)	*become detached*	A button **has come off** my coat.
come out	*appear*	The sun finally **came out** about noon.
come over/by	*visit informally*	**Come over/by** for lunch sometime.
come to	1. *total* 2. *become conscious again*	1. How much does the bill **come to?** 2. She quickly **came to** after fainting from the shock.
come up	1. *move near* 2. *happen or appear suddenly*	1. The man **came up** and introduced himself to us. 2. A big problem **has come up,** so I have to work tonight.
come up with	*think of an idea or plan*	John **came up with** a good idea for our class play.
cover s.t. **up**	*hide or keep s.t. secret*	Tobacco companies **covered up** the dangers of smoking.
cross s.t. **out**	*draw a line through*	The writer **crossed out** several sentences and rewrote them.

(continued)

PHRASAL VERB	MEANING(S)	EXAMPLE(S)
cut down (on)	*reduce the amount of*	I'm trying to **cut down** (on) the amount of meat I eat.
cut s.o. **off**	1. *drive a car in front of s.o.* 2. *stop s.o. from talking*	1. The reckless driver **cut** several people **off** on the freeway. 2. The teacher **cut** me **off** before I finished my speech.
cut s.t. **off**	*stop the supply of s.t.*	The phone company **cut off** my telephone service.
cut s.t. **out**	1. *remove by cutting* 2. *stop an annoying activity*	1. The movie editors **cut out** the most violent scenes. 2. **Cut** it **out!** Stop pulling your sister's hair!
do s.t. **over**	*do again*	Your work is unsatisfactory. Please **do** it **over.**
dress up	*put on special or formal clothes*	People generally **dress up** when they go downtown.
drop by/in	*visit informally*	I'll **drop by/in** on my way home from work tonight.
drop s.o./s.t. **off**	*take (s.o. or s.t.) to a place*	My father **drops** me **off** at school on his way to work.
drop out (of)	*stop attending*	My older brother **dropped out of** high school.
eat out	*eat in a restaurant*	I don't feel like cooking. Let's **eat out** tonight.
end up	*reach a particular place or situation, usually not planned*	Reckless drivers often **end up** in the hospital.
fall apart	1. *separate into pieces* 2. *stop functioning well*	1. The new toy **fell apart** one day after we bought it. 2. The company **falls apart** when the boss goes on vacation.
fall behind	*not stay at the same level*	Read one chapter a day, or you'll **fall behind** the class.
figure s.o./s.t. **out**	*understand after thinking about*	I can't **figure** this problem **out.**
fill s.t. **in**	*complete with information*	**Fill in** the blank in each sentence with a verb.
fill s.o. **in (on)**	*tell recent events*	Please **fill** me **in on** what you have been doing lately.
fill s.t. **out**	*complete a form*	**Fill out** the application in pencil.

PHRASAL VERB	MEANING(S)	EXAMPLE(S)
fill s.t. **up**	*fill completely*	I always drive to the same gas station to **fill** my car **up.**
find s.t. **out**	*discover information*	**Did** you **find out** her telephone number?
fool around	*play*	The students started **fooling around** as soon as the teacher left the room.
get s.t. **across**	*get others to understand an idea*	The speaker **got** his ideas **across** to the audience very well.
get ahead	*advance, make progress*	Hard workers usually **get ahead.**
get along (**with**)	*have a good relationship with*	She **doesn't get along with** her parents at all.
get away	*escape*	The police chased the robber, but he **got away.**
get back	*1. return from a place*	1. What day **will** you **get back** from your vacation?
	2. receive again	2. How much money **did** you **get back** from your landlord?
get by	*do or have enough to survive*	We're not rich, but we **get by.** I study just enough to **get by.**
get in/into	*1. arrive (at)*	1. The train **got in** at 3:30 in the morning. The train **got into** the station two hours late.
	2. enter a car or taxi	2. Never **get in/into** a stranger's car.
get off	*leave a bus, train, plane, bicycle, or subway*	We should **get off** at the next stop.
get on	*enter a bus, train, plane, bicycle, or subway*	Several people **got on** the bus at the last stop.
get out (**of**)	*1. leave a car or taxi*	1. He **got out** (of his car) and looked around.
	2. avoid doing work	2. My older sister always **gets out of** doing housework.
get over	*recover (from an illness or unhappy event)*	My daughter **got over** her cold in a few days. He never **got over** his wife's death.
get through	*finish*	It took me two months to **get through** that book.
get together	*meet*	Let's **get together** at my house the next time.

(continued)

PHRASAL VERB	MEANING(S)	EXAMPLE(S)
get up	*arise from a bed, chair, etc.*	People with young children **get up** early.
give s.t. **away**	*give without charging money*	That store is **giving away** balloons today.
give s.t. **back**	*return something*	The teacher **gave** our papers **back** the day after the test.
give in (to)	*surrender to s.o.'s wishes or demands*	She always **gives in** when her children beg for candy.
give s.t. **out**	*distribute*	The health center is **giving out** information about HIV.
give up	*stop trying*	I **give up!** I can't solve this problem.
give s.t. **up**	*stop doing or having s.t.*	She **gave up** her dream of becoming a dancer.
go after	*try to get for yourself*	Alan **is going after** his boss's job. He's also **going after** the boss's beautiful daughter.
go back	*return to a place*	I must **go back** home.
go back on	*fail to fulfill a promise*	He promised to pay back the money, but he **went back on** his promise.
go off	*explode (a gun, fireworks)*	The gun accidentally **went off** while he was cleaning it.
go on	*continue*	The party **went on** for hours after the host had gone to bed.
go out	*leave home for entertainment*	My husband and I **go out** for dinner every Friday night.
go (out) with	*date*	Mary **has been going (out) with** John for several months.
go over	*review*	**Go over** your paper again and check your punctuation.
go with	*harmonize in style, color, etc.*	**Does** this tie **go with** this shirt?
grow out of	*become too big for*	Children quickly **grow out of** their clothes.
grow up	*become an adult*	He **grew up** on a farm.
hand s.t. **down**	*give s.t. to a younger person*	My grandmother **handed down** most of her jewelry to my mother.
hand s.t. **in**	*give completed work to a teacher or boss*	Please **hand** your essays **in** on Wednesday.
hand s.t. **out**	*distribute*	The teacher **handed out** the test questions.

PHRASAL VERB	MEANING(S)	EXAMPLE(S)
hang up	*end a telephone conversation*	The caller **hung up** before I could find out his name.
hang s.t. **up**	*put on a hook or a hanger*	My brother never **hangs up** his clothes.
have on	*wear*	What color jacket **did** the robber **have on?**
help (s.o.) **out**	*help*	We **help out** at our parents' restaurant on weekends.
hold on	*wait on the telephone*	Don't hang up. Please **hold (on)** for a minute.
hold s.t. **up**	1. *rob* 2. *delay*	1. Two men **held up** the grocery store on the corner. 2. What **is holding up** my visa application?
keep (on)	*continue*	The students **kept (on)** working after the bell had rung.
keep s.t. **on***	*continue to wear*	We **kept** our coats **on** because it was so cold in the room.
keep up (with)	*stay at the same level as s.o. or s.t.*	Little Jack can't **keep up with** his older brothers.
kick s.o. **out (of)**	*force s.o. to leave*	They **kicked** him **out of** school for bad behavior.
lay s.o. **off**	*end s.o.'s employment*	The company **laid off** two hundred workers.
leave s.t. **on***	1. *not turn off (lights, machines)* 2. *continue to wear*	1. Please **leave** the computer **on** when you have finished. 2. We **left** our coats **on** because it was so cold in the room.
leave s.t. **out**	*omit*	You **left** the verb **out** of the last sentence.
let s.o. **down**	*disappoint*	She **let** her family **down** when she quit school.
let s.o./s.t. **in**	*allow to enter*	They **let** the dog **in** when it rains or when it's very cold.
let s.o. **off**	*allow to leave (a bus, train, car)*	Please **let** me **off** at the next corner.
let s.o./s.t. **out**	*allow to leave*	Please **let** the cat **out.**
lie down	*recline*	She **lies down** every afternoon to take a little nap.
light s.t. **up**	*illuminate*	A hundred candles **lit up** the church.

(continued)

PHRASAL VERB	MEANING(S)	EXAMPLE(S)
look after	*take care of*	Who **looks after** your cats when you go on vacation?
look down on	*feel superior to*	Snobbish people **look down on** people who aren't from their social class.
look into	*investigate*	The police **are looking into** the thefts.
look like	*resemble*	Both children **look** more **like** their mother than their father.
look out	*be careful*	**Look out!** Here comes a speeding car!
look out for	1. *watch for possible danger from* 2. *protect from harm*	1. You should **look out for** holes in the road. 2. The older children **look out for** the younger ones.
look s.o./s.t. **over**	1. *examine* 2. *review*	1. We **looked** the used car **over** carefully before buying it. 2. He **looked over** his notes before the test.
look s.o. **up**	*call or visit*	Please **look** me **up** the next time you are in town.
look s.t. **up**	*try to find in a book or on the Internet*	Should you **look up** every new word in a dictionary?
look up to	*respect*	Most boys **look up to** their fathers.
make up	*resolve a disagreement*	The young couple had their first argument, but they soon **made up.**
make s.t. **up**	1. *create in one's mind* 2. *do past work*	1. She **made up** a new excuse every day for not doing her homework. 2. He has to **make up** all the work that he missed when he was sick.
pass away	*die*	My favorite aunt **passed away** last year.
pass out	*become unconscious*	I always **pass out** at the dentist's office.
pass s.t. **out**	*distribute*	The teacher **passed out** the test questions.
pay s.o./s.t. **back**	*repay (a debt, an insult)*	Can I borrow five dollars? I'll **pay** you **back** tomorrow.
pay off	1. *pay a debt completely* 2. *bring success after effort*	1. The Smiths finally **paid off** their home loan. 2. His many years of hard work finally **paid off.**

PHRASAL VERB	MEANING(S)	EXAMPLE(S)
pick on	*tease, annoy*	Stop **picking on** your little brother.
pick s.t. out	*choose*	She **picked out** a scarf to match her dress.
pick s.o. up	*go to get s.o. in a car*	I'll **pick** you **up** in front of your house at eight-thirty.
pick s.t. up	*collect, gather*	**Pick up** your toys, children.
point s.o./s.t. out	*indicate, call attention to*	The students **pointed out** a mistake on the blackboard.
pull away	*drive away from a place*	The bus **pulled away** from the curb.
pull in/into	*drive into a certain space*	He **pulled in** behind my car and parked. He **pulled into** the garage.
pull out	*drive into a road from a place*	The taxi suddenly **pulled out** in front of several cars.
pull (s.o.) over	*(make s.o.) drive to the side of the road and stop*	We **pulled over** to check our tires. The highway patrol **pulled** me **over** for speeding.
put s.t. away	*put in an appropriate place*	**Put** your toys **away,** children.
put s.t. back	*put in its original place*	After examining the picture, we **put** it **back** on her desk.
put s.o./s.t. down	*criticize*	Alice's mother-in-law **is** always **putting** her **down** for one thing or another.
put s.t. off	*postpone, delay*	Ted and Ann **put off** their wedding until next May.
put s.t. on	*put on one's body (clothes, lotion, jewelry)*	Always **put** sunscreen **on** before you go out in the sun.
put s.o. on	*not tell the truth in a joking way*	You're **putting** me **on**—you aren't really going to get married tomorrow, are you?
put s.t. out	*extinguish (a cigarette, fire)*	Always **put** a campfire **out** completely.
put s.t. together	*assemble many pieces into one*	The class **put together** a great presentation. The father **put together** his son's new bicycle.
put s.t. up	*erect (a building, a sign)*	They **put up** a sign advertising puppies for sale.
put up with	*tolerate*	I don't know how she **puts up with** her mother-in-law.

(continued)

PHRASAL VERB	MEANING(S)	EXAMPLE(S)
run into / across	*meet or find by accident*	Last week I **ran into** my ex-boyfriend. I **ran across** a newspaper story about my old boss.
run out of	*finish all of s.t.*	We **ran out of** time and didn't finish the test.
run over	*hit and drive over s.o./s.t. with a vehicle*	The bus **ran over** the man.
set s.t. off	*unintentionally cause s.t. to start*	The children accidentally **set off** the fire alarm.
set off	*leave to go somewhere*	They **set off** this morning on their trip around the world.
set s.t. up	1. *start (a business)* 2. *make arrangements for s.t.*	1. Sara and her mother **set up** a beauty salon together. 2. My adviser **set up** several job interviews for me.
show s.t. off	*display s.t. for others to admire*	Jane **showed off** her diamond ring.
show off	*try to get others to admire you*	No one likes Tom because he is always **showing off.**
show up	*appear*	Several students didn't **show up** for the final exam.
shut s.t. off	*stop a machine, light, electricity, water*	The power company **shut off** our gas and electricity.
sign (s.o.) in	*put your name on a list to indicate that you are present*	Please **sign in** each time you visit the language lab.
sign (s.o.) up	*put your name on a list to indicate that you want to participate*	Have you **signed up** for the trip to Disneyland yet?
sit down	*get into a sitting position*	Let's **sit down** and discuss this calmly.
stand up	*get into a standing position*	A gentleman **stands up** when a woman enters a room.
start (s.t.) over	*begin (s.t.) again*	We didn't solve the math problem. Let's **start over.**
stay out	*remain away from home in the evening*	How late do your parents let you **stay out?**
stay up	*not go to bed*	The two friends **stayed up** all night talking.
stick to	*not quit*	She **stuck to** her decision.
stick with	*not quit, especially s.t. difficult*	Don't stop exercising. **Stick with** it, and you will get fit.

PHRASAL VERB	MEANING(S)	EXAMPLE(S)
straighten s.o. out	improve s.o.'s behavior	A year in the army **straightened** him **out**.
straighten s.t. out	resolve a problem	We need to **straighten out** our differences.
straighten s.t. up	make neat	They **straightened up** the living room before going to bed.
straighten up	improve one's own behavior	He had better **straighten up** soon, or his father will stop supporting him.
take after	resemble in appearance or behavior	She **takes after** her mother. They both like to talk a lot.
take s.t. back	return (to a store)	She **took** the shoes **back** because they weren't comfortable.
take s.t. off	remove clothing, makeup	In some cultures, you **take** your shoes **off** before entering a home.
take off	leave	They got in their car and **took off.** My plane **takes off** at noon.
take s.o. out	take s.o. on a date	John **took** Mary **out** last night.
take over	take control	The rebels **took over** the government.
take up	begin a new activity	When did you **take up** golf?
talk back	answer rudely	Children should never **talk back** to their parents.
talk s.o. into*	persuade s.o. to do s.t.	She **talked** her parents **into** letting her live alone.
talk s.t. over	discuss	Let's **talk** this **over** before we make any decisions.
tear s.t. down	destroy (a building)	The city finally **tore down** the old football stadium.
tear s.t. up	tear into pieces	They **tore up** the contract.
think s.t. over	think about carefully	She promised to **think over** his proposal of marriage.
think s.t. up	produce new ideas, names, etc. by thinking	He **thought up** several names for the new baby.
throw s.t. away/out	discard	I **threw out/away** the flowers because they were all dead.
throw s.o. out	force s.o. to leave	John's father **threw** him **out** after John was arrested.
throw (s.t.) up	vomit (bring food up from your stomach and spit it out of your mouth)	When you are seasick, you feel better after you **throw up.**

(continued)

PHRASAL VERB	MEANING(S)	EXAMPLE(S)
touch s.t. **up**	*improve by making small changes*	She **touched up** her makeup after lunch.
try s.t. **on**	*put on clothes to check the fit*	Always **try** shoes **on** before you buy them.
try s.t. **out**	*test*	They **tried out** the vacuum cleaner before they bought it.
turn s.o. **down**	*reject*	I applied for a job, but the company **turned** me **down.**
turn s.t. **down**	*decrease volume, heat*	**Turn** the music **down.** It's too loud.
turn s.t. **in**	*give an assignment to a teacher*	She always **turns in** her homework two days late.
turn in	*go to bed*	I'm sleepy. I think I'll **turn in.**
turn (s.o./s.t.) **into**	*change from one form into another*	Cinderella's coach **turned into** a pumpkin at midnight.
turn s.t. **off/on**	*stop/start (a machine, light, water, electricity)*	The power company **turned off** our gas and electricity. It's getting dark. I'll **turn on** some lights.
turn s.o. **off/on**	*destroy/arouse interest*	The lecture **turned** the students **off.** Rap music really **turns** young people **on.**
turn s.t. **out**	*turn off (light)*	Mother **turned out** the lights so that the children would sleep.
turn out	*have a particular result*	How **did** your party **turn out?**
turn s.t. **up**	*increase the volume, heat*	Please **turn** the heat **up.** I'm cold.
turn up	*appear after being missing*	Don't worry. Your car keys **will turn up.**
use s.t. **up**	*finish all of s.t.*	We **used up** all of the milk.
wait on	*serve*	Each server **waits on** six tables.
watch out (for)	1. *look for possible danger from s.t.* 2. *protect from harm*	1. You should **watch out for** holes in the road. 2. The older children **watch out for** the younger ones.
work out	*exercise in a gym*	She **works out** every day for an hour.
work (s.t.) **out**	*resolve differences, disagreements, problems, etc.*	The couple went to a marriage counselor to **work out** their problems.
write s.t. **down**	*write on paper*	Did you **write down** his telephone number?

49   Adjective + Preposition Combinations

This section lists many common adjective + preposition combinations. A good dictionary will give you information about other combinations not listed here.

absent from
accustomed to
acquainted with
addicted to
afraid of
amazed at/by
angry at/with
annoyed at/with
ashamed of
associated with
aware of
awful at

bad at
bored with/by
brilliant at

capable of
certain of
committed to
composed of
concerned about
confident of
connected to
conscious of
content with
convinced of
covered with
crazy about
crowded with
curious about

dedicated to
devoted to
different from
disappointed
 in/with/about
discriminated
 against
divorced from
dressed in

engaged to
envious of
equipped with
excellent at
excited about
exposed to

faithful to
familiar with
famous for
fed up with
filled with
finished with
fond of
friendly to/with
full of
furnished with

glad about
good at
grateful to/for
guilty of

happy about

impressed
 with/by
incapable of
innocent of
interested in
involved in

jealous of

known for/as

limited to
lucky at

mad at/about
made of/from
married to

nervous about

opposed to

patient with
pleased
 about/with
polite to
prepared for
proud of

ready for
related to
relevant to
remembered for/as

resigned to
responsible for

sad about
safe from
satisfied with
scared of
shocked at/by
short of
sick of
similar to
slow at
sorry about/for
sure of
surprised at/by
suspicious of

terrible at
terrified of
tired of

upset with/about
used to

worried about

50   Pairs of *-ing/-ed* Adjectives

Here is a list of pairs of participial adjectives that are sometimes confusing.

amazing	amazed	disturbing	disturbed
amusing	amused	embarrassing	embarrassed
annoying	annoyed	entertaining	entertained
boring	bored	exciting	excited
confusing	confused	exhausting	exhausted
convincing	convinced	fascinating	fascinated
depressing	depressed	frightening	frightened
disappointing	disappointed	horrifying	horrified
disgusting	disgusted	interesting	interested
distressing	distressed	irritating	irritated

(continued)

moving	moved	surprising	surprised
paralyzing	paralyzed	terrifying	terrified
pleasing	pleased	thrilling	thrilled
relaxing	relaxed	tiring	tired
satisfying	satisfied	touching	touched
shocking	shocked	troubling	troubled

51　Proper Nouns with *The*

Most proper nouns do not have articles. We say *Prince Charles, Friday, January, Mexico, Asia, Main Street,* and so on. This section lists the exceptions. Use *the* with the following proper nouns.

1. All proper nouns that contain an *of*-phrase

   the United States of America
   the Republic of Korea
   the Gulf of Mexico
   the Sea of Japan
   the Statue of Liberty
   the King of Thailand
   the Fourth of July (BUT **Christmas, New Year's Day**)
   the University of Texas
   the College of Notre Dame (BUT **Harvard University, Boston College**)

2. Certain geographic names

   - Geographic names that contain the word *kingdom, republic,* or *union*

     the United Kingdom
     the Dominican Republic
     the European Union

   - Plural geographic names (except waterfalls)

     the Americas (BUT *a single continent:* **South America**)
     the United Arab Emirates
     the Philippines
     the Hawaiian Islands (BUT *a single island:* **Oahu**)
     the Rocky Mountains (BUT *a single mountain:* **Mount McKinley**)
     the Great Lakes (BUT *a single lake:* **Lake Michigan**)
     BUT **Niagara Falls**

   - Bodies of water (except lakes and bays)

     the Pacific (Ocean)
     the Baltic (Sea)
     the Amazon (River)
     the Suez Canal
     the Persian Gulf (BUT **Lake Victoria, San Francisco Bay**)

• Regions	the Middle East the South the East Coast
• Points on the globe	the North Pole the Equator
• Deserts and forests	the Sahara (Desert) the Black Forest
3. Buildings, bridges, named roads, tunnels, towers, monuments (but not dams)	the Empire State Building the Brooklyn Bridge the Pan-American Highway the Chunnel the Eiffel Tower the Lincoln Memorial (BUT Aswan High Dam)
4. Hotels, theaters, movie theaters, libraries, and museums	the Hilton (Hotel) the National Theater the City Cinema the Abbey Library the Louvre
5. Historical periods and events	the Middle Ages the Tang Dynasty the Russian Revolution the Civil War (BUT World War II)
6. Names of organizations, departments of government, and political parties	the United Nations the Red Cross the State Department the Immigration and Naturalization Service the Republican Party
7. Names of historical documents	the Constitution the Magna Carta
8. Names of newspapers (Capitalize *the* if the newspaper uses *the* as part of its name.)	*The New York Times* the *San Francisco Chronicle*
9. Plural family names (used to refer to all of the members of the family)	the Smiths the Bushes
10. Adjectives naming nationalities that mean "the people from this country"	the British the Swiss the Japanese the Egyptians

11. Titles that refer to a unique person.

the Pope
the Dalai Lama
the President, the president
(*Capitalization is optional when "president" and "prime minister" appear without a name.*)

12. Electronic sources

the Internet
the World Wide Web

13. Ships and trains

the *Titanic*
the *Shanghai Express*

52　Connecting Words

Connecting words join ideas and show their relationship to one another. We divide connecting words into two main groups depending on the kind of relationship they express: (1) coordinating words, which express equal relationships, and (2) subordinating words, which express unequal relationships. Within each main group, there are subgroups.

Coordinating words

Coordinating conjunctions

Coordinating conjunctions connect grammatically equal elements and express equal relationships.

Addition in a positive sentence	and	John likes to fish **and** hunt.
Addition in a negative sentence	or	John doesn't like ballet **or** opera.
Contrast	but	I like to eat fish **but** not to catch them.
Result	so	I didn't eat breakfast this morning, **so** I'm a little hungry.
Choice	or	Do you prefer coffee **or** tea?
Surprise	yet	It's sunny, **yet** cold.
Reason	for	I'm a little hungry, **for** I didn't eat breakfast this morning.
Addition of a negative clause	nor	She doesn't eat meat, **nor** does she drink milk.

Correlative (or paired) conjunctions

Correlative conjunctions are always in pairs. Like coordinating conjunctions, they connect grammatically equal elements and express equal ideas.

Addition	both ... and	**Both** San Francisco **and** Sydney have beautiful harbors.
Addition	not only ... but also	Japanese food is **not only** delicious to eat **but also** beautiful to look at.
Positive choices	either ... or	Bring **either** a raincoat **or** an umbrella when you visit Seattle.
Negative choices	neither ... nor	My grandfather could **neither** read **nor** write, but he was a very wise person.
One of two choices	whether ... or	The newlyweds couldn't decide **whether** to live with her parents **or** to rent an apartment.

Conjunctive adverbs

Conjunctive adverbs can appear at the beginning, in the middle, or at the end of one independent clause, but we use them most often to connect two independent clauses.

Remember to put a semicolon before and a comma after the conjunctive adverb.

To add a similar idea	
also besides furthermore in addition moreover	Community colleges offer preparation for many jobs; **also (besides, furthermore, in addition, moreover)**,they prepare students to transfer to four-year colleges or universities.
To add a partial contrast	
however nevertheless nonetheless still	Most community colleges do not have dormitories; **however (nevertheless, nonetheless, still)**, they provide housing referral services.

(continued)

(*continued*)

To add a complete contrast	
in contrast on the other hand	Most community colleges do not have dormitories; **in contrast (on the other hand),** most four-year colleges do.

To show a result	
as a result consequently therefore thus	Native and nonnative English speakers have different needs; **as a result (consequently, therefore, thus),** most schools provide separate classes for each group.

To list ideas in order of time	
meanwhile afterward then subsequently	Police kept people away from the scene of the accident; **meanwhile,** ambulance workers tried to pull victims out of the wreck. The workers put five injured people into an ambulance; **afterward (then, subsequently),** they found another victim.

To give an example	
for example for instance	Colors can have different meanings; **for example (for instance),** white is the color of weddings in some cultures and of funerals in others.

To compare and show similarities	
similarly likewise	Hawaii has sunshine and friendly people; **similarly (likewise),** Mexico's weather is sunny and its people hospitable.

To indicate "the first statement is not true; the second statement is true"	
instead on the contrary rather	The medicine didn't make him feel better; **instead (on the contrary, rather),** it made him feel worse.
Instead also means "as a substitute."	They had planned to go to Hawaii on their honeymoon; **instead,** they went to Mexico.

To give another possibility	
on the other hand alternatively	You can live in a dorm on campus; **on the other hand (alternatively),** you can rent a room with a family off campus.
otherwise (*if not*)	Students must take final exams; **otherwise,** they will receive a grade of Incomplete.

To add an explanation	
in other words that is	Some cultures are matriarchal; **in other words** (**that is**), the mothers are the head of the family.

To make a stronger statement	
indeed in fact	Mangoes are a very common fruit; **indeed** (**in fact**), people eat more mangoes than any other fruit in the world.

Subordinating words

Subordinating words connect unequal ideas. A subordinating conjunction is the first word in a dependent clause. Common subordinating words include the following.

Subordinating conjunctions for adverb clauses

Time (*When?*)	
after	**After** we ate lunch, we decided to go shopping.
as, just as	**Just as** we left the house, it started to rain.
as long as	We waited **as long as** we could.
as soon as	**As soon as** the front door closed, I looked for my house key.
before	I thought I had put it in my coat pocket **before** we left.
since	I haven't locked myself out of the house **since** I was ten years old.
until	**Until** I was almost twelve, my mother pinned the key to my coat.
when	**When** I turned twelve, my mother let me keep the key in my pocket.
whenever	I usually put the key in the same place **whenever** I come home.
while	**While** I searched for the key, it started raining harder and harder.

Place (*Where?*)	
where	I like to shop **where** prices are low.
wherever	I try to shop **wherever** there is a sale.
anywhere	You can find bargains **anywhere** you shop.
everywhere	I use my credit card **everywhere** I shop.

Reason (*Why?*)	
as	I can't take evening classes **as** I work at night.
because	I can't take evening classes **because** I work at night.
since	I can't take evening classes **since** I work at night.

(continued)

(continued)

Result *(With what result?)*	
so + *adjective* + **that**	I was **so tired** last night **that** I fell asleep at dinner.
so + *adverb* + **that**	She talks **so softly that** the other students can't hear her.
such a(n) + *noun* + **that**	It was **such an** easy test **that** most of the students got A's.
so much/ many/little/ few + *noun* + **that**	He's taking **so many** classes **that** he has no time to sleep.

Contrast	
although	I love my brother **although** we disagree about almost everything.
even though	I love my brother **even though** we disagree about almost everything.
though	I love my brother **though** we disagree about almost everything.

Opposition	
while	My brother likes classical music, **while** I prefer hard rock.
whereas	He dresses conservatively, **whereas** I like to be a little shocking.

Manner *(How?)*	
as, just as	I love to get flowers **as** most women do.
as if	You look **as if** you didn't sleep at all last night.
as though	She acts **as though** she doesn't know us.

Distance *(How far? How near? How close?)*	
as + *adverb* + **as**	We will hike **as far as** we can before it turns dark.
	The child sat **as close as** she could to her mother.
	ALSO: The child sat **as close** to her mother **as** she could.

Frequency *(How often?)*	
as often as	I call my parents **as often as** I can.

Purpose *(For what purpose?)*	
so that	Many people emigrate **so that** their children can have a better life.
in order that	Many people emigrate **in order that** their children can have a better life.

Condition	
if	We won't go hiking **if** it rains.
unless	We won't go hiking **unless** the weather is perfect.

Subordinating words for adjective clauses

To refer to humans	
who, whom, whose that (*informal*)	People **who** live in glass houses shouldn't throw stones. My parents didn't approve of the man **whom** my sister married. An orphan is a child **whose** parents are dead.

To refer to nonhumans and things	
which	My new computer, **which** I bought yesterday, stopped working today.
that	Yesterday I received an e-mail message **that** I didn't understand.

To refer to a time or a place	
when	Thanksgiving is a time **when** families travel great distances to be together.
where	An orphanage is a place **where** orphans live.

Subordinating words for noun clauses

that	Do you believe **that** there is life in outer space?
whether whether or not whether . . . or not	I can't remember **whether** I locked the door. **whether or not** I locked the door. **whether** I locked the door **or not**.
if if . . . or not	I can't remember **if** I locked the door. **if** I locked the door **or not**.
who, whoever, whom, which, what, where, when, why, how, how much, how many, how long, how often, etc.	**Whoever** arrives at the bus station first should buy the tickets. Maria told us **which** teacher was the best. Do you know **where** the bus station is? I couldn't believe **what** I heard. I don't know **why** they didn't come to the party. Don't worry about **how much** they cost. We should ask **how long** the trip takes.

Notice that some subordinating conjunctions can introduce different kinds of dependent clauses. *That* can introduce either noun clauses or adjective clauses, and *where* can introduce either a noun, an adjective, or an adverb clause. It normally isn't important to know the kind of clause.

▶ I can't remember *where* **I put the house key**. (*noun clause; direct object of* remember)

▶ It's not in the place *where* **I usually put it**. (*adjective clause; tells* which place)

▶ I always put it *where* **I will see it when I go out the front door**. (*adverb clause; tells* where I put it)

53 Transition Signals

This section lists many of the transition signals used in English writing.

SENTENCE CONNECTORS	CLAUSE CONNECTORS		OTHERS
Transition signals and conjunctive adverbs	Coordinating conjunctions and paired conjunctions	Subordinating conjunctions	Adjectives, prepositions, verbs
To list ideas in order of time			
First, ... First of all, ... Second, ... Third, ... Next, ... Then ... After that, ... Meanwhile, ... In the meantime, ... Finally, ... Last, ... Last of all, ... Subsequently, ... Now ... Soon ...		before after until when while as soon as since	The first (reason, cause step, etc.) The second ... The third ... Another ... The last ... The final ...
To list ideas in order of importance			
First, ... First of all, ... First and foremost, Second, ... More important, ... Most important, ... More significant, ... Most significant, ... Above all, ... Most of all, ...			The first ... (reason, cause step, etc.) An additional ... The second ... Another ... A more important (reason, cause step, etc.) The most important ... The most significant ... The best, the worst

SENTENCE CONNECTORS	CLAUSE CONNECTORS		OTHERS
Transition signals and conjunctive adverbs	Coordinating conjunctions and paired conjunctions	Subordinating conjunctions	Adjectives, prepositions, verbs
To add a similar or equal idea			
Also, ... Besides, ... Furthermore, ... In addition, ... Moreover, ... Too As well	and both ... and not only ... but also		Another ... (reason, cause, step, etc.) A second ... An additional ... A final ... as well as
To add an opposite idea			
However, ... On the other hand, ... Nevertheless, ... Nonetheless, ... Still, ...	but yet	although even though though	despite in spite of
To explain or restate an idea			
In other words, ... In particular, ... (More) specifically, ... That is, ...			
To make a stronger statement			
Indeed, ... In fact, ...			
To give another possibility			

Alternatively, ...
On the other
  hand, ...
Otherwise, ...
	or
	either ... or
	whether ...
	  or		

(continued)

(*continued*)

SENTENCE CONNECTORS	CLAUSE CONNECTORS		OTHERS
Transition signals and conjunctive adverbs	Coordinating conjunctions and paired conjunctions	Subordinating conjunctions	Adjectives, prepositions, verbs
To give an example			
For example, ... For instance, ...			such as like an example of to exemplify
To express an opinion			
According to, ... In my opinion, ... In my view, ...			to believe (that) to feel (that) to think (that)
To give a reason			
For this reason, ...	for	because	as a result of because of due to
To give a result			
Accordingly, ... As a consequence, ... As a result, ... Consequently, ... For these reasons, ... Hence, ... Therefore, ... Thus, ...	so		the cause of the reason for to cause to result (in) to have an effect on to affect
To add a conclusion			
All in all, ... In brief, ... In short, ... In conclusion, ... To conclude, ... In summary, ... To summarize, ... To sum up, ... For these reasons, ...			

SENTENCE CONNECTORS	CLAUSE CONNECTORS		OTHERS
Transition signals and conjunctive adverbs	**Coordinating conjunctions and paired conjunctions**	**Subordinating conjunctions**	**Adjectives, prepositions, verbs**
To show similarities			

Likewise, ...
Similarly, ...
Also
	and
	both ... and
	not only ...
	  but also
	neither ...
	  nor
			alike, like, just like
			as, just as
			as well
			as well as
			compared with *or* to
			in comparison with
			  or to
			to be similar (to)
			too

To show differences			
However, ... In contrast, ... Instead, ... On the contrary, ... On the other hand, ... Rather, ...			instead of
To emphasize			

Most important, ...
Most significant, ...
Above all, ...
Most of all, ...
			The most
			  important ...
			The most
			  significant ...
			The best, the
			  worst ...

54   Troublesome Words

This section lists words that may cause difficulty for various reasons. They may cause difficulty because their pronunciation is similar (*custom, costume*), because they are similar in meaning but different in use (*because, because of*), or because they require a particular word order (*enough*), among other reasons.

a, an   *A* and *an* are indefinite articles. Use *a* in front of words and abbreviations that begin with a consonant sound. Use *an* in front of words and abbreviations that begin with a vowel sound.

▶ **a** book, **a** hole, **a** university, **a** VCR

▶ **an** egg, **an** octopus, **an** honest person, **an** MD degree.

(be) about to   Use with the base form of a verb to mean "going to . . . soon."

▶ Shh! The concert is **about to** begin.

▶ Hurry! The train is just **about to** leave.

accept, except   *Accept* is a verb that means "to take something that is offered." *Except* is a preposition that means "excluding."

▶ She **accepted** the job offer.

▶ Everyone **except** Tom passed the test.

advice, advise   *Advice* is a noun; *advise* is a verb. Their meaning is "(to give) an opinion about what someone should do."

▶ My parents gave me good **advice.**

▶ They **advised** me to finish my education before getting married.

affect, effect   *Affect* is a verb; *effect* is a noun. Their meaning is "(to) influence."

▶ Her parents' divorce **affected** her attitude toward marriage.

▶ It had a very bad **effect** on her.

ago, before   *Ago* tells how far back in the past something happened. Use *ago* after an amount of time: *two weeks ago, a little while ago, an hour ago, several years ago.* *Before* means "earlier than" and goes in front of a noun phrase or a clause. You cannot use *before* with an amount of time.

▶ We moved to New York six months **ago.**

▶ My parents got married **before** the war.

▶ We lived in a small town **before** we moved to New York.

alike, like   *Alike* is an adjective and an adverb meaning "similar" or "in a similar way." Use *alike* after nouns, not before nouns.

▶ Boys and girls **alike** enjoy video games.

Alike can also follow other kinds of words.

▶ No two snowflakes are exactly **alike.**

▶ My father and my uncle look **alike,** talk **alike,** and think **alike.**

Like is a preposition meaning "similar to." Use *like* before nouns and pronouns.

▶ The son looks **like** his father. He talks **like** him too.

(See also *as, like.*)

alive, live   *Alive* and *live* are both adjectives meaning "not dead." You can use *live* but not *alive* before nouns and pronouns. Put *alive* at or near the end of its clause.

▶ We bought some **live** crabs at the seafood store.
▶ The child was still **alive** when the searchers found him.
▶ Doctors are trying to keep him **alive.**

When *live* refers to sports events, televisions shows, or other performances of entertainment, it means that people are watching or hearing the event or performance at the same time it is happening or being recorded.

▶ The café on the corner has **live** music every Saturday night.
▶ Some television shows are taped in front of a **live** audience.

almost   *Almost* means "very nearly but not completely." You can use *almost* before verbs and before some (but not all) adverbs, adjectives, time expressions, and indefinite pronouns.

Verbs	▶ We're **almost** finished. My little niece can **almost** count to ten. I **almost** caught a fish.
Adverbs	▶ They said goodbye **almost** cheerfully. The coffee is **almost** too hot to drink. She's **almost** always late. BUT NOT She's almost usually late.
Some adjectives that follow a linking verb	▶ We were **almost** late. Dinner is **almost** ready. They seemed **almost** happy to see us leave. My little niece is **almost** three years old.
Adjectives that have an extreme meaning	▶ It's an **almost** impossible job. We warmed our **almost** frozen hands over the fire.
Certain time expressions	▶ We waited **almost** an hour. It's **almost** time for the movie to start. It's **almost** midnight in London.
Some indefinite pronouns	▶ She invited **almost** everyone to her party, but **almost** no one came.
	▶ **Almost** all of the students passed the test. BUT NOT Almost the students. (See Special Tips in *Section 14d.*)

already, yet, still   *Already* and *yet* mean "by or before now" and are usually used with simple present or present perfect verbs. Use *already* in positive sentences and questions. Put *already* after helping verbs and after *be* but in front of main verbs.

▶ She's **already** seen that movie three times. OR She's seen that movie three times **already.**
▶ It is **already** midnight.
▶ She **already** knows the truth.
▶ Have you **already** had dinner?

Use *yet* in negative sentences and questions. Put *yet* at the end of a clause.

▶ Have you had dinner **yet?**
▶ No, we haven't eaten **yet.**

Still means "up to and continuing through a particular time." You can use *still* in positive sentences, negative sentences, and questions. Put *still* after helping verbs, after *be,* in front of main verbs in positive sentences and questions, and in front of all negative verbs.

▶ You can **still** sign up for the field trip.
▶ He is **still** sick.
▶ I am **still** waiting for the doctor to call back.
▶ Is he **still** planning his trip?
▶ I **still** don't understand.
▶ He **still** hasn't called me back.

although, though, even though, despite, in spite of   *Although, though,* and *even though* are subordinating conjunctions followed by a clause. *Despite* and *in spite of* are prepositions followed by a noun, pronoun, or gerund. All five expressions have a similar meaning.

▶ The children wanted to play outside **although/even though/though** it was cold.
▶ The children wanted to play outside **in spite of/despite** the cold weather. (*The weather was cold, but the children wanted to play outside anyway.*)

Despite and *in spite of* are often followed by a gerund.

▶ The father jumped into the water to save his child **despite** not knowing how to swim. (*The father didn't know how to swim, but he jumped into the water to save his child anyway.*)

In informal spoken English, we often put *though* at the end of a sentence.

▶ I watched the entire movie. I didn't enjoy it, **though.** (*I watched the entire movie, but I didn't enjoy it.*)

among, between   Use *between* with two items. Use *among* with three or more items.

▶ The parents divided their property equally **between** their two children.
▶ The parents divided their property equally **among** their three children.

amount, number   Both words mean "quantity." Use *amount* with noncount nouns. Use *number* with count nouns.

▶ She owes a large **amount** of money.
▶ She has a large **number** of unpaid bills.

anymore, still   Use *not . . . anymore* to say that something happened or was true in the past but not now. Use *still* to say that something continues to be true. (See also **already, still, yet.**)

▶ I don't love you **anymore.**
▶ She **still** lives with her parents.

as, like   *As* (also *as if* and *as though*) is a subordinating conjunction and is used before a clause. *Like* is a preposition and is used before nouns and pronouns. In informal English, *like* is sometimes used as a conjunction, but it is not correct to do so.

▶ He wants to travel around the world, **as** his father did when he was a young man.
▶ He looks **like** his father.

because, because of *Because* is a subordinating conjunction. Use *because* to introduce a clause. *Because of* is a preposition. Use *because of* with a noun or noun phrase.

▶ We canceled our picnic **because** it was raining.
▶ We canceled our picnic **because of** the bad weather.

before, ago (See **ago, among.**)

beside, besides *Beside* is a preposition that means "next to, at the side of." *Besides* can be a preposition meaning "except" or a conjunctive adverb meaning "also, in addition to."

▶ The mother walked **beside** her child and held his hand.
▶ No one **besides** her sister knew her secret.
▶ I'm too tired to write my English essay tonight; **besides,** it's not due until next week.

between, among (See **among, between.**)

borrow, lend, loan *Borrow* is a verb meaning "take something that you will return later."

▶ I **borrowed** five dollars from Jim. I will pay him back tomorrow.
▶ May I **borrow** your dictionary for a minute?
▶ You can **borrow** five books from the library at one time.

Lend and *loan* are both verbs meaning "give something to someone, who will return it later." *Loan* is also a noun.

▶ Jim **loaned (lent)** me five dollars.
▶ Will you **loan (lend)** me your CD player for a couple of days?
▶ The bank gave us **a loan** to start our business.

bring, take, carry *Bring* includes the idea of direction toward a place or a person that is in the speaker's mind. *Take* includes the idea of direction away from a place. *Carry* does not include any idea of direction.

▶ Did you **bring** an umbrella? (*to the place where we are right now*)
▶ He didn't **take** an umbrella. (*when he left his house*)
▶ He **carries** a picture of his children in his wallet.

carry, bring, take (See **bring, take, carry.**)

close, near, nearly *Near* and *close* have similar meanings. Use *to* after *close* but not after *near.*

▶ I like to sit **close to** a window.
▶ I like to sit **near** a window.

You can add *-er* and *-est* to both *near* and *close*. *To* is required after *closer* but is optional after *the closest* and *nearer* and *the nearest.*

▶ I wish we lived **closer to** school.
▶ I wish we lived **nearer (to)** school.

Near and *close* can be adjectives.

▶ Where is the **closest** post office?
▶ Where is the **nearest** post office?

Nearly is an adverb meaning "almost."

▶ It's **nearly** midnight.

▶ I'm **nearly** finished with my homework.

come, go   Use *go* when the movement is away from the location of the speaker or writer. Use *come* when the movement is toward the location of the speaker or writer.

▶ Charles will **go** to England next month. (*The speaker is not in England.*)

▶ Charles will **come** to England next month. (*The speaker is in England.*)

custom, costume   A *custom* (plural: *customs*) is an activity that is normal, usual, or traditional for a person or group of people. The adjective is *customary* and the adverb is *customarily.*

▶ It is my grandfather's **custom** to take a short nap every afternoon.

▶ It is a good idea to know some of the **customs** of countries that you visit.

A *costume* (plural: *costumes*) is special clothing that you wear to look like someone or something unusual.

▶ She wore a cat **costume** to the Halloween party.

desert, dessert   A *desert* is a large area of dry, hot land. A *dessert* is a sweet food eaten after the main part of a meal.

▶ The Sahara is the world's largest **desert.**

▶ Would you like some ice cream for **dessert?**

despite, in spite of, although, though, even though   (See **although, ...**)

do, make   *Do* takes certain nouns and *make* takes others. There is no easy rule, but these suggestions may help you decide which verb to use with various nouns. In general, we use *do* to talk about activities involving some kind of work: *do homework, do a good job, do research.* Use *make* to talk about activities that create something that didn't exist before: *make a cake, make a decision, make a mess.* Here is a list of nouns that commonly occur with *do* and *make.*

do	**make**	
your best	an accusation	a mess
business	an appointment	a mistake
damage	an attempt	money
a dance	a change	a noise
your duty	a comment	an offer
a favor	a deal	progress
homework	a decision	a promise
housework (the cleaning, the dishes,	a demand	a recommendation
the laundry, the ironing, the	an effort	a request
vacuuming, the cooking, etc.)	an estimate	reservations
a job, a good job	an impression	a statement
research	a meal (breakfast,	a suggestion
a sport (BUT play baseball, tennis, etc.)	lunch, dinner, a	
work	snack)	

during, while, for, since   *During* and *while* both mean "through a period of time." Use *during* before a noun that names an event or a period of time. Use *while* before a clause.

▶ She works **during** the summer months.
▶ John slept **during** the lecture.
▶ John was sleeping **while** the teacher was lecturing.

Use *for* with an amount of time.

▶ John slept **for** an hour.
▶ They haven't seen each other **for** ten years.

Use *since* with a point in time.

▶ They haven't seen each other **since** 1995.
▶ She hasn't eaten **since** yesterday.

effect, affect   (See **affect, effect**.)

emigrate (from), immigrate (to)   When you *emigrate* from a country, you leave it permanently in order to live somewhere else. When you *immigrate* to a country, you enter it in order to live there permanently.

▶ My parents **emigrated from** Mexico ten years ago.
▶ They **immigrated to** the United States.

enough, too, very   (See *Section 12b.*)

especially, special   Don't use *especially* or *especial* when you mean *special*. *Especially* is an adverb that means "more than others." *Special* is an adjective that means "not ordinary or usual." *Especial* is not common in English.

▶ The weather is **especially** nice today.
▶ Mother prepared a **special** dinner for my birthday.

We usually put *especially* directly in front of the word or words it modifies.

▶ The test was difficult, **especially** the reading section.
▶ The reading section was **especially** difficult.
▶ The reading section was difficult, **especially** for me.

However, don't begin a sentence with *especially*.

▶ Redheads sunburn **especially** easily. (NOT Especially redheads sunburn easily.)

etc.   Avoid using *etc.* at the end of a list. Use "and so on" instead.

even   Place *even* directly in front of the word it modifies.

▶ She didn't **even** say goodbye.
▶ **Even** her mother didn't believe her.
▶ She didn't recognize **even** her own parents.

ever   *Ever* means "at any time." It is used mostly in negative sentences and questions.

▶ Have you **ever** been to Hong Kong?
▶ No, I haven't **ever** been there. (*I have never been there.*)

except, accept   (See **accept, except.**)

fairly   (See **pretty, fairly.**)

farther, further   Use *farther* for distances and *further* for quantity and degree.
▶ Let's walk a little **farther.**
▶ We'll discuss this idea **further** during our next class.

fewer, less   Use *fewer* with count nouns and *less* with noncount nouns.
▶ Since I changed jobs, I have **fewer** problems and **less** stress.

for, while, since, during   (See **during, while, since, for.**)

get / be / stay married to, marry   (See **marry, get / be married (to).**)

go, come   (See **come, go.**)

good, well   *Good* is an adjective. *Well* has two meanings. As an adverb, it means "in a good manner." As an adjective, it means "not sick."

          adjective   adverb
▶ This is a **good** book. The author writes **well.**

                                     adjective
▶ My father is in the hospital. He isn't **well.**

hard, hardly   *Hard* is both an adjective and an adverb. As an adjective, *hard* means both "not soft" and "difficult." As an adverb, *hard* means "with a lot of effort or force." *Hardly* is an adverb meaning "almost not."
▶ Do you like to sleep on a **hard** or on a soft bed? He has a very **hard** job.
▶ The whole class studied **hard** for the final exam.
▶ My grandmother is almost blind. She can **hardly** see.

hear, listen   *Hear* means that sound comes to your ears with no effort by you. *Listen (to)* means that you pay attention to the sound; you make an effort to hear it.
▶ Every morning, I **hear** the neighbor's cat meowing outside my window.
▶ **Listen!** Did you hear that noise?
▶ I like to **listen to** music when I am studying.

in, on, at   We use *in, on,* and *at* with both place and time expressions.

Place

in	Use *in* when something is enclosed—*in* **a box,** *in* **a room,** *in* **a drawer,** *in* **a window,** *in* **a picture,** *in* **a bed** (under the bedcovers), *in* **a garden,** fish are *in* **a lake.**
on	Use *on* when something is on the surface—*on* **a table,** *on* **a bed** (on top of a bed), *on* **a wall,** *on* **a lawn,** *on* **a street,** a boat is *on* **a lake.**
at	Use *at* when something is in a general area—*at* **school,** *at* **home,** *at* **an airport,** *at* **a store.**
	Also, use *at* with exact addresses: She lives *at* **2045 Main Street** (BUT *on Main Street*).

Time

in   Use *in* for months, years, seasons, and parts of a day—*in* **January,** *in* **2001,** *in* **(the) summer,** *in* **the morning,** *in* **the afternoon,** *in* **the evening** (BUT *at night*).

on   Use *on* for days—*on* **Saturday,** *on* **New Year's Day,** *on* **November 19** (ALSO *on* **Sunday morning**).

at   Use *at* for exact times—*at* **12:15,** *at* **three-thirty in the morning,** *at* **noon,** *at* **midnight.**

it's, its   *It's* is a contraction of *it is*. *Its* is a possessive word.

▶ **It's** hot today. (*It is hot today.*)

▶ The cat is licking *its* paw.

just   *Just* has three meanings. It can mean that something happened a short time ago.

▶ We had **just** finished our homework when the lights went out.

▶ The plane **just** arrived at the gate.

Just can also mean "only" or "exactly." In these meanings, put *just* directly in front of the word or phrase it modifies.

▶ We had finished **just** one part of our homework when the lights went out. (*only one part, not all of it*)

▶ **Just** one person answered my ad for a roommate. (*only one person, not two or three*)

▶ We saw him **just** a few minutes ago. (*only a few minutes ago, not several hours ago*)

▶ Jason looks **just** like his father. (*exactly*)

lay, lie   *Lay* is a transitive verb and always takes an object. Its principal parts are *lay, laid, laid.*

▶ A careful parent always **lays** a baby on its back, not on its stomach. He **laid** his book down, turned off the light, and went to sleep.

Lie is an intransitive verb and never takes on object. *Lie* has two meanings. In the meaning "to get into a flat position," its principal parts are *lie, lay, lain.* In the meaning "to say something that is not true," its principal parts are *lie, lied, lied.*

▶ My dog usually **lies** near the front door, waiting for my return. Yesterday he **lay** there all day.

▶ The boy **lied** to his parents about the broken window.

learn, teach   *Learn* means "to get knowledge." *Teach* means "to give knowledge."

▶ I **learned** how to swim when I was five years old.

▶ My mother **taught** me how to cook.

lend, loan, borrow   (See **borrow, lend, loan.**)

lie, lay   (See **lay, lie.**)

like, alike   (See **alike, like.**)

like, as   (See **as, like.**)

listen (to), hear   (See **hear, listen.**)

live, alive   (See **alive, live.**)

loan, lend, borrow   (See **borrow, lend, loan.**)

look (at), see, watch   *See* means that you perceive things through your eyes with no effort by you. *Look* means that you purposefully turn your eyes toward something or someone; you make an effort to see. *Watch* means that you look at something for a long period of time.

▶ We **saw** a terrible accident this morning.
▶ I can't find my glasses. I've **looked** everywhere for them.
▶ **Look at** this picture and describe what you **see.**
▶ Do you like to **watch** sports on TV?

loose, lose   *Loose* is an adjective meaning "not tight" or "not fastened." *Lose* is a verb meaning "not be able to find," "not have anymore," or "not win."

▶ His pants are **loose.** They look as if they will fall down.
▶ She **loses** her car keys at least once a week.
▶ We will **lose** our apartment if we don't pay the rent on time.
▶ Our baseball team **hasn't lost** a game all year.

a lot, lots, lots of   *A lot, lots,* and *lots of* are used in informal spoken English in place of *much, many,* and *a lot of.* Do not use them in formal writing.

make, do   (See **do, make.**)

marry, get/be married (to)   You *marry* someone and *get/are married to* someone (NOT *with* someone.) Use *get married* to talk about the time or place of the event. Use either *marry* or *get married to* to name the person. *Marry* is more formal than *get married to.*

▶ My sister **got married** last week.
▶ She **is married to** a doctor.
▶ She **married** her childhood sweetheart. She **got married to** her childhood sweetheart.
▶ My parents **have been married** for fifty years.

near, nearly, close   (See **close, near, nearly.**)

only   Put *only* directly in front of the word it modifies.

▶ They have **only** one child. (*They don't have two children.*)
▶ Tom **only** rented a car. (*He didn't buy one.*)
▶ **Only** Ann wanted to go camping. (*No one else wanted to go.*)

pass, passed, past   *Pass* is a verb with several meanings. Its past tense and past participle forms are *passed.*

▶ Please **pass** the salt and pepper.
▶ Time **passes** quickly when you are having fun.
▶ A police car **passed** us going very fast.
▶ I still **haven't passed** the test for my driver's license.

Past can be a preposition or an adverb meaning "farther than" or "later than."

▶ We walked **past** the restaurant where we had reservations.
▶ Don't work **past** midnight.

Past can also be an adjective or a noun meaning "before now."

▶ I have been living in New York for the **past** year.
▶ In the **past,** people married at younger ages.

pretty, fairly   *Pretty* is an adjective meaning "nice-looking, attractive." In informal English, *pretty* is also used as an adverb meaning "a little bit, not completely." Don't use *pretty* in this meaning in formal academic or business writing. Use *fairly* instead.

▶ The movie was **pretty** good. (*informal*)
▶ The movie was **fairly** good. (*formal*)

quiet, quite   *Quiet* is an adjective meaning "not loud." *Quite* is an adverb meaning "very" but is not as strong as *very.*

▶ Please be **quiet.** I am trying to get the baby to sleep.
▶ The movie was **quite** good.

When you use *quite* with a noun phrase instead of with a single adjective, put *quite* in front of the entire phrase. Compare the location of *very* and *quite:*

▶ It was a **very** good movie.
▶ It was **quite** a good movie.

quite a few, only a few   *Quite a few* means "many." *Only a few* means "not many."

▶ There were **quite a few** dogs in the park. (*There were many dogs.*)
▶ There were **only a few** dogs in the park. (*There were not many dogs.*)

raise, rise   *Raise* is a transitive verb and always has an object. Its principal parts are *raise, raised, raised. Rise* is an intransitive verb and never takes an object. Its principal parts are *rise, rose, risen.*

▶ The government is going to **raise** taxes next year.
▶ My grandfather **raised** cattle on his ranch.
▶ The sun **rises** in the east.

say, tell   Use *say* when you want to give the words that someone says or writes. You can give the person's words as a direct quotation or as reported speech. You don't have to mention the person spoken to, but if you do, always use a *to*-phrase.

▶ John **said,** "I'm leaving."

(See *Section 29a* for information about direct quotations.)

▶ John **said** that he was leaving.

(See *Section 11c* for information about reported speech.)

▶ John **said to me,** "I'm leaving."

You can also use *tell* as a reporting verb to quote or report someone's words. You must mention the person spoken to. Do not use a *to*-phrase with *tell* as a reporting verb.

▶ John **told me,** "I'm leaving."
▶ John **told me** that he was leaving.

Use *tell,* not *say,* with the words *a story, a joke, a lie, the truth.* In this situation, you may use either a *to*-phrase or a simple indirect object to mention the person spoken to. (See *Section 9c* for information about the word order of indirect objects.)

▶ The teacher **told a joke** *to the class.*
▶ The teacher **told** *the class* **a joke.**

scarce, scarcely *Scarce* is an adjective meaning "not plentiful, not easy to get." *Scarcely* is an adverb meaning "almost not."

▶ Food is **scarce** during a famine.
▶ My throat was so sore that I could **scarcely** talk.

see, watch, look (at) [See **look (at), see, watch.**]

set, sit *Set* is a transitive verb in the meaning "to put, to place" and always has an object. (BUT *Set* is intransitive in the meaning *The sun rises in the east and sets in the west.*) Its principal parts are *set, set, set. Sit* is an intransitive verb and never takes an object. Its principal parts are *sit, sat, sat.*

▶ She **set** a bag of groceries in the middle of the table.
▶ Don't **sit** on that chair; it's broken.

since, during, for, while (See **during, while, for, since.**)

so, so that *So* is a coordinating conjunction that connects a result clause to a main clause. Put a comma before *so. So that* is a subordinating conjunction that connects a purpose clause to a main clause. *So that* is usually followed by a modal verb such as *could.* Don't put a comma before *so that.*

▶ I studied hard**, so** I was accepted by a good college. (*result*)
▶ I studied hard **so that** I could go to a good college. (*purpose*)

so, very Informally, we sometimes use *so* in place of *very* to emphasize an adjective. In formal writing, use *very.*

▶ I was **so** tired last night. (*informal*)
▶ I was **very** tired last night. (*formal*)
▶ Thank you **so** much. (*informal*)
▶ Thank you **very** much. (*formal*)

special, especially (See **especially, special.**)

still, already, yet (See **already, yet, still.**)

take, bring, carry (See **bring, take, carry.**)

tell, say (See **say, tell.**)

than, then *Than* is a conjunction used in comparisons. *Then* is a time word.

▶ It's a lot cooler today **than** it was yesterday.
▶ We heard a loud crash, and **then** we saw two people running through the park.

they're, there, their *They're* is a contraction of *they are. There* is a place word. *Their* is a possessive word.

▶ **They're** late. (*They are late.*)
▶ Let's sit over **there** by the window.
▶ Tom and Mary forgot **their** tickets.

too, very, enough   (See *Section 12b.*)

until   *Until* means that something stops happening at a certain time or when something else happens.

▶ We waited **until** 3:30. (*We stopped waiting at 3:30.*)
▶ We waited **until** the last passenger got off the plane. (*We stopped waiting when the last passenger got off the plane.*)
▶ I won't get my paycheck **until** next Wednesday. (*"Not getting my paycheck" will stop next Wednesday.*)

very, too, enough   (See *Section 12b.*)

very, so   (See **so, very.**)

watch, see, look (at)   [See **look (at), see, watch.**]

weather, whether   *Weather* is a noncount noun meaning the temperature and other conditions such as rain, wind, sunshine, humidity, and so on.

▶ The **weather** is very pleasant today. The sun is shining and there is no wind.

Whether is a subordinating conjunction that shows that there are two choices. *Whether* often appears in a sentence with *or*, which connects the second choice.

▶ I can't decide **whether** to major in accounting **or** computer programming.

We often use *or not* with *whether* to indicate the second choice. *Or not* can come directly after *whether* or at the end of the clause.

▶ We haven't heard **whether or not** Sally is coming to the party.
▶ We haven't heard **whether** Sally is coming to the party **or not.**

well, good   (See **good, well.**)

what, which   The choice of *what* or *which* before a noun depends on your emphasis. Use *what* to ask for general information. Use *which* when you want to show that there is a choice.

▶ **What** jobs are available?
▶ **Which** math class should I take this semester?

when, while   *When* means "at a specific time." We never use *when* with a progressive tense verb. *While* means "during a period of time." We often, but not always, use *while* with a progressive tense verb.

▶ Everything was ready **when** their guests arrived.
▶ You can read a magazine **while** you are waiting.
▶ He set the table **while** she prepared dinner.

whether, weather   (See **weather, whether.**)

which, what   (See **what, which.**)

who, whom   (See *Section 16b* and *Section 23.*)

who's, whose   *Who's* is a contraction of *who is* (or *who has* in present perfect tense.) *Whose* is a possessive word.

▶ **Who's** coming to the party tonight? (*Who is coming . . . ?*)
▶ **Who's been waiting** the longest? (*Who has been waiting . . . ?*)
▶ **Whose** book is this? I don't know **whose** it is.
▶ The student **whose** picture was in the newspaper is in my class.

(be) worth   *Be worth* means "be equal in value to." *Worth* is a preposition, so it appears in front of nouns and pronouns except in questions beginning *How much . . . .* Put *worth* at the end of these questions.

▶ This piece of jewelry **is worth** a lot of money.
▶ How much **is** your car **worth?** It's **worth** $3500.
▶ **Is** it **worth** the extra money to fly first class?
▶ I don't think it's **worth** it.

Be worth + a gerund, such as *reading, trying, waiting for,* or *worrying about,* means "It is useful/helpful/valuable doing this."

▶ That movie **is worth** seeing.
▶ The damage **is** not **worth** worrying about.

yet, already, still   (See **already, yet, still.**)

you're, your   *You're* is a contraction of *you are. Your* is a possessive word.

▶ **You're** late. (*You are late.*)
▶ What is **your** name?

55   Editing Symbols

This section contains common symbols used by writing teachers on student papers. The numbers on the right refer you to sections of the handbook that contain information about the particular problem.

SYMBOL	MEANING	EXAMPLE OF ERROR	CORRECTED SENTENCE	SECTIONS
p	*punctuation*	^{p} I live, and go to school here. Where do you ^{p} work.	I live and go to school here. Where do you work?	24–32
◯ ∧	*missing word*	◯ I working in a ∧restaurant.	I am working in a restaurant.	

SYMBOL	MEANING	EXAMPLE OF ERROR	CORRECTED SENTENCE	SECTIONS
cap	*capitalization*	It is located at *cap* *cap* <u>main</u> and <u>baker</u> *cap* *cap* <u>streets</u> in the <u>C</u>ity.	It is located at Main and Baker Streets in the city.	33
vt	*verb tense*	*vt* I never <u>work</u> as a *vt* cashier until I <u>get</u> a job there.	I had never worked as a cashier until I got a job there.	11
s/v agr	*subject-verb agreement*	*s/v agr* The manager <u>work</u> hard. *s/v agr* There <u>is</u> five employees.	The manager works hard. There are five employees.	13
pron agr	*pronoun agreement*	Everyone works *pron agr* hard at <u>their</u> jobs.	All of the employees work hard at their jobs.	17
‿	*connect to make one sentence*	We work ‿ together. So we have become friends.	We work together, so we have become friends.	5–7, 8c
sp	*spelling*	*sp* The <u>maneger</u> is a woman.	The manager is a woman.	38
sing/pl	*singular or plural*	She treats her employees like *sing/pl* <u>slave</u>.	She treats her employees like slaves.	
✕	*unnecessary word*	My boss s̶h̶e̶ watches everyone all the time.	My boss watches everyone all the time.	
wf	*word form*	Her voice is *wf* <u>irritated</u>.	Her voice is irritating.	
ww	*wrong word*	The food is *ww* delicious. <u>Besides,</u> the restaurant is always crowded.	The food is delicious. Therefore, the restaurant is always crowded.	

SYMBOL	MEANING	EXAMPLE OF ERROR	CORRECTED SENTENCE	SECTIONS
ref	*pronoun reference*	The restaurant's specialty is fish. *ref* They are always fresh.	The restaurant's specialty is fish. It is always fresh.	18
		The food is delicious. *ref?* Therefore, it is always crowded.	The food is delicious. Therefore, the restaurant is always crowded.	
wo	*word order*	*wo* Friday always is our busiest night.	Friday is always our busiest night.	9, 19
rts OR	*run-together-sentence*	*rts* Lily was fired she is upset.	Lily was fired, so she is upset. Lily was fired; therefore, she is upset.	8b
cs	*comma splice*	*cs* Lily was fired, she is upset.	Because Lily was fired, she is upset. Lily is upset because she was fired.	
frag	*fragment*	She was fired. *frag* Because she was always late.	She was fired because she was always late.	8a
		frag Is open from 6:00 p.m. until the last customer leaves.	The restaurant is open from 6:00 p.m. until the last customer leaves.	
		frag The employees on time and work hard.	The employees are on time and work hard.	
choppy	*choppy writing*	*choppy* (I like the work. I don't like my boss. I want to quit.)	Even though I like the work, I don't like my boss, so I want to quit.	8c

SYMBOL	MEANING	EXAMPLE OF ERROR	CORRECTED SENTENCE	SECTIONS
not ‖	*not parallel*	Most of our regular customers are friendly and *not* ‖ generous tippers.	Most of our regular customers are friendly and tip generously.	6d
sub	*subordinate*	The tips are good, *sub* and all of the employees share them.	The tips, which all of the employees share, are good.	5, 8d
prep	*preposition*	We start serving *prep* dinner 6:00 p.m.	We start serving dinner at 6:00 p.m.	
conj	*conjunction*	Garlic shrimp, fried *conj* clams, broiled lobster are the most popular dishes.	Garlic shrimp, fried clams, and broiled lobster are the most popular dishes.	5
art	*article*	Diners in the United *art* States expect glass of water when they first sit down.	Diners in the United States expect a glass of water when they first sit down.	15
ⓣ	*add a transition*	The new employee ⓣ was careless. She frequently spilled coffee on the table.	The new employee was careless. For example, she frequently spilled coffee on the table.	41d
awk	*awkward*	*You can understand the meaning, but a native speaker would write it differently.*		
		Five basic flavors make Japanese food the special taste.	Five basic flavors give Japanese food its special taste.	
	awk			
nfs	*needs further support*	*You need to add some specific details (examples, facts, quotations) to support your point.*		41b
	nfs	Giant pandas are an endangered species. There are not many pandas living in the wild.	Giant pandas are an endangered species. Only about 1000 giant pandas live in the wild.	

ANSWER KEY

PART 1 The Basics

Practice—Section 1a, page 3

1. <u>Quebec</u> is a <u>province</u> in eastern <u>Canada</u>.
2. I usually get my best <u>ideas</u> in my <u>dreams</u>.
3. <u>Experience</u> is the best <u>teacher</u>.
4. <u>Exercising</u> immediately after <u>eating</u> is unwise.

Practice—Section 1b, page 4

1. <u>Whose</u> car can <u>I</u> borrow? <u>You</u> can borrow <u>mine</u>.
2. Is <u>that</u> <u>your</u> final answer?
3. <u>She</u> taught <u>herself</u> to play the piano.
4. <u>All</u> of <u>his</u> former girlfriends came uninvited to <u>his</u> wedding.

Practice—Section 1c, page 7

1. <u>Pardon</u> (MV) me. Your dog <u>is</u> (HV) <u>eating</u> (MV) my shoe.
2. Oh! <u>I'm</u> (MV) sorry! <u>I'll</u> (HV) <u>stop</u> (MV) him.
3. He <u>must</u> (HV) <u>be</u> (MV) very hungry. <u>Didn't</u> (HV) you <u>feed</u> (MV) him this morning?
4. Yes, I <u>did</u> (HV), but he <u>hasn't</u> (HV) <u>been</u> (HV) <u>eating</u> (MV) much lately. I <u>don't</u> (HV) <u>think</u> (MV) he <u>likes</u> (MV) dog food.
5. Well, he certainly <u>likes</u> (MV) my shoe. Maybe you <u>should</u> (HV) <u>try</u> (MV) a different brand of dog food.
6. Tom and I <u>are</u> (HV) <u>having</u> (MV) a potluck barbecue next weekend.
7. <u>That's</u> (MV) great! <u>Who's</u> (HV) <u>coming</u> (MV)? <u>Am</u> (HV) I <u>invited</u> (MV)?
8. <u>Didn't</u> (HV) you <u>get</u> (MV) our invitation? You <u>should</u> (HV) <u>have</u> (HV) <u>received</u> (MV) it long ago.
9. Well, it <u>hasn't</u> (HV) <u>come</u> (MV) yet.
10. <u>That's</u> (MV) too bad. I <u>hope</u> (MV) you <u>can</u> (HV) still <u>come</u> (MV).

Practice—Section 1d, page 9

1. <u>My</u> car isn't <u>new</u> or <u>beautiful</u>, but I love it anyway.
2. <u>Its</u> body is in <u>terrible</u> condition.
3. The <u>back</u> bumper is <u>rusty</u>, and the <u>front</u> window is <u>cracked</u>.

Practice—Section 1e, page 9

1. He said <u>a</u> neighbor's pet had escaped, and he was searching <u>the</u> neighborhood for it.

2. He showed us <u>a</u> picture of <u>the</u> escaped pet.
3. It was <u>an</u> enormous snake!
4. We closed <u>the</u> front door, turned on every light in <u>the</u> house, and sat with our feet in <u>the</u> air for <u>the</u> rest of <u>the</u> night.

Practice—Section 1f, page 10

1. I love the smell of <u>freshly</u> baked bread.
2. It <u>never</u> rains in July.
3. I can swim <u>fast</u>, but I can't swim <u>very far</u>.
4. The children went <u>outside</u> to play.
5. She <u>almost always</u> gets up <u>too late</u> to eat breakfast.

Practice—Section 1g, page 12

1. I usually buy a parking permit <u>for</u> my car <u>before</u> the first day <u>of</u> school.
2. Unfortunately, I was so busy that I forgot to buy one <u>at</u> the beginning <u>of</u> the semester.
3. <u>On</u> the first day <u>of</u> school, I walked <u>out of</u> the building <u>after</u> class and saw a police officer standing <u>next to</u> my car.
4. She was putting a ticket <u>on</u> the glass <u>under</u> the windshield wipers.

Practice—Section 1h, page 15

1. He opened his first store <u>when</u> he was still in high school, <u>and</u> now he owns three stores.
2. He <u>both</u> sells <u>and</u> rents computer hardware, <u>but</u> he doesn't sell software.
3. He is successful <u>because</u> he is honest <u>and</u> <u>because</u> he works hard.
4. Last year he made a lot of money; <u>as a result</u>, he was able to buy his parents a house.

Practice—Section 3b, page 21

1. American schoolchildren have a long summer vacation <u>because many families lived on farms at the beginning of the nation's history</u>.
2. The children worked on the farms during the busy summer growing season.
3. <u>Even though there are few farming families in the United States today</u>, schools still close for three months during the summer.
4. In modern times, some people think <u>that children don't need such a long summer vacation</u>.

414

Practice—Section 4a, page 23

1. <u>Snowboarding</u>, which is especially popular among young people, requires good balance.
2. <u>Special areas to be used exclusively for snowboarding</u> are now available in most ski resorts.
3. <u>A good skier</u> is not automatically a good snowboarder.
4. <u>The techniques of snowboarding</u> are different from the techniques of skiing.
5. <u>Most of the people in the world</u> eat rice as their staple food.
6. <u>Methods of cooking rice</u> differ from culture to culture.
7. Also, <u>different cultures</u> are accustomed to eating different types of rice.
8. <u>Asian people</u>, who use chopsticks to eat, prefer sticky rice.
9. Therefore, <u>short-grain and medium-grain rice</u>, which sticks together better than long-grain rice, is used in most Asian cuisines.

PART 2 Clear Sentences

Practice—Section 6a, page 36

Answers will vary. Sample answers:

1. Pit bulls, which are fighting dogs, can be very aggressive; *therefore, they* are not good pets for families with children.
2. Pit bulls must always be on a leash, *for they* are very unpredictable.
3. Never trust pit bulls; *they* can attack without cause.
4. Pit bulls are known to be dangerous, *and* rottweilers and giant schnauzers can also be problem dogs.
5. My little Chihuahua is small, *but he* thinks he is a pit bull.
6. He runs around and growls ferociously; *however, most* people just laugh at him.
7. Actually, Chihuahuas can be dangerous at times, *for they* are not very tolerant of children.

Practice—Section 6b, page 38

1. and	5. or	9. or
2. and	6. and	10. and
3. or	7. and	11. or
4. but (yet)	8. or	

Practice—Section 6c, page 39

1. neither . . . nor	4. either . . . or
2. Both . . . and	5. whether . . . or
3. not only . . . but also	

Practice—Section 6d, page 42

A. When deciding what kind of pet to get, most people consider only <u>dogs</u>, <u>cats</u>, or <u>fish</u>. Cats are <u>soft</u>, <u>cute</u>, and <u>playful</u>. Dogs <u>are fun</u> but <u>can be destructive</u>. They like to <u>dig holes in the garden</u> and <u>chew holes in the furniture</u>. Fish are excellent pets because <u>they don't make much noise</u>, <u>they don't eat a lot</u>, and <u>they won't ruin your carpets</u>.

B. If you prefer a more exotic pet, consider these choices. A giraffe is useful not only for reaching things from high shelves but also *for seeing* over the heads of people at a parade. A pet lion is a good choice if you live alone, for pet lions give their owners both companionship and home security. If you like water sports, cold weather, and *a companion* who is always well dressed, a penguin is the pet for you. If you have a new baby in your household, consider either a goat or a kangaroo. A "nanny" goat can baby-sit, *produce milk,* and *mow your grass.* You can use a kangaroo's pouch either for carrying the baby or *(for)* keeping the baby's bottle warm.

Practice—Section 7a (1), page 45

A. <u>After the war in Vietnam ended</u>, many Vietnamese came to the United States to live. Many of these newcomers wanted to settle <u>where they could live near others from their homeland</u>. As a result, large Vietnamese communities developed in the California cities of Los Angeles and San Jose.

B. *Answers will vary. Sample answers:*

Conflicts often develop in immigrant families *because* old and new cultures are different. For example, *a problem may occur* when young people want to choose their own careers and marriage partners. Although the children grow up learning the new culture, *their* parents and grandparents hold on to the customs of their homeland.

C. *Answers will vary. Sample answers:*

1. A friend of mine couldn't go to parties *because her* parents didn't allow her to go out.

2. *As soon as her* last class ended, she had to go directly home every day after school.
3. She had to help her mother *while her* brothers played sports and visited friends after school.

Practice—Section 7a (2), page 47

The island that most tourists visit is Oahu, where the capital city of Honolulu is located. The largest island is Hawaii, which is also the name of the state. One of the most interesting islands is Niihau, which is called the "Forbidden Island" because no one is allowed to visit the island without special permission. Niihau is privately owned by one family, the Robinsons. The Robinsons want to help the native Hawaiian families who live on their island to preserve their culture by keeping outsiders away. Although everyone can speak English, Hawaiian is the everyday language of Niihau.

Not many Americans know that Hawaii was once a monarchy. The most famous king of Hawaii was Kamehameha I, who united all of the islands into one kingdom about 1800. The last queen, whose name was Liliuokalani, ruled until 1893, when she was overthrown by a group of businessmen with the help of the U.S. military. Today, there are many native Hawaiian groups that want to see the United States give Hawaiian land back to their people.

Practice—Section 7a (3), pages 48–49

A. When I was young, I didn't know what I wanted to be. I wasn't sure whether I wanted to be a singer, an actor, or a musician. I just knew that I wanted to be famous. My parents, however, decided that I should study business.

B. My parents decided that I should become a businessman without asking me *what I wanted* to do with my life. My parents don't know me very well. They don't know *who I am.* They don't understand that I am an artist in my heart. I hope that I will find a way to fulfill their wishes and my dreams.

Practice—Section 7b, page 50

A. My teenage daughter saw the film Titanic twelve times. The film starred two of Hollywood's most popular young actors, Leonardo DiCaprio and Kate Winslet. The love story of the beautiful young heiress Rose and the handsome young artist Jack touched the hearts of young people everywhere. The film, one of Hollywood's biggest hits in years, received fourteen Oscar nominations.

B. 1. My mother, a professional chef, loves to cook.
2. She makes the best lasagna, a flavorful combination of ground beef, tomatoes, cheese, and pasta.
3. My father, a vegetarian, won't eat her lasagna.

Practice—Section 7d, page 53

A. Four-year-old Sarah loves to dress up in her mother's clothes and play "grown-up." One day, while wearing her mother's high-heeled shoes, Sarah fell down the stairs. Knocked unconscious, Sarah lay very still. Sarah's mother, believing that her daughter was dead, began to scream. Sarah woke up when her mother began screaming. Frightened by her mother's screaming, Sarah began screaming too.

B. *Finally realizing* that screaming was useless, Sarah's mother quieted down and called an ambulance. *While waiting* for the ambulance, she checked her daughter for injuries. Fortunately, she didn't find any. Just to be safe, however, the ambulance crew took Sarah to the hospital. Poor little Sarah, *strapped* to a gurney (a bed on wheels) and put into the ambulance, screamed all the way there. She stopped screaming only after her mother promised to bring her some ice cream. *Concerned* about broken bones, the doctor ordered X-rays. *After looking* at the X-rays, however, the doctor told Sarah's mother that nothing was broken and that she could take Sarah home.

Practice—Section 8a, pages 56–57

Four hundred years ago, a game began when people started throwing a ball against a church wall to entertain themselves during religious festivals. This game became known as jai alai, which means "merry festival" in the Basque language.

Jai alai is a ball game similar to handball and racquetball. *It was* invented by the Basque people, who live in the northern part of Spain. Although jai alai began in Europe, *it is* now popular in many Latin American countries. Especially in Mexico, *there are* many jai alai teams. Athletes who play jai alai must be very quick and have excellent eye-hand coordination *because* it is one of the fastest of all ball games. The ball, or pelota, has been clocked at over 180 miles per hour. *It is* the hardest ball used in any sport. Because the pelota is so hard, the walls of a jai alai court are made of granite *just* like the original church walls.

Practice—Section 8b, page 58

Answers will vary. Sample answers:

Teaching children good behavior is one of the main jobs of parents; schools also share this responsibility. Every culture has its own methods of doing this. In some cultures, parents and teachers hit children who misbehave. In other cultures, parents don't hit their children; instead, they exclude them from the family group. In U. S. schools, teachers may not hit children *because* physical punishment is against the law. They can make them do extra lessons or send them to the principal's office.

Practice—Section 8c, page 60

Answers will vary. Sample answers:

Washington and Lincoln were leaders during times of crisis. Washington was the top general of the army during the Revolutionary War, *which* began in 1776. Lincoln was president during the U.S. Civil War, *which* began in 1860.

The young country was in danger of breaking apart after these two wars. It needed a strong leader to stay united. *Both* Washington and Lincoln *were* strong presidents *who* believed in keeping the country together *and* worked very hard to keep the country from splitting apart. *After* America finally won its independence from England, Washington helped write the U.S. Constitution, *which* made the federal government strong. *When* the Civil War ended, Lincoln's strong leadership helped reunite the North and the South.

Practice—Section 8d, page 61

Answers will vary. Sample answers:

My family has always worked hard. *After* we came to the United States, we bought a small grocery store. My father worked in the store all day, and my mother, *who also took care of the house,* worked there for a few hours in the afternoon. There were five children in the family, and we all went to the store every day after school. *As* my oldest brother enjoyed selling things and I liked keeping the shelves neat, we enjoyed our afternoons in the store. *However,* our younger brothers and sisters hated being there because they wanted to be outside playing with their friends.

Practice—Section 9b, pages 64–65

Last week I received a letter from my best friend, who lives in Italy. He enclosed a funny photo of himself. The photo shows my friend holding both of his arms out to one side and his hands pointing up. In the background is the famous Leaning Tower of Pisa. It looks as if he is keeping *the tower from falling over.*

I was happy to get his letter. *I don't hear from this friend often*—usually just once a year at Christmas.

I am thinking about going *to Europe next summer.* If I go, I will certainly visit him. We haven't seen *one another for almost ten years.* We used to get together often, but since he moved to Italy, we have seen each other only once when he came home to attend his sister's wedding. *Not only did he move* to Italy, but he also got married. Now he is the father of two children and has no time to travel.

Practice—Section 9c, page 66

1. (*Correct*)
2. Could you please explain the difference between "lend" and "borrow" *to me*?
3. The polite student opened the door to the classroom *for the teacher.*
4. (*Correct*)
5. Every night, the mother reads *a story to the children* before they go to sleep.

Practice—Section 9d, page 68

Answers will vary. Sample answers:

Yesterday, I took the test for my first driver's license. I was so nervous during the driving test that I drove the wrong way on a one-way street. *To correct my mistake,* I made an illegal U-turn. I ran over the curb when trying to parallel park. I also forgot to signal before turning into the parking lot at the end of the test. *Even though I got 100% on the written test,* I failed to get my license.

Practice—Sections 10b–c, page 72

1. *Employees are* responsible for cleaning *their* own uniforms.
2. Each department elects a new *chair* every four years.
3. Yoshi *spends time* with several *friends* at the gym.
4. There are seven *children* in my family.
5. What time are you *going to* leave?

PART 3 Grammar

Practice—Section 11b (1), page 80

1. boils
2. is boiling
3. sits, is sitting
4. are you thinking about, have
5. begins

Practice—Section 11b (2), page 83

Verbs may vary. Sample answers:

1. has taught/has been teaching
2. has written
3. have Eric and Johannes taken
4. Have you ever seen
5. have you been waiting

Practice—Section 11b (3), pages 86–87

A. 1. shouted, didn't hear
   2. was talking, was driving
   3. wasn't paying attention
   4. were recovering, saw, jumped

B. 1. have you been having/have you had
   2. have ever had
   3. have you owned
   4. bought
   5. have you checked
   6. checked
   7. developed/has developed
   8. haven't learned

Practice—Section 11b (4), pages 88–89

1. arrived, had already taken off
2. had known, decided
3. got/had gotten, wanted
4. had been sleeping
5. was raining
6. have been sleeping
7. was having

Practice—Section 11b (5), pages 92–93

1. get there, will have already started
2. will remember, see
3. will call

4. Will we have, starts
5. is going/is going to go
6. will rain/is going to rain
7. is arriving/will arrive
8. am going to pick him up/will pick him up
9. lands, will have been traveling
10. is going to be/will be

Practice—Section 11b (6), pages 93–94

We finished dinner, washed our dinner dishes, and stored our leftover food in bear-proof metal containers before crawling into our tents for the night. We were almost asleep when suddenly, we *heard* the rattling of pots and pans just outside our tent. We looked out and *saw* an enormous black bear pawing through our campsite kitchen. Of course, it *was looking* for food. We *tried* to remember what to do: stay quiet, make noise, or run? No one could remember. Then I *realized* that I *had put* a candy bar in my shirt pocket during the afternoon and that I *was* still *wearing* the shirt with the candy in it. I *closed* my eyes, *said* my prayers, and *prepared* to die.

Suddenly, I *heard* the roar of a car engine and the screech of tires. Two park rangers *jumped* out of their truck and *began* banging cooking pots together. They *had heard* that a bear *was* in the area, so they *had been patrolling* the campground all night. The noise *scared* the bear away.

After I *was* sure that the bear had left, I *crawled* out of my tent. I was so happy to see those two park rangers! I *wanted* to give them something to thank them for saving my life, but they *were* not very pleased when I *took* the candy bar out of my pocket and *offered* it to them.

Practice—Section 11c (1), page 95

1. haven't seen, started
2. finished/had finished, asked
3. finish, will ask
4. have not slept, came

Practice—Section 11c (2), pages 99–100

1. wouldn't have gotten
2. knew
3. would be
4. aren't
5. will cancel
6. cancel
7. can sleep
8. had remembered
9. could have called
10. told

Practice—Section 11c (3), page 101

1. in the event that/in case
2. unless
3. in the event that/in case
4. as long as

Practice—Section 11c (4), page 106

1. The students said (that) they wouldn't be awake then.
2. The teacher told the students (that) they should eat breakfast before the test.
3. The students asked if they could bring coffee and bagels to the exam.
4. The teacher replied that they couldn't.
5. The students complained (that) they hadn't had time to eat breakfast.
6. The teacher said (that) the exam had started.
7. She told/asked them to be quiet.
8. The students said (that) they couldn't be quiet because their stomachs were growling.
9. The teacher said (that) they had done well on the exam.
10. Then she said (that) she was going to give all of them A's.
11. The students replied (that) they preferred A+'s.
12. The teacher smiled and said (that) that was not possible.

Practice—Section 11c (5), page 108

A. 1. The city water department ordered that homeowners not water their gardens.
   2. It also requested that no one wash his or her car.
   3. The mayor urged that each person recycle water whenever possible.
   4. It is vital that we all recycle water whenever possible.

B. It was important that John *call* home immediately because his wife was having a baby. When he called, his wife urged that he *come* home right away. He drove eighty miles per hour until a police officer stopped him for speeding. After he explained his urgency, the police officer smiled, tore up the ticket, and advised that he *not drive* quite so fast. "Your wife is probably feeling stressed," said the police officer, "so it is advisable that you *be* calm. Good luck!"

Another way to correct the paragraph is to use infinitive phrases:

It was important *for John to call* home immediately because his wife was having a baby. When he called, his wife urged *him to come* home right away. He drove eighty miles per hour until a police officer stopped him for speeding. After he explained his urgency, the police officer smiled, tore up the ticket, and advised *him not to drive* quite so fast. "Your wife is probably feeling stressed," said the police officer, "so it is advisable *for you to be* calm. Good luck!"

Practice—Section 11c (6), page 109

1. choose/to choose	5. to do
2. take care of	6. stopped
3. washed, changed, checked, tuned up	7. turned off
4. cut, take	8. carry/to carry

Practice—Section 11d (1), page 111

Because of the danger of international terrorism, passengers have to go through several airport security checks before they *can board* the plane. They *must arrive* at the airport at least two or three hours early. It *can take* a lot of time to check in all of the passengers, especially on an international flight. Passengers *must not leave* their luggage unattended because a terrorist *might put* a bomb inside. The ticket agent will ask three questions: Did you pack your luggage yourself? Has your luggage been under your control since you packed it? Has any person asked you to take anything on the airplane? Every passenger *must be able* to answer "no" to all three questions. Also, they *must show* a picture ID.

Practice—Section 11d (2), page 117

1. might be	9. can/will drive
2. could/can see	10. will we/are we going to get
3. could/can hike	
4. should/ought to/ must visit	11. should/ought to/ will be
5. Do we have to visit	12. Can we stop
6. would rather see	13. can/will stop
7. can do	14. must/should/ ought to be
8. can/will visit	

Practice—Section 11d (3), pages 119–120

1. should have fixed
2. may be/might be/must be/could be
3. may have taken/might have taken/could have taken
4. should have checked
5. should have been looking
6. may have/might have/could have
7. may be running/might be running/could be running
8. had better
9. may be spending/might be spending/will be spending
10. must be getting
11. must be wondering
12. should have arrived
13. could have called

Practice—Section 11e (1), page 123

A. 1. A Halloween party has traditionally been given by Mr. Randall's class every year.
  2. A huge party is being planned this year.
  3. All of the teachers will be invited.
  4. (*Not possible to change.*)

B. 1. Other students decorate the cafeteria.
  2. Everyone must wear a costume.
  3. Last year, the planning committee awarded a prize for best costume.
  4. Everyone had a good time at the party.

Practice—Section 11e (2), page 124

A. A young woman was murdered in our neighborhood last night. The woman had been seen walking her dog about ten o'clock by a neighbor. About midnight, a scream was heard. However, no one went outside to investigate. This morning, her body was found by another neighbor. The police were called right away. The crime is being investigated. We were told, "The murderer will be found."

B. X-rays were discovered quite by accident. *They were named* "X-rays" because "X" means "unknown" in mathematics and science. Indeed, the mysterious ray was unknown. When *X-rays were first used*, the dangers of radiation were not recognized and *X-rays were used* indiscriminately. Fifty years ago, even shoe stores had X-ray machines. Now *X-rays are used* more cautiously.

Practice—Section 12a (1), page 127

A. 1. Advertising encourages people to buy things.
  2. Buying things they don't need can cause people to go into debt.
  3. Staying out of debt should be everyone's goal.

B. 1. living
  2. coming home, working
  3. making

Practice—Section 12a (2), page 128

1. about sending
2. on staying in touch with
3. to . . . checking on

Practice—Section 12a (3), pages 129–130

Answers will vary. Sample answers:

1. being   **4.** handing it in
2. eating   **5.** do
3. doing   **6.** learning

Practice—Section 12a (4), page 131

1. sewing
2. getting along with
3. singing
4. searching

Practice—Section 12b (1), page 132

1. to have completed
2. not to go
3. to be lying
4. to be employed

Practice—Section 12b (2), pages 133–134

1. It is courteous to bring your hostess a gift of flowers in Germany.
2. It is essential to give an odd number of flowers.
3. It was embarrassing to me not to know this custom when I was in Berlin.
4. It is normal in many countries for guests to arrive late to a party.
5. In contrast, it is rude to be late in the United States.

Practice—Section 12b (3), page 135

Answers will vary. Sample answers:

A. 1. My mother said, "I can't bear *to see you leave.*"
  2. My friends promised *to write to me often.*
  3. I prepared myself *to be lonely for a while.*

B. 1. My mother told *me to eat regular meals.*
  2. I asked *my parents to call me often.*
  3. My friends urged *me to enjoy my new life.*

C. 1. He asked, "What have you decided *to major in?*"
  2. I answered, "If my parents permit *me to study art*, I will be very happy."
  3. "But if they force *me to study business*, I will be very sad."

Practice—Section 12b (4), page 137

A. 1. glad to help
  2. an easy way to learn English
  3. sorry to inform

B. 1. You could write an essay every week (in order) to improve your writing.
  2. You could write sentences using new words (in order) to improve your vocabulary.
  3. You could get an American girlfriend (in order) to improve your speaking ability.

C. Because of increased security at airports, you need to arrive at least two hours before your departure time *to pass* through all of the checkpoints. *To save time,* don't go to the check-in counters *to check* in your luggage; instead, use the skycap service. For a small fee, you can save yourself the trouble of standing in line. Even better, don't check luggage at all. If you pack carefully, you might be able *to travel* with only a carry-on bag.

Practice—Section 12b (5), pages 138–139

A. 1. too low
2. high enough
3. very heavy
4. too heavy
5. enough space
6. long enough

B. *Answers will vary. Sample answers:*
1. wide enough to get it through
2. too tired to cook
3. enough energy to go out

Practice—Section 12c, page 140

1. to make
2. to pay/paying; to make
3. making
4. paying
5. writing
6. to do
7. smoking
8. to buy
9. to take
10. taking

Practice—Section 12d, page 142

1. figure it out
2. aren't getting along
3. sit down
4. talk it over
5. putting it off
6. put up with her
7. get together
8. work out their problems/work their problems out
9. pick up something
10. letting me out

Practice—Section 13, page 149

1. were
2. was
3. is
4. is
5. costs
6. weren't
7. wasn't
8. is, takes
9. is
10. have, is
11. receives
12. is
13. satisfies
14. are
15. is

Practice—Sections 14a–c, page 152

Correct sentence completions:

1. some delicious Chinese food.
2. to a restaurant
3. steamed rice/ some steamed rice, vegetables, fish, some green tea
4. a healthy meal
5. some ice cream
6. a popular new TV show
7. television
8. an argument
9. some difficult math homework
10. a take-home test, help
11. honesty, independence

Practice—Section 14d, page 156

Correct sentence completions:

1. any, much, a great deal of, a lot of
2. little, some
3. Each, Every
4. many, several, a couple of, two, a number of
5. some, a lot of

Practice—Section 15a, page 157

1. G, G
2. NG, NG
3. NG, NG, NG
4. G, NG

Practice—Section 15c, page 161

1. a European show, the nineties
2. The European show, an island
3. The main idea, the longest time, a hostile place
4. the contestants, the island
5. The last remaining person, a million dollars
6. The biggest challenge
7. Ø fish
8. the winner, the million dollars

Practice—Section 15, pages 164–165

A. 1. Ø
2. Ø
3. the
4. the
5. Ø
6. Ø
7. Ø
8. A
9. Ø
10. a
11. a
12. the
13. Ø
14. Ø
15. a
16. Ø

B. 1. A
2. Ø
3. a
4. an
5. a
6. the
7. a
8. the
9. the
10. the
11. the
12. Ø
13. the
14. a

Practice—Sections 16a–b, page 168

A. 1. them
2. us, our
3. her, her

B. *Correct sentence completions:*
1. I
2. she
3. I
4. whom
5. who
6. me

Practice—Sections 16c–d, page 169

Correct sentence completions:

A. 1. each other
2. themselves
3. one another

B. 1. themselves
2. ourselves
3. himself
4. yourself
5. himself
6. (by) myself

Practice—Section 17, page 172

A. *Correct sentence completions:*
1. its
2. their
3. their
4. its
5. their

B. Our class had *its* end-of-semester party last Friday afternoon. Everyone came, and some students brought *their* children to join in the fun. Maria brought *her* son, and Omar brought *his* two daughters. At the beginning of the party, a few students provided entertainment. One student played the guitar and sang a song in English. Mr. Wolfe and his class performed a skit that *they* had written themselves. Everyone was a little embarrassed because neither Mr. Wolfe nor the students remembered *their* lines, but the audience applauded anyway.

Practice—Section 18, page 173

A. *Answers may vary. Sample revisions:*
1. Everyone in the class failed the test. When *the students* realized this, they complained.
2. My father told my brother that *my brother* was a lucky man to have found such a wonderful wife.

B. Recently, the government decided to raise taxes. *The president* said that a tax increase was necessary. Most citizens didn't believe *that an increase was necessary. The newspapers reported* that most people's taxes would rise twenty percent. My uncle told my father that *the tax increase* was *my father's* fault because he had voted for the wrong political party in the last election.

Practice—Section 19, page 176

1. (*Correct*)
2. They are excitedly building a snowman./They are building a snowman excitedly.
3. It is often foggy in London.
4. (*Correct*)
5. The boring lecture was finally over.
6. (*Correct*)

Practice—Section 20b, page 178

1. She baked a delicious chocolate cake for his birthday.
2. She also gave him several very expensive presents.
3. They were tired of the cold, rainy weather.
4. They asked their travel agent to find them a warm, sunny vacation spot.
5. The travel agent recommended the Caribbean, which has many beautiful white sandy beaches.

Practice—Section 20c, page 179

Correct participial adjectives:
1. surprised
2. interested
3. exciting
4. disappointing
5. boring

Practice—Section 21, page 184

A.
1. the biggest
2. (the) most luxurious
3. the smallest
4. the best
5. the same size as
6. the closest
7. longer than
8. earlier than

B.
1. Both *the* highest and *the* lowest points in the continental United States are in California.
2. Does it rain *more often* in the summer or in the winter in your country?
3. Most people like using e-mail because it is *faster* and *more convenient* than the postal service.
4. Jane and Joan are twins, but Jane's personality is quieter than *Joan's.*
5. Because she is *shyer,* Jane makes friends less easily *than* Joan.

C. I know I work as hard as for my English teacher as *I do for* my computer teacher, but I consistently get A's in computer science and C's in English. I often go to the writing center when I have a big assignment, but the tutors there don't help me as much as my roommate *does.* My roommate doesn't have *the* same problems with writing as I do. He is just naturally a better writer than *I (am),* so he doesn't have to work as hard or rewrite assignments as many times as *I (do).*

Practice—Section 22, page 186

1. My new sister-in-law *isn't* a good cook.
2. In fact, she *can* hardly pour milk and cereal in a bowl and serve it.
3. Since she and my brother returned from their honeymoon, she hasn't cooked *anything.*
4. She says she *doesn't have* time to learn.
5. (*Correct*)

Practice—Section 23, page 192

A. 1. In the year 2000, (when) the last census happened, the government mailed a questionnaire to every home and apartment in the United States.

2. Everyone (who) received a questionnaire had to fill it out.

3. The questionnaire contained questions about the number and ages of all of the people (who) lived at each address on a certain day.

B. 1. The census information, *which the government publishes,* is useful for planning.

2. For example, the number of people *who are 65 years or older* increased from three million in 1900 to over thirty-five million today.

3. The number of couples *who live together without being married* also increased.

C. 1. Her husband, *whom she met at work,* used to be her boss.

2. The company *where they worked* gave them a big party before their wedding.

3. Then the company, *which has a rule against married couples working together,* transferred her.

4. Her new office is in a city *that is 200 miles away.*

5. Her husband, *who is no longer her boss,* has asked for a transfer too.

PART 4 Punctuation

Practice—Section 24, page 196

1. Should we run, or should we just yell for help?
2. I decided to yell.
3. "Help! Robbers!" I yelled as loudly as I could.
4. The two men looked embarrassed and asked us very politely where the nearest ATM was.
5. Who was embarrassed then?

Practice—Section 25a, page 198

1. I was born in a small town, but my family moved to the capital when I was fourteen.
2. (*Correct*)

3. I was always good at sports, so physical education was my favorite class.
4. My worst subjects were physics and math.
5. I liked history and geography, but not English.

Practice—Section 25b, page 199

1. (*Correct*)
2. (*Correct*)
3. After three months, I began to help the doctor with examinations.
4. In addition, I sometimes watched her perform surgery.
5. Because I enjoyed this job a lot, I have decided to become a veterinarian too.
6. It is not easy to get into veterinary school.
7. First of all, there aren't many colleges of veterinary medicine, so admission standards are high.
8. (*Correct*)
9. There are always more applicants than the colleges have space for.

Practice—Section 25c, page 202

1. (*Correct*)
2. Planets that contain water can support life.
3. (*Correct*)
4. You don't often see men or women wearing hats these days.
5. Jennifer Lopez, wearing an old sweatshirt and jeans, was not recognized by the news photographers.
6. (*Correct*)
7. Business travelers like to fly Magic Carpet Airlines, which offers excellent food and gracious service.
8. (*Correct*)
9. Mary, his wife, sometimes accompanies him on these trips.

Practice—Section 25d, page 203

1. (*Correct*)
2. For example, my English teacher gave us fifty pages to read in one night.
3. My math teacher, on the other hand, gives very little homework.
4. As a result, I like math a lot better than I like English.
5. I'm not learning much math, however.

Practice—Sections 25e–f, page 205

1. (*Correct*)
2. He said, "Study hard, respect your teachers, and call home once a week."
3. "I will," I replied, "but please call me too."

4. I think about home every morning and every night.
5. I really miss my brother, my sister, my friends, and my mother's cooking.

Practice—Section 25g, page 208

1. Anyone can write to the U.S. president at this address: The President of the United States, The White House, 1600 Pennsylvania Avenue, Washington, DC 20500.
2. The United States declared its independence from England on July 4, 1776, in Philadelphia, Pennsylvania, and started a war.
3. Can I borrow the car tonight, Dad?
4. No, you can't.
5. (*Correct*)
6. It's a nice day today, isn't it?

Practice—Section 26, page 210

1. English has always borrowed words from other languages; for example, we take siestas, wear kimonos, and eat croissants.
2. Spanish is spoken in more countries; Chinese is spoken by more people.
3. Two hundred people came to his wedding; three attended his funeral.
4. Albert Einstein was one of the last century's most brilliant thinkers; however, he did not do well in high school.
5. Students brought many delicious dishes to the class party: paella, a Spanish seafood dish; kim chee, a mixture of pickled vegetables that is the national dish of Korea; guacamole, a Mexican dip made from mashed avocado, lime juice, chilis, and spices; and sushi, a Japanese favorite.
6. When the teacher does math problems on the blackboard, they are easy; when I do the same problems at home, they are hard.

Practice—Section 27, page 212

1. Girls in my country look forward to an important event in their lives: their fifteenth birthday.
2. The two causes of prejudice are ignorance and fear.
3. The next bus leaves at 12:27 and arrives at 2:15.
4. Whenever you go hiking, you should take the following items: a knife, a flashlight, a first aid kit, extra water, extra food, extra clothing, a map, a compass, matches or a lighter, and a whistle.

5. My strict parents didn't approve of smoking, drinking, dancing, watching television, or playing cards on Sundays.
6. The title of this book is *The Essentials of English: A Writer's Handbook.*

Practice—Section 28a, page 215

1. the moon's brightness
2. the stars' brightness
3. an hour's delay
4. six weeks' delay
5. my aunt and uncle's house
6. our son's and daughter's education
7. my sister-in-law's children
8. our children's safety
9. my boss's schedule

Practice—Section 28, page 217

1. Both of my aunts' birthdays are the same day.
2. The woman's purse was stolen.
3. The women's clothing department is on the third floor.
4. (*Correct*)
5. The cat hurt its paw, so it's licking it.
6. (*Correct*)

Practice—Section 29, page 219

1. My parents told me that I should do my best.
2. My parents told me, "Do your best, and you will be successful in life."
3. "Do your best," my parents told me, "and you will be successful in life."
4. The national song of the United States is "The Star-Spangled Banner," and the national song of Great Britain is "God Save the Queen."
5. People in many corners of the world use the Italian word *ciao* ("hello" and "goodbye") in informal speech.
6. In his poem "The Raven," poet Edgar Allen Poe repeats the phrase, "Quoth the Raven, 'Nevermore'" at the end of several verses.

Practice—Sections 30–31, page 221

1. She entered the room, greeted everyone with a cheerful "good morning," sat down at her desk—and burst into tears.
2. The Norman Conquest of England (1066) changed the English language forever.
3. The language of the conquerors (French) became the language of the upper classes.
4. The different greetings Americans use—*hello, hi, hiya, howdy,* and *how do you do*—have different levels of formality.

PART 5 Mechanics

Practice—Section 33, page 229

1619 Grand Avenue
Denver, Colorado 80207
January 1, 2002

Mr. Thomas B. Jackson
Jackson Computer Consultants
900 Park Avenue
New York, New York 10012

Dear Mr. Jackson:

I will graduate from the University of Denver in a few months and am looking for a position with a company such as yours. I will receive a master's degree in computer engineering in June.

Recently, I saw one of your company's advertisements in the *New York Times* newspaper. I plan to visit the East during the week of April 11-18 during my school's Easter vacation and would like to visit your offices then.

I will call your human resources director on Monday, January 10, to arrange an appointment. Copies of my resume and college grades are enclosed.

Very truly yours,

Dmitri Popovich

Practice—Section 34, page 233

1. (*Correct*)
2. The author of that book is *well known*.
3. (*Correct*)
4. A large group of soldiers arrived and attacked the *anti-American* demonstrators.
5. The recently discovered mummy is more than *two thousand* years old.
6. The *twelve-member* jury decided that the defendant was guilty.
7. Our gas tank was *two-thirds* full when we left.

Practice—Section 35, page 235

1. Hemingway's novel <u>The Old Man and the Sea</u> takes place in Cuba.
2. She spent the entire day preparing hors d'oeuvres for her guests.

3. <u>Humuhumunukunukuapua'a</u> is the very long Hawaiian name for a very small Hawaiian fish. Its Latin scientific name is even longer: <u>Rhinecanthus rectangulus</u>.
4. I always forget to put two <u>n</u>'s in the word <u>millennium</u>.
5. Two-year-old Mark can't pronounce the letter <u>y</u>, so he can't say the word <u>yes</u>; instead, he says "ess."
6. Did you read today's front-page story in the <u>Los Angeles Times</u>?
7. She subscribes to three news magazines: <u>Time</u>, <u>Newsweek</u>, and <u>U.S. News & World Report</u>.

Practice—Section 36, page 240

1. In the U.S., Thanksgiving is always on the fourth *Thursday* in *November*.
2. Our *chemistry* instructor will not hold office hours tomorrow *afternoon*.
3. My aunt is an assistant *manager* at Coca-Cola *Company*.
4. She works from 8:30 a.m. until 4:30 *p.m. Monday* through *Friday*.
5. Please send information about your health plan to *William J. Bryan, Ph.D.*
6. My address is 3015 Ninth *Avenue*, New York, NY 10021.

Practice—Section 37, page 243

1. *Three* classes were canceled last week.
2. The war cost several *million* dollars.
3. The U.S. flag has *thirteen* stripes and fifty stars.
4. Nearly *one-half* of the class has the flu.
5. They invited more than *one hundred* people to their wedding.
6. The company lost more than *$1.75* million last year.

Practice—Sections 38a–c, page 250

1. hands
2. eyes
3. glasses
4. boxes
5. brothers-in-law
6. fish
7. scissors
8. days
9. daisies
10. potatoes
11. videos
12. knives
13. beliefs
14. teeth
15. crises
16. 100s
17. CD-ROMs
18. X's

PART 6 Writing and Revising

Practice—Section 40a, page 260

Answers will vary.

Practice—Section 40b, page 263

Answers will vary. Sample answers:

Television: An Educational Tool

I. Introduction

II. Television keeps you informed about news and current events.
  A. Daily news programs
    1. CBS Nightly News
    2. The News Hour
  B. Weekly news programs
    1. 60 Minutes
    2. Washington Week in Review

III. Some television programs educate young children.
    1. Sesame Street
    2. Mr. Roger's Neighborhood

IV. There are many home improvement and repair programs.
      This Old House

V. Cooking programs are very popular.
    1. Cook the Italian Way
    2. The French Chef
    3. Chinese Cooking for Beginners

VI. Television also has many good programs about nature and science.
    1. National Geographic Explorer
    2. Stephen Hawkings' Universe

VII. Conclusion

Practice—Section 40, pages 270–271

Answers will vary. Sample answers:

A.   School Differences

High school in my country is very different from high school in the United States. *First,* the classroom atmosphere is very different. American classrooms are very informal. *For example,* students can wear jeans and T-shirts to school. The teachers dress casually too. In my country, high school students wear uniforms, and teachers wear business clothes. *Second,* discipline is different. American high school students talk during class and sometimes they don't pay attention. Our teachers are very strict. In my high school, we stand up when the teacher enters the room, and no one talks while the teacher is

talking. *Third,* students in my country have to study harder. We have to study more subjects. *For instance,* we take science classes for four years, but most Americans take only two years of science. Our math classes are more advanced, too. Students in my country reach the level of calculus. We take a difficult exam at the end of high school that covers all the subjects we have studied. In the United States, there are a lot of tests during the year but there is not a big test at the end of high school. ~~I think that in the U. S., activities like sports teams, clubs, community service projects, and dating seem more important than schoolwork. American high school students go out on dates.~~

B.   Driving Habits

Driving in my country is completely different from driving in United States. Our death rate from car accidents is the highest in world. Almost 8,000 people a year. In my country, driving is really dangerous ; no one pays attention to driving rules. In this country, drivers usually obey ~~it.~~ them

They stop~~ping~~ at stop signs and red lights. By contrast, when drivers in my country see a traffic light turning yellow , they ~~are driving~~ drive even faster! Also, everyone here wear s seat belts. In my wearing seat belts

country , is not "macho," so no one puts them on until they see a policeman. American drivers , are usually very polite and will let other drivers change lanes, make turns, and take a parking it's

space when ~~its~~ their turn. In my country , on the are

other hand , people ~~is~~ totally selfish behind the wheel of a car. They steal parking spaces, refuse s

to let other driver s into their lane, and honk when the car in front is too slow~~ly.~~ Pedestrians are not safe, either. I once saw a car cut across six lanes in heavy traffic and then drive onto a sidewalk was

because the driver wanted to greet a friend who ~~is~~ walking there. In conclusion, when you visit my country, be prepared to run for your life!

Practice—Section 41a, page 274

Sentence 2 is the best topic sentence: San Francisco is the perfect place to spend a vacation.

Practice—Section 41b, pages 276–277

Put checkmarks next to sentences 3, 4, 5, 7, 10.

Practice—Section 41c, page 278

Cross out these sentences: (1) She lives near the university where she works. (2) The scientists didn't use cats or other pets in the experiment.

Practice—Section 41d, page 282

1. Also
2. Then
3. As soon as
4. While
5. Most important

Practice—Section 41e, page 284

Sentence 3 is the best concluding sentence: It is clear that zoos must find ways to help pandas reproduce, or this much-loved species may soon disappear from Earth.

Practice—Section 42a, page 295

With an increasing population of elderly people, this country needs to find better ways to take care of them. Last month, an ambulance rushed an eighty-nine-year-old woman to the emergency room. A neighbor had found her on her living room floor, where she had been lying for two days after falling. In the same week, a ninety-year-old man burned to death in his home. Although there was a smoke detector in his home, the man's hearing was so poor that he couldn't hear its warning signal. He had left a pot on the stove, which started a fire. Experts who have studied the problem have proposed three possible programs.

Practice—Section 42c, pages 297–298

Conclusion 1 is the best conclusion.

PART 7   Formats

Practice—Section 45d, pages 343–344

Print sources: *Put checkmarks next to 1, 3, 5, 6.*
Internet sources: *Put checkmarks next to 1, 2, 4, 6.*

Practice—Section 45e, pages 350–351

Answers will vary.

Practice—Section 45g, page 358

1. "Genetic Engineering of Our Food." 12 Oct. 1999. DD MONTH YYYY <http://www.argonet.co.uk/users/john.rose>.
2. Kaufman, Marc. "Gene-Spliced Wheat Stirs Global Fears." The Washington Post 27 Feb. 2002: Al.
3. "Plant Disease." Encyclopedia Brittannica. 2000. DD MONTH YYYY <http://www.britannica.com>.
4. Walker, Robert. Frankenfood. Pasadena: Ross & Selvidge, 2000.
5. Wheelwright, Jeff. "Don't Eat Again Until You Read This." Discover Mar. 2002: 36–43.

INDEX